REGULATING FOR RIVALRY IN AFRICA

THE DEVELOPMENT OF COMPETITION REGIMES

Edited by Reena das Nair, Jonathan Klaaren, Simon Roberts

EMORY UNIVERSITY LIBRARY

Published by HSRC Press
Private Bag X9182, Cape Town, 8000, South Africa
www.hsrcpress.ac.za

First published 2025

ISBN (soft cover) 978-0-7969-2682-1
ISBN (pdf) 978-0-7969-2683-8

© 2025 Human Sciences Research Council

This book has undergone a double-blind independent peer-review process overseen by the HSRC Press Editorial Board.

The views expressed in this publication are those of the authors. They do not necessarily reflect the views or policies of the Human Sciences Research Council (the Council) or indicate that the Council endorses the views of the authors. In quoting from this publication, readers are advised to attribute the source of the information to the individual author concerned and not to the Council.

The publishers have no responsibility for the continued existence or accuracy of URLs for external or third-party Internet websites referred to in this book and do not guarantee that any content on such websites is, or will remain, accurate or appropriate.

Copy-edited by Jennifer Schnetler
Typeset by Simon van Gend
Cover design by Nadia Neethling
Printed by [Name of printer, city, country]

Distributed in Africa by Blue Weaver
Tel: +27 (021) 701 4477; Fax Local: (021) 701 7302
www.blueweaver.co.za

Distributed worldwide (except central and southern Africa) by Lynne Rienner Publishers, Inc.
Tel: +1 303-444-6684; Fax: +1 303-444-0824; Email: cservice@rienner.com
www.rienner.com

No part of this publication may be reproduced, stored in a retrieval system, or transmitted by any form or by any means, electronic, mechanical, photocopying, recording or otherwise, without prior permission from the copyright owner.

To copy any part of this publication, you may contact DALRO for information and copyright clearance.

Tel: 086 12 DALRO (or 086 12 3256 from within South Africa); +27 (0)11 712-8000
Fax: +27 (0)11 403-9094
Postal Address: P O Box 31627, Braamfontein, 2017, South Africa
www.dalro.co.za

Any unauthorised copying could lead to civil liability and/or criminal sanctions.

Suggested citation: Das Nair R, Klaaren J, Roberts S (Eds) (2025) *Regulating for rivalry in Africa: The development of competition regimes*. Cape Town: HSRC Press

Contents

Figures v

Tables vi

Abbreviations and acronyms vii

Foreword ix
Dr Willard Mwemba, CEO, COMESA Competition Commission

1 The development of competition regimes in Africa 1
   Reena das Nair, Jonathan Klaaren and Simon Roberts

2 The making of a competition agency: Lessons from the Competition Authority of Kenya's development from inception to enforcement 15
   Wang'ombe Kariuki

3 The fight against cartels in Zambia: Challenges and successes 27
   Chilufya P Sampa

4 Competition in the AfCFTA: Facing up to the core challenges of mergers and cartels? 38
   Grace Nsomba and Simon Roberts

5 'Buyer power' in emerging markets: Assessing the effectiveness of regulatory and enforcement developments in South Africa and Kenya 58
   John Oxenham, Michael-James Currie and Joshua Eveleigh

6 New thinking in competition regulation: Adjusting law and enforcement to address challenges of African markets 77
   Priscilla M Njako

7 Exploring a broader application of the 'substantial lessening of competition' standard: A South African perspective 95
   Jason Aproskie and Tessa Bleazard

8 Cartels under scrutiny 109
   Maletuma Malie

9 Developing thinking in merger assessment: Reflections from recent UK experience 130
   Genna Robb

10 Competition issues and regional integration in soybean and animal feed to poultry markets, within and across Kenya, Malawi and Zambia   147
Grace Nsomba, Angella Kachipapa Mhone, Inonge Mulozi, Rosebela A Oiro and Simon Roberts

11 Competition and the challenges of inclusive economic development: An apparent margin squeeze in poultry farming in Malawi   167
Timothy Gondwe, Grace Nsomba and Simon Roberts

12 An analysis of competition dynamics in South African digital markets for travel and tourism   184
Itumeleng Lesofe and Siphosethu Tetani

13 The other platforms, the other consumers: The missing bottom in the South African digital platforms policy debate   208
Jonathan Klaaren, Tlhalefang Moeletsi, Karissa Moothoo Padayachie and Thando Vilakazi

14 Is the introduction of competition between stock exchanges a good idea?   231
Paul Anderson and Andre Frauenknecht

15 E-commerce business models: Insights from micro- and small enterprises in South Africa   255
Aarti Krishnan and Reena das Nair

About the authors   286

Index   290

Figures

Figure 4.1   Regional extent of operations for companies with interests in Pure Oil   46

Figure 8.1   Companies by sector classification   115
Figure 8.2   The timeline for an event study   118

Figure 10.1   Commercial broiler poultry value chain in Malawi   149
Figure 10.2   Net exports in soybean and oilcake   152
Figure 10.3   APDL, Kenchic and Seaboard ownership links and alliances   153
Figure 10.4   Comparative prices for day-old chicks   155
Figure 10.5   Comparative broiler finisher feed prices   157
Figure 10.6   Comparative live chicken prices, per chicken   159

Figure 11.1   Prices of maize and soybean   171
Figure 11.2   Prices of maize and soybean against feed and day-old chicken costs, per kg of chicken meat   172
Figure 11.3   Diagram depicting the possibility of margin squeeze   173

Figure 12.1   Sources of traffic to travel and tourism platforms in South Africa   196
Figure 12.2   Google search results for hotels in Cape Town   200

Figure 13.1   Sample composition of digital platforms across sectors   212
Figure 13.2   Sample composition of digital platforms across business models   212
Figure 13.3   The number of local platforms established each year   214

Figure 14.1   Stylised illustration of the value chain for the provision of trading and post-trading services by the JSE for cash securities   234
Figure 14.2   Conceptual framework to assess the impact of competition   240
Figure 14.3   Summary of main findings   248

Figure 15.1   E-grocery value chain mapping for MSE 1   267
Figure 15.2   Restaurant marketplace value chain mapping for MSE 2   272
Figure A15.1 Diagram showing foodtech segments   285

Tables

Table 8.1   Summary of comparable empirical studies   112
Table A8.1   Summary of cumulative abnormal return results   127

Table 10.1   Summary market structure and supply   151
Table A10.1   Suppliers of day-old chicks (DoC) and market shares along the value chain, Malawi   164
Table A10.2   Breeding and supply of day-old chicks, Zambia   165
Table A10.3   Main breeders and day-old chick suppliers, Kenya   165
Table A10.4   Main suppliers of soy oilcake and commercial animal feed, Malawi   165
Table A10.5   Soybean processors and animal feed producers, Zambia   165
Table A10.6   Poultry feed producers, Kenya   166

Table 11.1   Commercial poultry producers and estimated market shares 2022, Malawi   169
Table 11.2   Soy oilcake, soymeal and commercial animal feed producers in Malawi, 2022   170
Table 11.3   Calculation of Central Poultry margins per 1.9 kg bird (Mwk)   177

Table 12.1   Accommodation platforms' estimated market shares based on commission revenues   188

Table 14.1   Summary of empirical literature on the impact of fragmentation from 2000 to 2021   244
Table 14.2   Examples of the impact of competition on innovation in selected countries   245

Table 15.1   Value chain actors in e-grocery and restaurant marketplaces   258
Table 15.2   Network architecture: From demand- and supply-side perspectives   261
Table 15.3   Network stability   262
Table 15.4   Foodtech segments in South Africa based on authors' compiled dataset (as of 2020)   264
Table 15.5   MSE 1: Network embeddedness (supply side)   269
Table 15.6   MSE 1: Economic and social value creation or lost/upgrading   270
Table 15.7   MSE 2: Network embeddedness (demand side)   273
Table 15.8   MSE 2: Network embeddedness (supply side)   274
Table 15.9   MSE 2: Economic and social value creation or lost/upgrading   276

Abbreviations and acronyms

AAC	Augmentative and assistive communication
AAMP	Agriculture and Agro-processing Masterplan
ACER	Annual Competition and Economic Regulation
ACF	African Competition Forum
AfCFTA	African Continental Free Trade Area
AI	Artificial intelligence
AIM	Alternative Investment Market
AMO	African Market Observatory
API	Application programming interface
ASEAN	Association of Southeast Asian Nations
CAC	Competition Appeal Court (South Africa)
CAK	Competition Authority of Kenya
CAR	Cumulative Abnormal Return
CC	Competition Commission
CCP	Central clearing counterparty
CCPA	Competition and Consumer Protection Act
CCPC	Competition and Consumer Protection Commission (Zambia)
CCSA	Competition Commission of South Africa
CEEC	Citizens Economic Empowerment Commission (Zambia)
CGCSA	Consumer Goods Council of South Africa
CMA	Competition and Markets Authority (United Kingdom)
COMESA	Common Market for Eastern and Southern Africa
CSD	Central Securities Depository
CSDPs	Central Securities Depository Participants
DoC	Day-old chicks
DPP	Director of Public Prosecutions
DRC	Democratic Republic of the Congo
DSMI	Data Services Market Inquiry
EAC	East African Community
EDM	Elimination of double marginalisation
ESA	Eastern and Southern Africa
EMH	Efficient-market hypothesis
ETG	Export Trading Group
EU	European Union
FISP	Fertiliser Input Support Programme
FSCA	Financial Sector Conduct Authority (South Africa)
GSMA	Global System for Mobile Communications Association
GVC	Global value chains
HACCP	Hazard Analysis Critical Control Points
ICN	International Competition Network

IFWG	Intergovernmental Fintech Working Group
IPCC	Intergovernmental Panel on Climate Change
ITU	International Telecommunication Union
JSE	Johannesburg Stock Exchange
MiFID	Markets in Financial Instruments Directive
ML	Machine learning
MMHS	Matlosana Medical Health Services
MNOs	Mobile network operators
MoUs	Memoranda of understanding
MSME	Micro, small and medium enterprises
MvNOs	Mobile virtual network operators
OECD	Organisation for Economic Cooperation and Development
OFT	Office of Fair Trading
OIPMI	Online Intermediation Platforms Market Inquiry
OTA	Online travel agent
PPC	Price parity clauses
PPPs	Public–private partnerships
REC	Regional economic community
RTCP	Retail Trade Code of Practice
SADC	Southern African Development Community
SEM	Search Engine Marketing
SEO	Search enging optimisation
SERP	Search engine results page
SLC	Substantial lessening of competition
SMEs	Small and medium enterprises
SPLC	Substantial prevention or lessening of competition
SRO	Self-regulatory organisation
STEM	Science, technology, engineering and mathematics
STK	Sim toolkit
ToH	Theories of harm
UNCTAD	United Nations Conference on Trade and Development
USSD	Unstructured Supplementary Service Data
WTTC	World Travel and Tourism Council
ZCC	Zambia Competition Commission
ZICTA	Zambia Information Communication and Telecommunication Authority
ZPPA	Zambia Public Procurement Authority

Foreword

Dr Willard Mwemba, CEO, COMESA Competition Commission

Establishing effective competition regimes in Africa is a crucial part of developing the institutions of economic policy. Competition laws have been passed by the great majority of African countries as well as some regional economic communities, notably the Common Market for Eastern and Southern Africa (COMESA). In addition, the African Continental Free Trade Area (AfCFTA) competition protocol has been agreed and its implementation is pending.

Cross-border markets, which are characterised by fair competition, are essential for regional integration just as they are important for national development. Anti-competitive arrangements such as cartels and vertical restraints that result in territorial restrictions can seek to divide markets along geographic lines, blocking the gains from intra-regional trade and raising prices. Anti-competitive mergers of multinational firms can mean monopolies or just a very few firms control the supply of goods and services across parts of the continent and have the power to exclude smaller African businesses to the ultimate detriment of consumers, which worsens the already high poverty levels on the continent. Therefore, competition enforcement on the continent is not just rhetoric but serious business that if well implemented can lift millions out of extreme poverty. The neglect of its enforcement may spell doom for most small businesses and perpetuate poverty, while large businesses, in most cases multinational corporations, continue to realise huge illegal and immoral profits.

If the anti-competitive effects on economies are to be addressed, it is important that laws must not exist only on paper. It is therefore crucial to understand how the authorities have exercised their powers in practice to ensure that markets are fair and open. This book critically engages with the key questions at a number of levels through chapters that address cross-country competition issues, chapters that focus on case studies in national jurisdictions, and chapters that tackle the interface of competition and economic development.

Building a common knowledge base through critical research is essential for effective competition regimes, especially given the relatively new and dynamic nature of the field. The research findings are drawn on for cases and inquiries. The research studies are also essential material for teaching and capacity building. The community of researchers includes those in competition authorities given the analytical- and knowledge-centred nature of the work. This is exemplified by the contributors to this book, many of whom are from competition authorities across the region. I am proud that the COMESA and indeed Africa has developed a cadre of researchers who appreciate the unique challenges of competition enforcement in Africa and propose unique recommendations to address the challenges. It is notable that the chapters draw from papers presented at the Annual Competition and Economic Regulation (ACER) weeks in East and Southern Africa, which were co-hosted by the COMESA Competition Commission (CCC). In addition, two chapters draw from research of the African Market Observatory in which the CCC has been a partner.

The two chapters on the critical issues of competition in agri-food markets, in the context of rising food inflation, shocks from COVID–19, the Russia–Ukraine war and the ongoing impacts of climate change, are very timely. The contributions point to the central role of regional competition enforcement give the cross-border nature of important markets and the international reach of the large firms involved. The COMESA Competition Commission has been closely involved with the research initiatives and is drawing on the findings for building regional competition enforcement and advocacy. The importance of research cannot be overemphasised. It is the bedrock of the generation of new knowledge required to address problems.

The book includes chapters from two trailblazers of competition enforcement – Chilufya Sampa and Wang'ombe Kariuki, who stood down in 2022/23 after around a decade as the heads of the Zambian and Kenyan authorities respectively. Each shares unique insights from the coalface of enforcement, combining practical lessons from tackling different forms of anti-competitive conduct with the challenges of building institutional capabilities. Their insights also include the challenges of building strong linkages between national and regional competition authorities.

There is a range of chapters assessing the appropriate tests to be applied in competition matters including in assessing buyer power, mergers and cartels. These chapters assess cutting-edge developments, drawing on experiences from different countries.

I also welcome the focus on digital markets with four chapter covering competition topics in this field. Digitalisation of economic activity is pervasive, with fundamental implications for how markets work for firms from micro and local to large and multinational in scale. The demands on competition authorities are ramping-up even further, meaning there is no time to lose. The chapters point to the importance of the issues and how authorities can respond to the challenges through tools such as market inquiries.

The editors are to be commended for their work and unwavering commitment in bringing these contributions together in a book that adds substantially to the body of knowledge in the field. This book is a must-read for all those wishing to make an impact in the lives of people through competition law enforcement.

1 The development of competition regimes in Africa

Reena das Nair, Jonathan Klaaren and Simon Roberts

The development of competition regimes in Africa may be partially tracked by the enactment of competition laws. In 2019, 33 of the 54 African countries already had competition laws (United Nations Economic Commission for Africa 2019). Since 2019, a further number of African jurisdictions, including Nigeria, have enacted competition laws. Competition laws regulate market power and economic concentration in the interests of economic development. The enactment of these laws across Africa has been bolstered by the growing international consensus that high levels of market concentration – where just a few companies account for the majority of the sales in a given market – mean that these companies have substantial market power. Ensuring that this power is not abused requires effective competition rules (see Aghion et al. 2021; Wu 2018; Eeckhout 2021).

However, rules and laws on their own are insufficient. Not only competition laws with teeth but also authorities with the power to enforce them are essential to ensure that markets are fair and open – for consumers to be charged reasonable prices and for firms to be able to enter and grow, based on the merits of their goods and services. Effective competition regimes consist of such laws and empowered enforcing authorities.

To understand how African competition regimes have developed and how they have worked in practice to date, the relevant context needs to be considered. Five major aspects of African competition regimes in context are particularly important – each of which is developed in chapters in this book. Here, we enumerate these aspects and motivate for why they are central to understanding the role of competition in the development of market economies in Africa.

First, competition authorities across Africa are generally young and with modest resources (Burke et al. 2019). They do not have a deep skills and knowledge base from which to draw, as competition law and competition economics have usually not been significant for these respective professions until the establishment of these authorities and the start of their enforcement work. We consider the experiences of the few African jurisdictions with leading and longstanding authorities below and in chapters 2 and 3, where the former heads of the Kenyan and Zambian authorities examine major areas of enforcement and the challenges they faced.

Second, as with many others around the world, African jurisdictions have to tackle entrenched dominant firms that have often obtained their position through prior government support. Economies of scale, scope and network effects mean that, given this history and the relatively small size of African economies, there are higher levels of concentration and a greater likelihood of dominant firms than in bigger and more open economies. Indeed, the recognition of the ability of such firms to exert superior bargaining power over suppliers, as well as customers, has led to African countries being pioneers in competition policy concerning abusive buyer power. Countries such as Kenya and South Africa have also been prompted to make use of market inquiries to consider the harm caused along value chains by large firms with substantial market power. We explicate this aspect further in this introductory chapter as well as in chapters 5 and 6 of this book.

Third, agriculture and food are extremely important in African economies given the contribution of agriculture to most countries' GDP and the importance of food expenditure in the budgets of African households. The shocks under Covid-19 and those linked to the Russia–Ukraine war have meant greater scrutiny by authorities on agri-food markets, while agriculture continues to be impacted by climate change. Competition regimes are increasingly being asked and expected to tackle these questions. How agriculture and food markets work, whether they are competitive, and what the role of competition authorities should be in these markets and in respect of climate change thus constitute a set of pressing questions. We explore the dynamics of barriers to entry and inclusion in these crucial sectors below and in chapters 10, 11 and 15 of this book.

Fourth, the relatively small size of most African economies belies and also contributes to the regional scope of competition concerns, as multinational companies with operations extending across borders are engaged in arrangements such as cross-border cartels operating at a regional level. Regional competition enforcement is required to tackle the scope of such arrangements and has led to competition authorities being established in some regional economic communities, such as the Common Market for Eastern and Southern Africa (COMESA). Over the past two years, in near record time, not only the principle but also the text of a competition protocol has been agreed to in terms of the African Continental Free Trade Agreement (AfCFTA). We assess the challenges of regional competition enforcement and the record to date below, as well as in chapter 4 of this book by Nsomba and Roberts (2023), which looks at AfCFTA, and chapter 10 of this book by Nsomba et al. (2022), which looks at regional poultry.

The fifth and final significant contextual aspect for the development of competition regimes across Africa is digitalisation. Network effects, platform competition and the rise of digital gatekeepers have significant implications for market outcomes and for competition enforcement (CCSA 2023; Andreoni & Roberts 2022). Competition regimes worldwide are grappling with these issues, and African competition authorities are similarly dealing with competition and regulatory problems arising in digital markets. However, the implications of market failures in digital markets in developing economies are even more pronounced, given small markets, entrenched dominant firms in highly concentrated markets, and limited resources and jurisdictional reach of competition authorities to effectively prosecute powerful global digital firms (Buthelezi & Hodge 2019). This book explores the effects of digitalisation and its dynamics from a competition perspective in South Africa and Kenya in chapters 12, 13, 14 and 15. Our claim is not that these five contextual aspects are exhaustive. Further empirical research would be supplemental and valuable. However, we do assert that any understanding of how African competition regimes – the practice of competition authorities in formulating and enforcing competition laws and policies within their societies – have developed needs to take into account the institutional, market, sectoral, national/regional and global features surveyed above.

A decade of building authorities

Africa has a relatively small number of existing and well-established competition authorities with a significant enforcement track record to date. In this section, we explore and detail how this group of authorities have established themselves over the decade or more since they started to operate effectively. For the six established African regimes we discuss here, their establishment and efficacy has been achieved through regular review of their internal processes, the strategic practice of prioritisation and the endowment of a sole mandate – rather than their emerging as a consequence of other components of institutional design, such as enforcement model and leadership structure.

Determining the set of 'established authorities' is of course, to a degree, a subjective exercise. One method is to cluster the regimes, grouping them at a high level. In their comprehensive book, Fox and Bakhoum assess the jurisdictions of Kenya, Zambia, Botswana and Mauritius as being in a cluster of regimes close to the continent-leading South African regime (2019). Their analysis categorises these five authorities as being established across Africa. For our purposes, in addition to the five identified by Fox and Bakhoum, we draw upon and consider the experience of the COMESA regime – making up a set of six. The institutional issues that we consider here, as well as in chapters 2 and 3, form a crucial part of the dynamics of the development of competition regimes both around the world and across Africa (Kovacic 1997).

One clear factor in establishing and maintaining institutional standing and success has been these authorities' capability to regularly adapt their internal processes. For instance, several of these established authorities have adapted their approach to merger evaluation to improve the efficiency in the process, particularly around 2015. South Africa reorganised its regime to devote more attention to large-scale mergers, Zambia embarked on a two-phase process, and Botswana instituted a fast-track system (Burke et al. 2019: 505).

Another clear factor in building the efficacy of this group of established African competition authorities is the strategic practice of prioritisation (Burke 2018). Through prioritisation, competition authorities make choices about what they regard as strategically important or not with respect to achieving their desired competition policy goals (Burke et al. 2019: 514). A majority of these agencies have established prioritisation plans, whether formally as sector specifications (South Africa), or informally with respect to specific sectors (Mauritius) or bid-rigging (Botswana and Zambia) (Burke et al. 2019: 516). Kenya has also engaged in prioritisation as part of its strategic planning (see chapter 2 by Kariuki, in this book).

Arguably, fitting within the practice of prioritisation, a number of these authorities focused in their early years not on cartel conduct nor on abuse of dominance, but rather on merger control. Such a focus is often advised in order to provide a young competition regime with the capacity, credibility, expertise and information base for overall competition enforcement. This advice to focus first on merger control has been followed with apparent success in some of the leading African jurisdictions including South Africa and Kenya (Lewis 2012; see chapter 2 by Kariuki, in this book).

Apart from prioritisation, a number of these regimes have demonstrated strategic conduct by showing significant responsiveness to country-specific challenges through amendments to their respective competition Acts. Some examples are revisions to the legal frameworks for buyer power in South Africa and Kenya, and for price discrimination in South Africa (discussed further and with narrative detail in 'Abuse of dominance issues' later in this chapter and in chapters 2 and 5 in this book). With its responsiveness to price gouging, South Africa also demonstrated responsiveness to the Covid-19 pandemic.

While important in a number of ways, institutional design appears to have had only a limited role to play in the development of the first cohort of established African competition authorities. Three significant components of institution design in the African context are an institution's enforcement model, its mandate or mandates, and the structure of leadership for the competition authority (Jenny 2016; Burke et al. 2019).

Regarding the first component of institutional design, half of the established cohort exhibit bifurcated agency enforcement models, where the prosecutorial and adjudicative functions are separated (either within a separate agency structure or entirely in the courts) (South Africa, Zambia and Kenya). The other half of the cohort demonstrates an integrated (administrative) agency enforcement model (Botswana, COMESA and Mauritius). A number of reasons for favouring the bifurcated model in the Southern Africa region have been identified (Burke et al. 2019: 507–509). In line with this leaning, one serious proposal has been made in the past decade – in Botswana – to move from an integrated agency enforcement model to a bifurcated agency enforcement model. However, this proposal does not appear to have been adopted.

With respect to the enforcement model, two important developments directly linked to the growth and effectiveness of the competition authorities are the use of corporate leniency policies and the use of market inquiries or market studies. The corporate leniency policy has been used with significant results in South Africa. Kenya and Zambia have had forms of a special compliance process akin to a corporate leniency and policy and addressing coordinated conduct, where firms could examine their conduct, such as through industry associations, and remedy it while not being fined. These regimes then later conducted investigations against cartels, with some leading to penalties. Market inquiries have, for instance, been used effectively in both Kenya and South Africa. As noted in chapter 12 of this book, in the 2022/2023 Online Intermediation Platform Market Inquiry, the Competition Commission of South Africa was able to identify competition concerns in several digital markets, even though some of these markets were still in their early stages of development.

With regard to the institutional design element of leadership structures, further research is needed to better understand the degree to which, if at all, this component influences the development and establishment of this cohort of agencies. Apart from South Africa (which has a unitary executive model of governance, recently amended to increase the number of deputy commissioners), the other jurisdictions here all have multimember boards responsible for the governance and oversight of their competition authority.

Abuse of dominance issues – rules for inherently powerful businesses

African competition regimes have been pioneers globally in introducing provisions within their competition laws that deal with the challenges faced by small and medium enterprises (SMEs). This is in recognition of the important role that SMEs play in African economies and in response to the challenges they face in entering and effectively competing in concentrated markets in which large, powerful firms dominate. Key new legislation against the abuse of buyer power was therefore introduced in countries with established competition regimes, like South Africa and Kenya.[1]

Buyer power is defined as the enhanced bargaining position of a buyer with respect to its supplier(s) of goods or services (Anchustegui, n.d.); or the ability for a buyer to capture a higher share of surplus when bargaining with a seller (Carlton & Israel 2011), or the ability of downstream firms to affect the terms of trade with upstream suppliers (OECD 2009). Intervention in cases of buyer power continues to be a controversial topic globally. Exerting buyer power can result in lower prices for consumers if cost savings are passed on to them and if the power of buyers countervails the market power of large sellers. Under these conditions, buyer power could therefore improve consumer welfare, which in many jurisdictions is the standard to which the core purpose of competition policy is held. However, there is growing recognition that the exercise of buyer power can substantially harm the competitive process in the long term if it leads to the exclusion of SMEs that are forced to take unfavourable prices and conditions of sale from a dominant buyer. The exercise of buyer power can severely hamper SMEs' ability to compete effectively, to invest in building capabilities and to innovate, harming consumers in the long term. The abuse of buyer power distorts the competitive landscape further in favour of dominant firms in what are already concentrated markets.

The abuse of buyer power also has distributional implications. Competition policy in developing economies aims for performance-based rivalry, which stimulates investment in capabilities and learning, while rewarding effort and creativity. This is closely related to opening opportunities and levelling the playing field for new participants, particularly SMEs. It is not simply overall growth in markets that matters. Who gets to participate in this growth and the nature of ownership also matter. Widening inequality, including in terms of economic participation, has damaging effects in developing countries, especially in countries like South Africa and others in Africa with a history of large economic and societal imbalances. As Baker and Salop (2015: 21) highlight: 'If growing concerns about inequality lead to the recognition that there are additional harms from market power, that recognition would justify reconsideration of the balance and the adoption of more interventionist antitrust rules.' High and growing concentration levels and pervasive barriers to entry and participation require rethinking the rules of the game from a competition enforcement perspective.

The Competition Authority of Kenya (CAK) and the Competition Commission of South Africa (CCSA) have taken bold steps to change the rules of the game through the introduction of buyer power legislation. Kenya was the first country in Africa and one of the first globally to add this to its Competition Act (No. 12 of 2010) with the introduction of the Competition Amendment Act in 2016. South Africa followed with amendments to its Competition Act (No. 89 of 1998) in 2018 (effective 2020). In both countries, a big stimulus for the provision stemmed from market inquiries and studies in the retail sector, in which powerful supermarket chains with their large store networks across countries, were 'gatekeepers' to suppliers accessing markets. These players govern participation and upgrading trajectories in supply chains, wielding considerable power over suppliers.

Persistent concerns over conduct such as delayed payments to suppliers, unreasonable and onerous trading terms and conditions imposed, passing of risks and costs onto suppliers, and the general extraction of rents from suppliers through various fees and requirements led to the realisation that the existing enforcement tools were inadequate to address these problems and that amendments to the competition laws were needed. This law-making action reflects the agility and flexibility of these African jurisdictions to be responsive to the realities in their economies. In Kenya, the CAK created a specialised buyer power department (or 'its specialised Buyer Power Department'), which was mandated to investigate buyer power cases filed under the provision. Over 217 investigations in 15 sectors have been undertaken as of 2023, with a concentration of cases in the retail and insurance sectors. In 2021, the CAK also gazetted the Retail Trade Code of Practice (RTCP), a voluntary undertaking encouraging self-regulation of signatories to ensure fair and ethical retailer–supplier trade relationships (see chapter 6 by Njako, in this book, on the CAK's treatment of buyer power cases). South Africa, by contrast, has yet to prosecute a case of an abuse of buyer power, although investigations are under way (see chapter 5 by Oxenham et al., in this book).

Competition, barriers to entry, and inclusion in food and agriculture

Competition is an essential part of understanding how food systems work, globally and across Africa (Clapp 2023; Roberts 2023).

Concentration has been increasing in food systems globally as in other sectors. Very few companies control the majority of inputs, trading of grain and agro-processing in key value chains. This means that market outcomes are largely the result of the decisions of a small number of firms (Béné 2022; Clapp 2023; Meagher & Roberts 2021). African countries are vulnerable to the exertion of market power by these firms as suppliers of inputs to farmers, as well as by international traders buying crops for export. As demonstrated in chapter 10 by Nsomba et al. in this book, the high levels of concentration and apparent anti-competitive conduct in African countries do appear to have squeezed farmers on both sides – the supply of inputs and the buying of outputs. Prices to supply staple foods to large urban areas have also increased by margins above the increases in international markets.

Concentration and market power have exacerbated the shocks associated with the Covid-19 pandemic and Russia's invasion of Ukraine, and substantially worsened outcomes (Nsomba et al. 2022). By comparison, resilience would be improved through a diversity of businesses and different business models, along with an appropriate framework to encourage a medium-to-long-term view to investing. It is therefore necessary to address barriers to the entry and growth of smaller participants as part of improving the resilience and sustainability of agri-food value chains (Roberts 2023; Vilakazi et al. 2020). Barriers include anti-competitive conduct by entrenched dominant firms and cartels to undermine smaller rivals and protect supra-competitive profits, market failures in access to finance, and obstacles in the main routes to market to build the brand profile required for consumer goods.

Addressing resilience in the face of climate change is particularly important for Africa. African countries are responsible for negligible emissions and yet face urgent challenges of adaptation to global warming and extreme weather events that threaten production. Areas in the continent are climate 'hotspots', where temperatures are increasing above the global average and rainfall is projected by the globally recognised the International Panel on Climate Change (IPCC) Assessment Reports to decline further (IPCC 2023). The extreme drought over the past three years in the Horn of Africa and East Africa has seen record food prices and heightened food insecurity (World Bank 2022).

At the same time, Africa includes some of the best areas in the world to sustainably expand food production, including regions in east and central Africa (Nsomba & Roberts 2023). The fact that many African countries are reliant on imports, despite this potential, points to the need to analyse how agri-food value chains and markets are working in practice, including understanding the political economy of food sectors and food security, regionally and globally. However, the work on food systems transformation required to respond to climate change has, with a few exceptions, not taken market power and market workings into account. This is notwithstanding the extensive evidence of anti-competitive conduct and high levels of concentration in agri-food markets.

In Africa, anti-competitive conduct includes a number of cartels uncovered in Zambia and South Africa in fertiliser, storage, milling of maize and wheat, poultry and fish breeding stock, and various food products (see chapter 3 by Sampa, in this book, on Zambia; Muzata et al. 2017 and Roberts 2020 on South Africa). Extensive competition concerns have also been raised relating to market power being exercised by supermarkets to govern value chains, including buyer power, discussed above. In addition, there have been examples of margin squeezes being exerted over smaller market participants such as in the Malawi animal feed and poultry markets (see chapter 11 by Gondwe et al., in this book).

Concentration and market power have a knock-on impact on the political economy of agri-food markets as large companies lobby to protect their positions (Mondliwa et al. 2021; Vilakazi & Roberts 2018). While competition law and enforcement are a realm that should be independent of government policy, a failure to tackle anti-competitive conduct that underpins excessive profits creates pressure on policymakers to skew the playing field in favour of incumbents. The lobbying by powerful interests is inevitable. The issue is that in fair, open and competitive markets, rents are disciplined by competitive rivalry.

The reach of the large companies in agri-food markets is international, as are the anti-competitive arrangements and effects of large mergers. We now turn to the regional competition challenges.

Regional competition challenges

The question of regional competition policy and its enforcement has long formed part of the comparative and global scholarship on competition and anti-trust (Drexl et al. 2012; Gal 2009, 2010). However, this scholarship developed initially largely without the benefit of African-based theory or evidence. Over the past 10 years, African-based scholars have increasingly turned their attention to regional matters and have pointed out that the gains from regional integration are much greater when the implications of imperfect competition are taken into account (Klaaren et al. 2019; Roberts 2016; Roberts et al. 2017).

One way to look at regional competition policy and enforcement across Africa and its current state is to see it as a two-level interactive process (Fox & Bakhoum 2019; Kigwiru et al. 2021; Waller & Gathii 2019). The two levels are the national and the regional (sub-continental) levels (Sucker & Klaaren 2021). Policy development and rule enforcement at these distinct levels of course take place within a global context (Hartzenberg 2013). Both the national and the regional levels have seen important developments on the two separate regime dimensions of policy/rules and of institutions/enforcement.

Both domestic and regional competition authorities face pressing challenges stemming from the broader context in executing their enforcement mandate. All African sub-continental regions are at best poorly integrated with respect to competition policy and its enforcement. For instance (and as explored further in this book), the cross-border agriculture and food markets in Eastern and Southern Africa are not working effectively (Nsomba et al. 2022). National policies are often not aligned with regional ones. In addition and worse than non-alignment, national policies can and occasionally do run counter to the regional integration initiatives (Hartzenberg & Kalenga 2015).

African and international firms with regional or even continental reach have been able to leverage control of infrastructure and inputs as well as promoting favourable regulation to sustain market power (Vilakazi & Roberts 2018). Nonetheless, these challenges are no longer flying completely under the radar. While most competition enforcement action takes place at the national rather than the regional level, there is a growing and significant caseload relating to enforcement action in competition matters with implications for regional economic development (Burke et al. 2019). Meeting the existing and developing regional challenges of competition enforcement across Africa will require cooperation among existing authorities as well as a strong African voice at the continental and global level. The example provided by COMESA and the importance of working on mergers and cartel enforcement at both regional and continental level are highlighted by Nsomba and Roberts (see chapter 4 by Nsomba & Roberts, in this book). An increasingly strong influence from continental processes, largely focused around the African Continental Free-Trade Agreement (AfCFTA), is felt particularly at the regional level (Kigwiru 2023).

Led by networks or associations of competition authorities, different African regions were and remain engaged in formulating policy regarding the AfCFTA and its competition protocol (Klaaren & Sibanda 2019; see chapter 4 by Nsomba & Roberts, in this book). These networks and the potential for cross-border coordination of enforcement efforts that they offer will undoubtedly play a leading role in enforcing the emerging content of an African competition policy. Along these lines, the leading international competition scholar Eleanor Fox recently underlined the significance of the AfCFTA protocol as establishing an institutional body 'with a voice' to articulate and enforce competition policy that is Africa-wide (Fox 2022).

Concluding thoughts and the rationale for the book

Understanding the development of competition regimes across Africa requires an appreciation of numerous factors. These regimes, whether established or nascent, do not generally benefit from well-resourced regulatory environments. Perhaps due to this need to do more with less, the efficacy of the most well-established of the regimes on the continent has been achieved in large part through regular review of their internal processes and the strategic practice of prioritisation.

Furthermore, competition authorities typically face markets with entrenched dominant firms, often due to a history of state support. This makes the pioneering role that Kenyan and South African authorities have played in formulating and setting into place pro-competitive rules addressing buyer power all the more important and timely. Exhibiting buyer power as part of their own particular dynamics, agriculture and food markets are simply crucial for households throughout African economies. Established African competition regimes recognise the operation of these markets as a key priority.

More generally, African competition authorities face firms operating across borders, in regions and at a wide scale, which pose particular enforcement challenges. Growing efforts are being made in networks such as the African Competition Forum and at the policy level to recognise, embody and work collaboratively on the basis of a continental scale. Finally, one should note that these regimes are hardly immune from global trends; indeed, the wave of digitalisation may be having particularly profound effects in Africa.

There is much that remains on the twin agendas of improving the enforcement records of competition regimes across Africa and understanding the dynamics of their development. While we have pointed to the benefits of internal review processes and strategic practices such as prioritisation, these may turn out to be relatively low-hanging fruit – factors with the most salience and impact in the early years of a developing and establishing a competition authority. Attention to agency design and to institutional factors more generally should thus remain firmly on any future research agenda (Jenny 2016). This is equally appropriate with a view to those African jurisdictions that remain with a law but no enforcement structure – and to those without either.

Greater enforcement will likely follow an increase in resources (financial and human capital) provided to the competition authorities. But the strength of this correlation is worth investigating. The substantial increase in agency funding provided to the SACC in the wake of the passage of the 2018 amendments in order to enforce those amendments provides one opportunity to research that presumed linkage and demonstrates one place where these agenda overlap.

As we have partially explicated above, the food and agriculture markets across Africa, as well as across the borders of its sub-regions, exhibit an entanglement of concentration, size and scope, and entrenched market power. This poses a near-existential challenge to the continent's population as well as its competition authorities. The challenge cannot begin to be addressed before there are investigations and enforcement actions of some type with respect to the firms in this industry. The market inquiry launched in Kenya in late 2023, which includes cross-border markets, is a good start and an example of how enforcement action has the potential to unlock potentially reinforcing market understanding.

About the book

This book brings together scholarship on the development of competition regimes in Africa, including drawing from papers presented at the Annual Competition and Economic Regulation week conference in east and southern Africa in 2021 and 2022. The chapters include those by researchers working in competition authorities and practitioners, which combine research insights and reflections from being at the coalface of competition cases. They critically reflect on key areas for the development of competition regimes, grouped as detailed below.

The first section of this book addresses the challenges of building authorities in practice, with chapters 2 and 3 by the former heads of authorities in Kenya and Zambia respectively. Chapter 4 tackles the requirements for building an effective African competition authority, especially in the areas of mergers and cartels.

The second section consists of chapters that analyse selected issues at the forefront of competition enforcement. These include chapters 5 and 6 on buyer power in Kenya and South Africa, while chapter 7 examines how the South African authorities have considered the 'substantial lessening of competition' standard in cases. Chapter 8 analyses the effects of cartel prosecutions on companies' shareholder value, while chapter 9 reflects on the experience of the United Kingdom for developing thinking in merger review.

In the third section, chapters 10 and 11 draw on the research by the African Market Observatory at the University of Johannesburg in conjunction with competition authorities to analyse competition issues in food markets in Kenya, Malawi and Zambia.

The fourth section is made up of four chapters that examine competition issues in digital markets. Chapter 12 reviews the South African Online Intermediation Platforms Market Inquiry, specifically highlighting the analysis and findings on international platforms in travel and tourism, which are relevant for countries across the continent (as well as further afield). Chapter 13 considers platforms 'from the bottom', meaning platforms that are local to South Africa, in areas such as e-hailing, food delivery and peri-urban accommodation services, to assess the potential for platforms to enhance inclusion. Chapter 14 looks at competition in a particular area – stock exchanges – where platforms have long operated in an analogue era and have now digitalised. Chapter 15 concludes by assessing how changes in technology under digitalisation have affected micro- and small enterprises in food in South Africa.

Notes

1   This draws from: Das Nair R (2022) The Competition Authority of Kenya: Trailblazers in the Enforcement of Buyer Power Regulations to Support MSMEs. In *11 Years of Competition Law Enforcement in Kenya*. Nairobi: The Competition Authority of Kenya.

References

Aghion PR, Cherif R & Hasanov F (2021) *Competition, innovation and inclusive growth*. Working Paper WP/21/80, International Monetary Fund

Anchustegui IH (n.d.) Buyer power: Global dictionary of competition law. Concurrences, Art. N° 12328

Andreoni A and Roberts S (2022) Governing digital platform power for industrial development: Towards an entrepreneurial-regulatory state. *Cambridge Journal of Economics* 46(6): 1431–1454

Baker J & Salop S (2015) Antitrust, competition policy, and inequality. *The Georgetown Law Journal Online* 104: 1–28

Béné C (2022) Why the great food transformation may not happen – a deep-dive into our food systems' political economy, controversies and politics of evidence. *World Development* 154 (June): 105881. https://doi.org/10.1016/j.worlddev.2022.105881

Burke M (2018) Prioritization in practice: Insights from the Competition Commission South Africa. *Journal of Antitrust Enforcement* 6(2): 261–280. https://doi.org/10.1093/jaenfo/jny001

Burke M, Paremoer T, Vilakazi T & Zengeni T (2019) Conclusion: Building institutions for competition enforcement and regional integration in Southern Africa. In J Klaaren, S Roberts & I Valodia (Eds) *Competition and regulation for inclusive growth in southern Africa* (1st edition). Johannesburg: Jacana Media. Accessed November 2023, http://oapen.org/search?identifier=1007876

Buthelezi T & Hodge J (2019) Competition policy in the digital economy: A developing country perspective. *Competition Law International* 15(2): 201–208

Carlton D & Israel M (2011) Proper treatment of buyer power in merger review. *Review of Industrial Organization*, 39(1–2): 127–136

CCSA (Competition Commission of South Africa) (2023) *Online intermediation platforms market inquiry final report and decision, July 2023*. Accessed November 2023, https://www.compcom.co.za/wp-content/uploads/2023/07/CC_OIPMI-Final-Report.pdf

Clapp J (2023) Concentration and crises: Exploring the deep roots of vulnerability in the global industrial food system. *The Journal of Peasant Studies* 50(1): 1–25. https://doi.org/10.1080/03066150.2022.2129013

Das Nair R (2022) The Competition Authority of Kenya: Trailblazers in the Enforcement of Buyer Power Regulations to Support MSMEs. In *11 Years of Competition Law Enforcement in Kenya*. Nairobi: The Competition Authority of Kenya.

Drexl J, Bakhoum M, Fox E, Gal M & Gerber D (Eds) (2012) *Competition policy and regional integration in developing countries*. Cheltenham: Edward Elgar Publishing

Eeckhout J (2021) *The profit paradox*. Princeton: Princeton University Press

Fox EM (2022) Integrating Africa by competition and market policy. *Review of Industrial Organization* 60(3): 305–326. https://doi.org/10.1007/s11151-022-09854-1

Fox EM & Bakhoum M (2019) *Making markets work for Africa: Markets, development, and competition law in Sub-Saharan Africa*. New York: Oxford University Press

Gal MS (2009) *Competition policy for small market economies*. Cambridge, Massachusetts: Harvard University Press

Gal MS (2010) Regional competition law agreements: An important step for antitrust enforcement. *University of Toronto Law Journal* 60(2): 239–261. https://doi.org/10.3138/utlj.60.2.239

Gerber DJ (2012) Regionalization, development and competition law: Exploring the political dimension. In J Drexl, M Bakhoum, E Fox, M Gal & D Gerber (Eds) *Competition policy and regional integration in developing countries*. Cheltenham: Edward Elgar Publishing

Hartzenberg T (2013) Competition policy in Africa. In C Herrmann, M Krajewski & JP Terhechte (Eds) *European yearbook of international economic law* (Vol. 4) (2013). Berlin, Heidelberg: Springer. http://link.springer.com/chapter/10.1007/978-3-642-33917-2_7

Hartzenberg T & Kalenga P (2015) *National policies and regional integration in the South African Development Community* (56th edition) (Vol. 2015). WIDER Working Paper, UNU-WIDER. https://doi.org/10.35188/UNU-WIDER/2015/945-9

IPCC (2023) Summary for Policymakers. In H Lee and J Romero (Eds) (Core Writing Team) *Climate Change 2023: Synthesis Report. Contribution of Working Groups I, II and III to the Sixth Assessment Report of the Intergovernmental Panel on Climate Change*. Geneva, Switzerland: IPCC. https://doi.org/10.59327/IPCC/AR6-9789291691647

Jenny F (2016) The institutional design of competition authorities: Debates and trends. In F Jenny & Y Katsoulacos (Eds) *Competition law enforcement in the BRICS and in developing countries: Legal and economic aspects*. Cham: Springer

Kigwiru V (2023) Supranational or cooperative? Rethinking the African Continental Free Trade Area Agreement Competition Protocol institutional design. *Journal of Antitrust Enforcement* 12(1): 98–125. https://doi.org/10.1093/jaenfo/jnad003

Kigwiru V, Klaaren J & Adham O (2021) Symposium introduction: Markets, competition and regional integration in the Global South – New perspectives. *Afronomics Law* (symposium post). Accessed November 2023, https://www.afronomicslaw.org/category/analysis/symposium-introduction-markets-competition-and-regional-integration-global-south

Klaaren J, Roberts S & Valodia I (Eds) (2019) *Competition and regulation for inclusive growth in Southern Africa* (1st edition). Johannesburg: Jacana Media

Klaaren J & Sibanda F (2019) Competition policy for the Tripartite Free Trade Area. In J Klaaren, S Roberts & I Valodia (Eds) *Competition and regulation for inclusive growth in southern Africa* (1st edition). Johannesburg: Jacana Media

Kovacic WE (1997) Getting started: Creating new competition policy institutions in transition economies. *Brooklyn Journal of International Law* 23(2): 403

Lewis D (2012) *Thieves at the dinner table: Enforcing the Competition Act, a personal account*. Johannesburg: Jacana Media

Meagher M & Roberts S (2021) The footprint of competition: Power, value distribution and exploitation in the food supply chain. In S Holmes, D Middelschulte & M Snoep (Eds) *Competition law, climate change & environmental sustainability*. Paris: Concurrences

Mondliwa P, Roberts S & Ponte S (2021) Competition and power in global value chains. *Competition & Change* 25(3–4): 328–349. https://doi.org/10.1177/1024529420975154

Muzata T, Roberts S & Vilakazi T (2017) Penalties and settlements for South African cartels: An economic review. In J Klaaren, S Roberts & I Valodia (Eds) *Competition law and economic regulation: Addressing market power in Southern Africa*. Johannesburg: Wits University Press

Nsomba G & Roberts S (2023) *Building competitive agricultural markets for Zambia: Unlocking export potential*. IGC Working Paper, LSE & Oxford International Growth Centre

Nsomba G, Roberts S, Tshabalala N & Manjengwa E (2022) *Assessing agriculture & food markets in Eastern and Southern Africa: An agenda for regional competition enforcement*. Working Paper No. 2022/1, Centre for Competition, Regulation and Economic Development, University of Johannesburg

OECD (Organisation for Economic Cooperation and Development) (2009) *Monopsony and Buyer Power: Key findings, summary and notes*. OECD Roundtables on Competition Policy Papers No. 98. Paris: OECD Publishing. https://doi.org/10.1787/36a2b824-en

Roberts S (Ed.) (2016) *Competition in Africa: Insights from key industries*. Cape Town: HSRC Press

Roberts S, Vilakazi T & Simbanegavi W (2017) Competition, regional integration and inclusive growth in Africa: A research agenda. In J Klaaren, S Roberts & I Valodia (Eds) *Competition law and economic regulation: Addressing market power in Southern Africa*. Johannesburg: Wits University Press

Roberts S (2020) Cartel enforcement – critical reflections from the South African experience. In D Healey, M Jacobs & RL Smith (Eds) *Research Handbook on methods and models of competition law*. Cheltenham: Edward Elgar Publishing

Roberts S (2023) Competition, trade, and sustainability in agriculture and food markets in Africa. *Oxford Review of Economic Policy* 39(1): 147–161

Sucker F & Klaaren J (2021) Trade and competition (laws): Interrelations from a Southern African perspective. In K Kugler & F Sucker (Eds) *International economic law: (Southern) African perspectives and priorities*. Cape Town: Juta and Company. Accessed November 2023, https://www.researchgate.net/publication/353826928_Trade_and_competition_laws_Interrelations_from_a_southern_African_perspective

United Nations Economic Commission for Africa (2019) *Assessing Regional Integration in Africa (ARIA IX)*. Accessed November 2023, https://www.uneca.org/sites/default/files/PublicationFiles/aria9_en_fin_web.pdf

Vilakazi T, Goga S & Roberts S (Eds) (2020) *Opening the South African economy: Barriers to entry, regulation and competition*. Cape Town: HSRC Press

Vilakazi T & Roberts S (2018) Cartels as 'fraud'? Insights from collusion in Southern and East Africa in the fertiliser and cement industries. *Review of African Political Economy* 46(161): 369–386. https://doi.org/10.1080/03056244.2018.1536974

Waller SW & Gathii JT (2019) Symposium on Eleanor M Fox & Mor Bakhoum, Making Markets Work for Africa: Markets, development and competition law in sub-Saharan Africa (Oxford University Press, 2019). *Afronomics Law Book Symposium III*. Accessed November 2023, https://ssrn.com/abstract=3604666

World Bank (2022) *Food Security Update LXXV*. Washington: World Bank Publications. Accessed November 2023, https://thedocs.worldbank.org/en/doc/40ebbf38f5a6b68bfc11e5273e1405d4-0090012022/related/Food-Security-Update-LXXV-December-15-2022.pdf

Wu T (2018) *The curse of bigness*. London: Atlantic Books

2 The making of a competition agency: Lessons from the Competition Authority of Kenya's development from inception to enforcement

Wang'ombe Kariuki

Chapter 2 first looks at the inception and operationalisation of the Competition Authority of Kenya, followed by a discussion of the strategic planning and prioritisation. Then the discussion focuses on new and dynamic markets, as well as enforcement during the Covid-19 pandemic. Next, the chapter examines buyer power concerns, addresses regional integration and finally concludes.

Inception and operationalisation

The establishment of an independent competition agency in Kenya was included in the government's *Economic Recovery Strategy for Wealth and Employment Creation* strategy paper, published in 2003. The then new government[1] was categorical that public administration is essential to economic recovery and the government committed to developing an appropriate competition law and creating an autonomous competition agency with an adequate budget. It is clear that the government appreciated the role of institutions in Kenya's economic growth in line with economic research on institutions and economic development (see, for example, Nobel prize winners Coase, North, Williamson and Ostrom).

The Competition Act No. 12 of 2010) (the Act) was assented to on 30 December 2010 and became operational on 1 August 2011. The Act's objective is to promote and safeguard competition in the national economy to 'enhance the welfare of the people of Kenya'. It provides for market structure regulation through control of mergers: prohibition of concerted practices and abuse of dominant positions: consumer protection: and competition advocacy. Subsequent amendments in 2016 and 2019 added control of abuse of buyer power.

The Act established the Competition Authority of Kenya (CAK) as an independent body guided by a non-executive board of nine persons and headed by a chairman. The board considers and determines all matters pursuant to investigations and mergers analysis under the Act. The decisions of the Authority can be reviewed by the Competition Tribunal and by the high court. This reflects an integrated agency/tribunal model.

The operationalisation process of the Authority was under the purview, first, of the cabinet secretary in the National Treasury. This was a strategic decision in order to not destabilise ongoing investments that were being finalised through the merger regime and to ensure an adequate budgetary allocation to the new agency in the subsequent financial year starting 1 July 2011. The second institution that was instrumental in operationalisation process was the State Corporation Advisory Committee, which categorised CAK on the then highest category of State Corporations in Kenya in order to be able to attract the specialised staff required. The committee also approved the Authority's organisational structure.

The director-general took office in January 2013, with the support of a skeleton staff, seconded from the National Treasury.

Strategic planning and prioritisation

To act immediately on its mandate, CAK developed its first four-year strategic plan. The period of the plan was informed by the need to have a short cycle to cater for any market dynamics and by the need to fast-track initiatives to build enforcement capacity. The plan stated very clearly that the enforcement capacity had to be credible, transparent and accountable, providing due process and rights of defence, reasons for every decision and rights of review.

Kenya's merger regime is suspensory and hence the Authority had to operationalise the merger regime immediately. Also, cognisant of the fact that the economy was moving from a controlled/mixed regime, advocacy was also prioritised in key economic sectors. The targeted sectors were those with the greatest impact on the poor and those that were investment enablers. This was in keeping with the national government's economic vision, Kenya Vision 2030.

Sector prioritisation to support the government's vision included addressing regulatory obstacles in the tea sector and pyrethrum sector.[2] This built awareness of the role of competition and supported Treasury funding for the Authority's budget.

Special compliance programmes for the financial and agriculture sectors raised awareness of coordinated conduct and provided for an 'amnesty' targeted at the associations in the sector.[3] Inquiries into each sector assessed common practices that undermined competition. Where industry associations proactively reviewed their own operations and made necessary changes, they would not be pursued under enforcement powers (Kariuki & Roberts 2016). This had the benefit of raising awareness and laying the basis for firmer enforcement in future if anti-competitive conduct were identified.

The retail sector, especially in urban areas, was also prioritised since concerted practices in this sector would have a significant detrimental impact on the urban poor. This focus led to the CAK imposing its first penalty on two retail outlets in the Nairobi CBD for participating in a concerted practice.[4]

In addition to attracting budget support from the National Treasury, CAK's approach was aimed at engendering the Authority's role to the policymakers including

Parliament. It was also aimed at creating awareness in the business community and among consumers about the mandate of the Authority.

CAK's strategy and prioritisation involved identifying and profiling the critical stakeholders nationally, regionally and internationally. As well as key stakeholders in Kenya, such as the media, government, business and consumer groups, institutions also included development partners and other competition agencies. The Authority has very active Memoranda of understanding (MoUs) with the Competition Commission of South Africa, which generally supports cooperation in case handling and capacity building, and with the Japan Fair Trade Commission, which has supported capacity building to CAK over the years. Individuals were also identified from academia and the research community as well as among practitioners whose main experience was in developing countries, particularly in Africa.

Accountability, buttressed by the citizen's right to information as enshrined in the Kenyan Constitution, motivated CAK to work closely with the media. The media was identified as an indispensable stakeholder to distribute information about CAK's work and decisions, while at the same time offering critique. On the other hand, the Authority has considered the media as a source of intelligence regarding competition law infringements. This is evident from the fact that the first concerted practice case where the Authority imposed a penalty was captured through a daily newspaper. The media outreach was cemented through the annual training focused on the press and recently expanded to bloggers and influencers. Legal advocates and other stakeholders are also targeted for specialised training programmes every year, while stakeholders' views are sought during the Annual Competition Symposium.

Work products of the International Competition Network have been central to developing the regulatory frameworks necessary to create transparency and predictability in CAK's enforcement process. However, CAK's approach to adapting these products has been more of a cross-pollination rather than simply transplanting the North to the South.

Good investigating and analysis capacity is non-negotiable for a competition agency to acquire the requisite credibility. This involves engaging the optimal number of staff with the necessary skills and ensuring continuous skills development. Having embarked on enforcement with an initial staff complement of 25, who were seconded from the National Treasury, CAK over the first decade was committed to ongoing skills development.

The first phase towards building the critical capabilities for enforcement was to conduct a job and skills needs analysis. Out of the initial 25 staff, only 12 were retained. The second phase was to progressively fill the 99 positions identified in different departments. Managers were recruited first, in order to give them an opportunity to recruit their teams. The recruitment process for professional staff focused on attracting young graduates, people who had worked with corporates and universities/research bodies, and public servants. The objective was to create a distinctive CAK culture while also blending the strengths of both the young and the experienced.

CAK developed internship and young professional programmes. These programmes have trained over 100 young people who were subsequently absorbed into corporates, law firms and universities. This has provided a pool of expertise and ensured more understanding for better self-regulation by corporates and for law firms to provide better advice.

Building a team with a common purpose and vision was critical in actualising CAK's mandate. A knowledge management infrastructure was established and complemented with regular communications, through periodic communiques and town hall meetings. Induction for all new staff was central to the onboarding process. This has included new employee' becoming familiar with the Authority's Strategic Plan, the Competition Act, and the other regulations and frameworks guiding the CAK's enforcement regime.

The use of short-term visiting consultants has supplemented expertise and transferred knowledge. The decision not to engage long-term resident consultants was informed by CAK's strategic objective aimed at developing its own internal capacity in as short a period as possible.

International engagements are important for improving the overall enforcement capacity of CAK. Staff thus participate in workshops and conferences, where they are invited as speakers or panellists. Papers that have undergone an internal peer review process have been presented at a number of international conferences. The review process ensures that the whole enforcement team is informed of the Authority's operations and helps the authors refine their thinking. Participation in regional conferences is aimed at driving the agenda of regional competition law, through CAK's taking a lead in the formulation of the regional regulatory frameworks.

As a result of these initiatives, CAK has progressively built staff capacity in terms of numbers and skills. This has allowed it to expand its competition work from merger determinations and advocacy initiatives to cases of abuse of dominance, consumer protection, cartel enforcement and control of abuse of buyer power over the first 10 years of its existence.

Shifting gears to include a focus on new and dynamic markets

All the strategic plans identified the need to progressively build capacity for cartel investigations and to tackle issues in dynamic markets, especially in digital services. The approach towards digital markets was to encourage innovation while controlling competition harm.

Kenya has been a trailblazer in leveraging technology to drive the economy and is a leader in payment platforms. The growth and success of Safaricom's M-PESA platform for payments and money transfers has been well documented, with

Safaricom being hailed by many researchers as a market leader driven by research and innovation. However, reviews have also found 'that these successes were achieved using strategies that have distorted and lessened competition (Macmillan Keck & Acacia Economics 2016).

When approaching the regulation of digital platforms, CAK has faced the challenge of facilitating innovation on the one hand and curtailing potential harm to competition on the other. The challenge is compounded by the fact that these are new and dynamic markets and there are no clear enforcement precedents globally.

CAK has had to craft its own regulatory approach, including decisions to rectify competition law infringements. This requires CAK to be flexible: Rather than having a purely legalistic approach, CAK focuses on understanding and appreciating the product/market offered, the needs and benefits to the consumers, elements of disruption and resultant innovation, and the general public interest benefits. This has been largely achieved through market inquiries (Kariuki & Roberts 2016).

With the growth of the new markets and the importance of market inquiries for understanding the related competition issues, CAK approached Parliament to make it mandatory for parties under consideration in a market inquiry to supply any information that has been requested.

Extinguishing a margin squeeze in USSD

The objective of the CAK market study into Unstructured Supplementary Service Data (USSD) in 2016 was to determine whether or not the terms of the provision of USSD services was detrimental to competition in financial services and to highlight issues, if any, relating to consumer protection.

USSD is a standard for transmitting information over a global system for mobile telecommunications (GSM) network. This is the common channel for provision of and access to mobile financial services in Kenya and is controlled by mobile network operators (MNOs). A short code is required for non-MNO companies to provide mobile financial services using USSD. In Kenya, USSD codes are assigned to MNOs, who more often provide secondary assignments to non-MNOs. Access can also be provided via the SIM toolkit (STK).

The market study considered four relevant markets. In retail mobile telecommunications services provided by MNOs and MVNOs (mobile virtual network operators), Safaricom PLC had a market share of 70%, based on subscriber base, while in terms of revenue it had a market share of 80–90%. The wholesale market includes provision of USSD and STK access by MNOs and MVNOs. The customers are banks and other mobile financial services providers who enter into agreements and pay MNOs to provide access via USSD. The study found that Safaricom's market shares in the wholesale USSD and STK markets were over 80%.

In the retail money transfer and payment services, Safaricom's M-PESA was more popular than any retail transfer service provided by the banks. Safaricom had a market share of over 70% of all mobile money subscribers. It is evident that Safaricom was dominant, with over 50% market shares in all markets. Safaricom had also expanded into the markets for providing savings and loan products, in partnership with some key banks. The inquiry indicated that Safaricom had over time accumulated 'considerable market share in this market.

The inquiry focused on possible excessive pricing, price discrimination and exclusionary conduct by Safaricom PLC, the dominant firm. The prices charged varied depending on customers. For banks with which Safaricom had a relationship in terms of supporting its M-Shwari and M-PESA products, no USSD or STK charges were levied, while the other banks were charged between Ksh2 and Ksh5 per session. Other mobile money-related service providers were incurring charges of up to Ksh10 per session. The assessment found that the conduct raised the costs of Safaricom's competitors and squeezed their margins to the extent that it was commercially unviable to supply downstream customers. Safaricom's position meant that it had both the *ability* and the *incentive* to exclude competitors, and its conduct had affected competition.

To address the conduct, the CAK reached a commitment decision with Safaricom for it to revise the USSD code access prices down to a maximum of Ksh1 (Paelo & Roberts 2022). This intervention has facilitated the growth of mobile financial services in Kenya, which was particularly beneficial during and after the Covid–19 pandemic.

In addition, during the inquiry it was noted that Safaricom did not provide all the information requested as it was not obligatory at the time. To remedy this, the Authority proposed amendments to the legislation that made it mandatory for parties under an inquiry to provide all information requested. The amendments were subsequently passed.

Enforcement in times of crisis – the Covid–19 pandemic

The Covid–19 pandemic was not only a challenge to the ability of competition agencies to continue their work. Agencies also had to ensure that governments did not undermine market economies due to global supply chain challenges. After the first coronavirus case was declared in March 2020, CAK's first priority was to keep its staff safe. This would make sure the enforcement capacity of CAK was not compromised and that its work in ensuring no price volatility as a result of infringements of the Competition Act would continue. The staff were guided to work remotely with periodic updates and virtual meetings. This arrangement was supported by the Authority's Case management system and Enterprise resources management, which the Authority had invested in earlier, informed by its Business Continuity Plan.

The Authority's top management was also in contact with the government's Coronavirus Emergency Response Committee for intelligence regarding any cases of supply chain constraints caused by competition restraints. In addition, both traditional and social media, including relevant influencers, were identified as credible sources of intelligence.

Unconscionable conduct case

After the first coronavirus case was identified, CAK issued a press statement cautioning firms that intended to increase prices of essentials in a way that was not informed by forces of supply and demand. This was followed by countrywide investigations targeting the pharmaceutical sector and basic commodities manufacturers. CAK applied a section under its consumer protection provisions, which states that 'it shall be an offence for a person in trade in connection with the supply or possible supply of goods or services to another person, to engage in conduct that is, in all the circumstances, unconscionable'.

The Authority considered a price hike, not informed by forces of supply and demand to be unconscionable conduct, especially when geographical markets had shrunk due to lockdowns. Consumers' bargaining position had also diminished, especially in relation to preventative necessities. CAK restrained itself from applying the excessive pricing provisions under the Act since it first required proof of dominance in the relevant market.

Pursuant to the investigation, the Authority issued a remedial order to Cleanshelf Supermarkets for unconscionably adjusting prices of sanitisers. The supermarket had stock of the sanitisers retailing at Ksh800 prior to the pronouncement of the first Covid-19 case. Immediately after the pronouncement, the prices were adjusted to Ksh1000. The Authority concluded that 'the retailer ... exploited its relative strength to the commercial detriment of consumers'[5] Consequently, the retailer was ordered to 'contact and refund all consumers who purchased nine hundred and sixty (960) pieces of the product above the usual selling price and submit evidence to support the same'. A compliance process was developed to ensure adherence to the order.

CAK also initiated a market surveillance framework in which it required all major retail outlets to forward the retail prices of essential commodities fortnightly, along with their suppliers' prices. (These included disinfectants, sanitisers, sanitary towels, toilet papers, gloves, masks and foodstuffs.) This surveillance mechanism was an excellent way of ensuring that retailers did not exploit their relative strength during the pandemic.

Further, CAK issued an order to major manufacturers and distributors of essential foodstuffs and commodities to negate any exclusive distribution agreements they may have been actualised without the Authority's explicit approval. Specifically, the order was directed to the manufacturers and distributors of maize/corn flour, wheat flour, edible oils, rice, sanitisers, toilet paper, gloves and masks. The order was meant to increase distributorship competition and allow new entrants in manufacturing to access distributors in order to facilitate their markets' access, and as a result allow consumers to access the products across the whole country.

The interventions by the CAK ensured uninterrupted supply chains in the economy and thus allowed consumers to access essential commodities. While the Covid-19 pandemic seriously affected the financial stability of most businesses, especially micro, small and medium enterprises (MSMEs), a competitive economy offered the best prospects for the post-Covid-19 economic recovery.

Buyer power concerns

The collapse of two major retail outlets in Kenya with huge suppliers' debt accumulated over long-term delayed payments, among others, motivated the Kenyan government to legislate to provide for the control of abuse of buyer power. The retailers were Uchumi, which collapsed in 2015, and Nakumatt Limited, which collapsed in 2018. The two cases brought to the fore policy concerns relating to how the big retailers were misusing their relative buyer strength against MSMEs. This could lead to the supplier becoming unsustainable and having to exit the market. With data from the Kenya National Bureau of Statistics indicating that approximately 40% of Kenya's GDP was supported by SMEs and that they constituted 98% of all businesses in the economy, a high rate of SMEs collapsing would thus have a huge effect on the Kenyan economy.

Policymakers were thus confronted with an emerging regulatory problem that could be catastrophic to the Kenyan economy and also affected most businesses owned and operated by local Kenyans. This called for an immediate regulatory intervention.

One school of thought was to create a new regulatory regime, with a new institutional dispensation. However, this approach would take much longer in legislative and operationalisation processes, and demand more budget outlay. The ministry responsible for trade and industry was advocating for this approach. However, the National Treasury's approach was for the minimisation of costs from regulation. The Treasury also viewed abuse of buyer power as an economy-wide challenge affecting all sectors of the economy, including the retail, insurance and construction industries. The government adopted the Treasury's position and the Competition Act was amended in 2019 to provide for CAK's control of abuse of buyer power.

Buyer power is defined as influence that a purchaser may exert in order to obtain more favourable terms than would usually pertain from a supplier. The conduct includes delays in payment, unilateral termination of commercial relationships, and transfer of costs or commercial risks. Notwithstanding the novelty of the regulatory challenge, the amendment was informed by the deliberations of the Organisation for Economic Cooperation and Development (OECD) Competition Committee.

To date, the Authority has applied these provisions to conduct investigations into incidences of abuse of buyer power in the retail and insurance sectors. In the retail sector, the provisions were invoked with regard to Tuskys Supermarket, which was subject to prudential and reporting requirements in 2021. The application of these provisions facilitated the recovery of Ksh2.1 billion from Tuskys Supermarket owed to the small and medium enterprise (SME) suppliers prior to its collapse in 2021. This was not the case when Uchumi and Nakumatt closed since the provisions had not been enacted. CAK has developed a code of practice for suppliers and buyers in the retail sector. This code provides for resolving disputes and the intervention of CAK is triggered when there is no agreement.

In the motor vehicle insurance sector, the provisions have resulted in the recovery of Ksh36 million in delayed payments owed by insurance companies to motor vehicle repairers and have managed to help salvage over 200 jobs.[6]

In December 2022, CAK entered into a settlement decision with Unilever Kenya Limited after the Authority conducted investigations under the abuse of buyer power provisions. It was agreed, among others, that Unilever would reduce payment periods for all existing SMEs from 90 to 60 days effective 1 January 2023, and subsequently to 45 days, effective 1 January 2025. Unilever also agreed to increase its procurement from SMEs by Ksh400 million and dedicate an annual budget of Ksh75 million to undertake supplier development training for its SMEs suppliers.[7]

These enforcement initiatives have been aimed at ensuring SMEs sustainability and removing some of the supply chain constraints that may hinder post-Covid–19 recovery. The three cases reflect an agency that is flexible in its enforcement capability and capacity, and that is determined to achieve results in all emerging sectors of the economy while driving the national economic agenda.

Informing regional integration

The success of a competition agency requires more than a focus on domestic challenges. CAK's development has been cognisant of globalisation and the resultant effects. Specifically, one strategic objective under its second Strategic Plan (2017/2018–2020/2021) was to 'deepen integration regionally and internationally through expanding market frontiers'.

Global markets and supply chains have an effect on the Kenyan economy, not only by exerting competition pressure on the local markets but also by meeting demand that is not adequately served by national industries. Some Kenyan firms also compete regionally and internationally.

Over the years, CAK has engaged the international community to develop its regulatory capacity, in both the human and legislative aspects. This has been done through MoUs, training and participation in conferences and workshops. It has also cooperated in case handling, especially with the Competition Commission of South Africa and the Common Market for Eastern and Southern Africa Competition Commission. The Authority has been a very active member of the International Competition Network (ICN) including participating in the development of various ICN work products, presenting at conferences and hosting ICN events. CAK joined the ICN Steering Group, where it can motivate for ICN work products that meet the needs of authorities in Africa. It is also active in OECD and United Nations Conference on Trade and Development (UNCTAD).

CAK is a founder member of the African Competition Forum (ACF), an informal network of competition authorities on the continent that was launched in Nairobi in 2011. The aim of the ACF is to promote competition across the continent in the interests of economic development mainly through adopting competition laws and building capacity to enforce it across the continent. The ACF also jointly conducts market studies to inform policy development and develop enforcement and research capacity.

The Kenyan government supports CAK's participation in the forum as a strategic way of creating consensus among competition agencies before the launch of any trade and competition negotiations, at the regional and continental level. This is evident in the negotiation of the African Continental Free Trade Area Competition Protocol, which was concluded in in 2023 in record time, compared with the time it took for the COMESA competition regulations and East African Community (EAC) competition protocol to be developed.

CAK has also been vocally in favour of the alignment of regional laws and provisions. CAK offered its views in the COMESA operationalisation process by articulating the need to create mergers thresholds, set merger filling fees that are commensurate with the costs of analyzing mergers, and develop a case referral and coordination mechanism with the National competition agencies. CAK took the view that these initiatives would be indispensable, not only to create predictability for firms but also to support enforcement cooperation between the regional and national agencies. As a result, COMESA has promulgated various rules and guidelines. Subsequently, CAK sought National Assembly approval through the amendment of the Competition Act and development of specific regulations to address the merger threshold and referral mechanism.

This arrangement has laid the foundation for a cooperation framework during the consideration of mergers. The framework implementation can be further enhanced by forums for shared analysis to reach the final common market merger determination, rather than the adoption and compilation of specific positions of national agencies.

The East Africa Competition Authority has started building regulatory capacity, albeit slowly. As of 2023, the Authority was yet to report any case since its inception in 2016. However, it is developing subsidiary legislation and attracting staff. CAK has offered technical support in this area. There is a challenge in the applicability of the EAC and COMESA laws due to dual membership of most EAC countries. CAK has noted this and advised the two regional competition agencies to create a coordination or referral mechanism to address the regulatory obstacle.

CAK's approach to enhancing regional integration has underpinned the technical assistance it has provided to the regional bodies and its active roles in the ACF and other global competition networks. In addition, five former employees of CAK moved to serve in the regional competition agencies as a way of building networks to improve the cooperation initiatives.

CAK's approach is also informed by Kenya's national interests, especially in improving the regional investment climate. The flexibility of CAK to support regional integration through ceding of regulatory powers donated to it by the National Assembly to achieve this objective is clear. On the other hand, CAK has supported the improvement of the investment climate in the common markets by curtailing regulatory overreach at the regional level.

Conclusion

CAK's development and enforcement over its first decade offer important lessons – some of which differ from the apparent consensus in the area of competition law enforcement.

First, the general view is that competition agencies in developing countries take long on the 'runway' because they are not supported in their take-off as governments lack appreciation of their role in the national economic agenda. CAK is only a decade old, but its prioritisation of enforcement and decisions have made policy-makers receptive to it and attracted the support of the government and Parliament. Internationally, CAK has been admitted to the ICN Steering Group. This shows an agency whose enforcement is visible both nationally and internationally.

Second, CAK's trajectory reflects the success of the focus on building internal capacity alongside an incremental enforcement strategy. This started with mergers and advocacy, which aimed at building coalitions of supporters. The focus then switched to digital platforms and other newly developing markets. CAK gradually placed itself 'at the table', ensuring it was noticed by the government rather than having to demand support.

The third lesson from the CAK experience is that business continuity plans should be a key feature in the governance of competition institutions. To illustrate this, the plans enabled the rapid switch to remote working and ensuring continuity in enforcement work during the Covid–19 pandemic.

The fourth lesson is that targeted, systematic and incremental enforcement can have an impact. CAK focused on general public needs and utilised commitment decisions, especially in dynamic markets. Credibility was created through a transparent, predictable, evidence-based process. This enabled CAK to take enforcement action in novel areas such as digital markets and abuse of buyer power, where it could not depend on existing precedents. Enforcement strategy informed by market inquiries can be effective as the inquiry process involves engaging with the regulated firms and presenting evidence. It also allows for an expansive and purposive interpretation, which is important in minimising regulatory costs and time.

By comparison, a legalistic enforcement approach will almost always be slow and adversarial. The CAK experience also highlights that the orthodox traditional parameters of competition law may be insufficient to address some market failures. CAK's approach to abuse of buyer power and the adoption of consumer protection provisions to enforce competition-related issues during the Covid-19 pandemic and recovery period show how an agency can create more competitive markets through utilising non-orthodox competition law provisions.

Finally, the Kenyan experience indicates the importance of domestic and international engagements, with stakeholders being structured and guided by a policy. This will ensure that the engagements are meaningful and the objectives are measurable. International stakeholders, whether individuals or institutions, should be identified purposefully in line with the competition agency's agenda. Unstructured international engagements will only drain the agency's resources and create unproductive duplication without enhancing the agency's capacity and visibility. Cooperation at the regional level should be facilitated further through setting of prioritisation enforcement areas between regional competition agencies and national agencies.

Notes

1   The government of President Kibaki had assumed power in August 2002.
2   See: CAK Annual Report, 2015/2016
3   See: CAK Annual Report, 2015/2016
4   See: CAK Annual Report, 2013/2014
5   See: CAK Annual Report, 2019/2020
6   See: CAK Annual Report, 2021/2022
7   See: Kenya Gazette Notice No. 581

References

Competition Authority of Kenya, Annual Reports, various years

Kariuki FW & Roberts S (2016) Competition and development: Insights into building institutions from the Kenyan experience. In EM Fox, H First, N Charbit & E Ramundo (Eds) *Antitrust in emerging and developing countries: Africa, Brazil, China, India, Mexico*. New York: Concurrences

Macmillan Keck & Acacia Economics (2016) *Competition inquiry into USSD service provision in Kenya*. Nairobi: The Competition Authority of Kenya

Paelo A & Roberts S (2022) Competition and regulation of mobile money platforms in Africa: A comparative analysis of Kenya and Uganda. *Review of Industrial Organization* 60: 463–489

3 The fight against cartels in Zambia: Challenges and successes

Chilufya P Sampa

Detecting and prosecuting cartels is a major challenge for competition authorities around the world, but in Africa the effects of such conduct are usually worse for the economy and the people. This is mainly because the economies are smaller and more concentrated and the people are poorer. Cartels are likely to be more widespread and longer-lasting, and therefore have a much greater impact on the population and economies of African countries. At the same time, where they have been established, the competition authorities are relatively young and under-resourced.

These constraints make learning from practical experiences even more important. In this chapter, I reflect on the experience of the Zambian competition authority, the Competition and Consumer Protection Commission (CCPC), under the new legislation enacted in 2010, which gave powers to the authority to investigate and penalise cartel conduct. As the Executive Director from 2011 to 2022, together with my team, I had to consider how to address cases of possible collusion, which is generally secret. In the decade that followed the new legislation, the CCPC undertook dawn raids of suspected cartels, penalised firms, and put in place a corporate leniency policy with mixed results. I reflect on some key cases and the lessons that can be learnt.

The harm caused by cartels is widely recognised, as reflected in a recent summary by the World Bank[1]:

> Anticompetitive business practices have been detected in various markets that are important for a country's overall competitiveness and poverty alleviation. Cartels, which increase prices in affected goods and services by at least 20 per cent, have been found in markets such as fertiliser, cement, and transportation services. Staple consumer products such as bread and sugar, and critical financial services ranging from electronic payment systems to insurance, cost consumers more due to cartels and abuse of dominance. Bid rigging in public procurement is prevalent in construction, transportation and health sectors. (World Bank 2023)

The incentive to coordinate behaviour in order to increase profits is a powerful one. Despite the now widespread legal prohibitions on explicit coordination, firms continue to form cartels to restrict output or set prices (Choi & Gerlach 2015). Thus, it is imperative for competition authorities worldwide to fight cartels, and more especially in Africa and developing countries, given the extent of the likely prevalence and resulting harm.

The essence of market competition is for firms to attract customers by delivering better and less costly products, and the goal of antitrust laws is to preserve competitive market environments to ensure that this is the case (Levenstein & Suslow 2012).

The increasing awareness of the role of competition law and policy in southern African countries has emphasised the role of competition in job creation, poverty reduction, and small and medium enterprise (SME) empowerment (Kaira 2017). These objectives of competition policy go mostly hand in hand with the traditional ones (ICN 2002) as cartels raise prices and restrict output which compounds poverty and undermines employment creation. Cartels also tend to exclude small and medium enterprises (SMEs) as their durability depends on raising barriers to entry.

The first cartel case busted by the Zambia Competition Commission (ZCC), as it was known then, was in the petroleum sector in 2004. Oil marketing companies had decided to price-fix fuel and petroleum products. Interestingly, the chairman of the cartel and managing director of Caltex Zambia blatantly stated that they had fixed prices, that they did not see anything wrong with this and that the government was aware of the collusion. This clear admission reflected the lack of awareness of competition law in Zambia and the need for advocacy to highlight the harm caused by cartels. Therefore, up until 2010, the ZCC used advocacy to deal with many anti-competitive trade practices, including cartels. The authority's enforcement powers were mainly employed in mergers and consumer protection. However, in 2010, there was an impetus to start enforcing laws to prevent anti-competitive conduct. With the repeal of the Competition and Fair-Trade Act and the passing of the Competition and Consumer Protection Act (CCPA) (No. 24 of 2010), came a new dawn.

Next, chapter 3 examines cartel enforcement, including key cases. The chapter then discusses the corporate leniency policy, highlighting key cases, and finally concludes and draws out some key lessons.

Cartel enforcement under the Competition and Consumer Protection Act of 2010

It must be noted that the change in strategies and priorities in fact happened just before the new Act was passed. The Commission initiated cartel investigations in the fertiliser sector and the auto repair industry in 2009. The evidence that was obtained could not be used under the new competition law regime from 2010. Nevertheless, the parties continued to engage in cartel behaviour even after the passing of the new Act and investigations were finalised by the new CCPC in each of these markets.

Under the new legislation, the CCPC was established and given the powers to investigate anti-competitive conduct, which may be covert, such as cartels. This included powers to obtain information. The CCPC is governed by a Board of Commissioners, which makes the initial decision on cases. Decisions can then be appealed to the specialist Competition and Consumer Protection Tribunal, while further reviews can be taken to the courts.

Six major cartel cases are described, based on information that is available in the public domain. The cases highlight features that are in line with international studies and experience, and point to issues for developing countries like Zambia in enforcing laws against cartels and the importance of doing so.

Auto repair cartel (2010–2013)

The significance of this cartel case is that it was the first time the Commission carried out a dawn raid, with great success for a young authority. An appeal challenged the legality of the raid, and the judgment formed the foundation on which future raids and cartel analysis and evidence would be based.

The case was initiated because of an awareness campaign that the Commission had carried out with insurance companies. One of the companies had reported to the Commission that auto repair companies had colluded to fix the terms and conditions for repairing accident-damaged vehicles that were insured. They had agreed to charge a commission whenever a consumer requested a quote to repair a vehicle. This commission amount was to cover the cost of preparing a quote if the company did not win the job of repairing the vehicle.

Equipped with the new law and the power to carry out a dawn raid, the Commission targeted three auto repair companies and carried out a raid. Although there were 19 companies altogether, human resource constraints confined the raid to the three companies that the Commission believed were the core conspirators of the cartel. Evidence in the form of an agreement document signed by all 19 auto repair companies was found at the cartel's ringleader, Top Gear. As collusion in the Zambian law is a per se prohibition, no evidence of effects was required to prove a violation. The Board of Commissioners penalised the companies at the rate of 5% of turnover, but on appeal, the Competition Tribunal reduced the fine to 2% for the ringleader and 1% for the other colluders.

This was a landmark case in that there was a challenge to the legality of a dawn raid in issuing a delayed investigation notice, citing natural justice for not having granted the players an opportunity to respond (per se prohibition). The court's decision upheld the authority's powers to conduct the search under the Act, as follows:

> Having considered the circumstances of his case and the evidence before us, we are satisfied that the Commission carried out its investigations in accordance with the provisions of the law, particularly Section 55 of the Act. The Commission used search warrants to search the premises of the Appellants in accordance with Section 55 of the Act which [requires] search warrants [to indicate] the subject matter and purpose of the investigations. We find that the nature of the issues raised in this matter are such that there was no need to call for witnesses at the hearing or to call the Appellants to make representations or to be heard in view of the fact that a horizontal agreement was established which was prohibited per

se and thus the law had been violated. We do agree with the Appellant's submission and authorities on the principals of natural justice. However, the Supreme Court clearly stated in the case of Frederick Jacob Titus Chiluba v Attorney General, Appeal No. 125 of 2002 that: *'It is not all cases where rules of natural justice are always applicable'.*[2] (Emphasis added)

Fertiliser cartel (2011)

The fertiliser cartel case is important as it showed how egregious cartel activity can be in harming large parts of the economy and that government policy can in fact facilitate cartel behaviour. The fact that the government saved millions of dollars after busting the cartel shows the importance of competition law and policy, and what an effective agency can do to help government advance its developmental agenda.

The Zambian government subsidises fertiliser for smallholder farmers under the Fertiliser Input Support Programme (FISP). The Commission prioritised investigations in the fertiliser sector because of the huge amounts of money being spent by the government. The Commission identified and penalised cartel conduct in 2011.

The cartel was enabled by the Zambia Public Procurement Authority (ZPPA), which made it impossible for other players to enter the market. The ZPPA tender document only allowed bidders who had supplied the government with fertiliser for the last seven years to be eligible to bid for the tender. This resulted in the disqualification of all but two companies, namely Nyiombo and Omnia. These two companies then fixed prices by providing cover bids and divided markets, with the north of the country going to Nyiombo and the south going to Omnia. The authority conducted a dawn raid on the two companies and found evidence that they had colluded. Before the Commission could finalise its investigations, the parties applied to the Competition Tribunal to stay the investigation. In its ruling, the Tribunal stated that it could not interfere with the investigation and that the appeal was premature. This was of paramount importance, as it became very clear that the Tribunal would not interfere with investigations of the Commission. The parties appealed the decision of the Tribunal, which the Supreme Court upheld.

Meanwhile, the Board made a finding of collusion in 2011 and decided to penalise the two companies with fines of 5% of each company's annual turnover. This decision was appealed to the Tribunal, which in its ruling stated the following (in para. 158):

> We recalled from our earlier consideration of grounds 1 and 2 and the findings we reached that Vincent Mkuyamba was the Appellants' Director and General Manager and Omnia Small Scale Limited General Manager. ... We concluded from these documents that both the Appellant and Nyiombo were awarded tenders to supply fertilisers under the FISP

for the farming seasons 2010/2011 right up to 2012/2013 when the investigations were launched and that they would therefore normally be competitors for the supply of fertilisers under the FISP. The following questions beg answers:

(a) Why would Nyiombo inform the Appellant's General Manager of trucks to be received by the latter for Eastern Province, and the latter request for the former to advise as to when the 'Eastern deliveries' would be concluded and to revert urgently 'as the Minister is expecting (the latter's) feedback' this afternoon?

(b) Why would Nyiombo be requesting the Appellant to 'send a report for all the receipts into the Omnia areas so as to analyse and follow up on the status of deliveries'?

(c) Why would Nyiombo communicate to the Appellant on the subject matter 'Urea allocations into Southern' and convey allocations for the Southern Province? Why would Nyiombo communicate to the Appellant that a consignment for some designated districts would follow and provide allocation of fertilisers to designated districts in Eastern and Southern Provinces?

(d) Why would Nyiombo 'facilitate Omnia with receiving 800 bags of Urea and 1200 bags of NPK'?

The only reasonable inference we draw is that the Appellant had the tender for the supply and delivery of fertilisers for those areas (Omnia areas or zones), such as Eastern and Southern Provinces, when in actual fact the secret arrangement between the two enterprises was that they decided who actually supplied which zone. Meaning that, secretly, the two enterprises conducted themselves as if they were one unit.[3]

The Tribunal ruled in favour of the Commission, citing price fixing, bid rigging and market allocation as conduct in which the Appellant and Nyiombo had been engaged. The impact of the fertiliser cartel was that in the year it was busted, the government was able to source cheaper fertiliser from other companies. This resulted in the government spending US$20 million less on fertiliser that year, which the Commission highlighted to stakeholders as constituting a significant saving. This precedent provided an incentive for the government to increase its funding to the Commission in years to come.

Bread cartel (2015)

After the Competition Commission of South Africa had busted the bread cartel in 2007 and highlighted the impact it had on the livelihoods of the poor, the CCPC took note of the ever-increasing prices of bread in the Copperbelt Province of Zambia. This case highlights the impact that cartels have on the poorest of the poor and was a priority for the Commission for this reason.

The Copperbelt Province is home to over 4 million of Zambia's population of around 20 million, due to the mining industry being mostly located there. In 2012, the Commission conducted a survey of the bakeries in the province but found little evidence to warrant further investigations. However, in 2015, after a complaint from the public about the uniform increase in the price of bread by 23% on the same day, the Commission conducted a dawn raid on the Copperbelt bakeries. Evidence was found suggesting that the bakeries were engaged in price fixing and raising the price of bread, a daily staple for many people, by over 20%. The Board ruled in favour of the Commission.

In its analysis of the impact of the cartel, the Commission stated the following:

> The population of the Copperbelt Province was about 2 362 207 in 2015 with 83% living in the urban and 17% in the rural area. The average number of households per family is five (5) members, most of whom require a loaf of bread per day. Before the Commission's intervention, 1 960 632 which represents the urban population spent K16 430 094.57 (US$1 643 009.5) on bread per day. After the Commission intervened and there was a reduction in the price of bread, K15 528 203.94 (US$1 552 820.4) was spent on bread. This made consumers save K901 890.63 (US$90 189.1) per day.[4]

During the bread cartel investigation, the Commission introduced a corporate leniency policy and this was offered to the cartel members to speed up investigations. The cartel members did not take up the offer and opted to settle the matter with the Commission. In an interview, the suspected 'ringleader' stated categorically that 'no member of the cartel would take up the leniency offer', without further elaboration.

Fish fingerlings cartel

This cartel case was brought to light by the Citizens Economic Empowerment Commission (CEEC), which had funded several fish farmers to develop the fish sector. At the time, the country was a net importer of fish. Through the CEEC, the government started an initiative to fund small-scale farmers to start fish farms. Information provided by the farmers to the CEEC suggested that the breeders of fish fingerlings were allegedly engaged in cartel activity, and that this was undermining the government policy to develop the sector.

More specifically, the Commission received a complaint from the CEEC that there was a likely cartel in the fish fingerling sector, where the prices of fish fingerlings had been fixed. As the market was still developing, there were only a few fish fingerlings breeding farms (producers) in the Siavonga, Lusaka and Kabwe districts. Due to limited resources, the Commission decided to target only the fish fingerling producers in the Kabwe and Lusaka districts, carrying out a dawn raid. The dawn raid on these companies yielded positive results. A key difference with this raid compared to others was that the evidence was no longer in paper format in files, but stored on electronic devices. This presented a new challenge to the Commission for how to access these electronic devices and social media accounts, which were used as platforms to fix prices.

With the help of the Zambia Information Communication and Telecommunication Authority (ZICTA), the seized devices were eventually accessed. The Commission's new procedure of offering leniency while undertaking a dawn raid was taken up by one of the cartel members. Electronic evidence showed that the producers had formed a 'WhatsApp group' where they discussed prices and costs of doing business in the country and suggested that a price increment be effected for fish fingerlings from K0.70 to K1.00 on an agreed date. They acted on the suggestion. The evidence obtained from the cartel member resulted in the cartel being busted. In 2021, the cartel members were fined 9% or 10% of their turnover.[5] Advocacy was also carried out to ensure that the cartel members understood the provisions of the CCPA.

Poultry cartel (2018)

A four-year investigation led to the CCPC fining four poultry hatcheries 7% of their annual turnover in 2018 for fixing trading conditions and setting production quotas.[6] According to the statement of the CCPC public relations officer, following the Board of Commissioners meeting of 1 March 2018, the companies involved in collusive practices were Hybrid Poultry Farm Ltd, Ross Breeders Zambia Ltd, Quantum Foods Zambia Ltd and Tiger Chicks.[7] The case is noteworthy as it involved multinational companies with operations across the region and with effects along a value chain that impacted SME producers downstream. The arrangements appear similar to those identified in the United States of America (USA) in 2021 (see Li & Weisman 2023; Sappington & Turner 2023).

Cement cartel (2021–2022)

The cement cartel involved three cement companies, with at least one also being involved in cartels around the world. High prices due to collusion have a major impact on the infrastructure investment required for Zambia's development.

The cartel was investigated over several years. In 2021, the Commission decided to undertake a dawn raid on four companies: Dangote Cement, Lafarge Cement, Sinoma Cement and Zambezi Cement. Dangote Cement had a plant on the Copperbelt, as did Lafarge and Zambezi. Lafarge Cement also had a cement plant in Lusaka, as did Sinoma. Sinoma Cement was barely a year old at the time.

After undertaking investigations, the Commission found that three of the cement companies – Dangote, Lafarge and Sinoma – had engaged in cartel conduct. Dangote quickly applied for leniency while it also recalled its managing director. This meant that the Commission had no access to him for interviews. Lafarge and Sinoma both denied being involved in a cartel. The allegations were that they had fixed the prices of cement to US$8 dollars for a 50kg bag while the pre-cartel prices had been US$4 dollars per bag. The Commission's decision not only penalised the two companies that did not apply for leniency but also ordered that the price of cement be dropped to the pre-cartel prices. All three companies appealed the decision of the Board (on Dangote's part the appeal was limited to the order to reduce the price to pre-cartel levels). As of October 2023, this case is still with the Tribunal.

Corporate leniency policy

In 2014, the Commission introduced the corporate leniency policy. The policy would allow enterprises engaged in anti-competitive conduct to self-report and be absolved from fines. The provision that provides for leniency does not limit it to cartels but applies any anti-competitive conduct. In later years, the Commission had a moratorium for a year on all restrictive business practices including cartels, provided the enterprises and individuals self-reported. However, this was not successful in inducing companies to come forward.

The Commission publicised the leniency programme, hoping that enterprises and individuals would take it up. Unfortunately, the industry has remained largely unresponsive to this new initiative, although there were leniency applications by members of both the fish fingerling and cement cartels described earlier in the chapter.

International experience and the literature point to the importance of factors such as legal certainty and the credible threat of detection behind the success of leniency programmes (see Lavoie 2010; Roberts 2020). Some of the reasons behind the low uptake of the leniency programme and moratorium in Zambia are as follows:

- Stakeholders lack trust in the system. The private sector does not believe that once companies shave self-reported or blown the whistle, they will not be prosecuted. This comes from the fact that while the Commission has the authority not to pursue civil cases, it does not have the authority to undertake not to prosecute criminal cases. Such authority lies with the Director of Public Prosecutions (DPP). While the Commission and the DPP have signed a memorandum of understanding, this is not legally binding on either party. This emerges as a weak point in the policy. Further, recent events at the DPP office seems to suggest that decisions of the DPP can be revisited and this can erode the confidence of the parties concerned. A different arrangement exists in the United States, where cartel investigations are undertaken by the Department of Justice and not the Federal Trade Commission, so they do not suffer from this lack of confidence. In South Africa, in the past, the Competition Commission of South Africa had full control of the whole policy because cartels were categorised as civil cases and not criminal cases. However, now that South Africa has criminalised cartels, it remains to be seen if the leniency policy is as successful as before.
- The private sector and their legal representatives believe that the Commission does not have adequate tools to detect cartels or restrictive business practices. The incentive to apply for leniency is to avoid a penalty, but this depends on there

being a credible threat of detection and a substantial penalty being imposed. Given the secret nature of most cartels, this means that authorities need to adopt cartel-screening practices to proactively identify markets of concern, which requires resources.
- The companies involved believe that any penalties will be postponed by extremely long court processes. The fact that a case takes an average of 10 years or more to be disposed of by the courts gives enterprises the impetus to 'wear down' the Commission. Thus, there is no incentive for them to apply for leniency on any anti-competitive conduct. This is especially true where the parties know that while the case is in court, they may continue to enjoy the fruits of a cartel.
- Most private sector companies in Zambia are not public institutions and therefore are not affected by bad publicity like public companies. Private companies do not have the same level of disclosures as public companies and therefore the reputation risk, while there, is not the same as for public companies. This was seen by the way in which a public listed company on the Lusaka Stock Exchange, Johannesburg Stock Exchange or even the London Stock Exchange would react to news of a dawn raid as opposed to private companies that might have been involved. Public companies are more accountable than private companies.
- Political connections on the part of companies mean that the companies believe that they can easily influence politicians, who in turn can instruct the Commission. While this may be true for other institutions in Zambia, it is not true for the CCPC, where the political influence by the minister is limited to appointment of boards and tribunals and not on the day-to-day running of the institution. However, it is clear from the 'threats' to report the Commission to the Minister that many in the private sector believe the minister has a lot of influence. These threats have not materialised.
- Where the leniency policy does not allow for leniency for the cartel instigator, companies know one or more parties will not apply for leniency and this undermines the incentives for others to apply. In consultations, some stakeholders have felt that even when new management has come in and decided to discontinue the anti-competitive conduct, there has been no incentive to report or apply for leniency, especially if the company is the instigator.

Having had a poor track record on leniency, the Commission relaxed its rules in this regard, allowing for companies under investigation (even while a dawn raid is happening) to apply for leniency. Further, applicants were allowed to apply after the fact, provided they presented evidence to the Commission, to reduce the time of the investigation. Two companies used this opportunity after the legal counsel failed to use political influence to stop the investigations. The two leniency applications – in the cement and the fish fingerling cartels – strengthened the CCPC's ability to investigate cases and bring culprits to book. Further review needs to be undertaken to increase the incentives to apply for leniency and strengthen the CCPC's ability to uncover and end cartels.

Conclusions and lessons from the Zambian experience

Cartel enforcement is critical for competitive open markets and to address substantial excess price mark-ups due to collusion. This is important to reduce poverty that is exacerbated by over-charges, and to support SMEs, which are undermined where the cartel is active in the inputs of these businesses. The incentive for cartels is to earn excess profits and it is for this reason that these syndicates will always be around. Even though laws have been passed to deter them, the high profits generally enjoyed by cartels means that proactive enforcement and penalisation are essential for the deterrence to have effect.

While cartels are likely to be more prevalent and have larger effects in developing country markets, the competition authorities in these countries are not well resourced, making the fight against cartels difficult. It is, however, pleasing that the international community and multilateral organisations have recognised this and have provided support to young authorities. Advocacy programmes must also continue to ensure that governments recognise the role of competition authorities, not only in fighting cartels but also due to the related effects on poverty reduction and development.

The authority in Zambia has made remarkable progress in cartel enforcement, especially in view of its limited resources. The experience of the CCPC shows that it is imperative that an authority prioritise cartel enforcement. The time and resource-intensive nature of cartel investigation mean that authorities need to carefully select cases with the greatest potential impact. The fertiliser case in Zambia was one such case, which clearly demonstrated the benefits from enforcement for the economy.

The second lesson is that the Zambian authority did not shy away from targeting powerful and politically connected businesses. The cement case is one example. The authority investigated and used the tools provided by the law to collect evidence. This is usually not an easy task to undertake, especially in situations where businesses are invited to invest in the economy, as the authority can be seen to be working against the country's drive to encourage investment.

In such a situation, the authority must prepare evidence to show the negative impact of the cartel. Without this, the authority will lose support from powerful stakeholders who may include the government. It is therefore not enough to say that cartels are bad; there must be sufficient evidence of that negative impact. So, with regard to the cement case, the government, which had embarked on road and infrastructure development, was provided with evidence of possible savings it would have made had there not been a cartel.

The third lesson is that cartel enforcement must be part of developing a competition culture. This implies following through on investigations where evidence has been brought to light even when the players involved are small. For example, the Competition Commission of South Africa has enforced small cases even while the penalties may not be as stiff.[8] Similarly, the Zambian authority, having found cartels in fish fingerlings, enforced the law while appreciating that the players were still small. Enforcement in such cases inculcates good behaviour, not only in the affected sectors but across the economy as a whole.

Notes

1. See: World Bank, Markets and Competition Policy. Accessed May 2023, https://www.worldbank.org/en/topic/competition-policy
2. See: 2013/CCPT/003 Top Gear and 9 others v CCPC
3. See: APPEAL NO. 2017/020/COM Omnia Fertilizer Zambia Limited vs. CCPC
4. See: CCPC Presentation to the ICN/World Bank Advocacy Contest, 2019
5. See: https://www.ccpc.org.zm/details/44
6. See: https://globalcompetitionreview.com/article/zambia-fines-chick-hatchery-cartel
7. See: https://diggers.news/business/2018/03/28/ccpc-fines-hybrid-ross-quantum-and-tiger-chicks-for-bad-business-practices/
8. See, for example, Competition Commission and Ikemele Egg Production 23/12/2021. Accessed May 2023, https://www.comptrib.co.za/cases-archived

References

Choi JP & Gerlach H (2015) Cartels and collusion: Economic theory and experimental economics. In RD Blair & D Sokol (Eds) *The Oxford handbook of international antitrust economics* (Vol. 2)

ICN (International Competition Network) (2002) Advocacy and Competition Policy. Report prepared by the Advocacy Working Group, ICN Conference, Naples, Italy 28–29 September

Kaira T (2017) Cartel enforcement in the southern African neighbourhood. In J Klaaren, S Roberts & I Valodia (Eds) *Competition law and economic regulation: Addressing market power in Southern Africa.* Johannesburg: Wits University Press

Lavoie C (2010) South Africa corporate leniency policy: A five-year review. *World Competition* 33(1): 141–162

Levenstein MC & Suslow V (2012) *Cartels and collusion – empirical evidence.* Ross School of Business Working Paper No. 1182, University of Michigan

Li D & Weisman D (2023) Ruffled feathers: The chicken cartel in the United States. *The Antitrust Bulletin* 68(1): 47–72

Roberts S (2020) Cartel enforcement – critical reflections from the South African experience. In D Healey, M Jacobs & RL Smith (Eds) *Research handbook on methods and models of competition law.* Cheltenham: Edward Elgar Publishing

Sappington D & Turner D (2023) Information sharing and collusion: General principles and the AgriStats experience. *The Antitrust Bulletin* 68(1): 10–23

4 Competition in the AfCFTA: Facing up to the core challenges of mergers and cartels?

Grace Nsomba and Simon Roberts

The competition protocol adopted under the African Continental Free Trade Area (AfCFTA) in 2023 provides for a continental competition authority to be established, working in conjunction with national and regional authorities.[1] In chapter 4, we consider the main gaps in merger review and cartel enforcement that a continental competition regime needs to address. A number of papers have weighed up the pros and cons of different potential models for a continental regime (see Dawar & Lipimile 2020; Fox 2022; Gachuiri 2020; Kigwiru 2024). We take it as given that a continental authority will be established and consider what its role should be in mergers and cartels. The experience of establishing competition regimes in Africa indicates that effective merger review is essential for building credibility and experience in the initial phases (Lewis 2012). We then consider cartels, given the indications of the extent of collusion and the associated harm to economies, including through undermining the gains from trade and regional integration (Roberts et al. 2017).

We draw on examples of cross-border cases from national authorities and the regional authority for the Common Market of Eastern and Southern Africa (COMESA) in order to consider the main challenges with merger review and cartel prosecution. Our review highlights that the challenges in merger review and cartel enforcement are quite different. Separate strategies are likely to be required for each at the continental level. We further assess the ways in which institutions at the continental, regional and national levels can work together in a mutually reinforcing manner and comment briefly on other restrictive practices and abuse of dominance at the continental level.

The chapter starts with a discussion on the importance of competition for economic integration in Africa. Then a focus on mergers examines the lessons that can be drawn from the COMESA Competition Commission, which covers the continent's largest regional economic community. This is followed by some case examples of mergers at both the global/continental level and the regional/national level, and ends with a focus on the public interest aspects of merger review. Next, the discussion on cartels unpacks the importance and complexities of cartel detection in international competition enforcement. It then gives an overview of the cross-border implications of other restrictive practices and abuse of dominance. Our concluding thoughts motivate for the prioritisation of mergers by the continental authority while supporting strong national and regional authorities through effective cooperation.

The importance of competition for economic integration in Africa

Regional integration on the continent is an opportunity to build competitive industries through realising economies of scale and linkages in regional value chains as well as overcome the legacy of colonial borders and open up markets to greater participation. This could perhaps be achieved through regional economic communities (RECs) (Roberts et al. 2017) in different parts of the continent and without a continent-level agreement. However, the RECs that do exist take very different forms, are overlapping, and substantial trade potential exists between as well as within them – thus providing the motivation for a continental agreement.

Realising the potential gains from economic integration at the continental and regional levels depends on healthy competition. If firms have substantial market power – either because a single firm is dominant or because there are a few large companies that are colluding – they can undermine fair markets through carving up regions to fix high prices, denying customers alternatives, extracting supra-competitive profits and undermining growth. To counter this, competition law and policy in Africa that consider inclusive growth and broad-based development ought to be an integral part of the development agenda (Fox & Bakhoum 2019).

Concerns about cross-border competition are raised by the increasing concentration at the global level, with large multinational companies accounting for a large share of sales in many markets (Eeckhout 2021; Wu 2018). African firms that were national champions are also expanding across state borders and competing with global firms on the continent, pointing to the importance of a supra-national perspective (Fox 2022; Boso et al. 2019). Factors affecting competition include the main locations of production and consumption, obstacles to trade including inadequate transport and logistics infrastructure, possible multi-market contact of firms across products and geographies, and barriers to entry. Taken together, these issues have an impact on the reach of firms and the degree to which market power can be exercised (Roberts 2016).

Challenges presented by mergers and cartels

The possible anticompetitive effects of mergers arise from either unilateral or coordinated effects, otherwise known as theories of harm to competition. There is a likely substantial lessening of competition when the merging parties have increased power to raise prices or exclude rivals. This can be the case where, prior to the merger, the companies were in different countries and competed against each other through international trade. By merging, they can remove competition between themselves. Coordinated effects can arise when a merger leads to market conditions that are conducive to tacit or explicit collusion between firms (Loertscher & Marx 2021). This market allocation may well happen at the regional level, where firms agree not to compete in each other's allocated geographic markets. This has been suspected to be the case with global mergers, such as Lafarge/Holcim in the cement industry, significantly affecting markets in Africa (Fox 2022). By requiring pre-merger notification by companies, the authority is able to stipulate that companies provide evidence on the merger to enable a review of its likely effects on competition. Research has found that as the depth of regional integration intensifies, mergers are likely to be encouraged, which means that effective merger review is essential (Wilson & Bala 2019).

Cartel conduct is where companies reach an understanding not to compete and this understanding is generally secret. Where companies are actual or potential competitors in cross-border markets, then a collusive arrangement would also be cross-border in scope. The secret nature of such arrangements means the enforcement challenge is quite different from that of merger review. Companies have no incentive to provide information and the authority may have no inkling of what is actually going on. Cartel enforcement requires proactive strategies for detecting collusion. The track record of regional cartel enforcement is weak, notwithstanding indications that a cartel in one country in traded products is in fact also likely to be a cartel in that regional economic block (Kaira 2017).

The need for a competition protocol in Africa

The objectives of the competition protocol in Africa are centred on promoting competition and economic integration by preventing restrictive business practices that deter the efficient operation of regional markets. This protects consumers against abuse of market power by large firms and guards against smaller firms being excluded from the markets. This is important, given the prevalence of highly concentrated market structures with high barriers to entry (Kigwiru 2020). Also, an effective competition law needs to have a geographical reach *as wide as the competition it is meant to address*, including where this reach is, through coordinated enforcement rather than a supranational authority (Fox 2022). This principle needs to guide the division of institutional responsibilities at different levels – continental, regional and national.

Implementing the protocol on competition in Africa requires demarcating the relationships between the continental, national and regional competition regimes (Fox 2022; Gachuiri 2020; UNECA 2019). It is necessary to strengthen the national and regional authorities, and support laws being passed and the establishment of national authorities in countries where they do not yet exist, alongside the continental body. This requires cooperation as well as the evolution of common approaches in the main areas of competition enforcement, suggesting the parallel development of effective regimes at national, regional and continental levels.

The ways in which different regional economic associations around the world deal with competition issues are instructive. On the one hand, in the Southern African Development Community (SADC) there is a cooperation model in place but not a supranational authority. It is noteworthy that there appear to have been few tangible results in terms of enforcement (Mwemba & Askin 2021). The Association of South East Asian Nations (ASEAN) also has a cooperation model. This ASEAN model has focused on developing regional competition policy such as strategies and advocacy tools that inform and guide how national competition authorities can best cooperate. It has the Experts Group on Competition to provide a regional platform for national competition authorities to cooperate with one another.[2]

On the other hand, in COMESA there is a supranational authority. The COMESA Competition Commission (CCC) operates as an autonomous regional institution insulated from any influence by member states (Mwemba & Askin 2021). Established in 2013, the CCC has made significant progress in the area of merger review. However, the CCC experience also shows that building strong institutions takes time (Fox & Bakhoum 2019; Gachuiri 2020). Thus, while supranational competition authorities theoretically have benefits such as tangible enforcement power, in practice this may not always be the case, so it is necessary to also have effective national competition authorities and cooperation arrangements.

Mergers

Mergers between firms that operate across two or more countries can be an important means for investment. However, they can also affect market composition and structure. Mergers can have an adverse effect on competition through consolidation of markets, which can result in the removal of actual or potential competitors. There is, therefore, a strong case for prior notification and review of mergers, and many national competition authorities in Africa have built their regulatory and enforcement expertise starting with merger review. For example, both the Competition Commission of South Africa and the Competition Authority of Kenya focused on merger enforcement in their first five years (Karanja 2016; Roberts 2004). The COMESA Competition Commission (CCC) has also focused largely on mergers in its first decade from 2013 to 2023 and we consider insights from its experiences in dealing with the challenges of cross-border competition enforcement.

Lessons from the COMESA Competition Commission

The COMESA Competition Regulations and Rules, which included the notification of cross-border mergers, came into force when the CCC was established in 2013. Initially, it was unclear whether notification of a merger needed to be made to the CCC, the national authorities or both, as the wording of Article 3(2)[3] stated that the CCC had 'primary jurisdiction' (not exclusive jurisdiction) for mergers in which the acquiring firm or target firm operate in two or more member states and a threshold of combined annual turnover or assets was exceeded. And, in section 3.4 of the COMESA Merger Assessment Guidelines published in August 2014, in effect the initial thresholds were set at zero (Mwemba 2020).[4] It was therefore unclear whether member states had in fact ceded their sovereignty to the CCC. The lack of any threshold meant that, in theory, all mergers involving one or more parties that had operations in two or more member states were notifiable to the CCC and subject to a filing fee (Mwemba 2020).

Multiple merger filings can be complex and onerous and incur filing fees for each filing. A further complication is that various authorities have different approval processes involving different timelines, which creates uncertainty about the implementation of a transaction. The upshot was that the CCC was notified about very few mergers and national authorities effectively did not cede jurisdiction. This impacted on the credibility of the CCC.

The CCC moved quickly to address the problems with two key changes. First, amendments to the regulations in 2015 established a non-trivial merger threshold of an annual turnover or value of assets in a member state exceeding US$5 million.[5] In addition, a target undertaking also operates in at least one member state. Second, a provision was made for a national nexus to be identified and the evaluation to be made by a national authority where the activities of the merging firms were predominantly within one country that had its own authority.[6] The national nexus was set out in regulations as where more than two-thirds of the annual turnover or value of assets in the Common Market of each of the merging parties is achieved or held within the same member state.[7]

As a result of these pragmatic measures, mergers are being notified to the CCC and member states with authorities have taken steps to cede decision-making to the CCC to avoid multiple merger filings in cross-border mergers. For example, in 2019, the Competition Authority of Kenya (CAK) enacted a merger threshold, which provided (under Section 8) that 'where a merger meets the threshold prescribed under the COMESA Competition Regulations and Rules, the parties shall notify the COMESA Competition Commission in the prescribed form and inform the Authority in writing regarding the notification'.[8] The Zambian Competition and Consumer Protection Commission (CCPC) also stipulated that mergers meeting the regional dimension test can only be notified to CCC.[9]

The CCC experience yields a number of lessons that are worth mentioning. First, national authorities with effective regimes in place will be unlikely to (and should not) cede jurisdiction over mergers with a substantial national effect to a supranational authority that is still being established. Countries with weaker regimes may also not cede jurisdiction on grounds of national interest. Second, it is undesirable to have multiple notifications and evaluations of the same merger in the same geographic area. Where the regulations are not sufficiently determined, firms will simply fail to notify. The delineation of jurisdiction must use readily provided and verifiable information and a mechanism for allocating the merger to the appropriate level of determination. Third, the application of the thresholds using assets and turnover is necessarily mechanistic and cannot anticipate the possible effects on competition that might be uncovered in the assessment. As illustrated in our review of actual merger cases below, it is therefore essential that there are systems in place for cooperation between authorities to ensure information on the likely effects on competition at different levels is shared.

Case examples

To illustrate the challenges and extract some practical recommendations, here we assess selected mergers that have had overlapping effects, first at the global and continental level, and then at the regional and national levels. For each merger, we describe the dynamics and outcome of the merger, and provide a short commentary on the geographic level at which there were likely competition effects.

Global and continental: Lafarge/Holcim (2014) and Bayer/Monsanto (2017)

The Lafarge/Holcim and Bayer/Monsanto cases represent mergers with substantial global, continental, regional and national effects. However, the full effects were not necessarily evident at the national and regional levels. In addition, imposing conditions on these transactions required a degree of institutional muscle that most national competition authorities in Africa lack. In addition, in the absence of a supranational authority, countries that do not have their own competition authority do not have a voice.

Lafarge/Holcim (2014)

The merger occurred in the context of apparent cross-border market division cartels in what is a cartel-endemic industry (Fox 2022). In an industry so prone to cartel conduct, the merger was likely to have extinguished rivalry between two of the most important potential competitors in Africa, even while they had restructured to reduce head-to-head competition *within* countries (Fox 2022).

The merger of the two leading global cement companies, Lafarge and Holcim, created the largest cement producer globally and in Africa (Fox 2022). At the time, the merging parties were active in 15 of the then 19 COMESA member states, and across Africa. Both companies were major producers of cement, aggregates and concrete. Because of its international nature, the merger was notified to authorities around the world, including in the United States (US), the European Union (EU) and Africa. In both the US and the EU, the merger was approved with conditions that Holcim divest its interests in competing firms.

Post-merger, Lafarge/Holcim would become the largest cement producer in Africa, with an annual production capacity of 22.5 million tonnes. Its closest competitor was Nigerian multinational Dangote Cement, with an annual production capacity of 20.7 million tonnes, along with smaller producers in some countries, including Afrisam.[10] Although this meant two large rivals on paper, a history of extensive collusive conduct in the cement industry in Africa and globally raised concerns that a reduction in the number of firms would increase the likelihood of coordination rather than competition in practice. Cases of collusion in the cement industry have been documented across the African continent, with cartels recurring because of the industry's inherent characteristics and incentives (Paelo et al. 2020; Roberts et al. 2023).

In Africa, after having found no competition problems, the COMESA Competition Commission (CCC) cleared the merger for all member countries without conditions. The exception was Mauritius (a COMESA member), whose Competition Commission found that the merger would result in a monopoly there.[11] Overall, the CCC based its finding on the absence of a geographic overlap between the firms, in large part due to Holcim's having already spun off plants into the separate Afrisam company grouping, in which it retained a very small shareholding. Afrisam had some producers in east and southern Africa. Potential competition, through entry or cross-border trade, was not discussed in the CCC decision. The merger review from the Competition Commission of South Africa (not a member of COMESA), however, identified the Holcim shareholding in Afrisam as a competition issue due to factors including technical assistance provided and information-sharing, which could continue.[12] This presented a significant concern for the CCSA in the context of the wider likelihood of coordination in the cement industry, and divestment was required of the shareholding in Afrisam.[13]

The Lafarge/Holcim merger was significant in being a major transaction in an industry with substantial competition concerns. It points to the importance of the merger review in such cases involving in-depth assessment of the different possible effects at different geographic levels. This needs to include coordinated effects that might have cross-border implications. Lafarge/Holcim and Dangote did indeed collude in 2019 in Zambia, with likely cross-border effects through regional trade (Roberts et al. 2023).

Bayer/Monsanto (2017)

The Bayer/Monsanto merger is an example of a global merger where the companies have limited production operations in Africa. However, African countries' substantial reliance on imports means they are affected by global concentration. Before the merger, Bayer was a global enterprise with core competencies in the life science fields of agriculture and healthcare. Monsanto was a global provider of agricultural products to farmers, including seeds. The companies competed in a number of important categories of products in markets that were already concentrated. The merged entity is in the top four in both seed and agro-chemicals in the world, which, combined, account for over 60% of proprietary seed sales globally (Clapp 2021; Shand & Wetter 2019).

The merger was evaluated in Africa by the CCC and a number of national authorities, which all approved the merger without substantial conditions. However, it is becoming increasingly clear that increased international concentration in markets through global mergers has potential anticompetitive effects in the long run, with possible impacts on prices and innovation (see Aghion et al. 2021; Clapp 2021; Lianos et al. 2022).

The competition dynamics in the market for agricultural inputs are especially relevant for Africa, due to the continent's high dependence on agriculture for national income. Concerns, including about this merger, stem from the nature of the agriculture and agrochemicals market, in that research and development and patent rights over varieties and processes become a significant factor in the way market players can compete (Bosiu et al. 2018; Lianos et al. 2022). The exercising of rights and patents serves to entrench the market power held by seed and agrochemicals companies, which increases structural and strategic barriers for new market entrants (Bosiu et al. 2018). The effects are complex and potentially far-reaching. Mergers such as Bayer/Monsanto point to the importance of sound institutional capacity and expertise in a continental competition authority, which needs to work closely with strong national and regional authorities that would make submissions and representations to the continental body.

Regional and national: National Foods/Pure Oil Industries (2016) and Zambeef/ Zamhatch (2016)

The case examples here point to the importance of cooperation between competition authorities alongside the appropriate allocation of the merger depending on the identification of a national or regional nexus. Authorities from countries in the affected regions need to provide evaluations that feed into the overall merger assessment, through mechanisms to be established under the AfCFTA protocol.

National Foods Ltd/Pure Oil Industries (Zimbabwe, 2016)[14]

The transaction involved the acquisition of a 40% stake by National Foods Ltd in Pure Oil Industries Ltd. This merger is an example of a transaction assessed at the national level, based on the thresholds, and was assessed and approved by the Competition and Tariff Commission Zimbabwe. However, it had regional effects and this required coordination between national and regional authorities.

The merger involved the largest food business in Zimbabwe, Innscor/Irvines, and the largest food company in South Africa, Tiger Brands (as the two major shareholders in National Foods Ltd Zimbabwe), together with ETG/Vamara and Parrogate.[15]

Tiger Brands has direct and indirect interests in international food businesses in Cameroon, Chile, Kenya, Mozambique, Nigeria, Zambia and Zimbabwe. National Foods manufactures and markets a wider range of foodstuffs and stock feeds in Zimbabwe.[16] The Export Trading Group (ETG) is a diversified agricultural conglomerate that owns and manages a vertically integrated supply chain across Africa, South East Asia, the Middle East, Europe and the Americas.[17] It is the largest agricultural commodity supply chain manager in Africa, with vertically integrated supply chain operations, processing plants, warehouses and a wide product portfolio of agro-commodities.[18]

The merger highlights the need to assess multi-market contact and common ownership across the region. In other words, a regional perspective is required to analyse the likely competition effects (Figure 4.1).

Figure 4.1 Regional extent of operations for companies with interests in Pure Oil

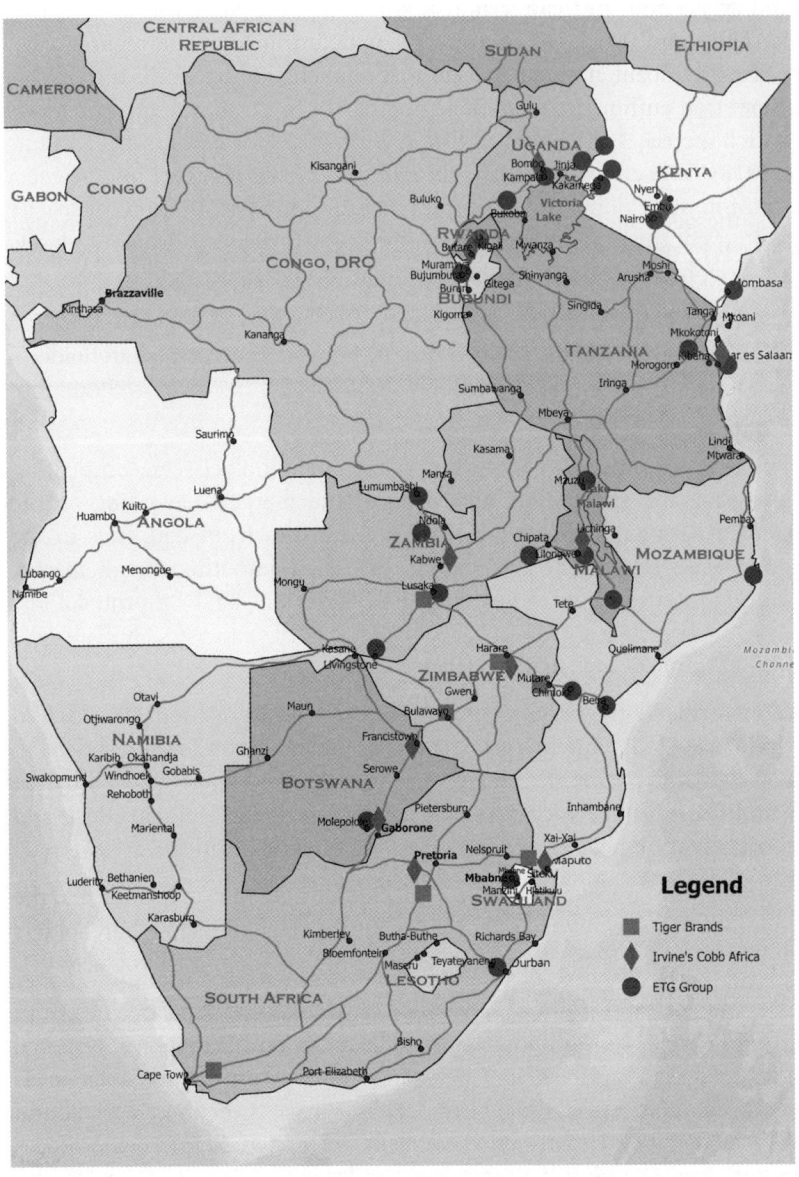

Source: Nsomba et al. (2022); redrawn by Enathi Motolwana, HSRC

High levels of concentration and multimarket contact mean a greater likelihood of coordination to divide markets and undermine vigorous competition, potentially undermining regional integration (Paelo et al. 2020). In terms of the merger filing, the necessarily mechanistic and administrative process may mean that notification is made to the national authority (as was the case with this merger).

However, cooperative processes must be developed where information on markets can be shared and authorities can make submissions on potential effects in their jurisdictions. The same is true when a merger is determined at the regional level; when there are significant national effects to be taken into account, the relevant national competition authorities need to be involved.

Zambeef/Zam Chick and Zamhatch (CCC, 2016)

In some cases, mergers may be notifiable to a regional competition authority even though the effects of the merger are largely national in nature. This appears to be the case with the Zambeef/Zam Chick and Zamhatch merger. The transaction involved Zambeef acquiring Rainbow Farms Investments' (RFI's) 49% shareholding in Zam Chick and its 51% shareholding in Zamhatch, to become the 100% shareholder in both entities. RFI is an investment vehicle for RCL Foods, the owners of Rainbow Chicken, and had invested as a joint venture partner with Zambeef to expand the poultry business in Zambia, as RCL is one of the two largest poultry producers in South Africa. The acquisitions by Zambeef meant it was effectively buying out its joint-venture partner.

Zambeef is a public company incorporated in Zambia and listed on the Lusaka Stock Exchange and the Alternative Investment Market (AIM) of the London Stock Exchange. It is the largest vertically integrated food brand in Zambia[19], with operations in Ghana and Nigeria. Zambeef produces, supplies and distributes beef and beef products, as well as pork, dairy and fish products. Zam Chick manages and operates Zambeef's broiler business in Zambia, including the broiler houses, chicken abattoir and processing plant. Zamhatch is the breeding operation set up in 2013 to feed into the broiler production of Zam Chick.

Zamhatch invested in hatchery operations and an animal feed mill in the Copperbelt region of Zambia to allow for exports of day-old chicks and animal feed into the Democratic Republic of the Congo (DRC) and Angola. In relation to the merger, the national nexus threshold in Zambia was presumably below the notification threshold, which meant that it was assessed and approved by the CCC. However, the competitive effects appear to be mainly relevant for Zambia.

A note on public interest in merger review

Public interest considerations are increasingly being incorporated in the merger provisions of the competition laws of developing countries as, for example, in Kenya and South Africa. These provisions typically include concerns with local industry development, employment and the participation of small enterprises. However, public interest considerations being incorporated into merger provisions at a continental and/or regional level are likely to be far more challenging.

The list of public interest factors in the AfCFTA competition protocol identifies four public interest factors (in a non-exhaustive list). These are: the potential to promote sustainable and inclusive socioeconomic and industrial development; employment; the ability of small and medium-sized businesses to become competitive; and the ability of industries in the market to compete in other international markets. Each of these would require a different set of tests and, while the protocol states that the competition assessment *includes* public interest grounds, they are conceptually very separate from the competition criteria for merger assessments. The competition assessment involves determining whether there is a lessening, prevention, restriction or distortion of competition. Aside from the impact on small and medium businesses' ability to compete, the other grounds are not, in fact, related to competition within the market. Attempts to include them will pose substantial challenges for the merger review and, in effect, represent a whole range of additional assessments to the competition tests. Given the challenges that have been identified for the cross-border competition assessment in an effective continental regime, it would appear to be more sensible to allow public interest factors to continue to be determined at the national level in a parallel process.

In the field of mergers, employment has typically been framed in terms of the employment losses anticipated following a merger. This has led to conditions being imposed where appropriate to restrict the losses and/or to provide for some retraining and other support to those employees who are most vulnerable, and for whom it is anticipated that finding similar employment elsewhere will be difficult. This category has been included most often in South Africa, where there are very high levels of unemployment and where specific provisions allow for trade unions to make representations to the competition authorities. The consideration is done separately from the competition assessment and does not form part of it. It can continue to be undertaken at a national level, where the necessity for employment protections can be evaluated.

The small and medium-sized business component in a merger assessment relates to the potential impact of the merger on barriers to entry and whether they would be able to be competitive post the merger. It can form part of the wider competition assessment where this takes into account barriers to the entry and growth of smaller firms. However, concerns about particular categories of small enterprises, such as those owned by historically disadvantaged persons in South Africa, would require national evaluation in a separate assessment.

Industrial development and competitiveness concerns may be interpreted relative to the policy objectives of a country. It is unclear how these are to be interpreted at a continental level. In addition, the competitiveness in one country may be relative to its neighbour to which it exports. The potential to promote sustainable and inclusive socio economic and industrial development is even broader and subject to multiple interpretations. It is unclear how a supranational body would make determinations on these grounds as they would likely cause major frictions with existing national and regional competition bodies. They would be more appropriately dealt with in separate national merger review processes.

Cartels, other restrictive practices and abuse of dominance

Cartels

Cartels are horizontal restrictive practices through which competing firms reach an understanding to divide markets, fix prices and/or rig bids. They should be separated out from other restrictive practices as a distinct category, especially when the roadmap for effective regional and continental enforcement is being developed. This is because cartels are generally per se offences, the evidence required is of the existence of the understanding between competitors, and there does not need to be evidence of effects on competition to make a determination. Other restrictive practices typically involve a rule-of-reason analysis, which weighs up the effects of the practices, and that poses different challenges.

In addition, cartel enforcement at the international level is important and necessary as companies may collude in market-division and price-fixing arrangements to allocate particular countries to different companies and charge supracompetitive prices internationally. These arrangements affect international trade flows and undermine regional integration. The market outcomes may not be readily identified or identifiable by national enforcement agencies and may require a supranational assessment in order for detection.

It has been estimated that, between 1990 and 2016, international private cartels that have been discovered overcharged to the value of more than US$1.5 trillion (Connor 2016). These cartels appear to be the tip of a large iceberg as only a small fraction of actual cartels are uncovered (Roberts 2020). In addition, even the cartels that have been discovered in one or more jurisdictions have not been tackled in many of the jurisdictions around the world where they have likely operated (Martyniszyn 2021). As research by UNCTAD (2021) concludes '[i]n fact, transnational restrictive business practices continue to be ungoverned at the multilateral level'. More than half of the transnational cartels recorded in Connor's database (now managed by the OECD) were fined in only one jurisdiction. This means that many of the cartels may continue to be operating in countries where they have not been prosecuted.

The importance of prioritising cartels in Africa is reinforced by the evidence from African countries. Of the global cartels uncovered in recent years in a variety of sectors (such as in auto parts, freight forwarding, refrigerator compressors), there are only a few isolated examples of prosecutions in Africa. In addition, many cartels uncovered in South Africa were evidently cross-border in nature and impacted other countries across southern Africa (Kaira 2017; Muzata et al. 2017). For example, the cement cartel extended across the whole of the Southern African Customs Union (SACU) (Botswana, Eswatini, Lesotho, Namibia and South Africa).[20] The concrete pipes cartel allocated countries including Mozambique, Zimbabwe and Malawi to particular members. The fertiliser cartel included export arrangements.

It also seems likely that cartels uncovered by authorities such as the Competition and Consumer Protection Commission (CCPC) in Zambia and the Competition

Authority of Kenya operated across borders. For example, the collusion between Dangote and Lafarge in Zambia would have impacted on these companies' exports from Zambia, without even considering the likely involvement of their plants in other countries (Roberts et al. 2023). Similarly, the cartels in Kenya in traded products such as paint and steel bars would also have likely affected trade by the companies within the East African Community.

The extensive operation of these cartels has important implications for the choices to be made in the application of the protocol. First, international experience shows that countries can and should pursue extraterritoriality in the application of their competition laws. This is now increasingly accepted by developing and developed countries (UNCTAD 2021). It means that cooperation is required to strengthen national regimes – to gather and share information on international cartels and the operations of transnational businesses, and simultaneously to build enforcement capacity. There is a strong case for screening for cartels, analysing market structures and considering publicly available information on market outcomes and firms' behaviour, at the regional and continental level through cooperation.

Second, while supranational enforcement can be developed at the level of regional economic communities and at the continental level, there are formidable legal obstacles to this being effective. Outside the EU, there is almost no effective multilateral cartel enforcement. Rather, there are initiatives through which various authorities work together on the basis of an 'enforcement patchwork'. This is understandable as cartel enforcement requires the exercising of invasive powers to compel the production of information and these powers typically have to be applied under national laws. Corporate leniency policies, where a colluding firm can come forward to expose a cartel in exchange for escaping penalty, have been very important tools in cartel detection. It means the competition authority can get insider evidence on how the secret arrangements worked. By their nature, the leniency policies are legal instruments that need to take account of the jurisprudence and laws of the country in question.

Effective cartel detection therefore requires five key conditions to be in place: strong national authorities enforcing enacted competition laws; information gathering for structural screening and behavioural screening; corporate leniency policies at the national level; a regional corporate leniency regime; and channels for cooperation with national authorities for investigations. It is possible to work on all these areas in parallel.

The question is whether there is the need for an AfCFTA authority in order to carry out the necessary enforcement against global cartels that have an impact on African countries. While this may be an ideal, it seems as if its success depends on the progress being made at national and regional levels. This is because the capabilities for cartel detection and enforcement, in the first instance, require effective national authorities who can cooperate together to build the tools to tackle cross-border cartels including on a regional basis.

There are concrete steps that can readily be taken for extraterritorial enforcement against transnational cartels, bearing in mind that legal provisions generally stipulate that cartels that have an effect in a particular jurisdiction should be tackled in that jurisdiction (Martyniszyn 2021; UNCTAD 2021). National authorities can cooperate in shared (non-confidential) information gathering for cartel screening in terms of structure and behaviour in priority markets. Collaborative relationships can be built to reinforce institutional capacity at regional and national levels. Cartel judgments in one jurisdiction can be drawn on in other jurisdictions with which there are trade flows and/or where the same companies operate in order to shift the onus onto companies to demonstrate that conduct has not had a cross-border impact. The likely impacts of cartels across countries can also be assessed through research as part of an advocacy strategy.

Cooperation at the continental level reinforces each of these steps. Mechanisms to ensure that this is effective include a shared information base on priority sectors, with a high likelihood of collusion based on literature and international cases; a common portal for tracking international cartel cases and their likely effects on African countries; joint studies under the African Competition Forum of authorities to identify red-flags based on market structure and outcomes; concerted advocacy programmes on cartel conduct; and studies on the links between trade and competition, including identifying where there may be contractual restrictions on parallel trade (such as through distribution agreements) that may be in place and that can be tackled by national and regional bodies working together.

A note on other restrictive business practices, abuse of dominance and market inquiries

Other restrictive business practices as well as abuse of dominance may operate across borders. However, there is much less consensus on how such conduct should be tackled than there is with cartels and mergers.[21] There is also no such obvious gap in regional enforcement.

Abuse of dominance relates to the unilateral exertion of substantial market power to exploit consumers and exclude rivals. It can generally be addressed by national authorities, so strengthening national and regional regimes alongside cooperation efforts is the appropriate approach. Regional vertical arrangements that have been identified by national authorities, such as distribution arrangements that restrict regional competition, can be prioritised at the regional level, including in countries that do not have their own competition authorities.

There are, however, two caveats. First, companies may be dominant in a country *because* of a regional cartel that has divided markets on geographic lines. Tackling horizontal collusion on a regional basis can therefore address what appears at a national level to be a unilateral abuse of dominance. Second, a single dominant firm in one country may exert its power across a wider geographic area, which could justify regional enforcement. However, one country may lead such an investigation of the effects in its territory and then, if findings of abuse are made, other national and REC authorities can consider whether the effects are also present in their countries and fast-track their own investigations. For example, in Europe, both approaches have been applied in investigations into digital platforms, with some at the national level (such as the UK's Competition and Markets Authority market investigations into digital advertising) and some at the EU level, such as the European Commission's cases brought against Google. The ongoing dialogue on digital markets among African authorities is likewise an important initiative for strengthening national enforcement.[22]

Market inquiries and studies have been a very effective tool in assessing market outcomes that appear to be inconsistent with effective competition, and avoid the need to launch an investigation into a specific type of possible infringement (see Bonakele et al. 2022). Making provision for national authorities and RECs to cooperate in joint market inquiries is thus important. Taking into account the increasing international scope of companies' operations and the potential for obstacles to competition existing at the cross-border level, a priority market or sector can be evaluated jointly by multiple authorities. The inquiry can lead to practical recommendations and/or, where appropriate, targeted investigations.

Market inquiries also provide any new competition authority that is set up, at both the regional and continental levels, with the opportunity to build its knowledge and credibility in cooperation with national authorities. It can draw on the experience of national authorities across the continent.

Conclusion

The internationalisation of business means that there is a need for supranational authorities with the powers to investigate and enforce against anti-competitive conduct that extends across national borders. This is especially important for Africa given: a) the increasing and high levels of market concentration globally (which affect African countries); and b) the growing evidence of anti-competitive arrangements that undermine regional integration through dividing markets. Africa needs a voice in the review of global mergers and in tackling international cartels. It is also important to focus a continental AfCFTA authority in the initial phase in the areas of greatest importance – mergers and cartels – as well as to set up the appropriate channels for cooperation with regional and national authorities.

The challenge of mergers

Effective merger review requires merger notification and regulations to allocate the merger review to the appropriate level (continental, regional or national) for evaluation. It also requires mechanisms to ensure cooperation between authorities. The case study examples of mergers involving the CCC and national authorities point to the importance of examining the international reach of firms' activities, even for instances where the merger is categorised for assessment at the national level. It is critical to understand the networks of relationships at different levels of value chains and the nature and extent of multimarket contacts (Nsomba et al. 2022).

The challenge of cartels

Cartels pose particular challenges for competition enforcement due to their generally secretive nature and good reasons to believe there is a high prevalence of collusion at the regional and continental levels. In contrast with mergers, companies will resist providing information on their arrangements. At the level of investigation capacity, priority should be placed on strengthening national and REC regimes, including the ability to initiate investigations and conduct enforcement actions regarding extraterritorial conduct. At the AfCFTA level, information gathering should be prioritised, with the AfCFTA starting with a market surveillance role to screen for likely cartel conduct for investigation at national and REC levels, including through parallel investigations (following the practice in, for example, the international auto parts cartel). Where companies have been found to collude in one country, a provision can require the companies to confirm under affidavit that the conduct did not have an impact in African countries. A database and portal on international cartels being identified by authorities should be put together.[23] This database should include cartels with a global reach identified outside Africa, and with likely effects on African countries given trade flows and companies' presence be scoped out. It should also include cartels identified by authorities within Africa, with likely cross-border effects.

Is a continental body the best way to meet the challenges?

The credibility of a continental competition regime will, in large part, depend on its ability to conduct effective merger reviews. If jurisdiction over cases shifts away from existing effective national and regional authorities to a nascent continental body that is not yet ready to enforce the regulations, then this would be a step backwards. Avoiding this situation would necessitate a continental authority to focus on the largest mergers with the widest geographic impact. The appropriate tests for determining where there is a regional nexus (if there is a regional authority), or national nexus, can be developed following the COMESA experience.

As it is unlikely that the long-established authorities will cede jurisdiction at the outset, there will continue to be multiple merger filings for the same transaction and concurrent jurisdiction in the initial phase. In time, as the continental authority proves itself, multiple filings should not be required. The thresholds can also be altered as the regime matures. Initially, the capacity of the supranational authority will be relatively limited and the thresholds for mergers to be notified to the AfCFTA should be correspondingly very high. In addition, at least in the initial phase, the focus should be on the core competition concerns and the AfCFTA authority should not take on public interest concerns, while national authorities should continue to evaluate the public interests.

The AfCFTA needs to be able to make representations on mergers being decided at REC and national levels. A strong research division will enable these representations and support cooperation. Research will also be essential for cartel screening at the continental level, working together with national and regional authorities. Coordination, research and capacity building are central to an approach that builds a common framework for a coherent competition regime, implemented at continental, REC and national levels. The African Competition Forum of competition authorities across the continent can play an essential role as a forum for developing cooperation.

Notes

1. The Committee on Competition Policy was established by the 5th Meeting of the AfCFTA Council of Ministers responsible for Trade held in Accra, Ghana on 3 May 2021.
2. See: https://www.asean-competition.org/aegc
3. See: Article 3(2) of the COMESA Competition Rules and Regulations 2004
4. See: https://www.comesacompetition.org/wp-content/uploads/2014/10/141121_COMESA-Merger-Assessment-Guideline-October–31st–2014.pdf
5. See: https://www.comesacompetition.org/wp-content/uploads/2015/04/Amendments-to-the-Rules-to-the-Determination-of-Merger-Thresholds-and-Method-of-Calculation-adopted-by-COM–26-March–2015.pdf
6. See the 2015 Amendment to the 2004 COMESA Competition Rules and Regulations.
7. See Article 23(4) of the COMESA Competition Rules and Regulations, as amended 2015.
8. See: https://www.cak.go.ke/sites/default/files/guidelines/Consolidated%20Merger%20Guidelines.pdf
9. See: http://www.ccpc.org.zm/mmdetails#section–3
10. See: https://www.competition.org.za/ccred-blog-competition-review/2015/2/18/consolidation-and-entry-changing-dynamics-in-the-regional-cement
11. See: https://www.comesacompetition.org/wp-content/uploads/2014/10/Decision-Holcim-and-Lafarge.pdf
12. The CCSA merger decision found that 'Holcim and Afrisam were party to an agreement in terms of which Holcim rendered certain technical assistance to Afrisam. This assistance also provided Holcim with information that it ordinarily would not have about a competitor's business.' http://www.compcom.co.za/wp-content/uploads/2014/09/Commission-approves-Holcim-Lafarge-merger.pdf
13. See: http://www.compcom.co.za/wp-content/uploads/2014/09/Commission-approves-Holcim-Lafarge-merger.pdf
14. See Nsomba et al. (2022) for more details and from which this case example is drawn.
15. Innscor Africa Ltd held 37.73% in National Foods Ltd and Tiger Brands held 37.45%. https://nationalfoods.co.zw/

16 See: https://www.world-grain.com/articles/557 tiger brands increases-stake-in-national-foods#:~:text=National%20Foods%20has%20the%20capacity,feeds%2C%20according%20to%20IH%20Securities

17 See: https://www.etgworld.com/

18 See: https://www.fmo.nl/project-detail/59075

19 See: https://zambeefplc.com/

20 See details on this and the following cartels in Roberts (2020).

21 In addition, they may involve in-depth effects-based analysis with cases taking very long periods, including through appeals.

22 See: https://www.compcom.co.za/wp-content/uploads/2022/02/Joint-Statement-of-the-Heads-of-Competition-Authorities-Dialogue-on-Regulation-of-Digital-Markets.pdf

23 This could draw on the existing OECD database, which is the continuation of the Connor database.

References

Aghion P, Cherif R & Hasanov F (2021) *Competition, innovation and inclusive growth*. Working Paper No. WP/21/80, International Monetary Fund

Bonakele T, Das Nair R & Roberts S (2022) Market inquiries in South Africa: Meeting big expectations? In M Motta, M Peitz & H Schweitzer (Eds) *A new competition tool for Europe?* Cambridge: Cambridge University Press

Bosiu T, Das Nair R & Paelo A (2018) Part VI: Case Studies Chapter 1: Insights from selected value chains in South Africa. In I Lianos (Principal Investigator) *Global food value chains and competition law BRICS draft report*. Centre for Law Economics and Society, UCL

Boso N, Adeleye I, Ibeh K & Chizema A (2019) The internationalization of African firms: Opportunities, challenges, and risks. *Thunderbird International Business Review* 61(1): 5–12. https://doi.org/10.1002/tie.21977

Clapp J (2021) The problem with growing corporate concentration and power in the global food system. *Nature Food* 2(6)

Connor JM (2016) *The private international cartels (PIC) data set: Guide and summary statistics, 1990–July 2016 (2nd edition)*. SSRN Paper. http://dx.doi.org/10.2139/ssrn.2821254

Dawar K & Lipimile G (2020) Africa: Harmonising competition policy under the AfCFTA. *Concurrences Review* 2(a93472): 242–250. ISSN 1773–9578

Eeckhout J (2021) *The profit paradox*. Princeton: Princeton University Press

Fox EM (2022) Integrating Africa by competition and market policy. *Review of Industrial Organization* 60(3): 305–326. https://doi.org/10.1007/s11151-022-09854-1

Fox EM & Bakhoum M (2019) *Making markets work for Africa: Markets, development, and competition law in Sub-Saharan Africa*. New York: Oxford University Press

Gachuiri E (2020) *African Continental Free Trade Area Phase II Negotiations: A space for competition protocol?* UNCTAD Research Paper No. 56 UNCTAD/SER.RP/2020/15

Kaira T (2017) Cartel enforcement in the southern African neighbourhood. In J Klaaren, S Roberts & I Valodia (Eds) *Competition law and economic regulation: Addressing market power in Southern Africa*. Johannesburg: Wits University Press

Karanja J (2016) *Competition Authority of Kenya flexes it muscles*. Accessed January 2024, https://www.bowmanslaw.com/wp-content/uploads/2016/08/Competition-DealMakers.pdf

Kigwiru VK (2020) The cooperation on competition policy under the African Continental Free Trade Area. *Manchester Journal of International Economic Law* 17(1): 98–121. DOI: 10.2139/ssrn.3591015

Kigwiru VK (2022) *Supranational or Confederate? Rethinking the AfCFTA. Competition Protocol Institutional Design*. DOI:10.2139/ssrn.4055877

Kigwiru VK (2024) Supranational or cooperative? Rethinking the African Continental Free Trade Area Agreement Competition Protocol institutional design. *Journal of Antitrust Enforcement* 12(1): 98–125

Kigwiru VK & Mwemba W (2021) *The COMESA Competition Commission, earlier experiences and lessons for regional competition regimes in the global South*. Accessed January 2024, https://www.afronomicslaw.org/category/analysis/comesa-competition-commission-ccc-earlier-experiences-and-lessons-regional

Lewis D (2012) *Thieves at the dinner table: Enforcing the Competition Act, a personal account*. Johannesburg: Jacana Media

Lianos I, Ivanov A & Davis D (Eds) (2022) *Global food value chains and competition law*. Cambridge: Cambridge University Press. DOI: 10.1017/9781108554947

Loertscher S & Marx L (2021) Coordinated effects in merger review. *The Journal of Law and Economics* 64: 705–744

Martyniszyn M (2021) Competitive harm crossing borders: Regulatory gaps and a way forward. *Journal of Competition Law and Economics* 17(3): 686–707

Muzata T, Roberts S & Vilakazi T (2017) Penalties and settlements for South African cartels: An economic review. In J Klaaren, S Roberts & I Valodia (Eds) *Competition law and economic regulation: Addressing market power in Southern Africa*. Johannesburg: Wits University Press

Mwemba W & Askin M (2021) *The role of regional competition regimes in supporting international enforcement cooperation*. Accessed February 2024, https://www.afronomicslaw.org/category/analysis/role-regional-competition-regimes-supporting-international-enforcement

Mwemba W (2020) Do supra-national competition authorities resolve the challenges of cross border merger regulation in developing and emerging economies? The case of the common market for Eastern and Southern Africa. Doctoral Thesis, University of Cape Town

Nsomba G, Roberts S, Tshabalala N & Manjengwa E (2022) *Assessing agriculture & food markets in Eastern and Southern Africa: An agenda for regional competition enforcement*. Working Paper No. 2022/1, Centre for Competition, Regulation and Economic Development, University of Johannesburg

Paelo A, Roberts S, Simbanegavi W & Vilakazi T (2020) *Understanding the role of competition in rethinking regional integration in Africa for inclusive and sustainable development.* AERC Paper. Accessed February 2024, https://static1.squarespace.com/static/52246331e4b0a46e5f1b8ce5/t/5f58bd766b1bea57547da66c/1599651199015/Regional+integration+and+competition_Paper_Final.pdf

Roberts S (2004) The role for competition policy in economic development: The South African experience. *Development Southern Africa* 21(1): 227–243

Roberts S (2016) Competition and development in Southern and East Africa. In S Roberts(Ed.) *Competition in Africa: Insights from key industries.* Cape Town: HSRC Press

Roberts S (2020) Cartel enforcement – critical reflections from the South African experience. In D Healey, M Jacobs & RL Smith (Eds) *Research handbook on methods and models of competition law.* Cheltenham: Edward Elgar Publishing

Roberts S, Simbanegavi W & Vilakazi T (2017) Competition, regional integration and inclusive growth in Africa: A research agenda. In J Klaaren, S Roberts & I Valodia (Eds) *Competition law and economic regulation: Addressing market power in Southern Africa.* Johannesburg: Wits University Press

Roberts S, Simbanegavi W & Vilakazi T (2023) Cementing regional integration or building walls? Competition, cartels and regional integration in the cement industry in Africa. *World Economy* 46(2): 303–495

Shand H & Wetter KJ (2019) *Plate tech-tonics: Mapping corporate power in big food.* ETC Group. Accessed October 2023, https://etcgroup.org/sites/www.etcgroup.org/files/files/etc_platetechtonics_a4_nov2019_web.pdf

UNCTAD (2021) *Developing countries' experience with extraterritoriality in competition law.* Geneva: United Nations

UNECA (2019). *Next steps for the African Continental Free Trade Area: Assessing regional integration in Africa.* Addis Ababa, Ethiopia: United Nations Economic Commission for Africa

Wilson M & Bala AP (2019) Regional integration and cross-border merger and acquisitions in Africa. *Journal of Economic Integration* 34(1): 109–132

Wu T (2018) *The curse of bigness.* London: Atlantic Books

5 'Buyer power' in emerging markets: Assessing the effectiveness of regulatory and enforcement developments in South Africa and Kenya

John Oxenham, Michael-James Currie and Joshua Eveleigh

As the Organisation for Economic Cooperation and Development (OECD) has confirmed, competition law typically places a larger amount of emphasis on the selling side of a market. This is particularly because there continues to be debate and scepticism as to the exact harm that an abuse of buyer power may cause to consumers and economic efficiency (OECD 2022: 6).

The concept and significance of buyer power in the field of competition generally and globally – in practice and law

While buyer power did not historically receive a significant amount of attention from competition agencies, one should not forget that conduct on the buyers' side of a market may, in fact, attract competition law scrutiny. In this regard, the OECD has highlighted that there appears to be a marked change in the stances adopted by leading competition jurisdictions, particularly, the United States and European Union, towards the enforcement of abuses of buyer power (OECD 2022: 6). While the purpose of this chapter is not to discuss the foreign developments in buyer power, we highlight that:

- in 2019, New Zealand's Commerce Commission took enforcement action against a real estate buyers' cartel;
- in 2019, the European Commission imposed fines exceeding EUR67 million on several firms for their engagement in a buyers' cartel relating to the market for scrap batteries; and
- in 2021, the United States' Department of Justice laid charges against 140 individuals for entering into bid rigging agreements at auctions for foreclosed real estate.

Evidently, the prevalence of contraventions on the buyers' side of the market is receiving increased priority than was previously the case. Given the enhanced focus that is being placed on abuses of buyer power globally, it is evident that there should be a similar trend across Africa in due course, with African competition agencies commonly following closely in the enforcement and jurisprudential developments of foreign competition authorities.

The issue of buyer power and buyer power abuse across Africa

While the exercise of buyer power typically has pro-competitive effects, generally likely to result in lower prices to consumers in the short term, in some contexts, substantial buyer power can also harm competition in the relevant upstream and downstream markets in the long term. This means that the context and market structure in which the alleged abuse arises must be more carefully scrutinised. Indeed, the rules regulating buyer power must ensure that overly strict enforcement of the rules does not dampen pro-competitive conduct. Lastly, and as mentioned above, it has been submitted by scholars that abuses of buyer power are more prevalent within emerging markets, and that this may be the reason for the apparent sudden interest in buyer power across Africa. While we acknowledge that this may be the case, particularly where there may be fewer downstream purchasers, there is a general lack of economic literature to support the assertion that abuses of buyer power are more prevalent in emerging markets than in to larger economies.

Rather, and similar to the lack of priority in enforcing anti-competitive practices on the buyers' side of a market by foreign competition authorities, there has in fact been an underwhelming historical level of enforcement of abuses of buyer power across Africa, as the majority of cases have focused on the supply side. There may be several reasons for this – including the fact that an abuse of buyer power may well result in reduced prices for consumers (to the detriment of the squeezed supplier). In this regard, African competition authorities most likely had to balance having to prosecute conduct that resulted in a net benefit to the consumer welfare against the harm incurred by suppliers. Given the various socioeconomic circumstances across the continent, the benefit to consumers most likely found favour with these competition authorities. This would not be dissimilar to the position in foreign jurisdictions where the 'exploitation resulting from buyer power was and still is ignored' and reliance on the consumer welfare standard has been regarded as limiting the scope of enforcement of abuses of buyer power (Carstensen 2017: 9).

A deeper dive into what buyer power means

Broadly, 'buyer power' describes a situation in which the relative bargaining position of a buyer, or a group of buyers, compared to that of a supplier, allows it to decrease the purchase price of input costs below the level at which the supplier supplies other firms (Anchustegui 2024). Further, buyer power can be characterised as either monopsony, or bargaining (countervailing) power (OECD 2022: 10).

Monopsony is the buyer's equivalent of a seller's monopoly (Blair & Harrison 1991: 301). In this respect, a monopsony arises where there is only a single buyer, or association of buyers, of a particular good or service despite there being a competitive market on the supply side of the value chain (OECD 2022: 9). Just as a monopolist has market power in selling its particular good or service, a monopsonist has buying power in respect of purchasing requirements (Blair & Harrison 1991: 301). Typically, a buyer, or group of buyers, is an effective monopsonist when it has a sufficient share of purchases that allow it to influence its purchasing price by adjusting its level of demand. A monopsonist exercises its buyer power through the withholding of purchases in order to decrease the purchase price that it would ordinarily have to pay if it were not for the withholding (OECD 2022).

Unlike a monopoly, however, where a supplier holding back on output will inevitably cause prices to rise, the anti-competitive effects of the monopsony model are applicable in only a limited number of contexts. This is because buyer power is not typically exercised through the strategic reduction of quantities; instead, it is exerted in bilateral negotiations between buyers and sellers over individual prices, which may often be subject to what is essentially a 'volume discount' (meaning that prices actually fall as more purchases are made).[1] In these situations, and without more context, the exercise of buyer power would have a pro-competitive effect (if certain of the discounts are passed on to consumers) or at the very least a neutral effect (if the welfare gains from the volume discounts are simply shifted from supplier to buyer).

Bargaining, or countervailing power, describes the situation in which a purchaser is able to obtain favourable prices or trading conditions as a result of its strengthened position in negotiations with suppliers (OECD 2022). Contrary to a monopsony, bargaining power is not exercised through the withholding of purchases. Instead, purchasers threaten to reduce demand from a supplier, or set of suppliers, in order to decrease purchase prices, with the objective of maintaining or increasing purchases of the input (OECD 2022: 13).

Generally, benefits associated with the reduction of input prices resulting from the exercise of buyer power are likely to be passed on by buyers to the end consumer, as long as there is sufficient downstream competition (OECD 2008). In this respect, there has been comparatively less intervention by competition authorities regarding abuse of power on the buyer side as opposed to the seller side of the market. This is particularly because many jurisdictions are premised on the 'consumer welfare' standard, justifying competition authority intervention when such intervention would either prevent harm to consumers or otherwise result in a benefit to the consumer (OECD 2022: 8).

In light of the above, and despite the historical scarcity of the enforcement of abuses of buyer power, there has been a recent increase in the amount of attention that these cases have received over the past few years. In this regard, there is a clear need for increased debate and discussion regarding abuses of buyer power, particularly as it may relate to the African context, to assist in the promotion of jurisprudence and regulation across the continent.

Of relevance are recent developments emanating from both South Africa and Kenya, home of some continent's most active competition agencies, the Competition Commission South Africa (CCSA) and the Competition Authority of Kenya (CAK).

While discussed in greater detail below, the topic of buyer power came to the fore within the South African context as a result of the Grocery Retail Market Inquiry (GRMI), which highlighted that because of a sizeable degree of concentration, large national retailers could extract favourable trading terms from their suppliers. Off the back of the GRMI, South Africa's Competition Act (No. 89 of 1998) was amended to expressly include, inter alia, the abuse of buyer power as a prohibited practice. While yet to be litigated before South Africa's Competition Tribunal (the Tribunal), this chapter will assess and discuss the implications of the provision's inclusion as both an abuse-of-dominance provision (particularly in light of recent cases on abuse of dominance being handed down by the Tribunal and the Competition Appeal Court) and a public interest provision. This amendment may have the effect of opening the floodgates for all suppliers to complain about a buyer on whom they are dependent abusing its position to obtain favourable terms and may even result in increased costs to end consumers, contrary to the consumer welfare standard.

In addition to South Africa's inclusion of the abuse-of-buyer-power provision, this chapter will also discuss jurisprudence from CAK, which dealt squarely with abuses of buyer power. As will become apparent, Kenya's abuse-of-buyer-power provision differs markedly from that of South Africa – particularly as it is not prohibited as an 'abuse of dominance'. While Kenya's competition authorities have, arguably, grappled more substantively with the issue of buyer power – jurisprudence handed down by Kenya's Competition Tribunal raises potential concern that there may be an unequal weighting of interests between buyers and suppliers, in favour of suppliers. This again may have the ultimate effect of increasing the costs of conducting business and, thereby, resulting in increased costs to end consumers.

Buyer power in South Africa

This section of the chapter aims to provide a high-level overview of how concerns of abuse of buyer power first became apparent to the CCSA, prompting the need to eventually prohibit such practices as an abuse of dominance. Thereafter, it continues with a specific assessment of the inclusion of section 8(4) as both an abuse of dominance and public interest provision and discusses the possible unintended consequences associated as a result.

In the South African context, the concerns of buyer power became increasingly evident in the findings following the GRMI, which specifically investigated, as a key objective, the prevalence of buyer groups and buyer power within the grocery retail sector (CCSA 2019). In fact, the findings outlined in the GRMI Report inspired the recent amendments to the Competition Act so that buyer power is now specifically included as one of the listed forms of 'abuses' in section 8(4) of the Act.

The Grocery Retail Market Inquiry (GRMI) and its impact

In 2015, the CCSA initiated the Grocery Retail Market Inquiry (GRMI). The inquiry sought to investigate, inter alia, the impact of buyer groups on small and independent retailers in the grocery retail sector (CCSA 2015). In addition, it aimed to determine the extent to which large supermarket chains had a degree of buyer power over their suppliers (CCSA 2019: 212).

In its findings, the GRMI noted that the grocery retail market was characterised by high levels of concentration among national supermarket chains as well as high barriers to entry. It considered both factors to be conducive to the exercise of buyer power due to the limiting of the amount of purchaser options available for suppliers (CCSA 2019: 248). As large national supermarket retailers constitute a significant route to market for suppliers, the GRMI identified that these retailers were able to obtain favourable trading terms from suppliers as a result of having limited purchaser options. The retailers were thus found to be exerting buyer power (CCSA 2019: 248).

In its assessment of the buyer power of the large supermarket retailers, the CCSA found that the retailers were in fact able to extract higher rebates from suppliers (CCSA 2019: 248). While rebates were typically afforded to large supermarket retailers to cover the costs associated with placing products in stores, it was found that these rebates were not extended to wholesalers as they do not offer the same services as larger retailers, including having distribution centres and merchandising allowances (CCSA 2019: 248). Crucially, the GRMI found that this resulted in harm to smaller retailers as they purchase products from wholesalers and do not benefit from rebates like those extended to larger supermarket retailers.

Importantly, while the GRMI found that large retailers are able to exert buyer power, not only on small suppliers but also on the largest fast-moving consumer goods suppliers, it is clear that the amendments to the Competition Act provide relief only for small suppliers. We believe that this was a significant missed opportunity. The Inquiry failed to recognise that an abuse of buyer power that has anti-competitive effects for consumers can occur regardless of whether the supplier is considered large or small. Naturally, the larger the supplier, the more countervailing bargaining power it may have, which would mitigate the risk of an abuse of buyer power in the first instance. We explore this further below.

The GRMI was significant in that it identified the existence of buyer power within the grocery retail market. It also confirmed the long-standing principle that buyer power only results in consumer harm in a limited set of scenarios, as well as the likely benefits of buyer power in that consumers may pay less for products in which the resulting cost saving has been passed on to end consumers (CCSA 2019: 249).

As part of its work, the GRMI conducted an assessment of the prevalence and impact of 'buyer groups' within the grocery retail sector. Here, it found there to be beneficial outcomes for the members of the buyer groups (CCSA 2019: 33). While this was not a surprising finding, an important question remains: How are buyer groups to be regulated in South Africa, which, uniquely, prohibits the fixing of a 'purchase price' by competitors as a per se hardcore cartel prohibition? Thus, just like competitors discussing and agreeing on a joint selling price, competitors are potentially at risk of cartel conduct if they jointly agree on a purchase price.[2]

Abuse of buyer power: The South African Competition Amendment Act of 2018

Before the implementation of the Amendment Act and the introduction of section 8(4) of the Competition Act, instances of buyer power were predominantly seen in terms of the per se prohibition of fixing purchase prices (CCSA 2019: 293). However, on 13 February 2019 when it was signed into law, the South African Competition Amendment Act (No. 18 of 2018) (the Amendment Act) broadened the framework of South African competition law to expressly address buyer power. The Competition Act was accordingly amended to include section 8(4), which:

> [prohibits] a dominant firm in a sector designated[3] by the Minister in terms of paragraph (d) to directly or indirectly, require from or impose on a supplier that is a small and medium business or a firm controlled or owned by historically disadvantaged persons, unfair —
>
> (i) prices; or
>
> (ii) other trading conditions.

These amendments mark a stark contrast to the conventional way that abuse of buyer power is regulated. This is evident in section 8(4), which is expressly included within the 'abuse of dominance' framework, and in the fact that it is considered against the public interest rather than against the consumer welfare standard (Van der Hoven et al. 2020: 140).

In addition to the Amendment Act, and as a means to introduce enhanced certainty as to how the CCSA would approach the enforcement of buyer power cases, the CCSA published the *Buyer Power Enforcement Guidelines* (Buyer Power Guidelines). Although these key provisions of the Buyer Power Guidelines are discussed throughout this section, it is important to note that these guidelines are not binding on either the CCSA or third parties, and are rather meant to indicate *how* the CCSA will likely approach enforcing the newly introduced section 8(4).

Abuse of buyer power as an 'abuse of dominance'

As explained in the background note to the Competition Amendment Act, the prohibition of an abuse of buyer power was specifically included to protect suppliers of dominant firms from being required to sell goods or services at prices that prevent them from being able to effectively participate in the market (CCSA 2017: 16). Thus, section 8(4) requires a purchaser to be dominant.

Section 7 of the Competition Act states that a firm is deemed to be dominant where it has a market share of at least 45%; between 35% and 45% market share (unless it can be established that the firm does not have market power); and less than 35% market share but has *market power*. Thus, for section 8(4) to be applicable, a firm must satisfy one of these thresholds.

However, as buyer power is largely dependent on relative bargaining positions, it can be exercised by firms that are not 'dominant' for purposes of the Competition Act. This is borne out in both the economic literature and international experience. Equally, a dominant firm will not necessarily hold substantial bargaining power in relation to its suppliers. This is why it is common for competition authorities to regulate the abuse of buyer power outside the ambit of their abuse-of-dominance frameworks (CCSA 2019: 144).

Despite the abuse-of-buyer-power provision requiring that dominance first be established, the CCSA has acknowledged in its Buyer Power Guidelines that buyer power cannot be exclusively limited to the market share of firms. It notes that even firms with less than 35% market share can have the requisite market power in the context of buyer power concerns (CCSA 2020: 8):

> Based on economic theory and experience in other jurisdictions, buyers with less than 35%, but still a material share, frequently have buyer power and would therefore be considered dominant under Section 7. This is because buyer power is strongly impacted by the outside options available to both the supplier and the buyer. (CCSA 2020: 8)

While non-binding on both the CCSA and third parties, the Buyer Power Guidelines show that CCSA will adopt the approach that the conventional dominance thresholds have been significantly reduced to include instances where a firm has a 'material share' in a market, which it considers to be 15% or more (CCSA 2020: 9). In addition to the market share assessment, the guidelines state that the CCSA is likely to consider three factors in determining dominance for the purposes of section 8(4): a supplier's dependency on alternative purchaser options; the availability of alternative suppliers available to purchasers; and the nature of supply negotiations between the purchaser and seller (CCSA 2020: 9–11).

It is important to note that the approach to determining dominance, and in particular a firm's 'market power', has become more open-ended and subjective. This is largely because of the CCSA's investigations into several 'price gouging' cases during the Covid-19 pandemic, which dealt with complaints regarding excessive pricing (and not abuses of buyer power). It means that the risk that firms in South Africa can be considered to be dominant, even if their market shares are well below 35%, has significantly increased.

To give further context to these developments, we believe it is important to look at the approach of both the Competition Tribunal (Tribunal) and the Competition Appeal Court (CAC) in assessing market power in the price-gouging cases. We look specifically at the cases of pharmaceutical retailer Dis-Chem and workwear manufacturer Babelegi.

The Competition Commission of South Africa vs Dis-Chem Pharmacies Limited

On 14 July 2020, the Competition Tribunal handed down its reasons relating to Dis-Chem's excessive pricing of surgical masks during the Covid–19 pandemic, in contravention of section 8(1)(a) of the Competition Act.[4] Although this was an excessive pricing case, in essence it was about determining whether Dis-Chem was in fact 'dominant' (Oxenham et al. 2020: 526). To this end, the CCSA had argued that it was not necessary to define the relevant market as Dis-Chem had 'market power', evident in its ability to substantively increase its prices, independently of its competitors, suppliers or customers.[5] The CCSA had thus sought to argue that market power may be inferred from Dis-Chem's conduct alone (*Competition Commission of South Africa vs Dis-Chem*, para. 81). In support of the CCSA's argument, the Competition Tribunal held that it was not necessary to define the relevant market, as the assessment into market power could be conducted just by looking at the prevailing market conditions (Anderson et al. 1999: 71; *Competition Commission of South Africa vs Dis-Chem*, para. 103).

The Babelegi case[6]

Separately from its decision in the Dis-Chem case, the Tribunal was later presented with a substantially similar case involving workwear manufacturer Babelegi, which also supplied FFP1 face masks. Its task here was to determine whether Babelegi was 'dominant', and whether section 7 of the Competition Act imposes time periods in the determination of a firm's dominance (Oxenham et al. 2020: 527). It was common cause that Babelegi held less than 5% market share for the supply of FFP1 face masks.

Drawing on what the CAC had ruled in the *Sasol Chemical Industries Limited v Competition Commission* case, Babelegi submitted that 'market power' must be regarded as the ability of a firm to raise prices above competitive levels, consistently and profitably.[7] However, the Tribunal held that, regardless of Babelegi's negligible market share: '*…as a matter of economics, in a crisis period such as Covid–19, the actual conduct of the firm can be used as a proxy to assess its market power*' (our emphasis).[8] The Tribunal went on to say that Babelegi's conduct must be assessed in light of the particular circumstances arising from the Covid–19 pandemic. Throughout the hearing, the Tribunal ultimately limited its assessment of the firms' market power to a period spanning little over a month – known as 'temporary market power'. The Tribunal noted that as the Covid–19 pandemic resulted in all competitors selling at capacity and no firm had an incentive to reduce prices to increase sales, even small firms could enjoy market power. The Tribunal thus found Babelegi to have had market power for the complaint period as a result of its ability to materially increase prices, and to be guilty of excessive pricing.

In hearing the appeal, the Competition Appeal Court found that the critical question relating to market power was 'how long a view must this court take of conduct which clearly is reflective of independence from customers and competitors?'

And it concluded that Babelegi's pricing practices over the complaint period were indeed reflective of its market power (*Babelegi*, paras 53–57).

Abuse of buyer power as a public interest provision

Section 8(4) of the Competition Act provides that it is an offence to require or impose unfair prices or trading terms against small or medium enterprises (SMEs) or firms owned by historically disadvantaged persons (HDPs).[9] Evidently, section 8(4) has a broader policy concern of protecting HDP and SME suppliers. However, very importantly, this has the potential to cause tension with the consumer welfare standard, albeit inadvertently. For instance, where a buyer's conduct results in consumer benefit or results in a net zero benefit, but otherwise prejudices an SME or HDP firm, this may be deemed to be an offence – despite intervention not being justified in terms of the consumer welfare standard (Van der Hoven 2020: 141).

Emphasising the CCSA's supplier-centric approach, the Buyer Power Guidelines offer a set of 'guiding principles' for when the CCSA has to make an assessment in terms of section 8(4). Specifically, the guidelines provide that:

> 2.2.1 An inquiry under section 8(4) is whether the prices and trading conditions imposed on suppliers in the designated class by a dominant firm are unfair or not. The focus of the inquiry is therefore on the treatment and welfare of suppliers in the designated class, and the application of a fairness principle to that treatment.
>
> 2.2.2 *The inquiry does not, in the Commission's view, require an assessment of the effects on final consumers.* For instance, it is not relevant whether an unfairly low price achieved through the exercise of buyer power is passed through to consumers or not. The legislation does not require any weighing up of the welfare of suppliers in the designated class against final consumers. (CCSA 2020: 5; own emphasis)

It thus seems that section 8(4) allows the CCSA to intervene only where a buyer extracts unfair prices or trading terms from SME or HDP suppliers, regardless of whether the intervention may result in increased costs to the end-consumer. Where consumer welfare is compromised as a result of favouring a group of identified competitors, this would clearly be untenable, even if it could be justified on grounds of public interest.[10]

As the Constitutional Court in *Competition Commission of South Africa vs Mediclinic Southern Africa (Pty) Ltd and Another* confirmed in 2021, an increase in prices is inherently against the public interest. The Court went on to state (para. 61): 'Lest we forget, to the overwhelming majority of South Africans, regard being had to our acute economic inequalities, even a 1% fuel or bread price hike probably constitutes a threat to their presumably shallow pockets and survival.'

While the Constitutional Court's approach in *Mediclinic* case is questionable in so far as it links an increase in prices to a public interest criterion, when an increase in price fits squarely within a traditional and well-accepted competition test, the key point that the Constitutional Court recognises is that any regulatory intervention that results in increased prices is in conflict with the public interest objectives enshrined in the Competition Act.

While it is easy to foresee the risk of tensions between public interest objectives and competition law objectives in respect of the amendments to the Competition Act's price discrimination provisions[11], it is less obvious that the amendments to the Competition Act's buyer power provisions will give rise to the same tensions.

If anything, the legislature failed to recognise that where a dominant buyer is able to exert its market power, which enables it to engage in the type of buyer power that gives rise to competition or public interest concerns, such buyer is effectively able to leverage that buyer power across all suppliers and not only small suppliers. Accordingly, in seeking to advance the participating and expansion of SME and HDP firms, the legislature has created a framework that does not fundamentally address the type of consumer harm that buyer power could cause in certain circumstances. While there is always the catch-all abuse-of-dominance provision contained in section 8(1)(c) of the Act, which prohibits general exclusionary conduct, this has always been available to a complainant.

The likely effect of the Dis-Chem, Babelegi and MediClinic cases on the application of section 8(4) and abuses of buyer power

There are a number of significant dimensions and implications in these decisions, some of which are problematic. In effect, the Tribunal and the CAC substantially lowered the threshold for dominance; they applied a limited complaint period; they failed to define any relevant market; and they failed to compare the prices of competitors during the same complaint period (Oxenham et al. 2020: 530). As the decisions from both bodies placed particular emphasis on a firm's ability to increase prices during Covid–19, they offer little guidance on the applicability of its assessment of dominance and market power within traditional abuse of dominance cases occurring outside these kinds of constraints. So, if for instance, an abuse of buyer power case was brought before them, it is not clear whether the Tribunal or the CAC would rely on such a limited complaint period or choose not to define a relevant market in their decision-making.

Given the transformation agendas of not only section 8(4), but also of the Competition Act and the mandate of the Competition Commission as a whole, it would not be surprising if the Competition authorities adopted a similarly broadened assessment of dominance in the context of potential abuse of buyer power.[12] Here, the notion of economic dependence is also of particular importance.[13] While market power traditionally refers to a firm's ability to act independently across a market *as a whole,* buyer power refers to a significantly reduced scope, involving the bilateral relationship between a buyer and seller. Here, the assessment of a 'dominant buyer' would not be identical to the conventional assessment of market power. So where the market share of a buyer falls below the 15% threshold provided in the Buyer Power Guidelines, the buyer may still be deemed dominant because of a particular supplier's dependence on it. The likely applicability of an 'economic dependence' doctrine may be inferred from the Buyer Power Guidelines themselves, which provides that the CCSA may consider the following in determining whether a buyer is dominant (CCSA 2020, para. 4.4.2.1):

> If suppliers are *financially dependent on a buyer* then they may not be able to replace those sales quickly or easily if the buyer threatens to not purchase in future. This position would provide the buyer with a strong negotiating position to extract favourable terms from the supplier (CCSA 2020, para. 4.4.2.1; own emphasis).

We, the authors, contend that, if implemented, this approach would be highly controversial and lead to significant debate in legal circles. It could result in the opening of the floodgates for all sellers to complain about a buyer on whom they are dependent (but who may not necessarily be dominant). And that's not all. While this problematic assessment of dominance and market power clearly has prejudicial effects on firms themselves, there may also be unintended consequences for consumer welfare. Thus, remedial measures that have been designed to protect inefficient market participants are likely to serve as a tax on large (or small firms).[14] This, in turn, has the potential to either be passed on to consumers or, very seriously, to even discourage investment within South Africa. We can only conclude that section 8(4) is generating a competing relationship between the public interest and consumer welfare.

Concluding comments

Based on the above analysis, we make four comments about the potential unintended consequences specific to the implementation of section 8(4) of the South African Competition Act and 2020 Buyer Power Enforcement Guidelines.

First, and as we have discussed, the South African Buyer Power Guidelines, in combination with the watered-down assessment of dominance, provide little clarity on the applicability of section 8(4) of the Competition Act to many buyers across South Africa. In this respect, the provisions of the Buyer Power Guidelines suggest that even firms below the 15% market share threshold may be considered dominant buyers where a supplier is financially dependent on them (CCSA 2020, para. 4.4.2.1). Naturally, this uncertainty is a cause of concern for many businesses within South Africa and is likely to be a source for lengthy and costly litigation.

Second, as the exercise of buyer power is inherently pro-competitive and the regulation thereof will have the likely effect of dissuading a large downstream firm from exercising buyer power in respect of its suppliers. Subsequently, firms will have less incentive to negotiate for better prices and terms, which will, in turn, have an adverse effect on consumers. A caveat to this, however, is that section 8(4) applies only to those sectors designated by the Minister and, thus, these unintended consequences are limited within those sectors specifically. To this end, it is understandable that the CCSA has sought to limit the applicability of section 8(4) to those sectors wherein there is a high degree of downstream concentration and where any efficiencies that may be extracted from suppliers are less likely to be passed on to the end consumer.

Third, the Buyer Power Guidelines require that the CCSA determine whether a price, in and of itself, is unfair (CCSA 2020: 12). One particular consideration that the CCSA may have in determining whether a price is unfair is the prices paid to other suppliers of similar goods or services, and whether such prices are higher (CCSA 2020, para. 6.1.1). In such an instance, where a buyer has a large supplier and various smaller suppliers, the buyer cannot provide the larger supplier with lower prices due to their having economies of scale and the buyer, as a result, being able to obtain volume-based discounts. Hence, where a buyer has both large and small suppliers, they are effectively prohibited from engaging in volume-based discounts as the lower price provided to the larger supplier will be relatively unfair to the smaller suppliers.

Last, potential unintended consequences may present themselves as a result of the regulation of non-pricing terms, such as rebates. With particular reference to rebates, non-pricing terms are generally associated with the delivery of efficiencies from the suppliers' end, which results in increased downstream competition and consumer welfare benefits. However, such efficiencies are only reasonably offered by larger suppliers and cannot necessarily be provided by smaller suppliers. We submit that although the buyer power framework seeks to regulate the conduct of buyers, issues regarding non-pricing terms may well become an issue that concerns the conduct of a supplier. To this end, we submit that there is likely to be a frustration between buyers and suppliers as to who bears the burden of ensuring that there is no differential treatment as a result of differences in bargaining power.

Buyer power in Kenya: Some key developments

Having discussed the buyer power framework in South Africa, this section will discuss the introduction of 'abuse of buyer power' as a prohibited conduct within Kenya's legislative framework and will also broadly comment on the Competition Authority of Kenya's (CAK) enforcement of this abuse-of-buyer-power provision.

Before South Africa's introduction of section 8(4) of the Competition Act, Kenya had been the first African jurisdiction to enact a separate provision within its competition law framework through which to specifically regulate an abuse of buyer power (Competition Authority of Kenya 2016: 7). Section 24A of the newly amended Competition Act (No. 12 of 2010) (Kenyan Competition Act) provides that '*Any conduct that amounts to abuse of buyer power* in a market in Kenya, or a substantial part of Kenya, is prohibited' (own emphasis).

Section 24A(5) provides a closed list of conduct that would constitute an 'abuse' of buyer power. Hence, it is not the ability to exert buyer power that is prohibited but rather the abuse thereof.[15]

In support of the amendments to the Kenyan Competition Act, the Competition Authority of Kenya (CAK) stated that abuses of buyer power were most prevalent within the Kenyan retail sector after it had received complaints from suppliers that certain buyers had refused to pay for goods or failed to honour general contractual obligations (CAK 2016: 4).

In comparison to the inclusion of buyer power into South Africa's Competition Act, section 24A of the Kenyan Competition Act does not expressly require that a firm be 'dominant' for the abuse-of-buyer-power provision to find applicability. Emphasising this point, the Buyer Power Guidelines, amended in 2022, state that 'even the least powerful buyer has a disciplinary effect on a supplier if there is a credible threat that it could switch to another supplier(s) to a sufficient extent and to the detriment of that supplier' (Competition Authority of Kenya 2022a: 3).

Moreover, the Competition Act (Kenya) section 2 defines 'buyer power' as:

> the influence exerted by an undertaking or group of undertakings in the position of purchaser of a product or service to—
>
> (a) obtain from a supplier more favourable terms; or
>
> (b) impose a long term opportunity cost including harm or withheld benefit, which, if carried out, would be significantly disproportionate to any resulting long term cost to the undertaking or group of undertakings.[16]

The Kenyan Act is further distinguishable from the South African Competition Act in that its applicability is not constrained to the extraction of favourable terms or prices from SMEs, despite CAK's recognising the pivotal role that SMEs have in safeguarding and sustaining the Kenyan economy (Competition Authority of Kenya 2022a: 3). Rather, the amended Buyer Power Guidelines provide that CAK will fast-track investigations involving SMEs or where an alleged abuse of buyer impacts numerous suppliers.

In November 2022, CAK announced that it was able to recover reneged payments worth KES38 million (approximately USD250 000) from 20 motor vehicle repairers and five motor vehicle assessors in favour of 1 000 Kenyans (Competition Authority of Kenya

2022b: 3). However, the first decision to be brought before the Kenyan Competition Tribunal (Competition Tribunal), *Majid Al Futtaim Hypermarkets Limited v Competition Authority of Kenya and Orchards Limited* (the *Carrefour* case), provided little clarity on the enforcement of Kenya's buyer power regime. Notably, the Competition Tribunal's decision in *Carrefour* has been criticised for focusing on fairness to suppliers rather than undertaking a robust assessment of concerns of foreclosure in any relevant market, the likely effect on consumer welfare and the existence of other pro-competitive efficiencies.

The Carrefour case

Briefly, on 26 April 2019, Orchards Limited (Kenya Orchards), active in the processing and sale of probiotic yogurts, alleged that Majid Al Futtaim Hypermarkets Limited (Majid) had abused its buyer power by transferring commercial risks to Orchards: refusing to receive Orchard's products: unilaterally and unjustifiably terminating its relationship with Orchards: applying rebates and listing fees marked as discounts: and requiring Orchards to deploy staff at its own cost.

Although the Competition Tribunal found Majid to have abused its buyer power, its judgment failed to provide much clarity on fundamental economic issues. First, the Tribunal failed to conduct a thorough and robust assessment into whether Majid, in fact, had abused its buyer power. In this respect, the Tribunal held that where a firm engages in conduct amounting to an 'abuse of buyer power', that firm has buyer power. 'In other words, the influence or power of the buyer becomes evident when the buyer engages in the offending conduct' (Majid 2021, para. 165).

Notably, by assessing the effects of a firm's conduct rather than the existence of buyer power, the *Carrefour* decision has had the effect of departing from the approaches of other competition law frameworks by seemingly adopting an *ex post* assessment to buyer power. As a result, the *Carrefour* decision had the likely impact of buyers' not being able to self-regulate, as ordinary commercial practices such as negotiating of terms could now be marked as an abuse of buyer power.

Second, the Tribunal adopted an approach that favoured fairness towards suppliers – undoubtedly tipping the law's favour in protection of suppliers as opposed to conducting a robust assessment of the relevant market, potential foreclosure concerns and consumer welfare or efficiencies.

The Unilever Kenya case

Emphasising its stance against abuses of buyer power, CAK entered into a settlement agreement with Unilever Kenya for allegedly revising its payment terms for 75 of its suppliers (principally consisting of local traders) from 60 days to 90 days. Additionally, Unilever Kenya's suppliers were provided with only a single week within which to accept the revised payment terms or otherwise be terminated as a supplier. Notably, Unilever Kenya's foreign and large suppliers were exempted from the revised payment terms.[17]

As part of the settlement agreement, CAK ordered that Unilever Kenya reduce its payment terms to be between 30 and 45 days, bringing its payment terms in line with Unilever Kenya's parent company, Unilever PLC. Further to improving payment terms, CAK also ordered that Unilever Kenya increase its local procurement by a minimum of KES400 million over three years, with Unilever Kenya also having committed to invite a minimum of two local suppliers to each of its tenders.[18] Although the Unilever Kenya settlement serves to emphasise the targeted approach of CAK in combatting abuses of buyer power, it does not provide any clarity on those questions left unanswered by the *Carrefour* decision.

CAK has stated that since the implementation of section 24A of the Kenyan Competition Act, it has noted significant obstacles preventing it from efficiently investigating and concluding complaints of abuse of buyer power. The main obstacle appears to have been the lack of understanding from various stakeholders about the processes and tools that CAK applies in assessing whether a purchaser has buyer power and, then, whether it has abused such a position (CAK 2022b: 18).

Concluding thoughts

As noted above, the *Carrefour* decision did little to provide comprehensive guidance on how to navigate the abuse of buyer power landscape in Kenya. In this regard, it is encouraging that the CAK's newsletter (*Ushindani*) emphasises the need for competition authorities to adopt clear and certain buyer power regulations to enable firms to self-regulate, which is particularly important as more competition authorities across the continent move towards increasing their buyer power enforcement.

In saying this, however, it is still incumbent on the CAK and Kenya's Competition Tribunal to objectively assess each abuse of buyer power on a case-by-case basis and without applying a supplier-centric approach towards enforcement to the unjustified prejudice of larger buyers.

Conclusions

It is evident from international and South African economic literature, as well as from the increasing interest being shown by the South African and Kenyan competition authorities in particular, that buyer power is a real-world issue and does not just appear in a few pieces of academic writing. Buyer power should be given far more due regard by all African competition authorities, as it seems that it is increasingly being exercised within developing countries – because of the specific economic dynamics in these countries' economies. However, as these competition authorities seek to amend their competition law frameworks to cover abuses of buyer power, they need to be mindful that amendments are implemented in line with international best practice (including foreign precedent) to ensure an enhanced degree of legislative certainty across numerous jurisdictions and to not overly favour the supply side to the detriment of the buyer – without which may cause buyers to exit the local market for having to substantially change their business models that they may have across their other geographic locations.

South Africa offers a cautionary tale for why this is so important. It is evident that that assessment of the public interest element in merger control has started to creep into assessments of prohibited conduct. Although the transformation agenda of South Africa's competition regime is laudable, the restriction of the recently included section 8(4) to cater only for abuses against SMEs and HDPs fails to accept that *all* firms are susceptible to abuse of buyer power. For example, if a buyer group was able to extract favourable terms or prices from a large supplier, their conduct would be immune from scrutiny under section 8(4). The failure to protect large firms from abuses of buyer power is arbitrary and may have the likely effect of discouraging investment because of an unfavourable regulatory environment. A reduction in investment may have a concomitant impact of consumer welfare due to a reduction of output.

It is evident from our analysis and discussion that the approaches of both the CCSA and CAK reflect a supplier-centric approach towards the treatment of buyer power. Both the South African and Kenyan competition Acts fail to consider the effect of the exercise of buyer power on the consumer welfare standard. Although it is otherwise common knowledge that developing countries tend to consider all market harms, as opposed to a pure consumer welfare standard, we argue that the effect on consumer welfare should be the overarching assessment measure and that the prejudice to suppliers and consumers and other efficiencies must at least be held in balance.

In light of the above, we strongly recommend that the adoption of a buyer power framework be premised on an objective assessment. This is to ensure clarity, certainty and equality, and to allow firms to self-regulate and engage in commercial operations without fearing that they may be unintentionally contravening buyer power regulations. Without a sufficient degree of certainty, coupled with increased enforcement initiatives where buyers are penalised for implementing the same purchase terms and conditions that they do in other jurisdictions, this may have an unintended consequence on foreign direct investment whereby large buyers exit the market and/or potential entrants decide to invest in more favourable regulatory landscapes.

Notes

1. See, for example, European Commission (2004) guidelines for the assessment of horizontal mergers under the Council Regulation on the control of concentrations between undertakings. Official Journal C31/5–18: 64; and Office of Fair Trading (2004) Assessment of Market Power. Competition Act Guidelines OFT516a:6.2; both refer to buyer power in the context of a bargaining framework.
2. On 31 August 2022, the Competition Commission published the Draft Block Exemption Regulations for Small, Micro and Medium-sized Businesses for public comment.

Of relevance, the Draft regulations expressly exclude, inter alia, joint purchasing agreements (which would otherwise be categorised as cartel conduct) from the prohibited horizontal and vertical agreement provisions of the Competition Act, being sections 4(1) and 5(1) respectively.

3 The following are included as 'designated sectors' (CCSA 2020):

(a) Grocery wholesale and retail sector

(b) Agro-processing sector

(c) Ecommerce and online services sector

4 Section 8(1)(a) of the Competition Act (South Africa) provides that it is 'prohibited for a dominant firm to— (a) charge an excessive price to the detriment of consumers or customers'.

5 Section 1 of the Competition Act (South Africa) defines 'market power' as 'the power of a firm to control prices, to exclude competition or to behave to an appreciable extent independently of its competitors, customers or suppliers'.

6 See: *Competition Commission vs Babelegi Workwear Overall Manufacturers and Industrial Supplies CC* Case No: CR003Apr20; and
Babelegi Workers and Industrial Supplies CC v The Competition Commission of South Africa Case No: 186/CAC/JUN20.

7 *Sasol Chemical Industries Limited v Competition Commission* 131/CAC/Jun14 at [2].

8 *Competition Commission v Babelegi Workwear Overall Manufacturers and Industrial Supplies CC* Case No: CR003Apr20 at [92].

9 Section 2 of the Competition Act (South Africa) defines 'historically disadvantaged persons' as, inter alia, 'a category of individuals who, before the Constitution of the Republic of South Africa, 1993 (Act 200 of 1993), came into operation, were disadvantaged by unfair discrimination on the basis of race…'

10 To this end, Van der Hoven, Anderson and Zwane submit that section 8(4)'s public interest agenda is likely to cause tension with a strict interpretation of the consumer welfare standard, but is nevertheless workable (Van der Hoven et al. 2020: 142).

11 See a comprehensive analysis in this regard in Currie's master's thesis (2020) 'South Africa's Amended Price Discrimination Provision: An Analytical Framework in Relation to the Grocery Retail Market', King's College London.

12 In this respect, the Minister of Trade, Industry and Competition, Ebrahim Patel, stated the following in respect of supporting local economic growth (gov.za 2021): 'The Competition Act has been amended to <u>place transformation at the centre of competition policy</u>, including through measures to address price discrimination against smaller businesses and firms owned by black South Africans, new curbs on abuse of power by dominant firms and new powers to the regulators to deal with economic concentration that results in exclusion of black South Africans in the economy' (own emphasis).

13 An abuse of economic dependence refers to the instance where one party (the buyer) abuses their relative power over another (the seller).

14 As confirmed in Babelegi where the Respondent had less than a 5% market share in the supply of FFP1 face masks.

15 For a full list of which conduct may constitute an 'abuse' of buyer power, see section 24A(5) of the Kenyan Competition Act.
16 See section 2 of the Kenyan Competition Act (No. 12 of 2010).
17 See: Ormandi D, Watchdog punishes Unilever Kenya for unfair trade deals, *Business Daily*, 19 December 2022. Accessed February 2023, https://www.businessdailyafrica.com/bd/economy/watchdog-punishes-unilever-kenya-for-unfair-trade-deals--4059484
18 See: Ormandi D, Watchdog punishes Unilever Kenya for unfair trade deals, *Business Daily*, 19 December 2022. Accessed February 2023, https://www.businessdailyafrica.com/bd/economy/watchdog-punishes-unilever-kenya-for-unfair-trade-deals--4059484

References

Anderson R, Daniel T & Heimler A (1999) Abuse of dominance. In RS Khemani (Ed.) *A framework for the design and implementation of competition law and policy.* Washington DC: World Bank; Paris: OECD

Anchustegui IH (n.d.) Buyer power: Global dictionary of competition law. Concurrences, Art. N° 12328. Accessed August 2024, https://www.concurrences.com/en/dictionary/buyer-power

Blair RD & Harrison JL (1991) Antitrust policy and monopsony. *Cornell Law Review* 76: 297

Carstensen PC (2017) *Competition policy and the control of buyer power: a global issue.* Cheltenham: Edward Elgar Publishing

Competition Authority of Kenya (2016) Newsletter 1. Accessed September 2022, https://cak.go.ke/sites/default/files/2019-06/Competition%20Authority%20of%20Kenya%20News%20Bulletin%20%2C%20October%202016-min.pdf

Competition Authority of Kenya (2022a) Buyer Power Guidelines, March 2022. Accessed September 2022, https://www.cak.go.ke/sites/default/files/Buyer_Power_Guidelines_2022.pdf

Competition Authority of Kenya (2022b) Newsletter 9. Accessed September 2022, https://cak.go.ke/sites/default/files/2022-06/CAK%20Newsletter%20Issue%209.pdf

Fox E (2013) *Imagine: Pro-poor(er) Competition Law, Organisation for Economic Co-operation and Development.* Paris: OECD. DAF/COMP/GF(2013)11/FINAL

OECD (Organisation for Economic Cooperation and Development) (2022) *Purchasing power and buyers' cartels.* Accessed September 2022, https://www.oecd.org/daf/competition/purchasing-power-and-buyers-cartels-2022.pdf

OECD (Organisation for Economic Cooperation and Development) (2008) *Policy roundtables: Monopsony and buyer power.* Accessed September 2022, https://www.oecd.org/daf/competition/44445750.pdf

Oxenham J, Currie MJ & Van der Merwe C (2020) COVID-19 price gouging cases in South Africa: Short-term market dynamics with long-term implications for excessive pricing cases. *Journal of European Competition Law & Practice* 11(9): 524–530

South African Government (2021) *Minister Ebrahim Patel on supporting local economic growth.* Accessed September 2022, https://www.gov.za/news/media-statements/minister-ebrahim-patel-supporting-local-economic-growth-03-jun-2021

Van der Hoven Z, Anderson P & Zwane K (2020) An economic perspective on the new South African buyer power provision and enforcement guidelines. *Competition Law International* 16: 139

Case law

*Babelegi Workwear and Industrial Supplies CC v Competition Commission of South Afric*a (186/CAC/JUN20) [2020] ZACAC 7 (18 November 2020). Accessed September 2022, http://www.saflii.org/za/cases/ZACAC/2020/7.html

Competition Commission of South Africa v Dis-Chem Pharmacies Limited CR008Apr20

Competition Commission v Babelegi Workwear Overall Manufacturers and Industrial Supplies CC Case No: CR003Apr20

Competition Commission of South Africa v Mediclinic Southern Africa (Pty) Ltd and Another (CCT 31/20) [2021] ZACC 35; 2022 (5) BCLR 532 (CC) (15 October 2021)

Majid Al Futtaim Hypermarkets Limited v Competition Authority of Kenya and Orchards Limited Case No. CT/006/2020 (20 April 2021). Accessed September 2022, http://kenyalaw.org/caselaw/cases/view/211430/

Majid Al Futtaim Hypermarkets Limited v Competition Authority of Kenya and Another (Civil Appeal E033 of 2021) [2024] KEHC 5812 (KLR) (Commercial and Tax) (23 May 2024). Accessed August 2024, https://kenyalaw.org/caselaw/cases/view/289845/

Legislation and guidelines

South Africa

Competition Commission of South Africa (2015) 'Grocery Retail Sector Market Inquiry: Terms of Reference'. Available at: http://www.compcom.co.za/wp-content/uploads/2015/06/GROCERY-RETAIL-SECTOR-MARKET-INQUIRY_ToR_final-3.pdf

Competition Commission of South Africa (2017) *Background Note on the Competition Amendment Bill*. Government Gazette No. 41294 (1 December 2017)

Competition Commission of South Africa (2019) 'Grocery Retail Market Inquiry'. Available at: https://www.compcom.co.za/wp-content/uploads/2019/12/GRMI-Non-Confidential-Report.pdf

Competition Commission of South Africa (2020) *Buyer Power Enforcement Guidelines* Available at: https://www.compcom.co.za/wp-content/uploads/2020/05/Buyer-Power-Guidelines.pdf

Minister of Trade, Industry and Competition (2022) *Draft Block Exemption Regulations for Small, Micro and Medium-sized Businesses* (31 August 2022). Available at: https://www.gov.za/sites/default/files/gcis_document/202208/46838reg11482gon2431.pdf

Kenya

Competition Authority of Kenya (2022a) *Buyer Power Guidelines* Available at: https://www.cak.go.ke/sites/default/files/Buyer_Power_Guidelines_2022.pdf

6 New thinking in competition regulation: Adjusting law and enforcement to address challenges of African markets

Priscilla M Njako

The world of competition enforcement is in flux across the globe. Increasing economic concentration and rapid technological change have led many to call for closer scrutiny of existing laws and how they are applied. A common thread in recent academic scholarship, as well as in political circles, seems to be questioning how adequate the law and the favoured enforcement model are in addressing the needs of contemporary markets.[1] The prevailing discourse at competition law forums globally reflects these concerns, with topics at recent forums such as 'Are market economies and the consumer welfare standard being overwhelmed by national interests, politics or progressive forces and policies?'[2]; 'Should competition authorities care about fairness and if so how?'[3]; 'The new regulatory landscape: How will the new regulations fit together and where does it leave competition law?'[4] and 'Sustainability and climate change: New dimensions in competition law.'[5] Essentially, the question asked is whether the law as presently applied is effective in keeping markets competitive or whether there is need to rethink both the content of the law as well as the widely applied welfare approach to enforcement.

Any effective change comes down to what the law should do. How should it position itself in addressing the two ends of the spectrum: that it is there to safeguard the process of competition on the one side, and on the other that the focus should be on the outcome of competition (Dunne 2015)? Put differently, should the law be designed to protect a process or to promote the maximising of value (Wu 2018)? Process-focused theories emphasise the functioning of the market mechanism, preferring a fragmented market structure. Outcome-focused theories are driven by the socially desirable distribution that competitive markets are said to yield, where market conduct that improves consumer welfare is sanctioned.

For African jurisdictions, the matter is more complex. The shift towards market-oriented economies and the assimilation of free market principles is relatively recent. Most African markets continue to be fairly rudimentary and characterised by a heavy reliance on agriculture and a large informal sector (Fox & Bakhoum 2019). Indeed, small domestic markets with low levels of industrialisation and diversification, high levels of concentration and high barriers to entry are some of the common characteristics of the continent's economies (Burke et al. 2017). High levels of concentration and high barriers to entry, in particular, have the effect of entrenching incumbents and depressing competition (Roberts 2017). African regulators are faced with the additional question of how to best employ a law that is premised on the characteristics of a developed economy, and how best it can effectively be applied to the actual circumstances on the ground (Waked 2016).

A review of the history of competition law in the pioneering jurisdictions of the West shows that the needs of a particular jurisdiction have influenced interpretation and enforcement. Competition policy has undergone many iterations of soul-searching, in attempts to ensure relevance, stability and coherence. So what may appear today as a novel concern, has easily had roots in an earlier time (Crane 2015a). Crucially, Western-based legislation is premised on existing markets that have large numbers of participants, fully rational economic agents and governments that are equipped to carry out redistribution or efficiently implement other measures (Waked 2016).

In African countries, framing goals is especially important for there to be effective competition legislation. Most African countries have fairly young laws without the benefit of years of accumulated jurisprudence. Developing countries are different in fundamental ways and, to be fit for purpose, competition law and enforcement must respond appropriately to the domestic context. This may, for example, involve an expansion of the law to ensure comprehensive solutions to the challenges of local markets.

An example is Kenya, which amended its Competition Act (No. 12 of 2010) in 2016 to incorporate the prohibition of abuse of buyer power.[6] On the available evidence, the enforcement of the abuse of buyer power provisions has been found to address a core need within this developing-country jurisdiction – namely, inclusive development. The overarching objective of Kenya's Competition Act is the improved welfare of the people of Kenya. This is to be realised by promoting and protecting effective competition in order to achieve increased efficiency in production, distribution and supply of goods and services; maximise the efficient allocation of resources; create an environment that is conducive to both foreign and local investment; and promote competitiveness of national firms operating in world markets.[7] Prohibiting the abuse of buyer power is a tool that contributes directly to these development goals.

This chapter uses the historical trends in American antitrust and European competition law to show that competition law has been fluid even in pioneering jurisdictions. The two examples illustrate that the law has always been used to address the specific economic needs of the jurisdiction at the given time. The chapter also examines the different priorities in western and African economies, and how competition law in African jurisdictions in particular needs to respond to their particular development needs. It uses the Kenyan experience to illustrate how the introduction and enforcement of abuse of buyer power provisions has been leveraged to enhance the usefulness of competition law for the country.

The chapter first looks at the current general global landscape of competition law. It then gives a historical overview of the development of competition legislation and policy, with a focus on the United States and the European Union (EU), and concludes with a review of Kenya's competition legislation and the value of inclusion of abuse-of-buyer-power provisions in that law.

Competition law at a crossroads

The general global landscape in which competition law is being enforced is a rapidly shifting one. A key force contributing to this change is the emergence of the digital marketplace. The digital economy has revolutionised the business landscape. With the internet so widely available, it has become a common channel that businesses rely on to market their brands and engage in transactions. The medium gives the benefits of closer connectivity to consumers, the collection of big data for insight on consumer preferences and additional ways to achieve sales and marketing goals.

Although they provide new ways of doing business, digital markets present a challenge to traditional models of competition enforcement. While in traditional markets we speak of market power, dominance or monopoly, in digital markets the language is different, with references to 'superior bargaining position'[8], 'uneven bargaining position'[9], 'strategic market status'[10] and 'gatekeepers'.[11] This is mainly due to the unique characteristics of digital markets such as their multisided nature, zero-price services, network effects and access to and monetisation of data. Traditionally, market shares have been used to assess market power. However, with digital markets, jurisdictions have adopted a range of measures to respond to the challenges of enforcement in these new markets. One common intervention has been to expand existing laws or to create separate statutes to support the existing ones.[12]

Merger regulation continues to generate vibrant debate. In the United States, for instance, antitrust generally, but more especially merger policy, is so hotly contested that it regularly features as a campaign issue. Vocal disagreements continue outside of the election cycles (Crane 2022; Waller & Morse 2020). The main criticism is that the pendulum has tended to swing too far in favour of non-intervention, with mergers being allowed to proceed on the basis of tenuous arguments about entry, expansion and efficiencies (Baker and Shapiro 2008; Hovenkamp 2017a). The end result, it is contested, is highly concentrated markets characterised by higher prices among other forms of consumer harm. The dominant view of enforcement of competition law is that it exists to promote some version of economic welfare – either total welfare or consumer welfare (Hovenkamp 2017b). The idea is that as markets usually work by themselves to attain efficient results, there must be intervention only when it is necessary to remedy a market anomaly that undermines consumer welfare. However, the economic welfare model has been criticised for being unduly accommodating of market players and implicitly overseeing increasing market concentration.

In the United States, antitrust enforcement is accused of encouraging 'overly cautious enforcement policies and overly demanding proof requirements'.[13] There have been growing calls for stronger enforcement as a way to revitalise the economy. By and large, these calls are for a return to stricter antitrust enforcement. Brandeisian tradition, described as a social or political theory supporting atomistic competition because of its beneficial effects on personal liberty and autonomy, is thought to be on the comeback, driven by the opinion that enforcement today is out of sync with the economic realities of the populace (Khan 2018; Leydecker 2021).

Historical trends in competition law and enforcement

This section covers the historical trends of competition law. It examines American and European enforcement of competition law over the years to illustrate how policy regimes have become established, and then have declined and been replaced by new ones. What we are seeing now is a continuation of these movements. This crossroads moment is giving African jurisdictions an ideal opportunity to review their enforcement paradigms and devise approaches that optimally serve their developing economies. Like all other legal disciplines, competition law is a social construct. To remain relevant and credible, competition law must be adjusted from time to time so that it is responsive to the context in which it is functioning and is thus better able to address the social and economic needs of a particular jurisdiction.

History shows that competition law has not only been the product of economic theorising, but also of the political economy. Competition legislation tends to be broad, providing a framework for the protection of competition but not actual guidance on how the concept of 'competition' is to be interpreted (Dunne 2015). The open-ended nature of most competition law has provided courts, enforcers and other stakeholders including scholars and bureaucrats with a blank canvas to paint on (Sidak & Teece 2009; Stucke 2012). It has enabled enforcers to adjust the application of the law to be more directly relevant to jurisdictional demands and courts to formulate a 'common law' of competition law (First & Waller 2012; Kovacic & Shapiro 2000). The downside is that the law has been open to misinterpretation (Cooper 2015). Successive political regimes have also deployed competition law to achieve predetermined goals (Ezrachi 2016).

This section addresses the issue from the angle of the US because a study of the normative foundations of competition law is essentially a journey through America's antitrust over the last century or so. Add to this the fact that competition legislation across jurisdictions, the EU included, typically takes the prototype of American law. Developing economies have been known to borrow their competition law regimes from American antitrust.[14] The structure, language and philosophy of South Africa's competition statutes and case law are said to have benefited from those of the United States and the EU (Munyai 2016). In turn, Kenya, Botswana and Namibia, among other African countries, have been inspired by the values of the South African system (Botchway 2011; Singh 2013). Alongside the law, developing countries have also tended to adopt the enforcement paradigms and institutions for administration of the US (Ezrachi 2016; Orbach 2013). With this reality, one can expect pertinent lessons from the trajectory of American antitrust.

The United States

Today, antitrust is caught up in increasingly political calls for a shift in the preferred model of enforcement. Stucke identifies four 20-to-30-year-long cycles that have marked antitrust policy from the early 1900s to the present date (Stucke 2011). These have been characterised by times of strict enforcement followed by seasons when the law was more accommodating of market conduct that would otherwise have been prohibited. A review of the enforcement of antitrust supports this position. The Sherman Act of 1890, a United States law that prescribes the rules of free competition for firms engaged in commerce, was a political tool right from the start, having been passed to counter amalgamation of economic and political power by big corporations (Ezrachi 2016; Orbach 2013). This was so much the case that strong public sentiment in favour of the law made voting against it a risky choice for politicians who were seeking re-election (Orbach 2013).

The Act picked up pace with the development of the *per se* rule in 1904.[15] When the courts established the rule of reason in 1911[16], Congress responded by passing the Clayton and Federal Trade Acts in 1914 to block the apparent softening of the law. Woodrow Wilson had two years earlier won the 1912 elections on the ticket of firm antitrust and the two Acts were a follow-through on his election agenda (Crane 2015a). A period of reinvigorated antitrust enforcement followed. However, firm antitrust took a step back with the advent of the First World War (Viscusi et al. 2018). Big Business was necessary for success in the War and therefore enforcers adopted a 'lite touch' approach to enforcement during the War years.[17] The Great Depression precipitated a season during which policy was reviewed to support the survival of struggling businesses, sometimes against their more efficient rivals (Meese 2013). Legislation was passed to support the policy position, the best known being the Robinson-Patman Act of 1936, whose purpose was the protection of small businesses from being driven out of the marketplace by bigger counterparts (Yonezawa et al. 2020). It is notable that after decades of dormancy, enforcement of this Act may be making a comeback.[18]

As the country began to move out of the Second World War, Brandeisian views on the dangers of bigness experienced a resurgence (Crane 2015b). The structure–conduct–performance touchstone, which endorsed a more interventionist antitrust to open up markets for participation by smaller players, anchored the enforcement programme that followed. Conduct was held to be anticompetitive, regardless of its actual effects.[19] The 'incipiency' standard was used to outlaw acquisitions that had the potential to create a monopoly or give the parties market power.[20] A structural presumption under which mergers beyond a certain threshold were presumptively held to be illegal was effected.[21] The structural presumption is today echoed in the language of legislation such as the EU's Digital Markets Act and the proposed American Innovation and Choice Online Act, where undertakings past established thresholds are characterised 'gate-keepers' in their respective markets.

The Chicago School, which advocated the consumer welfare standard, took prominence starting in the 1940s. Its proponents argued that the enforcement of the preceding years was unnecessarily interventionist and the proper focus of antitrust enforcement should be market power and the resultant ability to artificially raise prices and restrict output, thus harming the consumer (Bork 1978). It is this approach that is broadly applied but is currently under question. Today, the United States appears to be on the cusp of a direction shift in antitrust enforcement and indications are that the new policy cycle may bring with it a broadening of the ends of competition law to include political, social and ethical concerns (Hovenkamp 2018; Waller 2017).

The European Union

For the European Union, political and economic goals have influenced the levels and nature of competition law enforcement. Early decisions on EU competition law reflect interpretation in light of the EU's goal of market integration[22], so much so that the first definition of the European single market happened in a competition law case.[23] Market integration remained the key driver of the EU's competition law, which in practice has led to a focus on territorial restrictions that may undermine the creation of the Single Market (Ezrachi 2016).

However, over the decades, the enforcement of EU competition law has broadened from emphasis on market integration to protecting consumers. In *GlaxoSmithKline v. Commission*[24], the Court of Justice of the European Union acknowledged that the primary purpose of the law was shifting from a primary concern for an integrated market to a consumer-focused theory of protection. The Court observed that the primary objective of achieving the integration of national markets through the establishment of a single market had essentially been completed and therefore the law would now aim to protect the interests of competitors, consumers and the structure of the market.

Nonetheless, the issue of the purpose of competition law in the EU is not fully settled.[25] EU competition law is not monothematic and pursues multiple objectives. These include efficiency, consumer welfare, commercial or economic freedom and freedom to compete, market structure, fairness and protecting the competitive process (Stylianou & Lacovides 2022). Not only are the goals multiple, but they also reflect the evolving nature of the objectives of competition law.

Africa

During the past 20 years, many countries have adopted competition laws, driven by the global consensus on the value of competition and free markets supported by competition law to deter anticompetitive practices (Evenett 2015; Waked, 2016; Whish & Bailey 2018). At the beginning of the millennium, the majority of countries with competition law regimes were in the West. This number has since grown to over 140 in 2022[26], with the bulk of new competition law regimes being in the developing world.

Only three African countries – South Africa, Kenya and Gabon – had a competition law prior to 1990. Nine more African countries enacted competition laws up to 2010. As at 2020, 41 African countries had a modern competition law. However, out of this number, nine did not have an operational competition agency (Buthe & Kigwiru 2020). Virtually all of Africa's competition law regimes are fairly young and most are less than a decade old.[27] As an example, Nigeria's Federal Competition and Consumer Protection Act became effective in 2019.[28] Given the fairly recent addition of competition law into African Countries' statute books, it is not possible to pick out clear trends in terms of goals of enforcement. For most, the early days of enforcement have involved examination in order to establish how best to apply the law to support competition in their markets.

Though having similar competition law, with roots in the advanced jurisdictions, African countries differ in fundamental ways from jurisdictions in the developed world. Their foremost need is inclusive, sustainable economic development. As such, competition law should work in tandem with other policies that are geared towards this (Bakhoum 2011). It should support the development of competitive and inclusive markets. Effectiveness of enforcement can be measured from the ability of economic actors to enter and compete in markets (Budzinski & Beigi 2015). For Africa, enforcement needs to yield improved participation in economic pathways and therefore should be equipped to tackle practices that hamper inclusivity (Gal & Fox 2015).

The current trend in self-interrogation presents African countries with an opportunity to appraise their own laws and enforcement, and to find the best-fit models that take into account the unique challenges to competitiveness in their economies (Katsoulacos 2022).

Focus on Kenya: Abuse of buyer power in the Competition Act

Kenya's Competition Act was passed in 2010 to replace the Restrictive Trade Practices and Monopolies Act of 1988. It borrows extensively from legislation and experience of other jurisdictions and displays a strong orientation towards the promotion of economic efficiency (Mudida et al. 2015). The Act prohibits the archetypal anti-competitive conduct of restrictive trade practices and abuse of dominance and provides for merger regulation by the competition agency.[29]

What the Competition Act says about buyer power

The Act was amended in 2016 to introduce prohibition of abuse of buyer power.[30] In passing the amendments, Parliament was motivated by the need to deepen the Authority's ability to intervene against unfair market practices against small and medium enterprises in order to safeguard their sustainability as well as pre-emptively deter the abuse of buyer power in susceptible local markets.[31] The relevant provisions in section 24 of the Act were passed with inclusivity in mind.

Abuse of buyer power in a market in Kenya, or a substantial part of Kenya, is prohibited by section 24A(1) of the Act. Buyer power is defined as influence exerted by an undertaking in the position of purchaser of a product or service to either obtain from a supplier more favourable terms than would otherwise pertain or impose a long-term opportunity cost including harm or withheld benefit that, if carried out, would be significantly disproportionate to any resulting long-term cost to the purchaser undertaking.[32] The Act sets out conduct that, when engaged in by a party with buyer power, amounts to abuse of that power.[33] These include delays in payment of suppliers; transfer of costs or commercial risks meant to be borne by the buyer to the supplier; refusal to receive or return goods; and demands for preferential treatment. The list is not exhaustive and any conduct that is deemed to be unfair, unilateral, onerous or unrelated to the objective of the supply contract can qualify as abuse.[34]

The Buyer Power Guidelines

The Buyer Power Guidelines, published by the Competition Authority of Kenya, present the general principles and approach to analysis.[35] In determining any complaint in relation to abuse of buyer power, the Authority will take into account all relevant circumstances, including the nature and determination of contract terms between the concerned undertakings, any payment for access to infrastructure and the price paid to the supplier.[36] Conduct is considered against the overall perspective of promoting and maintaining fair competition.[37]

Analysis under the Guidelines comprises three levels: identification and definition of the relevant market; establishment of existence of buyer power or otherwise on the part of the buyer; and establishment of occurrence or otherwise of the impugned conduct.[38] Buyer power is determined by both the options available to the supplier and those available to the buyer. The criteria used for determining the options available to either party are the market share of the buyer, the actual position and concentration of buyer undertakings in the market relative to supplier undertakings, and the ability of the parties to credibly switch within a reasonable timeframe.[39] This is because a supplier who has limited options to replace sales to a buyer is likely to accept terms of supply from the buyer that they wouldn't otherwise accept and which may qualify as abuse of buyer power. Though market shares are important, they are not the determinant criteria, and dominance on the part of the buyer is not a requirement for liability. Economic dependency of the supplier on the buyer is assessed, as is the nature of the products and their commercial significance for the buyer undertaking.[40]

The Authority's determination against French retailer Carrefour in 2020 applied the standards as directed by the Guidelines and the assessment was affirmed by the Competition Tribunal in April 2021.[41] In that case, the Authority established that between the years 2015 and February 2019, Carrefour had in its engagement with Orchards Limited, an SME supplier of probiotic yoghurts, imposed terms as well as engaged in conduct that qualified as abuse of buyer power. The Authority found that Orchards was economically dependent on Carrefour as a gateway to consumers of probiotic yoghurts and similar health foods. It also established that Carrefour had transferred commercial risk to Orchard through returning goods already purchased, without a justifiable reason; refusing to accept delivery of goods ordered without a justifiable reason; and transferring costs by requiring the supplier to deploy permanent staff at the retailer's outlets.

Examples of effective enforcement to support MSME sustainability and to promote employment

Enforcement of abuse of buyer power has supported micro, small and medium enterprise (MSME) sustainability and competitiveness in a directly relevant manner. Of the prohibited conduct, the most pervasive has been delays in payment, making up 66% of all conducts investigated between June 2019 and June 2020[42]; 80% between June 2020 and June 2021[43]; and 85% between June 2021 and June 2022.[44] The effect of delayed payments is especially detrimental to small and micro-enterprises (SMEs). Liquidity challenges caused by delayed payment make it difficult to invest in innovation, and undermine efficiency and competitiveness. In 2021, the Authority recovered delayed payments amounting to KES2.25 billion (USD18 814 281) owed to suppliers of the then largest supermarket chain in the country,[45] and 2022 saw the recovery of KES38 million (USD318 000) owed to suppliers in the insurance sector.[46] Those affected were mainly SMEs employing between 7 and 20 employees, on average. In the words of one affected entrepreneur, delayed payments had meant 'delayed employee salaries and subsequent staff exits, overdue rent payments, lost business and frozen bank accounts'.[47] Putting money back into the pockets of these market players is critical to the Kenyan economy, which is heavily reliant on MSME sustainability and competitiveness.

Yet another contribution of the Authority's enforcement of abuse of buyer power is related to employment. Supporting the sustainability and competitiveness of small firms contributes directly to resolving the employment challenges faced by the economy. The country's employment statistics are grim, with only 9% of Kenyans having permanent full-time jobs and 28.5% working in casual or informal employment.[48] MSMEs are key to job creation, with the sector employing over 15 million people, where 7 out of 10 people are employed by MSMEs.[49] In the five years to December 2019, MSMEs in the informal sector are estimated to have created more than half of total new job opportunities.[50] In 2019, approximately 90% of new jobs created during the year were generated in MSMEs.[51] According to data submitted to the Authority by the association for motor repairers in the country, the Authority's intervention in the sector in 2021 led to their members being able to retain up to 1 000 employees.[52]

A settlement with Unilever PLC Kenya in January 2023 reflects the practical nature of remedies obtained through enforcement.[53] Under the settlement, Unilever will reduce the payment period for all its SME suppliers from 90 to 60 days and then to 45 days over three years, starting from 1 January 2023 and, in addition, procure from local SMEs to the value of KES400 million (USD3 151 591) over the three-year period. It has also committed to provide supplier development training to up-skill and build capacity within its MSME suppliers, to meet the qualification criteria for supplying multinational corporations. The firm will commit an annual budget of KES75 million (USD590 900) towards the training. While the standard remedy for a breach of competition law is the imposition of a pecuniary penalty, the remedies possible for abuse of buyer power as illustrated in the settlement of this case offer practical solutions that directly address the challenges of SMEs. With the shortened payment period for instance, SME suppliers have enhanced liquidity with which to support operations.

How the legislation has supported the pertinent needs of the Kenyan economy

For African countries, efficient development is given a wider meaning to encompass a wider group being enabled to enter markets and compete on their merits (Bakhoum 2015). This speaks to inclusivity. A competitive market is taken to denote one with many participants, low barriers to entry and returns that reward the investment made (Roberts et al. 2017). The understanding of efficiency in the developed world is different from that in the developing world, in the sense that the most urgent need for the latter is inclusive development. The goal of the law should be creating a dynamic and entrepreneurial economy.

A complexity, however, arises in cases where efficiency does not correspond with the outcome of enforcement and the agency may find itself forced to weigh the undesirable trade-offs between efficiency and the inclusion of a wider group in a market (Bakhoum 2011). The abuse-of-buyer-power provisions under Kenya's law are calculated as far as possible to prevent this eventuality. The Act keeps at a minimum the instances where the Authority must intervene, prioritising instead amicable sector-based solutions that guide players to conducting fair competition. Under section 24A(2), the Authority may require industries and sectors in which instances of abuse of buyer power are likely to occur to develop a legally binding code of practice, which is published in the public sphere.[54]

In June 2020, following a year of engagement with sector associations, the Authority published the Retail Sector Code of Practice, which was developed and agreed by both suppliers and buyers through their sector associations.[55] The Code sets out the Principles of Fair and Ethical Dealing, which are binding for all players. It also provides a first-tier dispute resolution mechanism, with the Authority intervening at the second tier. A code of practice with oversight provided by the Authority enables players to meet halfway so that where efficiency is a casualty, it is through consensus of the parties.

Unequal bargaining power means that suppliers often have to accept onerous terms or be subject to variation of contract terms mid-stream. Worse still, sometimes parties engage in business without recorded contracts, which places the supplier completely at the mercy of the buyer. To deal with this, the Act sets out a basic minimum for contracts, with five core basic minimum compulsory terms.[56] To this end, the Authority has prepared template contracts for the retail sector and insurance sector, which players may adopt and vary as necessary.[57]

SMEs in developing countries often punch above their weight in terms of their contribution to the economy. As an example, Kenya's MSME sector is projected to contribute 50% of the country's GDP over the next three years[58], in addition to the employment generation referred to above. The protection of small businesses should be a guiding principle for enforcement. However, providing indiscriminate protection without any checks and balances to small players could be dangerous. The checks and balances under Kenya's law are two-layered. First, the Act is clear on considerations in establishing abuse of buyer power, thus restricting the discretion of the agency.[59] Second, the Authority's Buyer Power Guidelines give detail on the matters that the Authority will take into account. As proof of effectiveness of the two safeguards, the Authority has not been quick to make findings of abuse of buyer power. In 2019–2020[60], the Authority made findings of liability in 59% of the cases investigated and 53% in 2020–2021.[61]

The Authority is also enabled to conduct sector surveillances to monitor the activities of sectors or undertaking with likelihood of incidences of abuse of buyer power.[62] This enables pre-emptive enforcement, which is more prudent than *ex post* intervention by which time it may be too late for the affected supplier. In the event of a finding that an undertaking or a sector is facing or is likely to face incidences of abuse of buyer power, the Authority may impose reporting and prudential requirements, a remedy that is much lighter than the penal ones provided at section 36 of the Act and more appropriate for supporting undertakings to adopt fair competition in their engagement with suppliers.

Conclusion

Competitive markets are fundamental. Without them, economic development, though possible, will remain below an economy's potential and adopting competition laws is a fundamental first step to increased competition in markets. More important, however, is ensuring that the law is directly relevant and its enforcement is directed towards the actual gaps that hinder competitiveness in domestic markets. Where necessary, the law should be expanded to better address these gaps. This chapter has established that currently competition law appears to be at crossroads with discourse around the effectiveness of the welfare standard. This debate has been precipitated by increasing concentration in markets and worsened by the advent of digital markets, which present a challenge to traditional methods of competition assessment. However, a study of historical trends in the US and EU shows that competition law objectives have not been static and enforcement in the past has been adjusted to address the direct jurisdictional needs. African jurisdictions have fairly young laws and as such, there is an opportunity to adjust the laws and enforcement to directly address jurisdictional priorities. The provisions in Kenya's Competition Act are an example of such adjustment. The chapter has established that enforcement of the provisions has directly supported the SME sector, whose contribution to inclusive development and economic growth is critical.

Notes

1   See, for example: Hovenkamp (2021), Klovers & Kulick (2022), Lande & Zerbe (2020), Marty (2020), Melamed & Petit (2018) and Orbach (2019). For an example of concerns in the political arena, see comments by Senator Elizabeth Warren calling for a return to the 19th-century approach to monopolies and mergers. Accessed November 2023, https://www.usnews.com/news/articles/2016-06-29/elizabeth-warren-calls-for-strong-executive-leadership-on-antitrust

See also Executive Order 14036 'Executive Order on promoting competition in the American economy' signed by President Joe Biden on 9 July 2021. Accessed November 2023, https://www.whitehouse.gov/briefing-room/presidential-actions/2021/07/09/executive-order-on-promoting-competition-in-the-american-economy/. In a departure from tradition, the order includes non-economic considerations such as democratic accountability, the welfare of workers, farmers, small businesses and start-ups as matters qualified for consideration under competition law.

2   Fordham's 49th Annual Conference on International Antitrust Law & Policy in September 2022: Among the notable speakers were EVP Margrethe Vestager, EU Commissioner for Competition; Jonathan Kanter, Assistant Attorney General, US Department of Justice; and and Lina Khan, Chair, Federal Trade Commission.

3   Fordham Competition Law Institute, 45th Annual Conference on International Antitrust Law and Policy, September 2018.

4   Informa Competition Law in the Digital Era Conference October 2022: Competition Law in the Digital Era: Adapting to the New Environment.

5   8th BRICS International Competition Conference 2023.

6   See: Amendment Act (No. 49 of 2016).

7   See: Section 3, Competition Act (No. 12 of 2010)0.

8   See: Japan's Guidelines Concerning Abuse of a Superior Bargaining Position in Transactions between Digital Platform Operators and Consumers that Provide Personal Information, etc. 2019; Korea's Fair Online Platform Intermediary Transactions Act (Online Platform Act) 2020.

9   See: Australia's Treasury Laws Amendment (News Media and Digital Platforms Mandatory Bargaining Code) Act 2021.

10 See: Consultation Document on Digital Market Unit, 6 May 2022. Accessed February 2023, https://www.gov.uk/government/consultations/a-new-pro-competition-regime-for-digital-markets/consultation-document-html-version#part-2-the-digital-markets-unit

11 See: EU Digital Markets Act; American Innovation and Choice Online Act.

12 Examples include the European Union's Digital Markets Act, Australia's Competition and Consumer Protection News Media and Digital Platforms Mandatory Bargaining Code, America's pending Innovation and Choice Online Act and United Kingdom's proposed

Digital Markets, Competition and Consumer Bill. See: UK government set to publish Digital Markets, Competition and Consumer Bill. Accessed February 2023, https://www.gov.uk/government/consultations/a-new-pro-competition-regime-for-digital-markets/outcome/a-new-pro-competition-regime-for-digital-markets-government-response-to-consultation#part–6-regulatory-framework; https://www.pinsentmasons.com/out-law/news/uk-government-digital-markets-competition-consumer-bill

13 Baker JB et al., Joint response to the House Judiciary Committee on the state of antitrust law and implications for protecting competition in digital markets. Congressional and Other Testimony, 30 April 2020. Accessed February 2023, https://digitalcommons.wcl.american.edu/pub_disc_cong/18

14 As an example, India has now repealed the Monopolies and Restrictive Trade Practices Act 1969 borrowed heavily from American antitrust (see Singh 2013; Shahein 2012).

15 See: *Northern Securities Company v United States Co.*193 U.S. 197 (1904), followed in 1911 by *Dr. Miles Medical Co. v John D. Park & Sons* 220 U.S. 373 (1911).

16 See: *Standard Oil Co. of New Jersey v United States* 221 U.S. 1 (1911) and *United States v American Tobacco Company* 221 U.S. 106 (1911).

17 See the decisions in *United States v United States Steel Corp.* 251 U.S. 417 (1920); *Board of Trade of the City of Chicago v United States* 246 U.S. 231 (1918); *United States v Colgate & Co.* 250 U.S. 300 (1919) and *Maple Flooring Manufacturers' Association v United States* 268 U.S. 563 (1925).

18 See: Federal Trade Commission *Statement of the Commission On the Withdrawal of the Statement of Enforcement Principles Regarding 'Unfair Methods of Competition' Under Section 5 of the FTC Act*. Accessed January 2023, https://www.ftc.gov/system/files/documents/public_statements/1591706/p210100commnstmtwithdrawalsec5enforcement.pdf. The Federal Trade Commission recently opened a preliminary investigation of PepsiCo and Coca-Cola Co. for potential price discrimination by the companies in violation of the Robinson-Patman Act. See: U.S. FTC probes Pepsi, Coca-Cola over price discrimination – Politico, *Reuters*, 10 January 2023. Accessed January 2023, https://www.reuters.com/business/retail-consumer/ftc-probes-pepsi-coca-cola-over-price-discrimination-politico–2023–01–10/

19 See: *United States v Socony-Vacuum Oil Co* .310 U.S. 150 (1940); *Northern Pacific R. Co. v United States* 356 U.S. 1 (1958); *Albrecht v Herald* 390 U.S. 145 (1968) and *Utah Pie Co. v Continental Baking Co.* 386 U.S. 685 (1967). *United States v Aluminum Co. of America (ALCOA)* 148 F.2d 416 (2d Cir. 1945); it did not matter how the firm had become a monopoly – the offence was simply becoming one.

20 See: *Brown Shoe Co. v United States* 370 U.S. 294 (1962) at 344.

21 See: *United States v Philadelphia National Bank* 374 U.S. 321 (1963) at 363.

22 See, for example: *Société Technique Minière (L.T.M.) v Maschinenbau Ulm GmbH (M.B.U.)*, Case 56–65; Cases 56 and 58, *Etablissements Consten SA & Grundig-Verkaufs-GmbH v Commission* [1966] ECR 299; Case 27/76 *United Brands & Co and United Brands Continental BV v Commission* [1978] ECR 207.

23 See: Case 26/76, *Metro SB-Großmärkte GmbH & Co. KG v Commission ('Metro I')*, EU:C:1977:167.

24 See: *GlaxoSmithKline Services Unlimited v EC Commission*, Case T–168/01.

25 Opinion of Advocate General Kokott in *T-Mobile Netherlands BV, KPN Mobile NV, Orange Nederland NV and Vodafone Libertel NV v Raad van bestuur van de Nederlandse Mededingingsautoriteit* C–8/08 at 71.

26 Membership of the International Competition Network (ICN) gives a close indicator of the actual number. As at October 2023 membership comprised 143 member agencies, 25 of which are from sub-Saharan Africa. The list of current membership is available at Members – ICN (internationalcompetitionnetwork.org) (accessed 23/11/2023).

27 See examples: Ethiopia Trade Competition and Consumers Protection Proclamation (813/2013); Mozambique Competition Law 10 of 2013; Angola Competition Act 2018.

28 See: Federal Competition and Consumer Protection Act 2019.

29 See: Parts III and IV of the Act.

30 See: Competition (Amendment) Act (No. 49 of 2016), which came into force through Kenya Gazette Notice No. 199 of 30 December 2016. The provisions of the Act were later amended through Competition (Amendment) Act (No. 27 of 2019), which came into force on 13 January 2020 through Kenya Gazette Supplement No. 202 of 2020.

31 See: Kenya National Assembly Hansard Report 13/12/2020 at 10, 43 and 46.

32 See: Section 2 Competition Act 2010.

33 See: Section 24A(5) Competition Act 2010.

34 See: Guideline 50 Abuse of Buyer Power Guidelines 2022. Accessed January 2023, https://cak.go.ke/mandate/buyer-power/rules

35 See: Part D of the Abuse of Buyer Power Guidelines 2022.

36 See: Section 24A(4) Competition Act 2010.

37 See: Guideline 17 Abuse of Buyer Power Guidelines 2022.

38 See: Guideline 23 and 43 Abuse of Buyer Power Guidelines 2022.

39 See: Guideline 47 Abuse of Buyer Power Guidelines 2022.

40 See: Guideline 48 and 49 Abuse of Buyer Power Guidelines 2022.

41 See: Case No. CT/006/2020 *Majid Al Futtaim Hypermarkets Limited v Competition Authority of Kenya and Orchards Limited*. The Tribunal's Determination is under appeal to the High Court at the time of publishing.

42 See: The Competition Authority of Kenya: Annual Report 2019/2020. Accessed February 2023, https://www.cak.go.ke/sites/default/files/annual-reports/FY_2019–2020_CAK_Annual_Report.pdf, pp. 60–61.

43 See: The Competition Authority of Kenya: Annual Report 2020/2021. Accessed February 2023, https://www.cak.go.ke/sites/default/files/annual-reports/CAK_Annual_Report_Financial_Year_2020_21.pdf, pp. 49–50.

44 See: The Competition Authority of Kenya: Annual Report 2021/2022, p. 50.

45 See: The Competition Authority of Kenya: Annual Report 2020/21, pp. 10 and 37.

46 See: Competition Authority of Kenya *Ushindani* 9 June 2022. Accessed February 2024, https://cak.go.ke/sites/default/files/2022–06/CAK%20Newsletter%20Issue%209.pdf

47 See: Competition Authority of Kenya *Ushindani* 9. Accessed February 2023, https://cak.go.ke/sites/default/files/2022–06/CAK%20Newsletter%20Issue%209.pdf

48 See: Central Bank of Kenya FinAccess Household Survey County Perspective November 2022. Accessed January 2023, https://www.centralbank.go.ke/2022/11/11/finaccess-household-survey-report-county-perspective-november–2022/

49 See: Central Bank of Kenya 2020 Survey Report on MSME Access to Bank Credit. Accessed February 2023, https://www.centralbank.go.ke/2021/07/15/2020-survey-report-on-msme-access-to-bank-credit/

50 See: Central Bank of Kenya 2020 Survey Report on MSME Access to Bank Credit Available. Accessed February 2023, https://www.centralbank.go.ke/2021/07/15/2020-survey-report-on-msme-access-to-bank-credit/

51 See: Central Bank of Kenya 2020 Survey Report on MSME Access to Bank Credit Available. Accessed February 2023, https://www.centralbank.go.ke/2021/07/15/2020-survey-report-on-msme-access-to-bank-credit/

52 See: Competition Authority of Kenya *Ushindani* 9. Accessed February 2023, https://cak.go.ke/sites/default/files/2022–06/CAK%20Newsletter%20Issue%209.pdf

53 See: *The Kenya Gazette*, 20 January 2023, Gazette Notice 581.

54 See: Section 24A(3) of the Competition Act 12 of 2010.

55 See: The*Kenya Gazette*, 11 June 2021, Gazette Notice 5725.

56 See: Section 24A(7) Competition Act 2010.

57 See: Template Contract for Retail Sector and Template Contract for Insurance Sector. Accessed January 2023, https://cak.go.ke/mandate/buyer-power/rules

58 See: Rotich K, Kenyan SME to contribute 50pc of GDP in next three years, *Business Daily Africa*, 21 June 2022. Accessed August 2022, https://www.businessdailyafrica.com/bd/corporate/marketplace/kenyan-sme-to-contribute–50pc-of-gdp-in-next-three-years--3836534

59 See: Section 24A(4) of the Competition Act 12 of 2010.

60 See: The Competition Authority of Kenya: Annual Report 2019/2020. Accessed February 2023, p. 63.

61 See: The Competition Authority of Kenya: Annual Report 2020/2021. Accessed February 2023, https://www.cak.go.ke/sites/default/files/annual-reports/CAK_Annual_Report_Financial_Year_2020_21.pdf, p. 46.

62 See: Section 24A(2) of the Competition Act 12 of 2010.

References

Baker J & Shapiro C (2008) Reinvigorating horizontal merger enforcement. In R Pitofsky (Ed.) *How the Chicago school overshot the mark: The effect of conservative economic analysis on U.S. antitrust.* New York: Oxford University Press

Bakhoum M (2011) A dual language in modern competition law? Efficiency approach versus development approach and implications for developing countries. *World Competition Law and Economics Review* (34)3: 495, 505

Bakhoum M (2015) The informal economy and its interface with competition law and policy. In MS Gal, M Bakhoum, J Drexl, EM Fox & DJ Gerber (Eds) *The economic characteristics of developing jurisdictions: Their implications for competition law*. Cheltenham: Edward Elgar Publishing

Bork RH (1978) *The antitrust paradox: A policy at war with itself*. New York: Basic Books

Botchway FN (2011) Mergers and acquisitions in resource industry: Implications for Africa. In FN Botchway (Ed.) *Natural sesource investment and Africa's development*. Cheltenham: Edward Elgar Publishing

Budzinski O & Beigi MHA (2015) Generating instead of protecting competition. In MS Gal, M Bakhoum, J Drexl, EM Fox & DJ Gerber (Eds) *The economic characteristics of developing jurisdictions: Their implications for competition*. Cheltenham: Edward Elgar Publishing

Burke M, Paremoer T, Vilakazi T & Zengeni T (2017) *Cross-cutting competition issues in regional industrial development*. Working Paper No. 20/2017, Centre for Competition, Regulation and Economic Development. Accessed January 2023, https://static1.squarespace.com/static/52246331e4b0a46e5f1b8ce5/t/59d5f22f8a02c7e2d816a295/1507193402807/AIDIRP+Cross-Cutting+Competition+Issues+in+Regional+Industrial+Development+Working+Paper+20-2017.pdf

Buthe T & Kigwiru V (2020) The spread of competition law and policy in Africa: A research agenda. *African Journal of International Economic Law* 1: 46

Cooper JC (2015) The perils of excessive discretion: The elusive meaning of unfairness in section 5 of the FTC Act. *Journal of Antitrust Enforcement* 3(1): 87

Crane DA (2015a) All I really need to know about antitrust I learned in 1912. *Iowa Law Review* 100(5): 2025

Crane DA (2015b) Rationales for antitrust: Economics and other bases. In RD Blair & DD Sokol (Eds) *The Oxford Handbook of International Antitrust Economics: Volume 1*. New York: Oxford University Press

Crane DA (2022) Antitrust as an instrument of democracy. *Duke Law Journal Online* 72: 21

Dunne N (2015) *Competition law and economic regulation: Making and managing markets*. Cambridge: Cambridge University Press

Evenett J (2015) Competition law and the economic characteristics of developing countries. In MS Gal, M Bakhoum, J Drexl, EM Fox & DJ Gerber (Eds) *The economic characteristics of developing jurisdictions: Their implications for competition law*. Cheltenham: Edward Elgar Publishing

Ezrachi A (2016) Sponge. *Journal of Antitrust Enforcement* 5(1): 49

First H & Waller SW (2012) Antitrust's democracy deficit. *Fordham Law Review* 81(5): 2546–2548

Fox EM & Bakhoum M (2019) *Making markets work for Africa: Markets, development, and competition law in Sub-Saharan Africa*. New York: Oxford University Press

Gal MS & Fox EM (2015) Drafting Competition Law for Developing Jurisdictions. In MS Gal, M Bakhoum, J Drexl, EM Fox & DJ Gerber (Eds) *The economic characteristics of developing jurisdictions: Their implications for competition law*. Cheltenham: Edward Elgar Publishing

Hovenkamp H (2017a) Appraising merger efficiencies. *George Mason Law Review* 24: 715

Hovenkamp HJ (2017b) Antitrust policy and inequality of wealth. *All Faculty Scholarship*. Philadelphia: Penn Carey Law. https://scholarship.law.upenn.edu/faculty_scholarship/1769

Hovenkamp H (2018) Whatever *did* happen to the antitrust movement? *Notre Dame Law Review* 93: 583

Hovenkamp H (2021) The looming crisis in antitrust economics. *All Faculty Scholarship*. Philadelphia: Penn Carey Law. https://scholarship.law.upenn.edu/faculty_scholarship/2151

Katsoulacos TY (2022) Why legal standards in antitrust enforcement in developing jurisdictions should differ from those in mature jurisdictions: A decision-theoretic approach. *BRICS Journal of Economics* 3(2): 63

Khan L (2018) The new Brandeis movement: America's antimonopoly debate. *Journal of European Competition Law and Practice* 9(3): 131

Klovers K & Kulick R (2022) Is concentration actually increasing, or are we just defining markets more narrowly? *Consumer Policy International*

Kovacic WE & Shapiro C (2000) Antitrust policy: A century of economic and legal thinking. *Journal of Economic Perspectives* 14(1): 58

Lande RH & Zerbe RO (2020) The Sherman Act is a no-fault monopolization statute: A textualist demonstration. *American University Law Review* 70: 497

Leydecker C (2021) A different curse: Improving the antitrust debate about 'bigness'. *New York University Journal of Law and Business* 13: 845

Marty F (2020) *Is the consumer welfare obsolete? A European Union competition law perspective.* Working Papers No. 2020–13, Groupe de Recherche en Droit, Économie et Gestion

Meese AJ (2013) Competition policy and the great depression: Lessons learned and a new way forward. *Cornell Journal of Law and Public Policy* 2(23): 256

Melamed D & Petit N (2018) The misguided assault on the consumer welfare standard in the age of platform markets. *Review of Industrial Organization* 54: 741

Mudida R, Ndiritu SW & Ross TW (2015) Kenya's new competition policy regime. *World Competition* 38(3): 244

Munyai PS (2016) A critical review of the treatment of dominant firms in competition law: A comparative study. LLD dissertation, University of South Africa

Orbach B (2013) How antitrust lost its goal. *Fordham Law Review* 81(5): 2253

Orbach B (2019) The consumer welfare controversy. *CPI Antitrust Chronical* 2(1): 22

Roberts S (2017) *(Re)shaping markets for inclusive economic activity: Competition and industrial policies relating to food production in Southern Africa*. Working Paper No. 12/2017, Centre for Competition, Regulation and Economic Development

Roberts S, Vilakazi T & Simbanegavi W (2017) Competition, regional integration and inclusive growth in Africa: A research agenda. In J Klaaren, S Roberts & I Valodia (Eds) *Competition law and economic regulation: Addressing market power in Southern Africa*. Johannesburg: Wits University Press

Shahein H (2012) Designing competition laws in new jurisdictions: Three models to follow. In R Whish & C Townley (Eds) *New competition jurisdictions: Shaping policies and building institutions*. Cheltenham: Edward Elgar Publishing

Sidak JG & Teece D (2009) Dynamic competition in antitrust law. *Journal of Competition Law and Economics* 5(4): 581

Singh R (2013) India's tryst with 'the Clayton Act moment' and emerging merger control jurisprudence: Intersection of law, economics and politics. In D Sokol, T Cheng & I Lianos (Eds) *Competition law and development*. Redwood City: Stanford University Press

Stucke ME (2011) Reconsidering competition. *Mississippi Law Journal* 81: 107

Stucke ME (2012) Reconsidering antitrust's goals. *Boston College Law Review* 53: 551

Stylianou K & Lacovides M (2022) The goals of EU competition law: A comprehensive empirical investigation. *Legal Studies* 42: 623

Viscusi WK, Harrington JE & Sappington DEM (2018) *Economics of regulation and antitrust*. Cambridge: Massachusetts: MIT Press

Waked DI (2016) Adoption of antitrust laws in developing countries: Reasons and challenges. *Journal of Law Economics and Policy* 12: 193

Waller SW (2017) Antitrust and democracy. *Florida State University Law Review* 45: 3

Waller SW & Morse JE (2020) The political face of antitrust. *Brooklyn Journal of Corporate, Financial and Commercial Law* 15: 77

Whish R & Bailey D (2018) *Competition Law*. Oxford: Oxford University Press

Wu T (2018) After consumer welfare, now what? The 'protection of competition' standard in practice. *CPI Antitrust Chronicle* 1: 12

Yonezawa K, Gomez MI & Richards TJ (2020) The Robinson–Patman Act and vertical relationships. *American Journal of Agricultural Economics* 102(1): 329

7 Exploring a broader application of the 'substantial lessening of competition' standard: A South African perspective

Jason Aproskie and Tessa Bleazard

A ubiquitous acronym across many countries with competition laws is 'SLC' (the substantial lessening of competition), or 'SPLC' (the substantial prevention or lessening of competition) or a variation of these.[1] We jointly refer to each of these as the 'SLC' test as it is applied in merger assessments. Mergers can be prohibited where they are expected to result in an SLC.

There are other areas of competition law where similar concepts are routinely spoken of. These include the abuse-of-dominance provisions where, in South Africa for instance, the conduct of the firm must have an 'anti-competitive' effect for it to be prohibited (although typically an *ex post* assessment). While there is no qualifier before the term anti-competitive effect, in practice this would have to be of a certain measurable magnitude or specific type to reach the threshold at which the dominant firm can be held to account through either an administrative penalty or other kinds of remedies.

Given the critical importance of these concepts for competition law enforcement, the wording of these concepts, and the SLC in particular, raises some questions. For example: what types of effects constitute an SLC? How much of an effect is sufficiently *substantial* to matter?[2]

Amidst the growing evidence of increasing corporate margins, and the hypothesis that this may reflect increased market power and therefore a gross under-enforcement of competition laws or policies (for example, Buthelezi et al. 2018; Thakoor 2020), we believe one crucial question needs to be asked: Is the current standard of SLC, or competitive effects – whether by definition or by application – sufficiently broad to deliver on the objective of competition policy to maintain and promote competition?[3] Our understanding and experience as practitioners suggest that the SLC, or any anti-competitive effect terminology more broadly, essentially captures only pricing and quality effects, while volume effects may also be relevant. However, in the merger assessment context across jurisdictions, the inquiry of whether an SLC would result from the merger in practice focuses almost exclusively on price effects from the merger.[4]

We explore these questions, primarily from a South African perspective. Through the examination of key selected cases and research from other jurisdictions, the chapter considers the bar for intervention in competition matters, in particular SLC standard used in merger control in many jurisdictions, and the anti-competitive effects requirement more generally. We conclude that a more expansive and inclusive interpretation of the SLC and anti-competitive effect terminology is both possible and reasonable.

The chapter[5] first looks at the nature of harm and the effects, and the unequal distribution of effects. It then examines the role of policy in determining effects, with a focus on the policy connection to the prioritisation of certain sectors. The chapter then looks at the importance of contextual factors in determining substantiality and magnitude, highlighting two key cases in South Africa. Through three illustrative cases, the final section examines the importance of taking into account the effects of the transaction versus the effects of a change in competition.[6]

The nature of harm and the effects

When considering harm or effects in terms of the SLC (or anti-competitive effect), one must certainly consider the nature of the harm. In particular, harm may not in practice be distributed equally across all consumers. Typically, competition investigations are concerned with the 'average consumer' (Mariuzzo & Ormosi 2021), but in fact the harm suffered by one consumer may be relatively more substantial than for another consumer. Therefore, considering only the 'average consumer' may mask the true harm. Mariuzzo and Ormosi (2021) use petrol-station-level data on fuel prices in Western Australia alongside data on acquisitions and concentration in the fuel retail markets to understand the impact of these mergers on different segments of the population.

Unequal distribution of effects

What the paper finds is instructive. Poorer consumers[7] in fact suffered more harm from the mergers than richer consumers. While fuel prices for richer consumers do not appear to be affected to any great degree by merger activity, fuel prices for poorer consumers tend to increase following concentration in the market. This means that there is an unequal distribution of effects in the market, with poorer consumers significantly affected and richer consumers experiencing hardly any change.

A merger that results in greater price impacts for richer consumers is objectively preferable to a merger that results in greater price impacts for the poor. This is not only because of a natural aversion to inequitable outcomes; in most cases, at least for more essential products, one would expect the practical impact of price increases on poorer consumers to be greater relative to their existing incomes or wealth, compared to the same price increase for richer consumers. Richer, higher-income consumers can more easily sustain price increases on a particular product.

Despite the product in the study (fuel) being homogenous, prices are not uniform. This is because consumers themselves engage with the market differently (Mariuzzo & Ormosi 2021). One reason the authors give for why we might observe such outcomes is search costs. They suggest in this case that higher-income consumers may be more able to search, or afford to search, for the lowest prices. Thus, in wealthier areas prices are more competitive, or at least less susceptible to increases following a merger transaction.

Two crucial messages emerge from the paper. The first is that there are dangers in considering only the 'average consumer'. The second is that, when assessing whether an SLC is likely to result from a merger, it is important to consider how specific consumer groups (such as the poor) may be affected.

This approach has been followed in practice. In 2019, the United Kingdom's Competition and Markets Authority (CMA) blocked the merger between Asda and Sainsbury over concerns that the merger would increase prices for consumers, and that it would further raise prices at the supermarket's petrol stations and lead to longer checkout queues (CMA 2019: 6–17). In this case, the CMA took into account the distributive effects when determining if the merger would likely lead to unilateral effects in the retail markets for fuel (petrol stations) and groceries in-store. The CMA found that products such as fuel or groceries are considered non-discretionary in terms of household expenditure items, and that these goods cover a large share of household expenditure. Even a small price increase for these products could cause significant harm to consumers, especially to low-income households. The CMA considered that price effects on these goods can therefore cause significant distributive effects. This is why it found that seemingly small price increases of between 1.5% and 2.75% on fuel and groceries represented a substantial harm to competition.

Another example of a greater focus on the effects on the poor specifically is the Competition Commission of South Africa's Data Services Market Inquiry (DSMI), completed in 2019 (CCSA 2019). The Data Services Market Inquiry was initiated following concerns from 'the public about the high level of data prices and the importance of data affordability for the South African economy and consumers.' (CCSA 2019: 13) The purpose of the inquiry was to understand the factors driving high prices and to make recommendations to address them.

Part of the DSMI's final report focused on what was termed 'anti-poor pricing'. The report showed that the incumbent operators, when looking at effective prices, priced smaller data bundles at exorbitant 'rand per megabyte' prices, compared with the larger data bundles. Smaller bundles tend to be associated with poorer consumers, whereas larger bundles tend to be associated with richer consumers. In essence, while one might consider whether pricing of data in a country is generally high by looking at pricing 'on average', an entirely different story might emerge when considering a specific group of consumers, such as the poor.

The role of policy in determining effects

The above examples appear to support placing more emphasis on one group of consumers over another (such as poorer consumers over richer) but on what basis? The underlying reason for supporting a different interpretation of SLC in favour of poorer consumers is likely an implicit acceptance among citizens and authorities that a policy position may justifiably inform the interpretation of substantiality in an SLC. For instance, if it is public policy to reduce inequality and/or uplift the conditions of the poorest citizens, then it is expected and arguably appropriate that one would factor this in to what is considered to be 'substantial' or meaningful – even if the policy is not necessarily directly expressed in the legislation.

Prioritising certain sectors as a reflection of policy

This perspective is also evident in the prioritisation of certain sectors by competition authorities. Most competition authorities set priorities in their work by identifying particular kinds of conduct or activities (such as fighting cartels) as well as priority sectors. The authorities choose sectors on the basis of certain criteria, which may relate to broader government policy. An example could be the sector's impact on consumer welfare and its alignment to government priorities – in this case, a clear nod to economic policy. In South Africa, the priority sectors frequently reflect government policy. These include the agriculture and transport sectors, which form a greater part of lower-income consumers' salaries. Groups that have been historically disadvantaged, such as the youth, face particular economic challenges and are therefore given focus in policy. It is these policies that can find expression in the enforcement of competition legislation by the competition authorities.

Identifying and prioritising particular work areas or sectors help to guide and operationalise the competition agencies' work. It helps authorities allocate and use resources to be the most effective and to have maximal impact (Bleazard et al. 2022; ICN 2021). How prioritisation is carried out can differ among competition agencies, depending on the function and powers set out in the law and the policy environment in which the agency operates (Bleazard et al. 2022).

Thus, public policy or economic policy, which clearly influences a competition authority's prioritisation strategy, should arguably be a relevant factor in interpreting what constitutes an SLC. Outside of questions relating to the magnitude of the effects, what can be considered as substantial is likely to be more readily judged through the lens of policy than anything else. This suggests then that the interpretation and application of the SLC standard can potentially be broader than a narrow, mechanical assessment of price effects. This is of course not to suggest that the application of the SLC standard in competition law be used for effecting policy outcomes or to create more uncertainty or subjective standards. However, in the specific context of a merger transaction, an appropriately weighted consideration of policy in the assessment of substantiality may be justified.

Substantiality and magnitude: The importance of context

A further area of uncertainty when considering whether there is an SLC, is the *magnitude* of the effects: Is it sufficiently large to warrant a prohibition or other action from the competition authority? If, for instance, one considers SLC in terms of pricing effects, how much of a price increase is 'sufficiently large'? Unsurprisingly, there is no simple rule for answering this. While case precedent in South Africa shows that an SLC cannot simply be non-trivial[8], what constitutes an SLC in terms of the magnitude of effect is less clear.

However, what *must* come into play is an understanding of the market context and the nature of the ultimate harm. Although not a merger scenario, the 'price gouging' cases pursued by the Competition Commission of South Africa in the midst of the initial stages of the Covid–19 pandemic (and associated lockdown) illustrate the importance of market context. The term 'price gouging' is used to describe a situation in which firms take advantage of the victims of a natural disaster or emergency by charging exorbitant prices for goods and services that are essential to the public during the crisis (Keleme & Moeketsi 2020). The Commission drew on the excessive-pricing provisions (section 8) in the newly amended Competition Act (No. 89 of 1998) to provide the legal framework for the first cases of price gouging in South Africa. It used these provisions to argue that in the specific market context, suppliers with access to certain personal protective equipment (PPE) items may possess a temporary form of market power, with consumers being unable to shop around due to the lack of supply in the short term.

Contextual factors in the Babelegi and Dis-Chem cases

The importance of market context in competitive assessment is also emphasised in the decisions by the Competition Tribunal (the Tribunal) and the Competition Appeal Court (CAC) in the most high-profile price gouging cases in South Africa, namely the *Babelegi*[9] case and the *Dis-Chem*[10] case.

The Tribunal found Babelegi Workwear and Industrial Supplies CC (Babelegi) contravened section 8(1)(a) of the Competition Act by charging excessive and exploitative prices for face masks to the detriment of consumers in early 2020, a decision that was ultimately confirmed by the CAC.[11] Similarly, in the *Dis-Chem* case, the Tribunal found that Dis-Chem contravened section 8(1)(a) of the Competition Act (the Act) in that it charged excessive prices for three types of surgical face masks to the detriment of consumers during March 2020.[12]

Neither of these cases related to mergers, but the structure of the assessment for excessive pricing was first for the Commission (as the complainant) to establish a *prima facie* case of excessive pricing, whereby the price is found to exceed the competitive price. After that, under section 8(1)(a), the burden of proof shifts to the respondent to show that the price is reasonably related to the competitive price. Importantly, this assessment of reasonableness evokes the concept of magnitude, much like the SLC. The Tribunal's decisions in *Babelegi* and *Dis-Chem*, and the CAC's decision in *Babelegi,* all of which were in the Commission's favour, revealed key insights into the thinking of the adjudicators.

The Tribunal, while acknowledging that some level of price increase would be acceptable (the Commission suggested that in the Covid–19 context a threshold of 10% should be used), noted that 'Babelegi's increases in both prices and markups are however so far above any acceptable level that they clearly are exploitative'.[13] The CAC similarly found that 'the price charged was manifestly far higher than the yardstick price, that is the price charged in a relatively competitive pre-Covid–19 market'.[14]

Lastly, the context of overpricing on key items of PPE and the specific nature of the harm in the midst of the Covid–19 crisis – face masks in both cases –appeared to be key factors in the decisions. In both the *Babelegi* and *Dis-chem* cases, the Tribunal highlighted the importance of the Covid–19 outbreak and that the pricing conduct of these firms during a crisis needs to be contextualised within the Tribunal's role in protecting public interest and the broader purpose of the Act. The Tribunal noted in the *Babelegi* case that:

> …one must have regard to context, including the nature of the conduct, or the theory of harm, as well as the economic and other circumstances, in this case the substantial hiking up of prices in the time of a health crisis. Such conduct by a firm at such a time should from a public interest perspective be regarded as offensive.[15]

In the *Dis-Chem* case, the nature of conduct and detriment to consumers was also emphasised within the context of the global pandemic and health crisis. The Tribunal agreed with the Commission's view that price increases during Covid–19 'have the most detrimental impact on poor individuals and families, who are already the most vulnerable during such crisis.'[16] Material price increases in the time of crisis (viewed as price gouging) are especially concerning as they could cut off poor consumers from accessing goods that are essential to their health (surgical face masks in the *Dis-Chem* case) by either making the goods unaffordable or imposing higher costs on poor consumers.[17]

In its judgment, the Tribunal emphasised that the excessive pricing conduct of Dis-Chem was to the detriment of consumers as 'material price increases of the magnitude of 47%–261% without corresponding increases in costs, of any goods in a country such as South Africa with a long history of economic exclusion and deep inequality would seriously affect the public interest adversely'[18]. The Tribunal further highlighted the skewed nature of more consumer harm towards poorer customers, noting that 'material price increases of surgical face masks … would seriously impact vulnerable and poorer consumers even more. Poorer customers would have been excluded from accessing the masks by such exorbitant increases, other customers would have spent more on these items as a percentage of their disposable income.'[19]

The importance of considerations around consumer detriment is further demonstrated in the CAC judgment in the *Babelegi* case, which states that:

> ...in this case, the excessive prices were charged at a time of crisis when the employment of a mask by every person in the country was seen as being essential to the protection of health, safety and welfare of others and therefore as critical to the reduction of the danger posed by Covid-19. The high prices of such a necessity unquestionably acted to the detriment of consumers in the country.[20]

The health and safety of individuals appears to have been a key contextual factor in the assessment of reasonableness (or magnitude) across the courts.

Effects of the transaction versus the effects of a change in competition

When considering whether the effects of a merger amount to an SLC itself, it appears that the courts routinely consider only the effects that directly result from a change in competition in the market. In light of our exploration of other seemingly important factors, it is pertinent to ask if there is room for a broader interpretation – such as where there is harm to consumer welfare as a consequence of the *transaction*, rather than competition itself. At first glance, this is already provided for to some extent by public interest provisions, such as those in the South African Competition Act. In South Africa, public interest provisions allow for a number of factors to be considered: the effect on a particular industry or region; employment; the ability of small firms and firms held by historically disadvantaged persons to participate and expand in the market; the ability of a national industry to compete in international markets; and the promotion of a greater spread of ownership.[21]

However, it is also clear that these public interest provisions, at least in South Africa, seem to steer clear of any consumer-centred effects. Indeed, broader public interest concerns are covered, as well as the effects on consumer welfare stemming directly from changes in competition. Yet other harms to consumer welfare, which may not stem directly from a change in competition, do not appear to be considered in the same light by legislators or at least the adjudicators of the legislation.

Three cases illustrate the potential for important merger-specific effects that may be candidates for a more expansive interpretation of SLC and competitive effects (or a change to the policy or legislation around this): the dialysis market in the United States; the Walmart case in South Africa; and the more recent Mediclinic/Matlosana Medical Health Services (MMHS) merger in South Africa.

The dialysis market in the United States

A study of acquisitions of outpatient dialysis facilities in the United States revealed an interesting conclusion. Eliason et al. (2020) studied the industry of dialysis treatment.

The study covered a period of 12 years and more than 1 200 acquisitions of independent dialysis facilities by 'large chains'. Given the acquisitions, the assessment shows that concentration levels naturally increased markedly over the period, with two firms ultimately accounting for 60% of all facilities. Whereas the industry was initially quite fragmented, it began to change as the larger players gradually acquired the independent players.

The study found that where an independent was purchased by the large firm, the quality of care fell substantially. Among other effects, the prescription of costly treatment medications (paid for by health insurance) increased, while recommendations for kidney replacements fell (enabling greater claims for treatment medication), patient loads per employee increased, and more highly skilled nurses were replaced with less highly skilled technicians in order to lower costs. This all translated into higher earnings for the acquiring firms and inferior patient outcomes (that is, a negative impact on quality[22]).

What is most interesting is that the study found that these effects were not driven by changes in competition or increased market power. Markets for dialysis treatment are narrow and local, as patients reside in the immediate vicinity of the facility and are unlikely to travel far for their treatment, or switch to a facility that is further away. However, the effects were apparent regardless of whether the large chain and the target were both present in the local market before the acquisition. Even where the target firm would be the only local facility in an area, the effects remained. What the chapter finds is 'that chains transfer several prominent strategies to the facilities they acquire' (Eliason et al. 2020: 221). The results for patients are not driven by competition but rather the adoption of the chains' strategies and practices following the acquisition. Many of the independents were not-for-profit, whereas the chains are for-profit, and the authors show that the change in strategy is also clear from the patient-level data.

Thus, in this case there is clear evidence of harm to consumer welfare from these acquisitions, and it therefore raises a question of how these transactions were assessed or allowed. However, it appears that there is little room for such transactions to be addressed under the current application of competition laws and the SLC test. Referring to the US Horizontal Merger Guidelines, Eliason et al. recognise that 'most acquisitions we study fall outside the scope of current antitrust laws, which prohibit acquisitions if "the effect of such acquisition may be substantially to lessen competition, or to tend to create a monopoly"' (Eliason et al. 2020: 261).

What this research may in fact suggest is that the acquiring firm (the large chain) was merely more willing to exploit the market power that the independent facility had already possessed due to the narrow, local geographic markets in which they operated. It is not apparent that the large chain did anything innovative or invested in the acquired businesses in any significant way – the effects were observed across the month prior and post the acquisition.

However, this does point to these mergers in fact resulting in a type of SLC – the substitution of a more competitive incumbent firm with a less competitive acquiring firm, or at least a firm more willing to take advantage of market power, to the detriment of consumer welfare. It is not clear therefore that such a case should be excluded from the SLC rubric, simply because the effects on consumers are not driven by an increase in concentration.

The Walmart case in South Africa

The Walmart[23] case in South Africa raised a similar issue. In this case, Massmart, a mass retailer, was to be purchased by US retail group Walmart. On the face of it, there were no competition concerns with the merger, as it involved a foreign entity with no operations in South Africa purchasing the local entity. However, objections were raised by labour unions[24], which argued that Walmart's acquisition of Massmart would result in harm to labour given its reputation for poor labour practices. The argument was that the merger would result in negative effects even if these were not directly a consequence of a change in competition.

So the relevance of public policy in assessing the nature of the impact of the merger became a key debate in the hearings of the case. Concerns from a policy perspective were expressed that the acquisition, or aspects of it, may not be in the best interest of consumers, labour and the economy more broadly. In response, in approving the merger with conditions, the Competition Tribunal ruled that it could only limit itself to the specific public interest considerations contained within the Competition Act[25], rather than any additional public policy concern beyond these provisions, regardless of how legitimate it may be.

Clearly, competition legislation can include certain public interest considerations. However, at the heart of the public interest provisions is public policy, which represents the government's social and economic policy agenda. The public interest provisions capture what policy-makers believe is in the public interest. More specifically, the public interest provisions capture what was considered as policy imperatives at the time the Competition Act was passed into law or at subsequent points when it was amended. Yet public policy is also fluid to some extent; public policy imperatives change over time, while legislation is more rigid. We need to then ask whether the public interest provisions in the competition legislation could have a broader reference to public policy, or whether the SLC itself can be interpreted more broadly to engage with public policy, as argued above.

Mediclinic/Matlosana Medical Health Services (MMHS) merger in South Africa

The *Mediclinic/MMHS* case in South Africa raised similar concerns as the Walmart case, but there were subsequent interesting developments. In this case, Matlosana Medical Health Services (MMHS), a small independent hospital group, was to be acquired by one of the three largest private hospital groups in the country, Mediclinic. Mediclinic's plans to acquire MMHS, based in Klerksdorp in the North West province of South Africa, were prohibited by the Commission in 2019. The Commission successfully argued that if the transaction was allowed, there would be an SLC in the area and prices would likely increase. In February 2020, after Mediclinic appealed the judgment, the Competition Appeal Court of South Africa (CAC) overturned the Tribunal's decision and ruled in favour of Mediclinic. The Commission then appealed to the Constitutional Court on the basis that the case involved the interpretation, protection and actualisation of the constitutional right of access to healthcare services, as the merger would result in higher healthcare costs, particularly for uninsured patients.

One aspect of the case was the Commission arguing that the acquisition would result in the acquiring firm (Mediclinic), a large national group of hospitals, enforcing its own pricing policies and strategies on the independent group. The argument was that the independent hospital was a lower-priced business, and the acquisition would result in higher prices for both insured and uninsured patients. However, in the appeal at the CAC, Mediclinic successfully argued that there was no competitive effect – no SLC – resulting from the merger, and thus it could not be prohibited.

On further appeal to the Constitutional Court, while continuing to argue that there was a competition effect, the Commission also argued that it would be unconstitutional for it not to consider the welfare effects of less access to healthcare overall due to the likely price increases. The Commission argued that the proposed merger would make the options outside of medical insurance schemes much less attractive, as it provides the merged firm with the ability to offer lower or no discounts on designated service provider networks (DSPs) and to deteriorate non-price factors in the relevant market. As stated by the Commission, 'Medical scheme members on low-cost options collectively are an important group from a public interest perspective since they are particularly vulnerable to increasing costs of private health care in South Africa'.[26]

The Commission also stated that the likely price effects of the proposed merger raised public interest concerns regarding the health care sector and the relevant region, with no positive countervailing public interest grounds that mitigate these concerns. The Commission emphasised that a particularly vulnerable group are uninsured patients in the area as, post-merger, they would have less choice (of cheaper hospitals) and less ability to switch to cheaper options.

Consequently, the argument is that to the extent that the impact of the merger is to restrict or impede human rights, there is effectively an SLC, and on this basis, the Commission must be able to prohibit such a merger. On 15 October 2021, the Constitutional Court upheld the Commission's appeal, setting aside the CAC ruling that had allowed the merger. The Court considered the effects on the healthcare costs of patients living in the relatively rural region, but especially the cost to uninsured patients as it would deny them the lower tariffs charged by the target hospitals while also limiting their ability to negotiate better prices or switch to cheaper hospitals.[27] The context and nature of the impact on uninsured persons who are relatively poorer consumers is an important aspect of the decision, and supports an emphasis on the distributive impact of mergers, in line with the discussion above.

What is also interesting, and more relevant for this chapter, is that the judgment appears to delink the SLC from a change in competition, or at least open the door for this. It found that the CAC:

> ...misdirected itself in a material respect by construing section 12A(1)(a) and (2) of the Act as requiring that a *price increase post-merger be shown to be the result of the market share changes, which it termed 'enhancement of market power'. This is not the test required by the Act*. And nothing in the language and context of section 12A(1)(a) and (2) allows for the assessment to be conducted with reference to the 'enhancement of market power', which is not even listed as one of the factors listed in section 12A(2)...All that section 12A requires in this regard is that a determination be made whether there is a substantial prevention or lessening of competition. And this is ordinarily measured with reference to a potential increase in price.[28] (Emphasis added)

While the impact of the Constitutional Court judgment on the application of the SLC is not yet clear, what the decision and discussion above suggests is that there may be room for the SLC, particularly in the South African context, to be interpreted more broadly. The decision shows that the SLC need not result from a change in market power but can also arise from other merger-specific changes to competition brought about by the transaction itself. This may potentially provide a basis for considering cases like those of the dialysis market discussed above, where the acquiring firm's differing strategy to the target firm resulted in adverse competitive outcomes. Indeed, not following this approach represents a potentially inadequate application of competition law in many jurisdictions, including South Africa. Where competition law does allow for the consideration of public interest provisions resulting from the *transaction* – like South Africa's in the Walmart case – it would be an odd position if negative effects on consumers as a result of the same *transaction* could not be considered in the application of the law.

Conclusions

This chapter has explored the rationale and possibility for a more expansive and inclusive interpretation of the SLC and anti-competitive effect terminology. There are essentially three key findings from this chapter.

First, it is arguable that public policy or economic policy should naturally be considered relevant to the question of what constitutes an SLC or anti-competitive effect. In some ways, the South African authorities and others may already be taking a broader approach, which would likely be driven further by the recent Constitutional Court ruling in the Mediclinic/MMHS case. However, there is also a question as to whether legislation could provide a more fluid provision for the consideration of public policy.

Second, any assessment of SLC must take account of context in assessing the relevant magnitude of effects that would constitute an SLC. The magnitude of what qualifies as 'substantial' depends on the context.

Third, policy-makers should consider providing for a broader definition of effects that includes more explicit provisions for prohibiting *transactions* based on the likely impact of the transaction itself on consumer welfare outcomes. Competition authorities may consider whether there are changes to the nature of competition through, for instance, a further or larger exploitation of market power and whether this is sufficient for a prohibition under an SLC standard. Importantly, where competition legislation provides for the assessment of public interest considerations as a result of the transaction itself, it must be the case that effects on *consumers* as a consequence of the transaction itself (such as increased prices, reduced quality and reduced access to essential services) must also be included in any consideration of a merger.

Moreover, there is a question as to whether a broader interpretation of the SLC or competitive effects may produce a more effective competition enforcement and regulation regime. This chapter has explored ways in which the SLC standard can be interpreted more broadly, but also raised the question of whether policy and legislation (or the application thereof) is sufficiently and comprehensively formulated, and thus whether further changes may be required.

Notes

1. Countries with an SLC test include the United States, United Kingdom, New Zealand, Australia, and Malawi. The SPLC is found in South Africa, Zambia and Canada. The European Union uses the Significant Impediment to Effective Competition (SIEC) standard (Niels et al. 2016).
2. A further question is how one then weighs this effect against any efficiency gains, but this is not addressed by this chapter.
3. In South Africa, competition policy is also reflected in the objectives of the Competition Act, which include aspects such as promoting small and medium enterprises and a greater spread of ownership.
4. See OECD Policy Roundtables (2009) Standard for Merger Review.
5. An earlier version of the paper on which this chapter is based was first published as part of a compendium following the 7th CUTS-CIRC Biennial Conference on Competition, Regulation & Development: 'Building Blocks for an Inclusive and Resilient Economy', CUTS International, 2022, publication #2207.
6. Jason Aproskie and Tessa Bleazard are economists at the Competition Commission of South Africa. The views of this chapter reflect those of the authors and not necessarily those of the Competition Commission of South Africa.
7. The study tested the pricing effects according to the average income for the area. Thus price effects in lower-income areas are used as a clear indicator of price effects for lower-income consumers. Therefore, 'poorer consumers' here can be understood to be consumers from poorer areas.

8 The South African Nationwide Poles case and appeal dealt with this issue. It was found by the Competition Appeal Court that 'substantial' does not equate to non-trivial.
9 See: *Competition Commission v Babelegi Workwear and Industrial Supplies CC* (Tribunal Case no. CR00Apr20, at para. 159).
10 See: *Competition Commission v Dis-Chem Pharmacies Limited Competition* (Tribunal Case No. CR008Apr2).
11 See: *Competition Commission vs Babelegi Workwear and Industrial Supplies CC* (Tribunal Case no. CR00Apr20, para. 159).
12 See: *Competition Commission v Dis-Chem Pharmacies Limited* (Tribunal Case No. CR008Apr2)
13 See: *Competition Commission vs Babelegi Workwear and Industrial Supplies CC* (Tribunal Case no. CR00Apr20), para. 171.
14 See: Competition Appeal Court decision on the Babelegi case (Case no. 186/CAC/JUN20), para. 59.
15 See: *Competition Commission v Babelegi Workwear and Industrial Supplies CC* (Tribunal Case no. CR00Apr20), para. 169.
16 See: *Competition Commission v Dis-Chem Pharmacies Limited* (Competition Tribunal Case No. CR008Apr20), para. 226.
17 See: *Competition Commission v Dis-Chem Pharmacies Limited* (Competition Tribunal Case No. CR008Apr20), para. 226.
18 See: *Competition Commission v Dis-Chem Pharmacies Limited* (Competition Tribunal Case No. CR008Apr20), para. 228.
19 See: *Competition Commission v Dis-Chem Pharmacies Limited* (Competition Tribunal Case No. CR008Apr20), para. 228.
20 See: *Competition Appeal Court decision on the Babelegi case* (Case no. 186/CAC/JUN20), para. 67.
21 See: South Africa's Competition Act 89 of 1998, section 12A(3).
22 A negative impact on quality is equivalent to an increase in price while quality remains constant.
23 See: *Competition Tribunal, Walmart Stores Inc v Massmart Holdings Ltd* (73/LM/Dec10) [2011] ZACT 42 (29 June 2011).
24 This included the South African Commercial, Catering and Allied Workers Union (SACCAWU), the Food and Allied Workers Union (FAWU), and Southern African Clothing and Textile Workers' Union (SACTWU).
25 Section 12A of the Competition Act (No. 89 of 1998) (as amended) details the public interest provisions that may be considered, including: (i) the effect on employment, (ii) the effect on a particular industrial sector or region, and (iii) the ability of small business those owned by historically disadvantaged person to be competitive.
26 Application for Leave to Appeal Volume 1 (CCT Case No. 31/20). Commission Founding Affidavit p. 14. See: Application for leave to appeal.1pdf (concourt.org.za).

27 See: *Competition Commission of South Africa v Mediclinic Southern Africa (Pty) Ltd and Another* CCT 31/20. P. 33–34.

28 See: *Competition Commission of South Africa v Mediclinic Southern Africa (Pty) Ltd and Another* CCT 31/20. P. 22, para. 53–54.

References

Bleazard T, Mahuma A & Aproskie J (2022) Competition Commission Brief: *Prioritisation: An overview of international approaches*

Buthelezi T, Mtani T & Mncube L (2018) *The extent of market concentration in South Africa's product markets*. Working Paper No. CC2018/05, Competition Commission of South Africa

CCSA (Competition Commission of South Africa) (2019) Final report: *Data services market inquiry*. Pretoria: CCSA

CMA (Competition and Markets Authority) (2019) Final Report: *Anticipated merger between J Sainsbury PLC and Asda Group Ltd*. London: CMA

Eliason PJ, Heebsh B, McDevitt RC & Roberts JW (2020) How acquisitions affect firm behaviour and performance: Evidence from the dialysis industry. *The Quarterly Journal of Economics* 135(1): 221–267

ICN (2021) Report on: *ICN Agencies' Case Prioritisation and Initiation*. ICN Agency Effectiveness Working Group

Keleme M & Moeketsi N (2020) *Excessive pricing in the time of COVID-19: Insights from a regulator's perspective*. Pretoria: CCSA

Mariuzzo F & P Ormosi (2021) *Do the poor pay more for increasing market concentration? A study of retail petroleum markets*. CCP Working Paper No. 21–08, University of East Anglia

Niels G, Jenkins H & Kavanagh J (2016) *Economics for competition lawyers* (2nd edition). Oxford: Oxford University Press

Thakoor V (2020) *Market power, growth, and inclusion: The South African experience*. Working Paper 2020/206, International Monetary Fund

8 Cartels under scrutiny

Maletuma Malie

Cartel conduct is widely viewed by competition authorities as the most egregious of competition infringements. This is because cartels reduce the levels of competition and create the opportunity for members to wield market power collectively, which allows them to raise prices and constrain supply (Maphwanya 2017). Cartels seek to pursue collective profits similar to those that would be enjoyed by a monopoly in the same industry. In this way, a cartel can be viewed as a simulation of a temporary merger among rival companies, with the ultimate goal of generating monopoly profits (Connor 2008).

When a cartel is detected and penalised, one can expect this to have a negative impact on the implicated companies' share prices. This negative impact may not reflect any altruistic motives on the part of investors, but is more likely to be attributed to three key factors. First, the litigation that results from the suspected cartel activity could lead to legal costs and penalties, which in turn would negatively affect the company's profits. Second, post-cartel, the company may not generate the large profits that motivated the cartel in the first place. Third, the reputational damage to the company resulting from cartel activity may have a detrimental impact on customer relations (Bianconi et al. 2015).

The effective implementation of anti-cartel laws is an imperative for most competition authorities worldwide. This stems from the fact that when competitors form a cartel, the pressure of competing is overtaken by coordinative efforts that allow them to achieve collective market power. Such market power enables these cartel members to raise prices and restrict supply. The harmful effects of cartel conduct become a burden to consumers who will face higher prices, limited product choices and diminished quality of products or services. An effective competition regime thus creates an environment that discourages market participants from engaging in cartel activity, as it would result in significant negative consequences. To discourage cartel conduct, the role of the competition authorities is then to use all the tools at their disposal to detect and prosecute cartels (Maphwanya 2017).

Administrative penalties are a critical tool used by competition authorities to penalise cartel conduct. If they are sufficiently high, the penalties should effectively deter cartel conduct, as they could significantly impact the finances of the implicated companies (Aguzzoni et al. 2013). To gain some perspective on the effectiveness of enforcement measures by the competition authorities in South Africa, it is important to assess the cost of the penalties incurred by companies when found guilty of cartel conduct.

In light of this, the study aims to determine the impact on company share prices of enforcement interventions in the form of investigations and penalisation when a cartel is uncovered. Using event study analysis, the study quantitatively examines 15 companies listed on the Johannesburg Stock Exchange (JSE) to analyse the changes in company share prices after a cartel enforcement announcement is made public. The outcome of this research provides insight into the extent to which investors view cartel activity as detrimental to the valuation of a company.

In summary, the study finds that investigation and penalty announcements do not consistently result in negative and significant returns for the implicated cartel members. There are a number of reasons for this, some of which point to the effectiveness of the enforcement measures. This study seeks to add to the existing literature by offering a perspective on the effectiveness of cartel enforcement measures in the South African competition landscape.

The chapter starts by providing an overview of cartel legislation in South Africa and provides a brief history of event studies.

Cartel legislation in South Africa

Competition legislation can be described as the policies and rules that seek to ensure that competition in the economy is not restricted to the detriment of society (Motta 2004). The widespread and global implementation of competition legislation was initiated in part due to cartel activity being identified as one of the reasons for inflation, trade restrictions and stunted economic growth in the post-World War II period (Connor 2008). By the early 2000s, more than 100 countries globally, including South Africa, had adopted some form of competition law.

The South African competition regime is in line with international best practices in that it encourages free trade, while closely monitoring the actions of companies for anticompetitive behaviour. The South African Competition Act (No. 89 of 1998) (the Act)[1] was promulgated to address high concentration levels, ineffective antitrust policies and restrictions on equitable economic participation following years of exclusion under apartheid (Wise 2004).

The Act promotes competition, economic development, consumer access to products at competitive prices, social and economic welfare, international market integration and fair opportunities for small and medium enterprises through three statutory bodies: The Competition Commission investigates and evaluates anticompetitive practices, the abuse of dominant positions and large mergers. The Commission makes recommendations to the Competition Tribunal. The Competition Tribunal adjudicates competition matters referred to it by the Competition Commission. Appeals relating to the Competition Tribunal decisions are heard by the Competition Appeal Court (Hartzenberg 2006).

This study is primarily concerned with cartel conduct, which is prohibited on a per se basis under section 4(1)(b) of the Act, whether it is in the form of price fixing, market division or collusive tendering. Under the Act, the Competition Tribunal may impose administrative penalties on those parties found to have engaged in cartel activity. The penalty liability depends on, inter alia, the extent of the cartel conduct, the duration of the cartel conduct and the amount of damage that results from the conduct. However, the penalty is capped at 10% of the company's annual turnover in the preceding financial year. Companies found guilty of recidivism can face penalties of up to 25%.[2] The objective is to deter companies from engaging in cartel conduct.

A brief history of event studies

An event study analyses the impact of specific events on the value of a company using that company's financial information in specified timeframes. The main premise of this kind of study is that the impact of an event reflects immediately in the share price, given that investors are expected to act rationally (MacKinlay 1997).

Event study analysis dates back to the early 1930s, with some of the early work being attributed to Dolley (1933), cited in Campbell et al. (1997) for a study on the impact of stock splits on prices. In the decades that followed, more advanced event studies were published. The seminal works of Ball and Brown (1968) and Fama et al. (1969) were instrumental in developing the event study methodology still used today. Ball and Brown (1968) review the content of accounting information to determine which measures can be used for analysing earnings. Fama et al. (1969) analyse the impact of stock splits when confounding effects are excluded. The use of event study methodology has since expanded beyond finance and economics to other disciplines such as environmental, corporate and governance studies (Cheung 2011; Klassen & McLaughlin 1996; Lundgren & Olsson 2010; Tamechika 2020).

From the perspective of companies, event studies provide some insight into the extent of abnormal profits (or losses) to shareholders following an event of interest. In competition law and economics, this approach has been used to determine the effectiveness of regulation and to assess damages in liability cases (Aguzzoni et al. 2013; Kothari & Warner 2007). It is therefore possible to observe the impact of company-specific as well as industry-specific events such as mergers and acquisitions, changes in legislative frameworks and enforcement of regulatory policies.

Event studies have been used in competition law to analyse the impact of competition infringements and penalties on company share prices. Table 8.1 gives a summary of the key outcomes of a sample of event studies with a focus on the financial impact of antitrust enforcement on cartels – the subject of this study.

Table 8.1 Summary of comparable empirical studies

Author/s and year	Title	Objective of paper	Findings
Mariuzzo F, Ormosi PL & Majied Z, 2020	Fines and Reputational Sanctions: The Case of Cartels	To assess the deterrence effect of public and reputational sanctions due to cartel activity in Europe.	On average, dawn raids resulted in a 0.85% decline in share price; penalty decisions resulted in a share price decline of 0.35%.
Bos I, Letterie W & Scherl N, 2019	Industry Impact of Cartels: Evidence from the Stock Market	To evaluate the impact of dawn raids and infringement decisions on the share price of cartel and non-cartel companies in Europe.	The study finds a significant negative impact on the share price of cartel members, with decreases ranging from 0.60% to 1.41%, following the interventions by competition authorities. However, the results for non-cartel members were ambiguous.
Aguzzoni L, Langus G & Motta M, 2013	The Effect of EU Antitrust Investigations and Fines on a Firm's Valuation	To assess the share price impact of investigations and fines relating to cartel conduct in Europe.	On average, dawn raids resulted in a decrease in the share price of 2.89%; infringement decisions resulted in a 3.57% decrease in the share price.
Günster A & Van Dijk M, 2016	The Impact of European Antitrust Policy: Evidence From the Stock Market	To analyse the response of share prices to investigation announcements, infringement decisions and appeals in Europe.	On average, dawn raids resulted in a 5% decline in share price; successful appeals resulted in approximately 4% increase in share valuation.
Beverley L, 2007	Stock Market Event Studies and Competition Commission Inquiries	To evaluate the impact on share prices of specific announcements by the European competition authority.	The study did not find conclusive evidence of the responsiveness of share prices to announcements by the competition authorities.
Bosch JC & Eckard Jr EW, 1991	The Profitability of Price Fixing: Evidence from Stock Market Reaction to Federal Indictments	To estimate the impact on the share price following a cartel indictment announcement in the United States of America.	On average, company share prices decreased by 1.08% following announcement of price-fixing indictments.

Source: Author's compilation of selected empirical studies

Event study methodology

The key objective of event studies is to establish if there are any abnormal returns on the company share price following specific events. An abnormal return in this context is the difference between an observed return and the counterfactual (Peterson 1989). The counterfactual, or the expected return, refers to the return that would have been observed had the event in question not occurred (Cichello & Lamdin 2006). To the extent that share prices reflect the valuation of a company's assets, changes in these equity values can be expected to reflect the anticipated changes in the company's financial performance. Therefore, news about a company that is expected to result in a positive share price movement stimulates investment in the company and, *ceteris paribus,* is expected to result in a share price increase. Conversely, *ceteris paribus,* news that is expected to negatively affect the value of the company is expected to result in a share price decline (Bos et al. 2019).

Central to event study analyses is the efficient-market hypothesis (EMH), which states that a market is efficient if it fully reflects all relevant and available information (Fama 1970). If this is the case, share prices are a true reflection of the fundamentals of a company. As all participants are assumed to have the same information, it is therefore not possible to make profits solely based on such information (Campbell et al. 1997).

In terms of EMH, markets are assumed to be efficient such that, when company news is announced that is material enough to affect the value of a company's share price, the share price should adjust rapidly to reflect the new expected value of future cash flows. The EMH thus assumes that in determining share prices, the capital market fully and accurately reflects all relevant company information (Campbell et al. 1997). Additionally, any new information that impacts on the fundamentals of the company will reflect immediately as a share price adjustment (Langus & Motta 2007). So, following a market announcement, the share price will provide the best estimate of the event's impact on the market value of the company.

Event study analysis requires knowledge of the exact date on which information is disseminated to the market. It is assumed that there are no information leaks prior to the formal announcement. In reality, however, material information about a company may reach some investors sooner than others, which may dilute the results of an event study (Beverley 2007). Uncertainty about the precise timing of an event can lead to underestimating its true impact, potentially resulting in a Type II error, where the event is falsely concluded to have no effect on the company's share price. A redeeming feature of the event study methodology is that where an event is found to have influenced a share price, despite a low-powered test that may affect the level of significance, the results may still be credible provided there is sufficient background information to substantiate the findings (Cichello & Lamdin 2006).

Event study methodology also assumes that there are no other confounding effects that could have influenced the company's share price at the time of the announcement or event of interest (McWilliams & Siegel 1997). Confounding effects could be factors such as the announcement of dividends, the resignation of a director or an impending merger, which could all impact the performance of the share price. Such events should therefore be recognised and understood, as they may affect the estimates and the validity of the findings.

In this study, the events of interest relate to two types of cartel enforcement actions against a company. The first is the announcement or a dawn raid, indicating that a company is under investigation for suspected cartel activity. The second is the imposition of a penalty on the company for involvement in cartel conduct. The objective of the event study is therefore to isolate the abnormal return that results from the events of interest. This is to determine if investigations that relate to cartel activity matter to investors and whether the announcement of penalties has an adverse impact on the valuation of the company.

The building blocks of an event study

The quintessential event study follows seven key steps: event definition, selection criteria, calculation of normal and abnormal returns, estimation procedure, testing framework, presentation of empirical results, and finally, interpretation and conclusions (Beverley 2007). What follows is a description of each stage, with a short summary for this particular study.

Event definition

The initial stage of an event study defines the event of interest and determines the period over which share prices of the company(s) involved in this event will be analysed. The time frame for each event is based on the identification of an event window, which is the period over which the impact of the event on a company's share price will be observed. As stated above, in theory, the EMH holds that all value effects of announcements on price would reflect immediately after the information relating to the event is announced publicly. In practice, however, it is understood that the impact of the event may be observed before the actual day if the market is anticipating the announcement or after the day of the announcement if it takes time for the effects of the event to fully pass through to the company's share value (Beverley 2007). The choice of an event window is key to the accurate observation of the market reaction. An event window that is too narrow may under-represent the impact of the announcement. Conversely, if it is too wide, there is a greater probability that it will include confounding events that may produce biased results (Cichello & Lamdin 2006).

The conventional approach is to observe the estimation window as the period before the event window, to estimate the normal or expected returns. The hypotheses of interest are then tested in the event window (Jeng 2015).

In this study, the events of interest relate to enforcement actions on competition law infringements by companies. The focal areas for each case were the investigation announcement or dawn raid for potential cartel conduct by companies, and the final decision, which culminates in the imposition of a penalty by the Tribunal.

Selection criteria

The second task in the event study analysis is to determine the selection criteria for inclusion of companies in the study. The key determinant for particular companies being included in the study is the availability of tradeable share price data. Ideally, the share price data in an event study should be consistently available and sufficiently liquid, which is often the case with companies that are listed on a formal stock exchange (Beverley 2007). It is worth acknowledging that the liquidity of the various shares could differ significantly, even within the same markets. This is a common feature of stock market trading. The qualifying criteria may also be dependent on the areas of interest for analysis, such as industry, market capitalisation and time period (Campbell et al. 1997).

For the current study, the first qualifying criterion for inclusion of companies was that they were listed on the main board of the JSE. Out of the approximately 370 companies listed on the main board, 23 were prosecuted for collusion between 2009 and 2019. Eight of these companies were excluded from the study due to insufficient share price history. The final list that formed the core focus of the study therefore comprised 15 JSE listed companies that had been involved in and were successfully prosecuted for cartel activity. Figure 8.1 below represents these companies by sector classification.

Figure 8.1 Companies by sector classification

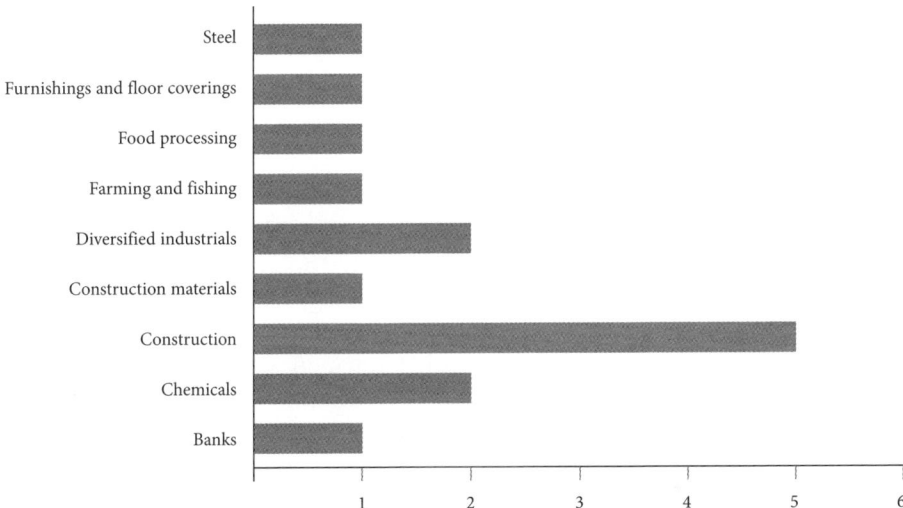

Source: Author's compilation from JSE listed companies

Even though construction companies were disproportionately represented in the sample, as illustrated in Figure 8.1 above, the study included various other sectors, and the results are consistent across these sectors. The dominance of construction and construction material companies in the sample is partly due to the Competition Commission's strategic focus on seven priority sectors, including construction and infrastructure, food and agro-processing, and intermediate industrial inputs[3]. Additionally, industries such as banking and telecommunications are highly regulated, with prices and other key measures often set by sectoral regulatory bodies, making it more challenging to identify and prove cartel conduct. Despite these factors, the findings in sectors such as food processing, chemicals, and diversified industrials align with those in construction and construction materials companies.

Therefore, while construction companies make up the larger proportion of the sample, the study demonstrates that these findings are broadly applicable across different sectors.

Key to event study analysis is the ability to differentiate between the factors that affect the company(s) under study, such as the news of a dawn raid vis à vis those that impact the entire market, such as changes in legislation (Corrado 2011). This separation allows for the observation of abnormal share performance resulting from the impact of the relevant event on the valuation of the company in question.

Calculation of normal and abnormal returns

The third stage involves calculating the normal and abnormal returns. This involves estimating the parameters for the period preceding the event, that is, the estimation window. The event dates for this study were determined based on when the news of the infringement or judgement became publicly available. In this study the JSE Stock Exchange News Service (SENS), the Competition Commission's media releases, and company financials were used to determine the event dates.

Estimation procedure

There is no consensus in the event study literature as to the ideal number of days to include in the estimation window. Estimation periods in the literature range from 100 to 300 days for daily studies. The decision to use a longer estimation window balances the need to get the most reliable and robust parameters with the risks of including potential structural shifts in model parameters over extended periods (Günster & Van Dijk 2016). In this study, the estimation window was taken as the number of trading days in a typical South African year, which is 115 days. The approach was similar to that used by Aguzonni et al. (2013), Bosch and Eckard (1991) and Günster and van Dijk (2016). There is no standard length for event windows, but the length should sufficiently accommodate potential leaks in the market and still be able to limit confounding effects (McWilliams & Siegel 1997). The event window includes the day of the event as well as the days leading up to, and following that event, enabling the examination of the periods surrounding the event (Mackinlay 1997).

This study used an 11-day event window that included 5 days before and 5 days after the event date. For comparative purposes, it also included a 16-day event window, covering 5 days before and 10 days after the event. The 5 days before the event are included in the event window to capture potential information leakages prior to the event date. The days after the event are included to account for the impact of announcements that are made after the stock market closes (Mackinlay 1997). In addition, SENS announcements are in some instances issued after the competition authority's announcement.

To ensure that any confounding effects were identified and accounted for, the SENS company announcements were screened during the event window for events such as dividend payouts, changes in executive management, and mergers and acquisitions.

Testing framework

Once the estimation and the event windows had been determined, a testing framework was devised for any abnormal returns calculated. This included defining the null hypothesis and establishing procedures to aggregate the calculated outputs over time and across the various companies. The test of significance approach was adopted to reject or fail to reject the null hypothesis. The decision to reject or fail to reject the null hypothesis is based on the test statistic, as outlined below. The null hypothesis H_0 states that the event does not have an impact on the mean or variance of the share price returns. This implies that under the null hypothesis, the abnormal returns are expected to equal zero (Campbell et al. 1997).

The test statistic is calculated and compared to its expected distribution under the null hypothesis. If the test statistic exceeds the critical value, which is typically at 10%, 5% or 1%, then the null hypothesis is rejected and it can be concluded that the abnormal returns are not equal to zero (Kothari & Warner 2006).

For this study, the null hypothesis was that the news of an investigation by the Competition Commission would not have an impact on the company's share price. Similarly, the news of an adverse finding and accompanying penalties by the Competition Tribunal would have no impact on the share price.

Presentation of empirical results

The findings of the analysis can then be presented, including diagnostics for testing the validity of the model. The quantitative findings of this study are presented in detail in Appendix A. This includes the regression analysis results for each of the 15 JSE listed companies covered in this study, as well as the associated significance tests.

Interpretation of results

The final step involves making inferences based on the results of the study. Reflections of the implications of the findings and concluding remarks complete the analysis. The empirical results of this study will therefore illustrate whether investigations and penalties by South African competition authorities are viewed as negative and/or material by investors. The findings of this study are discussed in detail later in the chapter.

Econometric approach

An assessment of how information about anti-cartel interventions affects a company's share price using event study analysis requires an accurate measurement of the abnormal return on the share price. This is the difference between the actual return and the expected return on the share (Dombrow et al. 2000). The abnormal return represents the investors' expectations of the future earnings of the company given the new information (Bos et al. 2019). In this study, the new information refers to the investigation or the penalty announcements relating to cartel conduct.

A commonly used statistical model for estimating the abnormal return is the market model (Aguzonni 2013; Bosch & Eckard 1991). The section that follows provides an overview of the market model and a non-parametric alternative model for robustness checks.

The market model

The market model is adopted to determine the counterfactual or the normal returns of a given share. This model relates the return of a particular share relative to that of the market portfolio. Under the market model, market-wide factors that affect share performance during the event window are held constant, enabling the isolation of the impact of company-specific events (Cichello & Lamdin 2006). The abnormal return is the observed return on the share price during the event window minus the counterfactual share price during the same period. The market model seeks to eliminate the influence of factors that affect the entire market (Van den Broek et al. 2012).

The model can be represented as:

$$R_{it} = \alpha_i + \beta_i R_{mt} + \varepsilon_{it} \quad [8.1]$$

With $E[\varepsilon_{it}] = 0$; $Var[\varepsilon_{it}] = \delta^2_{\varepsilon_i}$

Where R_{it} and R_{mt} are the returns on share i at time t, and the returns on the market are represented by an index of the stock exchange where the share is listed. ε_{it} is the zero mean disturbance term. α and β are the Ordinary Least Squares (OLS) estimates of the slope and the intercept of the market model regression.

The timeline for the event is represented schematically in Figure 8.2 below.

Figure 8.2: The timeline for an event study

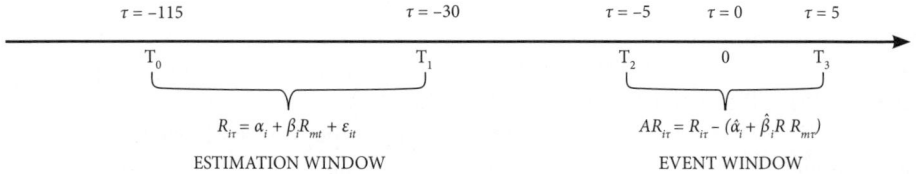

Source: Reproduced from Van Den Broek (2012)

The date of the event is defined as τ = 0. This is the day on which the news of the event reaches the market. In this study, the SENS announcements were the primary reference used to determine when information was provided to the investors. The predictive model estimates the parameters α and β during the estimation window.

The estimation of the normal return was calculated from $\tau = T_0 (\tau = -115)$ to $T_1 (\tau = -30)$ relative to the date of the event. The abnormal returns were then calculated at $\tau = T_1$ to $\tau = T_2$, which is the event window. Typically, the estimation window and the event window do not overlap (Van den Broek et al. 2012). This is important because the estimation of the normal return seeks to exclude the influence of the event.

Using the market model, the abnormal returns in the event window were constructed as the difference between the counterfactual and the actual return (Günster & Van Dijk 2016):

$$AR_{i\tau} = R_{i\tau} - (\hat{\alpha}_i + \hat{\beta}_i R_{m\tau}) \quad [8.2]$$

where the abnormal return for share i at time τ is the disturbance term of the market model.

The cumulative abnormal return (CAR) for the event window is calculated on the individual shares as follows:

$$CAR_i = \Sigma_{i=1}^{t} AR_{i\tau} \quad [8.3]$$

To test the hypothesis that abnormal returns are equal to zero, the following t-statistic was then computed:

$$t = \frac{CAR_i}{\sigma_i} \quad [8.4]$$

where σ_i is the standard deviation of abnormal returns during the event window.

This study adopted the market model in line with Aguzonni, Langus and Motta (2013), Beverley (2007), and Bosch and Eckard (1991). In this study, the FTSE/JSE All Share index (ALSI)[4] was used to represent the market.

An alternative to specifying abnormal returns as prediction errors in the market model can be extended to include dummy variables.

The specification of equation 8.1 including the dummy variable is:

$$R_{i\tau} = \hat{\alpha}_i + \hat{\beta}_i R_{m\tau} + \Sigma_{a=1}^{A} \gamma_{pa} D_{at} + u_{pt} \quad [8.5]$$

where $R_{i\tau}$ is is the return on the share during period t, $R_{m\tau}$ is the return on the market portfolio in the period, and β and γ are the estimated parameters. u_{pt} is the error term. The dummy variable D_{at} represents one or more dummy variables for each event window. It assumes a value of 1 during the event window and 0 otherwise. The coefficient of the dummy variable will therefore measure the average abnormal return for the company across all the event periods (Cichello & Lamden 2006).

Theil's non-parametric approach

The Ordinary Least Squares (OLS) methodology used in the estimation of equations 8.2 and 8.5 relies on the assumption that the error terms are normally distributed.

However, daily share price data have often been found to vary from this assumption, with empirical evidence suggesting that daily returns exhibit fatter tails than is typical of normal distributions (Brown & Warner 1985). If the normality assumption is violated, this can produce biased estimates of the abnormal returns (Saleh 2007).

To overcome this challenge, for robustness checks the study used a non-parametric estimator using Theil's approach to estimate the market model (Aguzonni et al.2013); Saleh 2007).

Contrary to the OLS methodology, Theil's approach does not make any assumptions on the distribution of the error terms.

Using the market model equation [8.1, on page 118], this approach followed the six steps discussed below.

The first step in this process was to sort the N data pairs of (in ascending order of the market return, where N is the number of data points in the estimation window. Second, the data pairs were separated into two equal groups of size j based on the median. If N is an odd number, the middle point was excluded. The third step calculated a slope parameter β for each of the data pairs in each group using:

$$\beta\left(j, j+\left(\frac{N}{2}\right)\right) = \frac{R_{\left(j+\left(\frac{N}{2}\right)\right)} - R_j}{Rm_{\left(j+\left(\frac{N}{2}\right)\right)} - Rm_j} \quad \text{for } j = 1 \text{ to } \frac{N}{2} \quad [8.6]$$

The median value $\hat{\beta}_i$ was then chosen as the best estimate for β.

The fourth step was to use the estimated $\hat{\beta}_i$ to estimate the N parameters:

$$\alpha_{i\tau} = R_{i\tau} - \hat{\beta}_i R_{m\tau} \quad [8.7]$$

At step five the median of the intercepts $\hat{\alpha}_{i\tau}$ was selected as the best estimator of α.

Finally, for each day and company in the event window, the nonparametric abnormal returns were calculated as:

$$\widehat{AR}_{i\tau}^* = R_{i\tau}^* - (\hat{\alpha}_i + \hat{\beta}_i R_{m\tau}^*) \quad [8.8]$$

The Theil estimators are median-based, offering an additional benefit of excluding outliers from the estimation, which would be on the extreme ends of the ranking. This may help eliminate bias in the estimates that could occur due these outliers. On the other hand, by excluding these outliers, some detailed information contained in the original dataset may be lost in the process of ranking (Vaughan 2001).

Potential limitations in the methodology

A limitation of this study relates to the sample size. In order to be included in the study, companies were required to be listed on the JSE. This meant that a large proportion of successfully prosecuted cases could not be included, as they were not listed on the exchange. The second limitation is that the sample had a disproportionate representation of construction and construction material companies due to widespread collusion in the construction industry during the period under review, which caused increased focus by the competition authorities. This indicates that broad conclusions could not be drawn on all companies or industries as to the effect of enforcement announcements on the valuation of their companies. However, the redeeming aspect of this study is that it included companies from other sectors, and the results remained consistent across these sectors, reinforcing the validity of the findings. These limitations are not unique to this study.

Findings: The effectiveness of anti-cartel enforcement in South Africa

The aim of this study was to analyse the impact of news of interventions of the Competition Commission on the share prices of the affected companies. The results of the study and their interpretation are discussed in this section, first in terms of the technical outcomes, and then by examining their implications for the effectiveness of anti-cartel interventions undertaken by the Competition Commission. The results of this study provide the output of the OLS and the Theil methodology. The percentage cumulative abnormal return (CAR) is calculated in the 11-day and the 16-day event windows. The results reflect the share price movement at the investigation announcement and the penalty announcement stages. The results are assessed against the null hypothesis that the news of interventions by the Competition Commission has no impact on the valuation of companies, that is, the CAR on the company share price is equal to zero.

The company level results are presented in Appendix A. In a vast number of the cases, the OLS and Theil estimates have the same sign. However, in terms of the value of the CAR, the results suggest that the Theil method is more conservative and, as such, in most instances reflects a lower value than the one calculated using OLS. This may be due to the exclusion of outliers that is built into the Theil method.

Implications for anti-cartel enforcement in South Africa

The general results of the study indicate that, in most of the cases, the news of an investigation or the imposition of a penalty in South Africa does not result in a statistically significant negative movement in share prices. Several factors may contribute to this outcome. First, in many instances, the Commission investigates and prosecutes each company's case independently. This means that two members of the same cartel may have different timelines for when their case is initiated and eventually concluded. As a result, news of the cartel may reach the market when one cartel member is prosecuted, and this could be long before other members of the cartel have been investigated. By the time the investigation and penalties occur, such news has already been priced into the affected company share price(s). For example, in the case of the much-publicised bread cartel of the late 1990s to 2000s involving Tiger Brands, Premier Foods (Pty) Ltd, Pioneer Foods (Pty) Ltd and Foodcorp (Pty) Ltd[5], Premier Foods was first to approach the Commission and indicate its willingness to cooperate with the investigation into the alleged cartel conduct. While Tiger Brands and Premier Foods had concluded their cases by 2007, Pioneer Foods continued to contest the matter until it was eventually concluded with a penalty in February of 2010.

Second, many cases take several years to be concluded, and this also results in the news of a penalty being neither new nor shocking to the market. Nkosi and Boshoff (2022) find that the average cartel prosecution period in South Africa is 44 months, although the duration for some of the cases in this study extended up to a decade. For instance, with the construction companies that were involved in cartel activities during the construction of the 2010 FIFA Soccer World Cup stadiums, the initial cases against Aveng Ltd, Wilson Bayly Holmes-Ovcon Ltd (WBHO) and others commenced in 2009, with many of them not being concluded until seven years later.[6]

Third, the size of the penalties may be viewed by investors as not material enough to erode the value of their investment in a company, even if it is found guilty of cartel conduct. Section 59(2) of the Competition Act specifies that the penalty for cartel conduct may not exceed 10% of a company's turnover, including exports, in the preceding financial year. It is often the case that the penalty eventually imposed is lower than the 10% threshold. If investors expect a penalty amounting to 10% of revenue, then the news of a significantly lower penalty relative to the originally expected penalty may be received favourably. A lower penalty will have a lower impact on the company's immediate profitability. In addition, in some cases, both the Commission and the Tribunal have been amenable to payments being made over a few years, usually three years, which also lessens the impact on profitability in one single year. A key insight from the study is that the size of the penalty on its own, as well as relative to the size of the company's revenue, particularly matter to companies that form part of a group of companies. For instance, for their involvement in the bread cartel, Tiger Brands was issued a penalty that constituted 5.7% of the national turnover of their bakery division which was less than 1% of the group's revenues.

Finally, in some markets where widespread collusion is detected and where some firms are repeat offenders, it is possible that announcements of additional cartel conduct do not lead to further negative impacts on share prices. Investors may already have priced in a culture of collusion into the company's share price. In addition, if company profitability had proven resilient to previous findings and penalties, investors may take the view that the latest penalties are unlikely to be detrimental to the company's profitability. This applies even more if the company has already made provision for potential penalties in its preceding annual financial statements, which is routine when it is likely that the company will be penalised.

Concluding remarks

Typically, cartel conduct, if successfully prosecuted, results in a loss in profitability as companies no longer enjoy supra-competitive profits. In addition, since penalties are an expense, there is also a short-term impact on the profitability reported in the period/s in which it is paid. The expectation is that company share prices will exhibit negative returns on the news of an investigation, and upon the imposition of penalties for cartel conduct. This decline in share price can be attributed to investor perceptions about the company's future prospects, stemming from potential legal fees and penalties, reduced profits due to the end of supra-competitive pricing, and reputational damage due to the company's involvement in cartel activities. A decline in the share price may be an indicator that enforcement actions by competition authorities are sufficiently impactful to deter cartel conduct due to the potential revenue loss if detected.

The findings of the study indicate that, on average, the news of an investigation and penalties for cartel conduct resulted in negative returns. However, in most instances, these negative returns were not statistically significant. Three key factors may have affected the results. First, the effective penalties imposed on individual divisions or subsidiaries within a group's company structure were relatively low compared to the company's revenues. This suggests that penalties are not significant enough to have a meaningful impact on the overall valuation of a company. Second, due to delays in the process between the investigation and the penalty stages, the present values of the penalties were discounted, leading to lower effective fines. During the investigation process, delays may also have meant that investors could have already priced in the penalties by the time the case was eventually concluded. Third, as different cartel members were prosecuted at different times, information relating to the enforcement process may have reached the markets before all pending investigations were finalised.

The results of this study highlight the need for more punitive measures to achieve meaningful deterrence from cartel conduct. Competition authorities may therefore consider the following revisions to the existing cartel enforcement framework. First, where applicable, the 10% threshold for penalties associated with cartel conduct should be applied to the entire group under investigation, not just one of their divisions or subsidiaries. Extending the penalty threshold to the entire group may put more pressure on shareholders and management to ensure that compliance measures are in place to combat cartel activity at all levels throughout the company. Second, competition authorities should be stricter in terms of payment terms so that penalties are paid over shorter periods and not over several years, as can be the case. The risk of the pain inflicted by significant penalties and reductions in profitability should serve to discourage cartel conduct. Finally, competition legislation relating to cartels should place the onus of proof on the accused colluding companies as opposed to the applicants, who may be small businesses or individuals. This would create a further incentive for companies to ensure that their policies and culture are compliant with anti-cartel laws.

The policy recommendations of this study are pragmatic and achievable as they do not necessitate a complete overhaul of the existing framework, but rather encourage stricter enforcement on the part of the competition authorities, for instance by imposing harsher penalties and being less amenable to extended payment terms.

From a long-term perspective, the South African Competition Commission may consider increasing focus on personal liability as an additional penalty for cartel conduct. This may increase individual accountability, which could result in a change of behaviour. However, this would require a well-capacitated and efficient prosecution authority as such matters would be dealt with by the National Prosecuting Authority, with the Competition Commission solely providing referrals.[7]

There are promising areas for future research that would add depth to this study's analysis. First, the long-term effect of successful prosecution provides further insight into the effectiveness of anti-cartel enforcement. If company share prices tend to revert to their cartel levels over time, this could indicate that cartel conduct has not been sufficiently deterred and may recur in the future. Second, further research into the effectiveness of individual prosecutions in deterring cartel conduct will provide insights into the efficacy of that proposed approach to combat cartel conduct. Finally, due to the nature of the cases that the South African competition authorities have focused on in the period of study, this research covers mainly the manufacturing and construction sectors. There is therefore further scope in future research to assess the impact of cartel news in other sectors such as pharmaceuticals and retail.

Notes

1 See: http://www.compcom.co.za/wp-content/uploads/2017/11/pocket-act-august-20141.pdf
2 See: The South African Competition Amendment Act 18 of 2018. Accessed November 2020, https://www.gov.za/sites/default/files/gcis_document/201902/competitionamendment-act18of2018.pdf
3 The seven priority sectors of the Competition Commission are: food and agro-processing; healthcare; intermediate industrial inputs; construction and infrastructure; banking and financial services; information and communication technology; energy (Competition Commission 2009).
4 The ALSI includes 150 companies listed on the JSE and is the exchange's largest index in terms of market capitalisation (Johannesburg Stock Exchange Limited 2020).
5 See: *Competition Commission v Pioneer Foods (Pty) Ltd* (15/CR/Feb07, 50/CR/May08) [2010] ZACT 9 (3 February 2010).
6 See: *Competition Commission v Aveng (Africa) Ltd* (016931) [2013] ZACT 76 (23 July 2013).
7 See: Section 73A of the South African Competition Act 89 of 1998. Accessed June 2020, http://www.compcom.co.za/wp-content/uploads/2017/11/pocket-act-august-20141.pdf

References

Aguzzoni L, Langus G & Motta M (2013) The effect of EU antitrust investigations and fines on a firm's valuation. *The Journal of Industrial Economics* 61(2): 290–338

Ball R & Brown P (1968) An empirical evaluation of accounting income numbers. *Journal of Accounting Research* 6(2): 159–178

Beverley L (2007) *Stock market event studies and competition commission inquiries*. CCP Working Paper No. 08-16, University of East Anglia

Bianconi M, Richards D & Yuan H (2015) *Equity prices and cartel activity*. Discussion Papers Series, Department of Economics, Tufts University

Bos I, Letterie W & Scherl N (2019) Industry impact of cartels: Evidence from the stock market. *Journal of Competition Law & Economics* 15(2-3): 358-379

Bosch JC & Eckard Jr EW (1991) The profitability of price fixing: Evidence from stock market reaction to federal indictments. *The Review of Economics and Statistics* 73(2): 309-317

Brown SJ & Warner JB (1985) Using daily stock returns: The case of event studies. *Journal of Financial Economics* 14(1): 3-31

Campbell JY, Lo AW & MacKinlay AC (1997) *The econometrics of financial markets*. Princeton, New Jersey: Princeton University Press

Cheung AWK (2011) Do stock investors value corporate sustainability? Evidence from an event study. *Journal of Business Ethics* 99(2): 145-165

Cichello M & Lamdin DJ (2006) Event studies and the analysis of antitrust. *International Journal of the Economics of Business* 13(2): 229-245

CCSA (Competition Commission of South Africa) (2009) *Annual Report 2008/2009*. Accessed November 2020, http://www.compcom.co.za/wp-content/uploads/2019/10/annual-report-2008-2009.pdf

Competition Tribunal (2013) *Matter between Competition Commission and Aveng Limited (Case ref: 016931)*. Accessed November 2020, https://www.saflii.org/za/cases/ZACT/2013/76.html

Competition Tribunal (2016) *Matter between Competition Commission v WBHO Construction (Pty) Ltd (CR234Feb16/SA049Jun16)*. Accessed November 2020, https://www.saflii.org/za/cases/ZACT/2017/51.html

Connor JM (2008) *Global price fixing* (2nd updated and revised edition). Berlin, Heidelberg: Springer

Corrado CJ (2011) Event studies: A methodology review. *Accounting and Finance* 51(1): 207-234

Dombrow J, Rodriguez M & Sirmans CF (2000) A complete nonparametric event study approach. *Review of Quantitative Finance and Accounting* 14(4): 361-380

Fama EF (1970) Efficient capital markets: A review of theory and empirical works. *Journal of Finance* 25(2): 383-417

Fama EF, Fisher L, Jensen MC & Roll R (1969) The adjustment of stock prices to new information. *International Economic Review* 10(1): 1-21

Gopane TJ & Mmotla RM (2019) Stock market reaction to mega-sport events: Evidence from South Africa and Morocco. *International Journal of Sport Finance* 14(4): 193-210

Günster A & Van Dijk M (2016) The impact of European antitrust policy: Evidence from the stock market. *International Review of Law and Economics* 46: 20-33

Hartzenberg T (2006) Competition policy and practice in South Africa: Promoting competition for development symposium on competition law and policy in developing countries. *Northwestern Journal of International Law and Business* 26(3): 667-686

Jeng JL (2015) *Analyzing event statistics in corporate finance: Methodologies, evidences, and critiques*. New York: Palgrave Macmillan

Johannesburg Stock Exchange Limited (2020) *What is the JSE All-Share Index*. Johannesburg: JSE. Accessed June 2020, https://www.jse.co.za/grow-my-wealth/what-is-the-jse-all-share-index

Klassen RD & McLaughlin CP (1996) The impact of environmental management on firm performance. *Management Science* 42(8): 1199–1214

Kothari SP & Warner J (2007) *Econometrics of event studies*. In B Espen Eckbo (Ed.) *Handbook of corporate finance: Empirical corporate finance*. Amsterdam: Elsevier/North-Holland

Langus G & Motta M (2007) *The effect of EU antitrust investigations and fines on a firm's valuation*. CEPR Discussion Papers No. 6176, Centre for Economic Policy Research

Lundgren T & Olsson R (2010) Environmental incidents and firm value – international evidence using a multi-factor event study framework. *Applied Financial Economics* 20(16): 1293–1307

MacKinlay AC (1997) Event studies in competition and finance. *Journal of Economic Literature* 35(1): 13–39

Maphwanya R (2017) Cartel likelihood, duration and deterrence in South Africa. In J Klaaren, S Roberts & I Valodia (Eds) *Competition law and economic regulation: Addressing market power in Southern Africa*. Johannesburg: Wits University Press

Mariuzzo F, Ormosi PL & Majied Z (2020) Fines and reputational sanctions: The case of cartels. *International Journal of Industrial Organization* 69: 102584

McWilliams A & Siegel D (1997) Event studies in management research: Theoretical and empirical issues. *Academy of Management Journal* 40(3): 626–657

Motta M (2004) *Competition policy: Theory and practice*. Cambridge: Cambridge University Press. DOI:10.1017/CBO9780511804038

Nkosi WW & Boshoff WH (2022) Characteristics of prosecuted cartels and cartel enforcement in South Africa. *Review of Industrial Organization* 60(3): 327–360

Peterson P (1989) Event studies: A review of issues and methodology. *Journal of Business and Economics* 28(3): 36–66

Saleh W (2007) Investors reaction to dividend announcements: Parametric versus nonparametric approach. *Applied Financial Economics Letters* 3(3): 169–179

Tamechika H (2020) Effects of environment-related stimulus policies: An event study approach. *Case Studies on Transport Policy* 8(3): 895–900

Van den Broek S, Kemp RG, Verschoor WF & De Vries AC (2012) Reputational penalties to firms in antitrust investigations. *Journal of Competition Law and Economics* 8(2): 231–258

Vaughan L (2001) *Statistical methods for the information professional: A practical, painless approach to understanding, using, and interpreting statistics*. Medford, New Jersey: Information Today, Inc.

Wise M (2004) Competition law and policy in South Africa. *OECD Journal: Competition Law and Policy* 5(4): 7–69

Appendix A

Table A8.1 Summary of cumulative abnormal return results

Company	Case and duration (years)	Method	Investigation announcement						Penalty announcement			
			Event window (–5.5)		Event window (–5.10)				Event window (–5.5)		Event window (–5.10)	
			CAR (%)	P-value	CAR (%)	P-value			CAR (%)	P-value	CAR (%)	P-value
ArcelorMittal	Case 1 (8)	Parametric	–13.0007**	0.015	–9.448	0.177			–6.491	0.342	–4.032	0.612
		Theil	–20.154***	0	–23.016***	0			–1.489	0.495	0.004	0.990
Aveng	Case 1 (1)	Parametric	13.856*	0.076	10.489	0.334			2.751	0.792	17.710	0.214
		Theil	1.436*	0.065	2.593	0.331			1.490	0.743	8.106	0.191
	Case 2 (4)	Parametric	1.203	0.886	6.053	0.583			–7.804	0.326	–6.755	0.453
		Theil	–3.982	0.362	–1.292	0.82			–2.737	0.379	–1.614	0.646
	Case 3 (3)	Parametric	–2.998	0.6	–0.176	0.979			–2.728	0.519	–3.669	0.584
		Theil	–0.726	0.771	0.597	0.837			–0.093	0.589	–1.730	0.551
Basil Read	Case 1 (4)	Parametric	–8.244	0.12	–9.141	0.182			2.993	0.568	2.509	0.667
		Theil	–4.304	0.129	–5.063*	0.093			0.524	0.799	–0.381	0.874
KAP Industrial	Case 1 (9)	Parametric	15.213	0.429	15.22	0.427			2.105	0.765	11.367	0.188
		Theil	5.172	0.533	4.523	0.585			0.131	0.965	3.705	0.306
Murray & Roberts	Case 1 (4)	Parametric	–2.67	0.52	–7.364	0.32			–2.635	0.768	–1.534	0.878
		Theil	–0.492	0.714	–2.548	0.435			–0.071	0.985	0.801	0.853
	Case 2 (6)	Parametric	–6.567	0.34	–8.31	0.374			–3.962	0.439	–10.273	0.317
		Theil	–2.833	0.334	–3.859	0.53			–2.620	0.237	–5.684	0.206
Oceana	Case 1 (4)	Parametric	–8.776*	0.051	–0.939	0.903			–4.384	0.538	–6.911	0.340
		Theil	–5.429**	0.008	–2.228	0.512			–1.907	0.714	–1.142	0.545

Company	Case and duration (years)	Method	Investigation announcement				Penalty announcement			
			Event window (−5,5)		Event window (−5,10)		Event window (−5,5)		Event window (−5,10)	
			CAR (%)	P-value	CAR (%)	P-value	CAR (%)	P-value	CAR (%)	P-value
Omnia	Case 1 (13)	Parametric	−1.104	0.722	0.27	0.937	−4.838	0.418	−3.662	0.551
		Theil	0.106	0.936	1.018	0.502	−2.482	0.345	−2.117	0.431
PPC	Case 1 (11)	Parametric	5.067	0.520	3.301	0.686	−0.742	0.873	3.432	0.542
		Theil	2.708	0.519	2.256	0.424	−0.756	0.709	0.839	0.730
Raubex	Case 1 (4)	Parametric	6.894	0.398	9.904	0.236	−4.703	0.446	−2.635	0.723
		Theil	2.762	0.404	3.662	0.276	−1.650	0.530	−0.446	0.888
RMB Holdings	Case 1 (3)	Parametric	−3.112	0.792	0.014	0.999	−3.710	0.234	−5.037	0.220
		Theil	0.24	0.961	2.123	0.704	−1.328	0.279	−2.154	0.208
Sasol	Case 1 (2)	Parametric	4.36	0.261	1.37	0.781	−8.117	0.196	−8.622	0.288
		Theil	0.538	0.749	−0.509	0.798	−4.166	0.135	−4.720	0.197
	Case 2 (10)	Parametric	2.582	0.722	2.636	0.736	3.629	0.367	8.809	0.140
		Theil	1.798	0.571	2.128	0.532	0.900	0.703	2.723	0.284
Stefanutti	Case 1 (2)	Parametric	−2.636	0.499	0.23	0.961	−3.389**	0.040	−4.552	0.188
		Theil	−0.387	0.758	−2.252	0.632	−0.918	0.164	−1.150	0.435
	Case 2 (4)	Parametric	0.869	0.918	0.884	0.921	16.196	0.127	21.56*	0.091
		Theil	0.947	0.798	1.202	0.756	9.293*	0.053	12.603**	0.030
Steinhoff	Case 1 (9)	Parametric	−3.544	0.539	−10.11	0.124	0.789	0.822	−5.142	0.273
		Theil	−1.472	0.546	−4.32	0.114	0.618	0.689	−2.025	0.344

Company	Case and duration (years)	Method	Investigation announcement				Penalty announcement			
			Event window (–5.5)		Event window (–5.10)		Event window (–5.5)		Event window (–5.10)	
			CAR (%)	P-value	CAR (%)	P-value	CAR (%)	P-value	CAR (%)	P-value
Tiger Brands	Case 1 (3)	Parametric	3.193	0.387	–1.159	0.793	–3.037	0.519	–3.093	0.584
		Theil	2.643*	0.083	0.186	0.927	–0.116	0.954	0.415	0.865
	Case 2 (1)	Parametric	–11.403	0.16	–13.924	0.111	–2.243	0.790	–0.722	0.937
		Theil	–4.79	0.183	–5.869	0.131	–0.357	0.921	0.506	0.898
WBHO	Case 1 (4)	Parametric	–7.166	0.429	–8.319	0.364	3.754	0.403	4.484	0.384
		Theil	–2.235	0.57	–1.966	0.623	0.941	0.667	2.337	0.341
	Case 2 (5)	Parametric	–0.472	0.402	–7.057	0.299	–10.163	0.044	–10.953	0.122
		Theil	–1.547	0.561	–1.855	0.525	–3.986*	0.080	–3.957	0.229
	Case 3 (7)	Parametric	–0.472	0.402	–7.057	0.299	–3.007	0.644	–4.712	0.463
		Theil	–1.547	0.561	–1.855	0.525	–1.077	0.712	–1.807	0.530

*Significant at 10%; ** Significant at 5%; ***Significant at 1%.
(Source: Author's compilation from Stata output)

9 Developing thinking in merger assessment: Reflections from recent UK experience

Genna Robb

A theme of recent work on the effectiveness of merger control has been the need for competition policy to evolve in the light of changing markets and the risk of under-enforcement, particularly in digital markets. For example, the Furman Report (Digital Competition Expert Panel 2019) noted that while, in the 10 years to 2018, the five largest digital firms have made over 400 acquisitions globally, none of these was blocked by competition authorities and very few had conditions attached to them. Ex-post evaluations of merger decisions and empirical studies have suggested there is scope for greater caution regarding the likely efficiency benefits of mergers and the ability of entry to offset the anticompetitive effects of otherwise problematic mergers.

This chapter aims to reflect on some aspects of the economics of merger assessment, which have been the subject of recent discussion, and examine how the approach to these issues is evolving in United Kingdom (UK) merger control. It is particularly concerned with elements of merger assessment that are relevant to the assessment of dynamic markets and with digital platforms. Under three main themes, it will consider some of the recent literature, commentary and ex-post studies before analysing cases considered by the UK's Competition and Markets Authority (CMA) and Competition Appeals Tribunal (CAT)[1] and drawing out issues, challenges and learnings on each theme. The aim is not to provide a full literature review on each issue, but to highlight recent debates and reflect on how some of the relevant issues have been tackled in cases.

The chapter will proceed as follows. First, it will look at how UK authorities have evaluated horizontal mergers in markets with changing competitive dynamics and how the inherent uncertainty in such forward-looking assessments has been dealt with. It will focus particularly on highly concentrated markets or where there is evidence of pre-existing market power, including in mergers involving digital platforms. Second, recent vertical mergers will be reviewed, with a particular focus on the consideration of new or non-traditional mechanisms for foreclosure and practical approaches to the assessment of incentives for foreclosure. Finally, it will consider the approach to evaluating the likelihood of entry and expansion in recent cases. In conclusion, the chapter will draw out some cross-cutting themes and lessons.

Potential competition and dealing with uncertainty

An important recent debate in merger policy has been how to better capture the potential for horizontal mergers to have a harmful effect on innovation and future competition. Federico et al. (2020) explain that the unilateral innovation effects arising from a merger are closely analogous to unilateral price effects. They describe what are known as 'business-stealing effects' where, as part of the dynamic competitive process between rivals, firms gain customers at the expense of rivals, by offering them better value. Mergers are more likely to lead to higher prices (or lower levels of quality and service) where internalised business-stealing effects are high, where firms have competed closely to win customers from one another pre-merger. This is because the merger will reduce the pressure on the merged firm to improve its offering to customers. In the case of innovation, business-stealing is through undertaking 'risky investments to develop new and improved products or production processes' and, similarly, innovation is more likely to be harmed where this is an important feature of competition between the merging firms.

Federico et al. (2020) explain three scenarios in which innovation competition may be affected by a merger. The third of these – where a large firm with a dominant position may acquire a smaller rival with the potential to be an innovative or disruptive competitor in future – presents a particular challenge for competition authorities: it involves an attempt to assess the potential for competition in the future in circumstances where current or historical information may provide limited insight into how competition is likely to evolve.

Dominant incumbent firms may have strong incentives to acquire nascent competitors who could grow to become significant rivals.

> As a general principle, the greater and more durable is the market power of an incumbent firm, the larger is the payoff from preventing that firm from acquiring the smaller firms that, if left to grow on their own, would become its strongest challengers. (Shapiro 2018)

Research commissioned by the CMA into past UK merger decisions in the digital sector found that Amazon, Facebook and Google acquired 5, 6 and 16 companies per year on average between 2008 and 2018, and that the targets were typically very young firms, four years old or younger in nearly 60% of cases (Lear 2019). This suggests that many of the target firms were not necessarily well established as strong competitors at the time of the merger but could have become so in future.

These concerns are particularly relevant in digital markets. A report by the Stigler Centre on digital platforms explains that one of the challenges for merger enforcement with respect to digital platforms is that such platforms are often in winner-take-all/most markets, meaning that competition is largely for the future or 'leapfrog' competition (Stigler Center 2019). In such markets, competition from nascent firms could be an important source of competition and the acquisition of such a firm by a dominant incumbent may have a significant impact on competition, even though the entrant is small.

As noted above, one challenge for competition authorities is how to evidence and assess whether a target is likely to be an important competitor in future. In its study of past merger investigations, Lear (2019) found that in assessing potential competition (most notably in the Facebook/Instagram and Google/Waze mergers), the UK competition authorities had considered the right evidence and found that the target firms had been growing and had promising business models and expansion plans. Nonetheless, they ultimately dismissed this evidence due to uncertainty around the future growth of the target. This highlights one of the main challenges with assessing potential competition theories of harm (ToH):

> Rarely, if ever, will the Authorities find conclusive evidence of future growth: potential competition ToHs will always entail a certain degree of uncertainty. If the Authorities wish to pursue this type of ToH in the future, then they should be willing to accept a greater degree of uncertainty in their evaluations. (Lear 2019)

In a similar vein, Shapiro (2020) makes the following argument in the case of potential competition:

> Sound competition policy would tolerate some false positives – blocking mergers involving targets, only to find that they do not grow to challenge the incumbent – in order to avoid some false negatives – allowing mergers that eliminate targets that would indeed have grown to challenge the dominant incumbent. (Shapiro 2020)

Merger control always involves balancing the risk of over- or under-enforcement. However, the danger of false negatives may be particularly acute in the case of some digital platform markets as high barriers to entry and network effects may make it unlikely that entry will occur in future in a manner that is sufficient to undo the harm due to the merger.

The CMA's revised merger guidelines, published in early 2021, talk about the challenge of assessing dynamic theories of harm in the context of uncertainty about the outcome of investments and innovation efforts absent the merger (CMA 2021, paras 5.20–5.23). They explain that the CMA will consider evidence of any direct response by an incumbent firm to the threat of entry or expansion but also evidence on their incentive to respond to such a threat. They go on to explain that the elimination of a competitor that is making efforts to enter or expand may cause harm to competition, even if the entrant is ultimately unsuccessful, if the removal of the threat of entry could lead to a significant reduction in innovation by other firms.

Merger assessments by the CMA

Illumina/PacBio

This reflects the way the CMA has assessed recent mergers. In Illumina/PacBio[2], the CMA considered whether the acquisition by Illumina (a global leader in DNA sequencing) of smaller competitor Pacific Biosciences of California (PacBio) could harm competition. Illumina was by far the largest provider of DNA sequencing, with an estimated market share of 80–90% globally, using what is termed 'short-read' DNA sequencing technology. PacBio had developed 'long-read' technology – a different kind of technology from the incumbent – and had a very small market share of less than 5% worldwide.

The CMA's assessment focused on a few key questions. First, the assessment considered the extent to which long-read and short-read technology competed with one another and how closely they were likely to compete in future. It found that, although in some instances the different types of sequencing were used for different applications, half of customers already found that long-read and short-read technology were substitutable for at least some of their work. The evidence suggested that over time, long read was presenting a growing constraint on short read. Internal documents from Illumina showed that it reacted and responded to what it saw as a competitive threat from long-read technology.

Second, the possibility of Illumina developing its own long-read technology, in direct competition with PacBio, was considered. Internal documents suggested that Illumina was keen to develop or acquire long-read technology. The CMA considered that, while there was some uncertainty about if or when Illumina would enter the long-read segment, it had a clear incentive to enter in order to protect its strong position in DNA sequencing. There were high barriers to entry, but Illumina was well placed to overcome these relative to other potential entrants. The CMA also considered that the threat of entry by Illumina could have spurred innovation by other competitors.

Finally, the CMA considered whether Illumina and PacBio would have competed closely in future. Despite the uncertainty, considering the evidence, the CMA thought it was likely that they would compete closely. PacBio had recently improved its technology and customers had given positive feedback on these improvements. CMA analysis of PacBio's patents found that it was ranked highly in terms of its External Competitive Impact3, which measures how often the patent is cited in later patents and the global market size protected by the patent. This supported the finding that PacBio had an attractive product. Furthermore, Illumina's internal documents showed that it thought PacBio would become more of a threat in future. The CMA provisionally[4] found that the parties would have been important innovation competitors of each other and so the merger was likely to result in a loss in incentives to innovate. Other competitors were provisionally found to offer only a limited competitive constraint and were considered insufficient to offset the loss in competition that would result from the merger.

PayPal/iZettle

In PayPal/iZettle[5], the situation was slightly different. Although PayPal was a large incumbent provider of online payment services, its intended target, iZettle, was active in the adjacent market for mobile point-of-sale (mPOS) services in which PayPal already had a presence. mPOS services consist of a card reader that is connected, physically or by Bluetooth, to an app downloaded onto a smartphone or tablet, which enables merchants to accept card payments. It was introduced as an alternative to traditional POS services, which operate through stand-alone devices. The question was not whether mPOS devices would compete more closely with online payment services in future, but about two other scenarios: first, whether, absent the merger, PayPal would have become a stronger competitor in the mPOS market (in which it had historically been perceived as a weak competitor) in competition with iZettle; and second, whether PayPal and iZettle would have competed in an emerging 'omnichannel' market for integrating the two types of services to allow customers to take all payments through a single provider.

As in the assessment of Illumina/PacBio, the parties' internal documents were an important source of evidence on their future plans. PayPal's internal documents showed that it wanted a strong mPOS offering in order to be able to compete in the omnichannel market. The CMA considered that it had the incentive and resources to be able to find a way to achieve this and that there were a range of ways in which this could have been achieved, for example through acquisition or partnership. However, it also found that iZettle was unlikely to expand much in the omnichannel market, based on its current plans, and that there were several other competitors growing rapidly in mPOS or with entry plans and which would have presented a meaningful constraint. There was also some constraint from traditional POS providers. In this case, therefore, the CMA found that the merger would not be likely to lead to a substantial lessening of competition.

Meta/GIPHY

In Meta/GIPHY[6], the CMA considered whether the merger could lead to a loss of potential competition in display advertising.[7] Display advertising is where advertisers pay for their content to be displayed within defined ad units on a particular web page or app. This is distinct from search advertising, where advertisers pay for their company website to be linked to a specific search word or phrase so that it appears in relevant search engine results (CMA 2020). Meta is a multi-sided platform offering social media services and messaging as well as digital advertising. The CMA found in its digital advertising market study in 2019 that Meta had market power in display advertising. GIPHY was the world's leading provider of free GIFs and GIF stickers, which are used on social media platforms. However, relevant to the potential competition between Meta and GIPHY was the fact that GIPHY had introduced a product called paid alignment, which provided advertisers with GIF-based advertising. This was introduced in 2017 and had been used by a number of leading international consumer brands. The CMA considered whether GIPHY's paid alignment model had the potential to compete with display advertising.

Again, the CMA looked into the parties' plans and other internal documents. GIPHY's forecasts did not envisage it becoming anything like the size and scale of Meta in the medium term and there was considerable uncertainty around the success of paid alignment. However, the CMA considered that GIPHY's efforts to innovate and monetise its services before the merger were valuable, even if paid alignment was not certain to be successful. The reason given was that this provided a form of dynamic competition, which could have spurred further innovation and competitive responses from Meta and GIPHY itself. In the context of Meta's significant market power in display advertising and GIPHY's strong position as a leading provider of an important social media engagement tool, and given the network effects present in social media and high barriers to entry in display advertising, the CMA found that this loss of dynamic competition was likely to lead to a substantial lessening of competition (SLC).

Meta asked the Competition Appeal Tribunal to review the CMA's decision on a number of grounds, including challenging its finding that the merger would lead to a horizontal SLC due to a loss of dynamic competition.[8] The CAT acknowledged that an assessment of dynamic competition is bound to involve uncertainty: 'Assessment of impairment to dynamic competition will almost always involve consideration of expectations (that is, an outcome with a more than 50% chance).'[9] Overall, the CAT found that the CMA had correctly directed itself to the test it had to apply. According to the CAT, whether there will be a loss of dynamic competition should be assessed by considering four factors. First, the motives of the merging firms should be investigated. For example, is the acquiring firm seeking to kill off a rival? In the case at hand, it considered that although GIPHY was not in a strong position and its value was declining, it had done a lot of the hard work to establish the paid alignment model. Also, in spite of challenges, the CMA was justified in concluding that it would be able to further grow the model.

For Meta's part, the evidence showed that it was prepared to pay a premium for GIPHY and that part of the reason for this was its need to ensure that its social media platforms continued to have access to a supply of GIFS. However, the monetisation of paid alignment was also part of Meta's rationale for the merger. The CMA's report found that GIPHY's paid alignment was likely to compete closely with Meta's display advertising services for several reasons. It found that paid alignment was closer to display advertising than search advertising as it was less likely to directly prompt a purchase of the product and more likely to increase the user's brand awareness. In addition, ads were not generated by search terms; instead, users experienced the ads selected for and displayed to them by GIPHY. Other evidence, including from one of GIPHY's largest customers, suggested that GIPHY and Meta were likely to compete for display advertising budgets. The CAT noted that, while Meta did not acknowledge this competition between the services, it accepted that paid alignment could be monetised', which is tantamount to the same thing'[10] as advertising spend is ultimately limited. Also, if more is spent on paid alignment, then less would be spent on other forms of advertising, particularly those that are close substitutes.

The second factor that the CAT deems relevant is the market's evaluation of the value of the dynamic element. If there is a lot of interest in the target firm from other market participants because of its plans, this may be an indicator of its valuable dynamic potential. GIPHY had the support of its investors to continue developing paid alignment, but the CAT considered the evidence suggested it was a business that was declining in value.

Third, the contestability of the market is relevant to the assessment as it indicates whether other entrants could easily replicate the position of the target. The CAT considered that GIPHY had generated a substantial user base, which would be hard to replicate.

Fourth, the ability to monetise the dynamic element should be assessed. The CAT found that there was considerable advertiser enthusiasm for paid alignment, but that this had to be set against difficulties GIPHY would face in growing the business, such as lack of funds. The CMA's decision had considered these factors but nonetheless came to the conclusion that GIPHYs efforts to monetise its service were valuable to dynamic competition.

Analysis

These cases demonstrate some of the challenges in assessing the impact of mergers on potential competition. In all the cases, the acquiring firm was a large, established firm and the target firm was a smaller entrant, making it difficult to use backward-looking evidence of rivalry to inform the assessment of the likely impact of the merger on competition in the future. In such circumstances, it may be appropriate to place more weight on evidence from customers (in cases where they are likely to have an informed view of the dynamic trends in competition) and internal documents, especially the merging parties' future plans. However, this may not prove informative in all cases, and a lack of documented concern by the acquiring firm about the potential impact of the rival on future profits may not preclude such an impact from being possible or even likely. Uncertainty is inherently a feature of such assessments, but evidence that sheds light on the incentives of the merging firms is likely to prove helpful, as discussed by the CAT in Meta/GIPHY.

Vertical effects

Another area that has been the subject of debate in the literature is the approach to assessing the vertical effects of mergers. Salop (2018) suggests that there has been under-enforcement with respect to vertical mergers in the US, arguing that Chicago-school narratives, which cast vertical mergers as largely benign and efficiency-enhancing, have been the source of an inappropriately permissive approach. Salop (2018) argues that this approach rests on three main claims that do not have a strong basis in economics.

First is the argument that vertical mergers simply realign vertical relationships: a vertically integrated firm may choose to self-supply and provide less of the input to competing downstream firms, but downstream competitors will simply purchase more from other suppliers in response. The situation may be different though where there is existing market power and barriers to entry. In these circumstances, unintegrated rivals may face lower input volumes or higher prices.

Second, it is often claimed that a monopolist cannot gain additional profit by monopolising a second vertically related market and so has no incentive to foreclose rivals. However, this result only holds under extreme assumptions, including that there is a monopolist upstream and that the downstream market is perfectly competitive. In other circumstances, vertical mergers can lead to anti-competitive effects. For example, a vertical merger may provide a firm that has market power upstream with the opportunity to acquire a downstream firm with the potential to enter upstream itself or to sponsor entry. The incentive for foreclosure downstream arises from the need to protect its incumbency position in the upstream market.

Third, the elimination of double marginalisation (EDM) is often used as a defence of vertical mergers, as it is claimed a vertically integrated monopolist will charge a price equal to marginal cost for the upstream input, which will lead to lower downstream prices. There are a number of scenarios in which this is unlikely to be an optimal strategy for the monopolist (Baker et al. 2020). Kwoka and Slade (2020) highlight that, while empirical studies have shown that vertical integration can reduce costs and yield benefits to producers and consumers, this has usually been in competitive or monopolistically competitive settings and there is little empirical evidence about the outcome in imperfect market settings.

Other recent papers highlight the need for careful consideration of the competitive effects of vertical mergers. Beck and Scott Morton (2020) consider the empirical evidence on the welfare effects of vertical mergers. They find that it demonstrates a variety of effects, including foreclosure and efficiencies, and that this suggests that the effects of mergers should be considered on a case-by-case basis. Motta and Fumagalli (2020) consider a dynamic rationale for vertical foreclosure where a vertically integrated incumbent faces the threat of entry in the downstream market in the current period and in the upstream market in the following period. They demonstrate that the incumbent may have an incentive to foreclose a more efficient downstream rival, sacrificing profits in the short term, in order to deter the threat of upstream entry. Even if upstream entry cannot be prevented, they demonstrate that it may be optimal to foreclose the downstream competitor. The aim is to obtain a downstream monopoly and use this position to extract rents from the more efficient upstream entrant. The conduct of the incumbent is able to affect the future market structure and results in higher profits.

Other studies highlight the need for vertical merger control to adapt to the challenges of digital markets. In the UK, a review by the Digital Competition Expert Panel (2019) concluded that it would be appropriate to reconsider the presumption that non-horizontal mergers will typically be benign and broaden the consideration of anti-competitive incentives to account for the fact that 'digital companies often seek to maximise growth over profits for many years'. It also recommended that attention should be given to the relevance of data assets in digital market competition.

E.CA Economics (2022) explains that since digital markets often involve two-sided platforms and ecosystems that are changing rapidly, it can be difficult to make a distinction between horizontal and vertical concerns.[11] However, the authors argue that the issue of 'killer acquisitions' has an important digital dimension. They give an example of a social media network buying an input provider to prevent it from expanding into social networking or to deny rival social networks an essential input. Having studied four recent CMA cases in detail, they find that 'the CMA (and other competition authorities) might have a tendency to pursue weak, less well-defined horizontal effects over the potentially stronger, more logical vertical effects of the same merger' (E.CA Economics 2022).

In addition to the fact that traditional thinking on the effects of vertical mergers may not be appropriate in digital markets, traditional tools for assessing these effects may be less useful. One tool that is often used for assessing the incentive to foreclose is vertical arithmetic, whereby the potential benefit to the incumbent of foreclosure in one market is quantified and contrasted with the potential losses in the other. In the case of input foreclosure, for example, the incumbent will likely lose some sales and profits upstream but gain downstream as customers divert purchases to the merged entity. A purely static assessment of these costs and benefits may miss important dynamic elements of the incentive to foreclose such as those discussed above. Further, the benefits of some partial foreclosure strategies that may be relevant in digital markets, such as foreclosure through incompatibility or the use of data, may be particularly difficult to quantify. Foreclosure strategies may not be implemented in isolation and to consider their costs and benefits in such a way may therefore also lead to an incomplete understanding of their likely effect.

The CMA's Merger Assessment Guidelines (2021) indicate that, where appropriate, it will take a broad approach to considering the elements, both short-term and long-term, which may influence the incentive to foreclose and that a robust quantification of the benefits and costs of foreclosure is unlikely to be possible, or appropriate, in all cases.[12]

The guidelines also consider the potential for anti-competitive vertical effects to arise as a result of the merger firm gaining access to rivals' data:

> Another possible concern is that the merged entity may gain access to commercially sensitive information of its rivals through its role as their supplier or customer. Depending on the industry context, this could include data on specific sales and bids, overall pricing strategies and algorithms, technical product specifications or innovation plans. This could allow the merged entity to compete less aggressively, [for example,] with prices or product specifications only marginally better than its rivals and may also deter rivals from innovating. The CMA may assess this concern as a separate theory of harm, or as part of a broader foreclosure theory of harm.[13]

Relevant merger assessments by the CMA
Tobii/Smartbox

In Tobii/Smartbox[14], the CMA considered the potential for anticompetitive vertical effects due to the merger in the market for augmentative and assistive communication (AAC) solutions, which are communication aids catering to the needs of those with communication difficulties such as people with congenital disabilities such as cerebral palsy. The CMA considered that the 'end-users of the products supplied by the Parties are unusually dependent on technology to communicate and are therefore particularly vulnerable to any deterioration in the way the market for AAC solutions operates, and consequently can be regarded as vulnerable consumers.' The solutions consist of several components including hardware, software and a means of access such as an eye gaze camera, and both parties supplied complete solutions to customers as well as supplied individual components to some of their competitors.

In addition to concerns about the horizontal effects of the merger in the market for dedicated AAC solutions, the CMA considered the merger would lead to a substantial lessening of competition due to vertical effects. First, the CMA found that Smartbox's 'the Grid' had a strong position in the upstream market for the supply of AAC software and that the merged entity would have the ability and incentive to use that position to foreclose downstream competitors by making their access to the Grid more expensive or through deteriorating its quality. It considered that the constraint from alternative software providers was weak and that downstream rivals would not be able to switch away from the Grid without significantly weakening their competitive position in the supply of dedicated AAC solutions. It found that it was likely to be a profitable strategy for the merged entity since customers would switch from rivals' dedicated AAC solutions to the parties' solution.

Second, it found that the merged entity would likely also have the ability and incentive to foreclose competitors of Tobii's eye gaze cameras through limiting the compatibility of the Grid with rival cameras. It found there were limited routes to market for eye gaze cameras other than through dedicated AAC solutions based on the Grid software and that customers would be likely to switch to Tobii's cameras if rival cameras have limited compatibility with the Grid. The CMA also found that this was likely to be profitable as dedicated AAC solution providers were unlikely to switch to a different type of software. This could lead to reduced innovation in eye gaze cameras, higher prices and the worsening of price and quality of AAC solutions, of which eye gaze cameras are a key component.

The parties asked the CAT to examine the CMA's decision on a number of grounds, including that the CMA's finding of an SLC as a result of vertical effects was unreasonable or irrational.[15] The CAT referenced its decision in ICE/Trayport, which clarified its view that:

> vertical mergers can and do raise competition concerns. Whether a
> particular merger is likely to give rise to an SLC is fact specific. Here we

do not consider that there is any special elevated evidential burden on the CMA in deciding whether this merger gives rise to a SLC.[16]

In respect of the input foreclosure theory of harm, the CAT found that the CMA was justified in finding that Smartbox had a strong position in the upstream market due to its control of Grid. It did not accept Tobii's submission that an input must be 'indispensable, critical or "must have"' in order for there to be ability to foreclose. However, it considered that the CMA had not fully evaluated the potential impact of partial foreclosure as it had only asked customers and competitors what would happen if Grid was no longer available, and not what they would do if it increased in price or worsened compatibility. It therefore did not have information on whether suppliers would pass through any increases in the price of Grid to customers. This meant it could not properly assess if the merged firm had the ability to engage in partial foreclosure through an increase in the wholesale price of a Grid licence. It had, however, gathered sufficient evidence to conclude that the merged entity would have the ability to engage in partial foreclosure through reducing the extent to which Grid supported rival dedicated AAC hardware.

In terms of the incentive to foreclose, again the CAT felt that in this case the CMA's enquiries had not gone far enough, as it had based its analysis on total rather than partial foreclosure. The CMA had calculated that for total foreclosure to be profitable, 10–20% of the lost upstream sales of the Grid would need to be recaptured through downstream customers switching away from rival dedicated AAC solutions towards the parties' dedicated AAC solution. The CMA argued that the critical level of diversion would be lower in a partial foreclosure scenario. The reason it gave was that the higher price charged for the Grid (in the case of partial foreclosure based on price) or engaging in less software development and support (in the case of partial foreclosure based on degrading compatibility with rival hardware) would lead to gains upstream relative to a total foreclosure strategy. It also contended that the level of diversion was likely to be high since the Grid was a key driver of sales for dedicated AAC solutions. In this case, the CAT considered the CMA could have asked rival suppliers of dedicated AAC solutions how they would have reacted to either of the partial foreclosure scenarios. It also stated that the evidence in relation to total foreclosure was not sufficient to conclude that there was an incentive for partial foreclosure. For the same reasons, the CAT found that the CMA did not have sufficient evidence to conclude on the effect of foreclosure on competition.

With respect to customer foreclosure, the CAT found that the CMA had sufficient grounds for concluding that the merged entity would have the ability and incentive to foreclose rival providers of eye gaze cameras and that this would result in an SLC. It confirmed that the CMA was not required to quantify the SLC and recognised that the CMA's competition concerns regarding the merger were not confined to price but included the impact on other competitive parameters such as product range, customer service levels and the development of new products.

Meta/GIPHY

In Meta/GIPHY[17], in addition to the potential competition theory of harm discussed above, the CMA also considered whether the merger could have vertical effects on competition in the supply of social media arising from foreclosure in the supply of GIFs. The CMA found that Meta had a significant share of the social media market in the UK (73% in 2020) and may have been able to disadvantage its rivals in social media by limiting their access to GIPHY in some way. This could either be through preventing them from accessing GIPHY or worsening the terms on which they were able to do so. The CMA also considered whether Meta would have an incentive to disadvantage rivals by reprioritising innovation and development of GIPHY's services towards the requirements of its own platforms, rather than rival social media platforms or by requiring them to provide more data (for example, on individual or aggregate user behaviour) as a condition of accessing GIPHY.

The CMA found that Meta would have the ability to foreclose rival social media platforms. Based on evidence from industry players and internal documents, GIFs were found to be an important feature of social media platforms, particularly in relation to encouraging user engagement. Apart from GIPHY, there was only one other significant provider of GIF-based services, Tenor, which was owned by Google. In addition, the CMA found that the acquisition of GIPHY would give Meta access to data that could place its rivals at a competitive disadvantage if they continue to use GIPHY. For example, Meta could use the data to analyse activity on rival apps in such a way that would allow it to identify competitive threats or react to emerging market trends before other rivals. Although GIPHY's data may be incrementally small compared to Meta's existing databases, the CMA found that GIPHY's data could refine Meta's existing market intelligence sources and that 'given Facebook's significant and enduring market power in social media and display advertising, and its existing significant data advantages, even a small data increment further strengthens its ability to limit competitive threats'.[18]

The CMA also considered that Meta had an incentive to foreclose rivals, as limiting the features available on a rival social media platform is likely to mean that users switch at least a proportion of their time to other platforms. Given that Meta had such a strong position in the market, customers were highly likely to switch to a Meta platform and this could lead their friends and family to switch as well. The CMA found that such a strategy could have a limited cost for Meta as, although GIPHY benefited from having a large user base which made its product more attractive to brand partners and other content creators, Meta's own platforms also had a large user base and so GIPHY would remain prominent and attractive. The CMA found, in this instance, that it was able to reach a view on the incentives to foreclose without conducting a quantitative assessment as the evidence showed that the benefits of foreclosure would be positive while the costs would be limited. It also considered that a quantitative assessment would not be feasible due to the difficulty of estimating the importance of network effects in both social media and GIF provision, and the complex and dynamic nature of the relevant markets. The CMA considered that the merger would have the effect of strengthening Meta's significant market power in social media and reducing competition faced from others.

Analysis

The literature and cases reviewed above illustrate the challenges in assessing vertical mergers and highlight that traditional thinking on the economics of vertical mergers may fail to capture the potential for harm to competition, particularly in the case of fast-changing and digital markets. In this context, a presumption that vertical mergers are likely to be benign is inappropriate, and that competition authorities should not hold vertical mergers to a higher standard when assessing whether they are likely to lead to a substantial lessening of competition. As noted by the CAT, each case needs to be considered on its own merits, and with reference to its own facts and evidence including where there may be efficiencies to consider.

In addition, the discussion above highlights some issues that are likely to be increasingly relevant in the context of mergers in digital markets. In particular is the need to carefully consider firms' incentives in a dynamic setting and move beyond the consideration of purely static effects. While in some cases the benefits and costs of foreclosure can be usefully estimated quantitatively, precise quantification of the incentive to foreclose is unlikely to be possible in many cases, particularly in more dynamic settings. However, as the CAT found in Tobii/Smartbox, gathering qualitative or quantitative evidence from customers and competitors on their likely reaction to partial foreclosure strategies may be informative. It is also important to consider a broad range of possible foreclosure strategies, particularly those concerning interoperability and the use of data.

Entry and expansion

A study commissioned by the CMA conducted ex-post evaluations of eight mergers reviewed by the Office of Fair Trading (OFT), Competition Commission (CC) and CMA[19] with the aim of drawing lessons about the CMA's assessment of entry and expansion in merger control.[20] It found a mixed picture: in three of the cases, the authorities predicted that entry or expansion would be timely, likely and sufficient to prevent an SLC, and the review showed that this prediction was realised following the merger. In the other five cases, for various reasons, the authorities' assessment had not proven to accurately predict market developments. In two cases out of the five, the authority placed significant weight on entry or expansion occurring and the review found this had not materialised and that prices had increased following the merger. In the third case, the authority placed weight on the barriers to entry and expansion being low but there was limited entry following the merger and the merging parties' prices increased. In the final two cases where the authority put weight on a particular firm entering or expanding, this did not materialise to the degree expected by the authority, although in one of the cases another firm expanded and appeared to constrain the merger parties.

The study found that in the cases considered, entry by suppliers already operating in closely related markets and entry or expansion by suppliers with new or innovative products were the main characteristics of entry that occurred. The authorities were better at predicting the former than the latter. In some cases, potential new entrants had been too optimistic about their prospects for entry.

The study presents a series of recommendations, including that the CMA should continue to consider carefully whether entry or expansion from closely related markets is likely following the merger. It states that '[i]n particular, specific evidence on factors such as costs of entry being relatively low, consumer preferences supporting such entry, and plans for entry being particularly well-progressed, all appeared to be important predictors of sufficient and timely entry or expansion.'[21] It further recommends that the CMA have more systematic regard for the possibility of entry or expansion by suppliers with innovative products.

The CMA's Merger Assessment Guidelines (2021, paras 8.30 and 7.19) reflect the need to make a careful assessment of potential entry and expansion:

> The CMA will seek to ensure that the evidence is robust when confronted with claims of entry or expansion being timely, likely and sufficient to prevent an SLC from arising. It is likely to place greater weight on detailed consideration of entry or expansion and previous experience of entry and expansion (including how frequent and recent it has been). (CMA 2021)

This approach has been followed in recent cases. For example, in CHC/Babcock, a merger in the market for oil and gas offshore transportation services in the UK (for example, helicopter services used to transport crew to and from oil and gas platforms)[22], the CMA found that there were a number of barriers to entry including significant set-up costs, the availability of hangar space, regulatory and licensing requirements, and customer preference for track record and experience. In addition, it considered that the recent decline in the industry, together with low margins and significant barriers to entry, would make entry unappealing. Potential entrants made it clear that they were not interested in entering the UK market, even if profitability were to improve. The CMA considered that the key factors to take into consideration were the timeliness of entry and its sufficiency to replace the constraint lost as a result of the merger.

The ex-post study commissioned by the CMA suggests that the UK competition authorities have, at times, placed too much weight on entry or expansion which either has not occurred, or has occurred later or in a more limited way than expected. Placing a greater emphasis on the entry plans and capabilities of firms in related or adjacent markets as well as evidence of past, successful entry is likely to be appropriate, as has been reflected in recent cases. In addition, the analysis in CHC/Babcock highlights the importance of considering the incentives for entry, as well as the barriers firms have to overcome. Even where barriers are surmountable, entry may be unlikely to occur if it will not lead to sufficient returns for a potential entrant.

Conclusions

While this discussion has focused on three distinct elements of merger assessment, there are a few cross-cutting themes that we can draw out. First, the issue of how to deal with uncertainty is relevant to all aspects of the assessment. This is inherent in all merger assessment due to its forward-looking nature, but poses a particular challenge in the case of dynamic markets. There are several ways in which competition authorities can deal with this. As highlighted in the literature and the ex-post review commissioned by the CMA, it may be necessary to accept a higher degree of uncertainty in such cases to counteract the risk of potential competition being eliminated. This is particularly the case in markets with pre-existing dominance and high barriers to entry such as many digital platform markets.

In addition, the case examples demonstrate that it will often be useful to focus on understanding and evidencing firms' incentives rather than seeking evidence of what is likely to happen in future, which may not exist. Dynamic incentives are particularly important, especially in 'winner takes all/most' markets. The probability of disruption by a nascent competitor may be low, but the harm to the incumbent's position and future profitability could be very substantial if it did occur and this may create the incentive to snuff out potential threats at an early stage. On the other hand, attempts made by a potential disruptor to enter and expand may drive a competitive response from the incumbent even if they are not ultimately successful.

The discussion also highlights the importance of thinking carefully about the relevant theories of harm and taking account of the potential non-price effects of mergers. With regard to horizontal mergers, the need to consider possible effects on innovation has been a theme of recent literature and cases. The ex-post review of vertical mergers found that the UK authorities had not done a good job of characterising theories of harm in all cases, making it more difficult to assess the likelihood of an SLC. Both the literature on competition in digital markets and the CMA's recent experiences highlight the importance of considering a broad range of foreclosure mechanisms.

Finally, the discussion highlights the usefulness of ex-post reviews in helping competition authorities to understand the impact of their decisions. This is likely to be particularly important in dynamic markets and may help to deal with the problem of uncertainty by providing an evidence base on the impact of interventions in different markets.

Notes

1. The United Kingdom Competition Appeals Tribunal is a specialist judicial body with cross-disciplinary expertise in law, economics, business and accountancy. It hears and decides cases involving competition or economic regulatory issues. Among its functions, the CAT hears and decides applications for the review of merger decisions made by the CMA.

2. Anticipated acquisition by Illumina, Inc. of Pacific Biosciences of California, Inc.: Provisional findings report, 24 October 2019.

DEVELOPING THINKING IN MERGER ASSESSMENT

3   This analysis was based on data provided by PatentSight GmbH. See paragraphs 9.27 and 9.28 of the Provisional Findings.

4   It should be noted that the merger was abandoned after the CMA's provisional findings were published, so the following discussion of the case is based on its provisional findings and not a final decision.

5   Completed acquisition by PayPal Holdings, Inc. of iZettle AB: CMA Final Report, 12 June 2019.

6   Completed acquisition by Facebook, Inc (now Meta Platforms, Inc) of GIPHY, Inc., CMA Final report, 30 November 2021.

7   At the time of writing, the CMA was considering the remittal of the case at the direction of the CAT on procedural grounds in relation to the redaction of confidential information. The Remittal Group adopted the CMA's Phase 2 Final Report as its provisional findings in the Remittal and, at the time of writing, was awaiting comments from interested parties on these findings. The discussion in this chapter is therefore based only on the information available in the CMA's original Final Report (and Remittal Group provisional findings report) and the CAT judgment of June 2022.

8   See: Competition Appeals Tribunal, case no: 1429/4/12/21.

9   See: CAT judgment, paragraph 105.

10 See: CAT judgment paragraph 124(3).

11 See: E.CA Economics (2022) Ex-post evaluation of vertical mergers: Report for the Competition and Markets Authority. https://www.e-ca.com/wp-content/uploads/2023/04/ex-post-evaluation-of-vertical-mergers.pdf

12 See: Note 9, paragraphs 7.18 and 7.19.

13 See: CMA 2021, paragraph 7.3.

14 See: Completed acquisition by Tobii AB of Smartbox Assistive Technologies Limited and Sensory Software International Ltd: Final report, 15 August 2019.

15 See: Competition Appeal Tribunal, case no: 1332/4/12/19.

16 See: Competition Appeal Tribunal, case no: 1271–1272/4/12/16.

17 See: Completed acquisition by Facebook, Inc. (now Meta Platforms, Inc.) of GIPHY, Inc.: Final report, 30 November 2021.

18 See: CMA's Final Report, paragraph 8.102(a).

19 In 2014, the Office of Fair Trading and Competition Commission were merged to form the CMA.

20 See: Entry and expansion in UK merger cases: An ex-post evaluation. KPMG LLP, April 2017. https://assets.publishing.service.gov.uk/media/5a82b3b440f0b6230269c40a/entry-and-expansion-in-uk-ex-post-evaluation-kpmg.pdf

21 See: Entry and expansion in UK merger cases: An ex-post evaluation. KPMG LLP, April 2017. https://assets.publishing.service.gov.uk/government/uploads/system/uploads/attachment_data/file/606693/entry-and-expansion-in-uk-ex-post-evaluation-kpmg.pdf

22 See: Completed acquisition by CHC Group LLP of Offshore Helicopter Services UK Limited, Offshore Services Australasia PTY Ltd and Offshore Helicopter Services

Denmark A/S: Final report, 1 June 2022. https://assets.publishing.service.gov.uk/media/62978706d3bf7f0375568de4/Final_report_-_CHC_Babcock_1.6.22.pdf

References

Baker JB, Rose NL, Salop SC & Scott Morton FM (2020) Recommendations and comments on the draft vertical merger guidelines. *Scholarship at Georgetown Law* 2245. http://dx.doi.org/10.2139/ssrn.3543736

Beck M & Scott Morton F (2020) Evaluating the evidence on vertical mergers. *Review of Industrial Organization* 59(2): 273–302

CMA (Competition and Markets Authority) (2020) *Online platforms and digital advertising market study*. London: CMA

CMA (Competition and Markets Authority) (2021) *Merger assessment guidelines (CMA 129)*. London: CMA

Digital Competition Expert Panel (2019) *Unlocking digital competition: Report of the Digital Competition Expert Panel, March 2019*. London: HM Treasury Publications

E.CA Economics (2022) Ex-post evaluation of vertical mergers: Report for the Competition and Markets Authority. Accessed 2022, https://www.e-ca.com/wp-content/uploads/2023/04/ex-post-evaluation-of-vertical-mergers.pdf

Federico G, Scott Morton F & Shapiro C (2020) Antitrust and innovation: Welcoming and protecting disruption. *Innovation Policy and the Economy* 20: 125–190

Kwoka J & Slade M (2020) Second thoughts on double marginalization. *Antitrust* 34(2): 51–56

Lear (2019) *Ex-post assessment of merger control decisions in digital markets*. Rome: Lear

Motta M & Fumagalli C (2020) Dynamic vertical foreclosure. *The Journal of Law and Economics* 63(4): 763–812

Salop S (2018) Invigorating vertical merger enforcement. *The Yale Law Journal* 127(7): 1962–1994

Shapiro C (2018) Antitrust in a time of populism. *International Journal of Industrial Organization* 61: 714–748

Stigler Center (2019) *Stigler committee on digital platforms final report*. Chicago: Stigler Center for the Study of the Economy and the State

10 Competition issues and regional integration in soybean and animal feed to poultry markets, within and across Kenya, Malawi and Zambia

Grace Nsomba, Angella Kachipapa Mhone, Inonge Mulozi,
Rosebela A Oiro and Simon Roberts

The agricultural sector is key to fostering economic growth, reducing poverty and improving food security in eastern and southern Africa (ESA). It is necessary to sustainably increase food production to meet the demand from rapidly expanding urban populations. However, over the last decade, Africa as a whole has run a food trade deficit averaging around US$30bn a year (Nsomba et al. 2022). Many countries in the ESA region are net food importers, despite good soils, land availability and favourable growing conditions in much of the region (Annan et al. 2015; Kaziboni & Roberts 2022). Africa as a whole has around 60% of the arable land in the world.[1]

Poultry production exemplifies these patterns. Urbanisation and rising incomes mean an increased demand for chicken meat as the main source of animal protein (Nakamura et al. 2016). Commercial poultry production relies on the competitive supply of maize and soybean for animal feed, as well as investments in breeding operations for the supply of day-old chicks. Despite higher levels of production in soybeans in Malawi and Zambia since 2015, along with increased levels of investment in breeding operations across the region, this has not translated into a competitive regional poultry value chain. This is evidenced through substantial poultry imports that compete with expensive domestically produced poultry products, along with high levels of concentration along the value chain.

We attribute these outcomes in Kenya, Malawi and Zambia to the structure of poultry markets, which we find to be largely oligopolistic in nature. Moreover, regional alliances and cross-ownership relationships exacerbate the effects of these extremely high concentrations at different levels of the value chain, including the extent of participation by small- and medium-scale producers being undermined.

Scale economies play an important role in low-cost production at certain levels in the value chain, such as breeding and processing. In addition, vertical integration can assist with coordination along the value chain. This means that it is not surprising to find high levels of concentration with a few large firms participating in more than one level of the value chain across the three countries studied. The development of the value chain therefore depends on the conduct of these firms and the extent to which markets are competitive. In order to consider the state of competition and the firms' conduct, in this chapter we analyse market outcomes at different levels of the value chain, within and across borders in the region.[2]

The chapter first provides an overview of the value chain and the main firms in each of the countries, looking specifically at value chain linkages, value chain concentration in Kenya, Malawi and Zambia, and patterns of co-ownership and networks of alliances. It then analyses the market outcomes, with a focus on breeding stock, feed and consumer effects. Next, the chapter discusses a summary of the findings and the implications for competition, and finally concludes with some recommendations.

The poultry value chain and main firms

Value chain linkages

The poultry value chain has multiple levels – from the production and processing of agricultural commodities for animal feed (mainly maize and soybean) through to quasi-industrial processes of production in the rearing, processing and distribution of poultry in live, fresh and frozen form (Figure 10.1; Goga & Bosiu 2019). There are large-scale commercial producers that are generally vertically integrated from the key inputs of breeding stock and feed through to the sale of poultry products. The integrated large commercial businesses operate alongside smaller and medium-sized producers who may operate only in broiler production. For smaller commercial producers to expand, they need to source their inputs on competitive terms from third parties.

Poultry feed and breeding stock are by far the most substantial inputs in the value chain, while labour, energy, drugs and chicken litter comprise smaller proportions. Feed accounts for between 60 and 70 per cent of the total input costs for broiler production, while breeding stock is estimated to account for up to 20 per cent of input costs (Goga & Bosiu 2019; Ncube et al. 2017).

The main components of poultry feed are milled maize and soybean (including in meal or oilcake form), with salt, vitamins and mineral premixes, and synthetic amino acids accounting for a relatively smaller proportion of the feed mixture. In the three countries we are analysing, the main components of feed are sourced from millers and oil-seed crushers, who also produce vegetable oil and for which oilcake or meal is a co-product, with Kenya importing from Zambia, Malawi and Uganda.

In terms of breeding stock, there is a global duopoly with two main breeds of chickens that are used worldwide in the broiler production industry. These are the Ross breed, supplied by EW/Aviagen, and the Cobb breed, supplied by Tyson subsidiary Cobb-Vantress (Goga & Roberts 2023). Typically, the holder of the intellectual property sells great-grandparent stock of the breed under licence to a company in a given geography who then breeds grandparents to supply parent stock to hatcheries. The parent stock produce what are known in the industry as 'day-old

Figure 10.1: Commercial broiler poultry value chain in Malawi

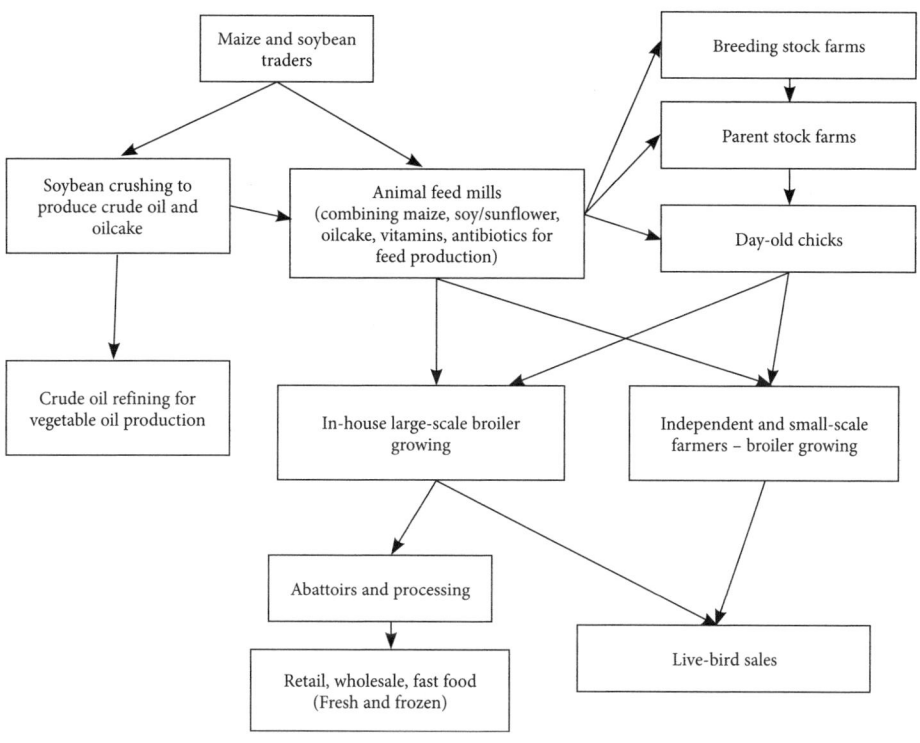

Source: Adapted from Bagopi et al. (2016) and interviews in Kenya, Malawi and Zambia

chicks' to rear as broiler chickens in around 35 to 42 days. The breeding companies with the licence may also be vertically integrated into broiler production as well as supplying independent broiler producers.

Value chain concentration in Kenya, Malawi and Zambia

In the ESA region, broiler breeding and distribution rights are licensed by the two multinationals to a few breeding companies, with South Africa and Zambia being key locations for licence holders. Poultry producers need to purchase breeding stock from these licence holders. Becoming a licence holder is costly, as setting up breeder farms requires significant research and investment, as well as special phytosanitary care (Goga & Roberts 2023). It also takes time to produce commercial day-old chicks, estimated at a year from the delivery of the grandparent breeding stock to the first commercial level broiler day-old chicks for rearing to produce poultry meat.

Malawi has no breeding operations at the grandparent level and suppliers of day-old chicks obtain parent stock from neighbouring countries, either from Cobb Africa (mainly through Irvines in Zimbabwe) or from Country Bird Holdings (mainly from

Ross Breeders Zambia, RBZ) for the Cobb and Ross breeds respectively. While there are at least five suppliers of day-old chicks for broiler production in Malawi, the largest, Central Poultry, accounts for 87% of the day-old chick supply (see Appendix Table A10.1). This estimate includes what Central Poultry supplies into its own production of broiler birds and what it supplies to independent producers across Malawi. Central Poultry is also vertically integrated into feed production.

Zambia, on the other hand, appears to have much less concentration than Malawi at the level of breeding and supply of day-old chicks, with six suppliers of day-old chicks (see Appendix Table A10.2). However, only three of these firms can access grandparent breeding stock and hold distribution licences – Hybrid (for the Cobb 500 breed), RBZ (for the Ross 308 breed) and Tiger Chicks (for the Indian River breed at parent stock level). All other players in the poultry value chain source their parent stock or day-old chicks from these three firms.

In Kenya, the level of breeding and supply of day-old chicks is also highly concentrated, with only two major suppliers of day-old chicks that each have links to regional and international breeding companies and animal feed producers. Kenchic is the largest supplier of day-old chicks, holding 70% of the market share (Appendix Table A10.3). Kenchic is also vertically integrated into feed (through a partnership with Unga Feeds, the largest supplier of animal feed) and into the production of broilers at the downstream level. Unga supplies Kenchic and its contract farmers with feed, while the contract farmers sell their chickens back to Kenchic for processing.[3] This then guarantees offtake for both Kenchic and Unga. Contract farmers are required to buy feed from Unga, while other independent farmers sourcing day-old chicks from Kenchic are not subject to restrictions on where they buy feed. We unpack the effects of alliances such as this below.

Poultry feed production also exhibits high levels of concentration across all three countries, despite Kenya and Zambia having a number of independent feed producers of various sizes. In Malawi, two feed producers, Central Poultry and Kelfoods, account for around 80% of total supply (Appendix Table A10.1 and Table A10.4).[4] Central Poultry is also fully integrated into soybean crushing activities through its sister company, Sunseed Oil (a vegetable oil producer), with an annual soybean crushing capacity of 180 000 metric tonnes (Appendix Table A10.4). In Zambia, there are around seven sizable feed producers (Appendix Table A10.5) while soybean crushing required for key inputs is in the hands of four companies. In Kenya, there are four large feed suppliers and many smaller and medium-sized companies (Appendix Table A10.6), however, the largest Unga is estimated to account for around half of all supplies in the country. Across the three countries there are relatively high levels of concentration and, as discussed below, indications of market power (see Table 10.1 for a summary).

Table 10.1 Summary of market structure and supply

	Malawi	Zambia	Kenya
Breeding	• One dominant supplier (CP) with GP to parent, supplying Cobb 500 day-old chicks, 87% share. • All other players supply Ross 308, import fertilised eggs from Zambia at PS level.	• Cobb 500, Ross 308 and Indian River main breeds. • Concentrated: three licensed producers at GP level, additional three suppliers at PS level.	• One dominant supplier (Kenchic) supplies Ross 308, from RBZ in Zambia GP, 70% day-old chick share. • Isinya, supplies Cobb 500.
Feed	• Sufficient maize and soybean grown locally; net exports. • Production concentrated, two producers with 80%; horizontal links to storage, trade and veg oil production.	• Sufficient maize and soybean grown locally; net exports. • Production concentrated, few large suppliers with horizontal links to storage, trade and veg oil production.	• Bulk of inputs imported, regional soymeal processors crucial. • One dominant producer with 50% share, a few other large producers and many smaller ones.
Broiler production	• One integrated producer (Central Poultry) commands 80% of the market. • Commercial and rural farmers compete in downstream retail of live chickens.	• Mainly contract farming – production contracts between poultry producers and contract growers. This means broiler production is relatively concentrated and is linked to upstream breeding stock.	• Mix of integrated and independent producers.

Source: Compiled by authors

Co-ownership and networks of alliances

The regional extent of operations of the main firms in key inputs across countries is essential to understanding their market power, given the licensing arrangements and trade flows in key products along the value chain. In particular, Zambia and Malawi are the major producers and exporters of soybeans and soy oilcake for animal feed (Figure 10.2), while Zambia is a major breeding hub. While Zambia and Malawi have exported to meet demands in Kenya, they have also exported substantial volumes to South Africa, Tanzania, Zimbabwe, the United Arab Emirates (UAE) and India (Nsomba et al 2022). There are only a few major traders of soybeans and producers of oilcake in each country (with common major companies across countries). The main companies are Central Poultry in Malawi, and Mount Meru, ETG and Global Industries/Wilmar, which are global and regional commodity traders with extensive operations across Kenya, Malawi and Zambia. They are integrated into soybean crushing for vegetable oil production and into storage and logistics, which ensures they have stocks throughout the year.

Figure 10.2 Net exports in soybean and oilcake

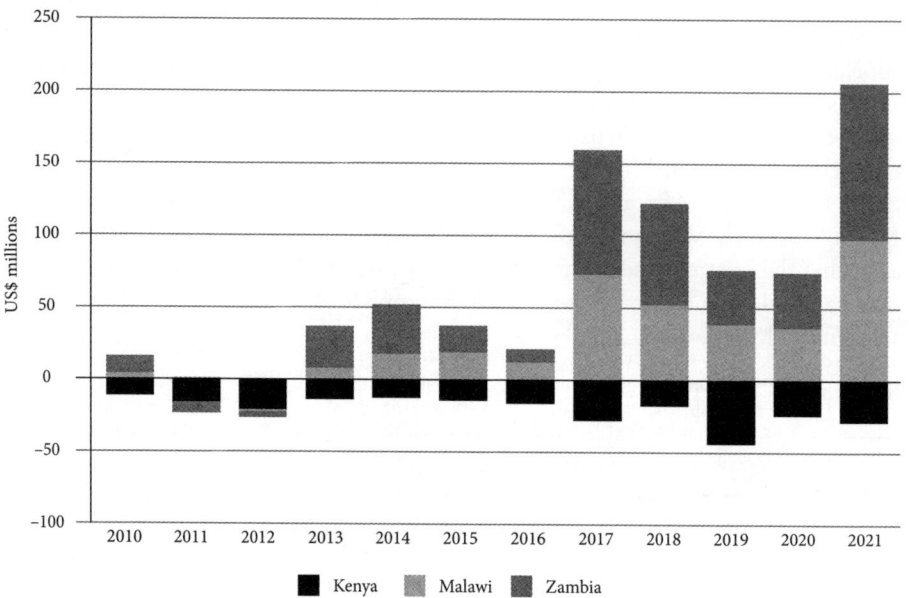

Source: Trademap

The sourcing of inputs is key for competitiveness in the production of feed. Given low levels of production in the country, Kenya relies heavily on the imports of maize and soymeal (as well as minerals and vitamins) for the production of feed.[5] Key sources of maize and soymeal imports are Zambia and Uganda, and Malawi to a lesser extent. Prices of the commodities in these markets, along with the related costs to transport them to Nairobi, play a critical role in the ability of Kenyan feed producers to compete.

There are extensive ownership relationships and inter-firm linkages across the region. It is important to note that while these can help firms realise efficiencies, such as by reducing transaction costs, they can also be the basis for coordination and the exertion of market power.

In poultry breeding stock, the relationships between companies across the region reflect the ownership structures of the two multinational companies, Tyson and Aviagen, which together account for more than 90% of global supply, as well as regional multinational companies in ESA. Tyson, which has the Cobb breed, has shareholdings through Buchan and Cobb Africa, together with regional multinational Irvines (Goga & Roberts 2023).

Aviagen, which has the Ross breed, forms part of the complex layers of shareholdings between African Poultry Development Limited (APDL), Country Bird Holdings (CBH), Aviagen Central Africa, Aviagen East Africa and Ross Central Africa

(Goga & Roberts 2023). APDL also has a shareholding in Hybrid in Zambia (an important Cobb breeder), which means there are direct ownership relationships between suppliers of competing breeds. APDL, incorporated in Mauritius[6], is reported to represent the largest group of integrated poultry companies in Zambia and East and Central Africa.[7] In Kenya, APDL is the shareholder in Kenchic, while its shareholder Seaboard owns Unga. APDL is in a joint venture with Aviagen, and is owner (together with Country Bird Holdings, which owns RBZ) of Aviagen East Africa. Aviagen East Africa consists of grandparent farms and parent stock hatcheries of Aviagen breeds, which include Ross 308 (Figure 10.3).[8] These relationships also mean that the upstream companies with strong associations (Aviagen, CBH, APDL and Seaboard) can track day-old chicken supplies across borders in the region, including in Kenya.

Figure 10.3 APDL, Kenchic and Seaboard ownership links and alliances

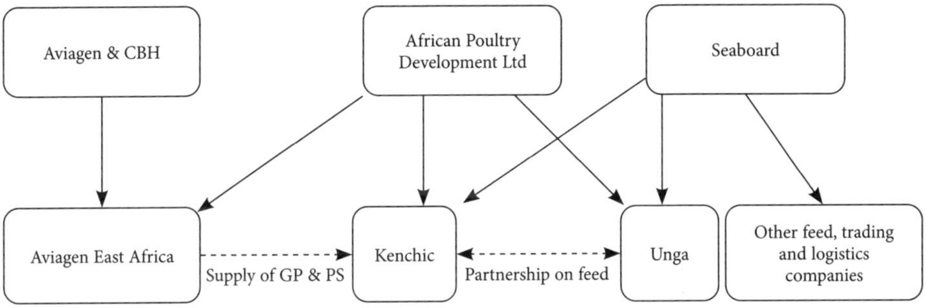

Source: Compiled by authors

In feed, there are also networks of shareholdings, which increase concentration when viewed at a regional level. These include the major producers and traders of oilcake across the countries, such as Seaboard's ownership links with Unga and its trading operations across Kenya, Zambia (where it is an owner in National Milling and United Africa Grains), Uganda (where it is an owner in Unga Milling), South Africa and Mozambique. Seaboard partnered with South Africa's largest soybean crusher through a merger in 2021.[9] Pembe, another substantial feed producer in Kenya, also has soybean crushing operations in Zambia (see Appendix Tables A10.5 and A10.6).

Together with the licensing of breeds, these relationships point to a network of intertwined companies across the poultry regional value chain. Unga supplies Kenchic with feed for its breeding and hatchery business, and it supplies Kenchic's contract poultry farmers who sell their chickens back to Kenchic for processing.[10] This then guarantees offtake for both Kenchic and Unga. Kenchic's contract farmers are also required to buy feed from Unga. Sigma Feeds in Kenya is reported to have close relations with CP/Sunseed Oil in Malawi.[11] ETG owns processing and trading businesses in all three countries.

Comparative analysis of market outcomes in Malawi, Kenya and Zambia

In this section, we compare the market outcomes in the studied countries at levels of feed production, day-old chick supply and chicken prices to understand the competitiveness of the value chain at the country levels and in regional terms. We analyse information and data collected through in-depth semi-structured interviews in Kenya, Malawi and Zambia, as well as desktop research and previous research conducted by the authors. This is done in order to assess competition and competitiveness in the regional animal feed to poultry value chain.

The interviews were carried out with a range of industry stakeholders across the three countries, including government departments, industry associations, vertically integrated poultry producers, independent poultry producers, animal feed producers, commodity traders and processors, and customers. Information and data were collected on various aspects of the poultry industry, including market structure and concentration, national and regional trade along the poultry value chain, production and prices along the value chain (including of maize, soybean, animal feed and poultry products) and local and regional markets for inputs and poultry products. The interviews were carried out between March and October 2022.

The analysis also draws from a knowledge base of market structure and pricing data from the African Market Observatory (AMO), housed at the University of Johannesburg. The AMO is an initiative that tracks and analyses prices of staple foods in the ESA region. This initiative also conducts in-depth assessments of markets to pinpoint problems and make recommendations to achieve a more inclusive and sustainable food production system in the face of climate change.

In the following subsections, we conduct a comparative analysis of the breeding stock and feed levels of the poultry value chains across the three countries.

Breeding stock

Figure 10.4 shows the pattern of day-old chick prices between January 2021 and August 2022. Zambia is a net exporter of day-old chicks and apparently a low-cost producer (given the low prices of maize and soybeans as feed inputs). The graph shows that in the first half of 2021, Zambia had the lowest prices of the three African countries, at between $0.45 and $0.52 per chick. This is also close to prices in South Africa of around $0.56 for the whole of 2021. In the last quarter of 2021, however, Zambian prices doubled to above $0.90, before falling back somewhat (Figure 10.4). Similar sudden price increases were observed in Malawi from May 2021, surpassing prices in Kenya, an apparently high-cost producer. The effect of the higher breeding stock prices is that the costs of poultry producers are directly increased, which undermines their competitiveness both in relation to imports as well as with vertically integrated poultry companies.

Figure 10.4 Comparative prices for day-old chicks

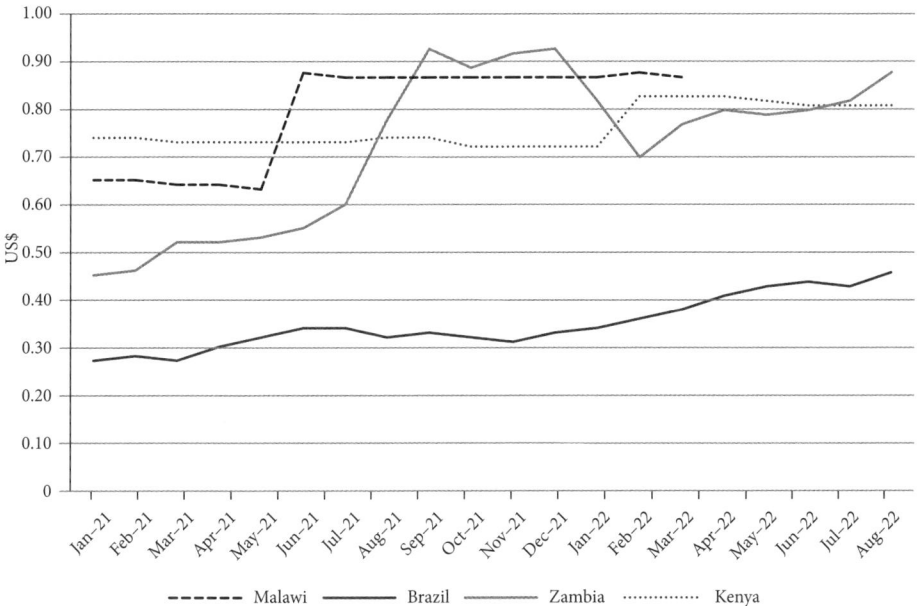

Source: Poultry Association of Zambia, interviews in Kenya and Malawi, and Conab via Brazilian researchers

We use prices in Brazil as an international comparative benchmark. Brazil is the largest poultry exporter in the world due to its competitive costs base, including competitively priced day-old chicks (Goga & Bosiu 2019). Prices in Brazil in 2021 were around $0.30, which was close to levels in the EU, and far below those that we see in the ESA region.

The increased prices in Zambia have been attributed to constraints in the supply of chicks. However, Zambia is an export hub for breeding stock to the region, including to Kenya – so it is not clear why there should be supply limitations and what could justify the very sharp price increases to levels above prices in Kenya. Small-scale producers in Zambia have been reporting shortages, particularly since late 2020 through to mid–2022, while exports of day-old chicks have been rising throughout the period. This has had implications on their downstream competitiveness against vertically integrated producers.

Three companies across the region hold distribution rights to the main breeds, which has meant extensively high levels of concentration in the supply of breeding stock across the region. These companies supply parent stock, and thus monitor the production capacity of a very few other companies. The increase in prices, together with increases in exports (as shown in Goga & Roberts, 2023) implies an exertion of market power by breeders in the Zambian market. The price increase in the Malawian market is from a single dominant firm that is able to set prices for the day-old chicks it produces from breeding stock sourced from Irvine's (under the Cobb Africa licence).

The concentrated nature of distribution rights of the commercial breeds raises competition concerns, given that these firms have the ability to control who accesses which breeds and at what price. The vertically integrated poultry producers are both the suppliers to, and the competitors of, independent producers. Given the essential nature of high-performing breeding stock for commercial broiler production, the large producers are able to undermine or exclude independent producers if they exert collective or unilateral market power. Such concerns were part of the competition case brought by the Zambian Competition and Consumer Protection Commission (CCPC) in 2018. Indeed, the regional footprint of the main companies is an important dimension to consider when evaluating both the arrangements and their effects.

Feed

Increased production of soybeans with prices in Malawi and Zambia at harvest substantially below world prices has not translated to competitive market prices of poultry feed (Nsomba et al. 2022). The high levels of concentration, especially in the trading and crushing of soybeans, mean that just a few traders and producers control the volumes and set the prices in different markets. In particular, it is evident that substantial volumes of soybeans and cake were being exported out of the region, and that the prices on these exports were lower than those being charged to arms-length buyers in Kenya, Malawi and Zambia.[12] This illustrates the need for regional competition enforcement that tracks markets across borders, including through sharing information and coordination with national competition authorities.

For feed (for which we use broiler finisher feed for comparisons), Kenyan prices remained relatively stable between January 2021 and April 2022, hovering between $0.53 and $0.55 in that period despite significant fluctuations in the prices of maize and soybean (Figure 10.5). The graph also shows that Kenyan feed prices were 30% higher than feed prices in Malawi and Zambia in the first half of 2021. Feed prices in the net exporters, Zambia and Malawi, then increased and surpassed Kenyan prices in August and November 2021 respectively. This occurred even though maize and soybean prices in Zambia remained consistently much lower than in Kenya over 2021 and 2022. While Malawi also continued to be a substantial net exporter of soybeans and oilcake, the soybean prices to independent buyers in Malawi increased sharply from May 2021 to peak in January 2022, along with the increasing feed prices. Given that soy oilcake is a significant cost component in production, this has negatively impacted the competitiveness of small- and medium-scale producers of feed and poultry.

Figure 10.5 Comparative broiler finisher feed prices

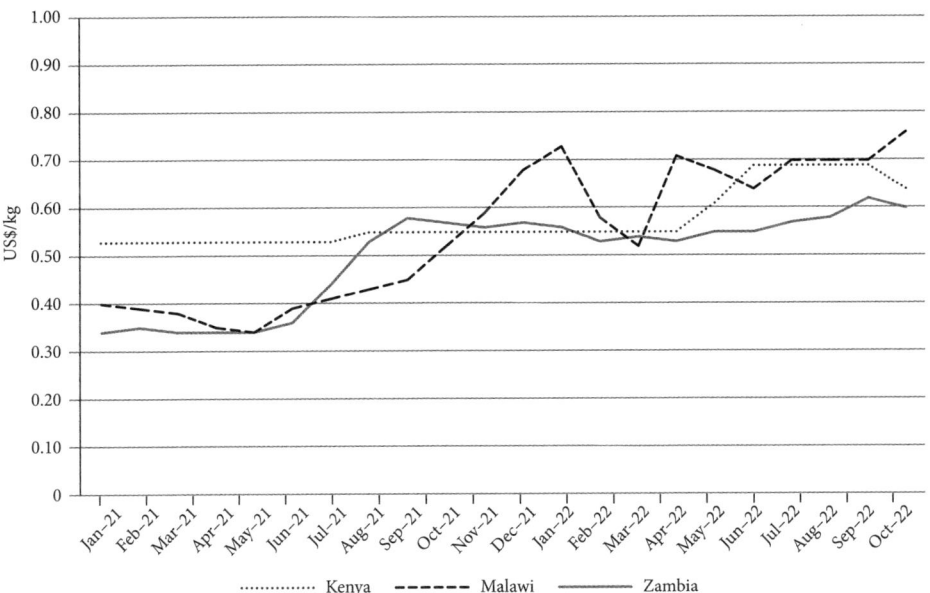

Source: Prices of feed of the main feed suppliers in each country, from interviews with market participants

Notes: Kenyan prices appear to have been set in US dollar terms as the local currency prices fluctuated. The Zambia price increase in US$ terms from June to September 2021 was due to an appreciation in the local currency while local prices stayed stable. The Malawi price increases were in both local and foreign currency terms as the currency was stable until a 25% depreciation in May 2022 that was matched by pass-through to local prices.

Prices across all three countries do not reflect what would be expected from cost-reflective competitive markets. In Zambia and Malawi, price-setting appears to reflect market power and price-setting by the major feed producers that are integrated into the soybean crushing. In Kenya, the feed producers are subjected to the prices from the main sources of soymeal, namely the small number of large crushing companies operating across the region.

The Kenyan feed producers that are integrated with these businesses are in a favourable position compared to independent buyers. Over the year to October 2022, feed manufacturing in Kenya was reported to have contracted by around 20% in volume terms, with an estimated 30 smaller feed producers reported to have gone out of business.[13] The contraction has been attributed mainly to the rising and fluctuating costs of importing inputs amid the drought that Kenya experienced in 2021 and 2022.[14] Despite this, the larger producers (in tier one, Appendix Table A10.6) have not experienced significant contractions in terms of production volumes, and interviews have suggested that their margins have been maintained, as prices were adjusted upwards when input prices rose.[15] In these price adjustments,

Unga appears to be the price leader, with all the other major players following its price movements.[16]

Transport costs are an important part of the cost of feed constituents being imported for Kenyan feed. In the interviews conducted in Kenya, there were big differences between the estimates of efficient transport costs such as those incurred by large integrated processors and traders with fleets of trucks, compared to the costs that smaller feed customers reported being charged (CAK, 2019). Efficient road freight rates of around $80/t to $120/t have been estimated from Lusaka and Nairobi between 2021 and 2022 compared to $200/t that smaller feed customers reported.[17] The implication is that at the regional level, there are potentially very high margins being made by traders and/or processors.

Consumer effects

High input prices flow through to higher consumer prices of chicken. In all three countries, chickens can be purchased live by consumers. In line with the feed and day-old chick prices, the prices of live chickens were considerably higher in Kenya in 2021 than in Malawi and Zambia (Figure 10.6). Prices came into line across all the countries in 2022, as Kenyan prices fell and prices in Malawi and Zambia increased. Zambian live poultry prices increased by around 70% from May to September 2021. For much of the following 12-month period, Zambian prices were higher than in Malawi, even while feed prices were substantially lower. This suggests that higher input costs have been passed onto consumers of live chickens in Zambia. By comparison, in Malawi from late 2021, the increased day-old chicken and feed prices with poultry prices remaining stable meant that small independent producers had negative margins (see chapter 11 by Gondwe et al., in this book).

Kenyan prices by comparison were consistent with a squeeze on independent producers of live chickens from February 2022, as reported in interviews with smaller producers going out of business and an overall contraction in the industry.

Overall findings and implications for competition

The potential for substantial expansions in soybean and maize production to ensure competitively priced animal feed and poultry production across the region is being stymied by markets that are not working at all well. Farmers are receiving low prices for their produce, while smaller downstream producers and consumers of poultry products are charged high prices. The prices of maize in Zambia and Malawi have been substantially below international prices and the prices of soybeans in Zambia have also been in line with international prices or lower at harvest times. However, at the same time, prices to poultry producers of feed, as well as day-old chicks, have been very high and the poultry industry within and across countries is not competitive or inclusive.

COMPETITION ISSUES AND REGIONAL INTEGRATION

Figure 10.6 Comparative live chicken prices, per chicken

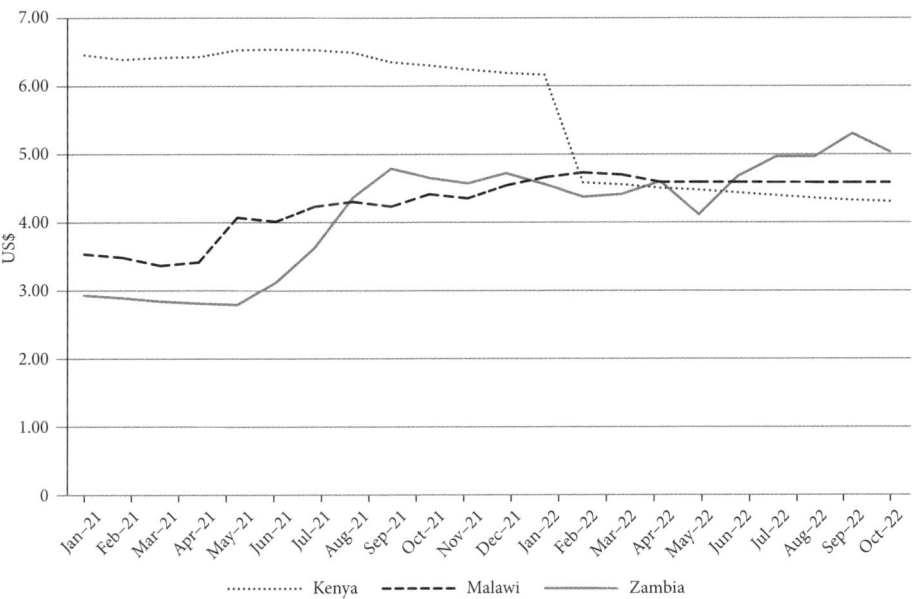

Source: Interviews in Kenya and Malawi and Poultry Association of Zambia

There are high levels of concentration in breeding stock and in feed supply within and across the countries. The pricing observed is consistent with the exertion of market power. In large-scale commercial soybean crushing to produce oilcake and soymeal for animal feed, along with vegetable oil, there are very few regional producers, with apparently very high mark-ups being charged. These high prices have undermined independent producers across the region, including in Kenya, where there is the largest demand. The main oil crushers and millers are integrated with large traders and are exchanging pricing information across the region through the East African Grain Council's platform.

In Malawi, there is a tight oligopoly in soybean processing and feed supply, and a single dominant firm in breeding stock through to commercial poultry production. The escalation of soybean prices throughout the year after the harvest in 2021, even while there are exports at lower prices, indicates the exertion of market power to subject independent producers to a margin squeeze (see chapter 11 by Gondwe et al., in this book).

Zambia has oligopolistic market structures in soybean processing, feed supply and day-old chick supply. High feed and day-old chick prices are being charged, along with high poultry prices (even while prices of frozen poultry are relatively constrained by competition from imports). Independent producers are subject to the high feed and day-old chicks prices, and constrained supply of day-old chicks, which undermine their ability to compete. Large integrated producers extract high margins from selling inputs as well as from poultry sales.

The concentration at the national level in each country is reinforced by the regional reach of the major producers, and common ownership and associations between them. There are therefore substantial policy and competition concerns in each country. These require attention at the regional level. The market structure and the market outcomes that we have described are consistent with the literature on cartel screening and require proper investigation (see Harrington 2007; Marshall & Marx 2012; Roberts 2020). Our assessment also suggests exclusionary and possibly discriminatory conduct, including through the exertion of unilateral market power.

Conclusions and recommendations

The competition issues that we have identified in this study ought to be addressed as part of wider strategies that aim to ensure the improved competitiveness in poultry production across east and southern Africa. In so doing, the benefits from agricultural production of the main components of feed will flow through to lower costs of poultry production. A regional view of competition issues and increased regional integration are necessary in order to ensure that agricultural potential in countries such as Malawi and Zambia lead to improved competitiveness in poultry production across the region.

We also see that the development of the industry depends on the decisions and behaviour of large enterprises, which are influenced by economic policies. Similar to the findings of Bagopi et al. (2016), the development of the poultry value chain highlights the challenges of ensuring both local investment and competitive outcomes. Large-scale investments are required in key activities such as breeding and processing of soybeans, yet the concentrated nature of the industry has undermined wider participation of small and medium enterprises, and the realisation of substantial economic gains to local economies.

Given these findings, we propose the need to reshape the poultry value chain, and agricultural markets more widely, through three closely related areas for action.

First, we need appropriate policies to support resilient and inclusive regional value chains. This means investing in the necessary infrastructure and support for farmers and agro-processors, including irrigation, storage and logistics. This can link expanded agriculture with better transport logistics for competing regional production. Barriers to entry for smaller producers should be reduced through a package of measures tackling access to market, development finance and effective support for skills and technology adoption (Vilakazi et al. 2020). These are part of green and inclusive industrial policies tailored to sectors and value chains, investing in shared infrastructure, advisory services and finance as part of a green industrial policy for food (Andreoni et al. 2021).

Second, it is essential to monitor markets in real time as climate change implies more frequent and deeper shocks. The effects of frequent and deeper market shocks can be exacerbated by the conduct of firms that are able to control the terms of supply along value chains, subsequently harming participation of small producers and the choices of consumers. Through collating prices within and across countries at different levels of value chains, the African Market Observatory can assess where markets are not working well. It can identify where there are excess margins and obstacles that harm smaller producers and consumers, in particular.

Third, we need effective referees for markets. This is the role for competition authorities. Some African countries have built strong national competition institutions and the Competition Commission of COMESA (the Common Market of Eastern and Southern Africa) has established a regional merger review and is extending its work to enforcement. However, our assessment points to the imperative to ramp up the powers and capacities of these institutions to make regional markets work more effectively. This means that national authorities need to tackle national arrangements alongside cross-border market division and price fixing cartels. Inquiries need to place the onus on dominant firms to justify conduct that undermines smaller businesses.

These three main areas are mutually reinforcing if we are to achieve healthy, growing regional food value chains based on investment in the future. Moreover, they are central to realising the vision of the African Continental Free Trade Area of sustainable and inclusive continental development with efficient regional trade.

Notes

1. According to the International Fund for Agricultural Development (IFAD) Field Report; see: https://www.ifad.org/thefieldreport/#:~:text=More%20than%20half%20of%20the,yields%20with%20currently%20available%20technology
2. The chapter draws on a working paper by the same authors (Nsomba et al. 2022) where additional context can be found.
3. Interview with Kenyan feed producer, 26 October 2022.
4. Interview with Malawian oil producer, 18 March 2022.
5. Interview with poultry feed producer, 25 October 2022.
6. Incorporated in 2007, with parent company Seaboard Corporation; see: https://opencorporates.com/companies/mu/C073845/statements/subsidiary_relationship_object ; https://www.seaboardcorp.com/investors/seaboard-portfolio/
7. See: https://tmea.aviagen.com/news-room/press-releases/aviagen-secures-local-supply-through-a-greenfield-investment-in-east-africa-with-the-establishment-of-aviagen-east-africa-limited/
8. APDL is also a holding company for Interchick Ltd and Tanbreed Poultry Ltd in Tanzania, and Kenchic Uganda Ltd in Uganda; see: https://tmea.aviagen.com/news-room/press-releases/aviagen-secures-local-supply-through-a-greenfield-investment-in-east-africa-with-the-establishment-of-aviagen-east-africa-limited/

Cobb Europe has held workshops in March 2019 with RCL Foods in South Africa, and with Hybrid on behalf of APDL Group, the holding company of Hybrid; see: https://www.poultryproducer.com/cobb-europe-drives-innovation-in-southern-africa/

9   See: https://www.seaboardcorp.com/investors/seaboard-portfolio/
10 Interview with Kenyan feed producer, 26 October 2022.
11 Interview with poultry feed producers, 25–27 October 2022.
12 See: Nsomba et al. 2022.
13 Interview with market participants 25–27 October 2022. There has also been a sizeable new entrant.
14 Interview with poultry feed producers, 25–27 October 2022.
15 Interview with poultry feed producers, 25–27 October 2022.
16 Interview with poultry feed producers, 25–27 October 2022.
17 Nsomba, Jangale and Vilakazi (2019) and Competition Authority of Kenya (2019) found $0.04/ton/km to be in line with an expected efficient transport rate along the main corridors in east and southern Africa, taking into account crossing multiple borders, which yields $80/t from Lusaka to Nairobi. With the fuel price increase in 2022, this increased to $120/t. These costs compare with road freight transport costs over the same distance within Brazil (and so without any border crossings) of around $60/t before international fuel price increases in 2022, and $90/t after the 2022 fuel increases.

References

Andreoni A, Mondliwa P, Roberts S & Tregenna F (2021) (Eds) *Structural transformation in South Africa: The challenges of inclusive industrial development in a middle-income country.* Oxford: Oxford University Press

Annan K, Conway G & Dryden S (2015) African farmers in the digital age: How digital solutions can enable rural development. *Foreign Affairs* November/December (special issue)

Bagopi E, Chokwe E, Halse P, Hausiku J, Humavindu M et al. (2016) Competition, agro-processing and regional development: The case of the poultry sector in South Africa, Botswana, Namibia and Zambia. In S Roberts (Ed.) *Competition in Africa.* Cape Town: HSRC Press

CAK (2019) *Competition in shipping, trucking and haulage sector study in East Africa, final report, July 2019.* CAK and Maritime Business and Economic Consultants

Gereffi G & Fernandez-Stark K (2011) *Global value chain analysis: A primer.* Durham, NC: Centre on Globalisation, Governance and Competitiveness

Goga S & Bosiu T (2019) *Governance of poultry value chains: A comparative perspective on developing capabilities in South Africa and Brazil.* Working Paper Series 10/2019, Centre for Competition, Regulation and Economic Development, University of Johannesburg

Goga S & Roberts S (2023) *Multinationals and power in poultry value chains in South Africa, Zambia and Malawi.* Working Paper Series 2023/11, Centre for Competition, Regulation and Economic Development, University of Johannesburg

Gondwe T, Nsomba G & Roberts S (2022) *Competition and the challenges of inclusive economic development: An apparent margin squeeze in poultry farming in Malawi*. Working Paper Series 2022/10, Centre for Competition, Regulation and Economic Development, University of Johannesburg

Harrington JE (2007) Behavioural screening and the detection of cartels. In C-D Ehlermann & I Atanasiu (Eds) *European competition law annual 2006: Enforcement of prohibition of cartels*. Oxford: Hart Publishing

Kaziboni L & Roberts S (2022) *Industrial policy for a just transition to a green economy: The importance of regional food value chains in Southern Africa*. Working Paper Series WP 2022–01. SARChI Industrial Development, University of Johannesburg

Marshall R & Marx L (2012) *The economics of collusion: Cartels and bidding rings*. Cambridge, Massachusetts: MIT Press

Nakamura S, Harati R, Lall S, Dikhanov Y, Hamadeh N et al. (2016) *Is living in African cities expensive?* Policy Research Working Paper No. 7641, World Bank, Washington, DC

Ncube P, Roberts S, Samboko P & Zengeni T (2017) *Identifying growth opportunities in the Southern African Development Community through regional value chains – the case of the animal feed to poultry value chain*. WIDER Working Paper 2017/4, Helsinki, UNU-WIDER

Nsomba G, Jangale E & Vilakazi T (2019) *Assessing competition and political economy dynamics in the transport and logistics sector in Malawi*. Working Paper No. 2019/12, Centre for Competition, Regulation and Economic Development, University of Johannesburg

Nsomba G, Kachipapa Mhone A, Mulozi I, Oiro R & Roberts S (2022) *Competition issues and regional integration in soybean and animal feed to poultry markets, within and across Kenya, Malawi and Zambia*. Working Paper Series 2022/09, Centre for Competition, Regulation and Economic Development, University of Johannesburg

Nsomba G, Roberts S, Manjengwa E & Tshabalala N (2022) *Assessing agriculture and food markets in East and Southern Africa: An agenda for regional competition enforcement*. Working Paper. No 2022/1, Centre for Competition, Regulation and Economic Development

Nsomba G, Roberts S & Tshabalala N (2021) *Assessing agriculture markets in Eastern and Southern Africa: Implications for inclusion, climate change and the case for a market observatory*. Working Paper 2021/07, Centre for Competition, Regulation and Economic Development, University of Johannesburg

Roberts S (2020) Cartel enforcement – Critical reflections from the South African experience. In D Healey, M Jacobs & RL Smith (Eds) *Research handbook on methods and models of competition law*. Cheltenham: Edward Elgar Publishing

Vilakazi T, Goga S & Roberts S (2020) *Opening the South African Economy: Barriers to entry, regulation and competition*. Cape Town: HSRC Press

Appendix B

Table A10.1 Suppliers of day-old chicks (DoC) and market shares along the value chain, Malawi

Company	Operations	DoC market share	Feed	Broiler production
CP Feeds	Parent operations Obtain parent DoC from Irvines (Cobb)	~87%	~40%	~80%
Kelfoods	Parent Operations Obtain parent DoC from RBZ (Ross)	~11%	~40%	<4%
Others: – Conforzi/Glenae – Charles Stewart – Thanzi	Parent operations Obtain parent DOC from RBZ (Ross)[a]	~1% each	Very small	Very small

Source: Goga and Roberts (2022) and interviews with market participants

Table A10.2 Breeding and supply of day-old chicks, Zambia

Company	Operations	DoC Production Volumes	Feed production
Licence and distribution rights holders			
Hybrid Poultry	Sole rights to distribute Cobb500 breeding stock in Zambia; grandparent stock supplies parent stock, day-old chicks, live and dressed broilers, layers and village chicken	550 000	
Ross Breeders Zambia (RBZ)	Sole rights to distribute Aviagen's Ross 308 breeding stock for Country Bird Holdings in southern Africa; grandparent stock, parent stock, day-old chicks, processed chicken	450 000	Nutrifeeds
Tiger Chicks	Rights holder to Aviagen's Indian River grandparent stock, supplies parent stock, DoC, production and distribution of chicken products	200 000	Tiger Animal Feeds
Buyers of parent stock, supplying day-old chicks			
Zamhatch	Hatchery and breeding of day-old chicks, processed chicken: Cobb 500 (from Hybrid); Ross 308 (from RBZ)	450 000	Novatek
Quantum Foods	Hatchery and breeding of day-old chicks, processed chicken: Ross 308 (from RBZ)	60 000	Nova Feeds
Zamharvest (Heartland)	Hatchery and breeding of day-old chicks, processed chicken: Ross 308 (from RBZ); Sasso (from Tyson/Hendrix)	n.a.	

Source: Compiled by authors

Table A10.3 Main breeders and day-old chick suppliers, Kenya

Kenchic	Isinya
• Estimated 70% market share of supply of day-old chicks, holding Ross 308 from GP level • Largest commercial broiler producer • APDL is parent company, Seaboard also shareholder • APDL in Aviagen East Africa JV • Partnership with Unga Feeds, common shareholding	• Likely to source Cobb 500 from Irvines (Zimbabwe) at parent stock level • Vertically integrated into feed and broiler production

Source: Compiled by authors

Table A10.4 Main suppliers of soy oilcake and commercial animal feed, Malawi

Company	Animal feed production	Supply of oilcake	Production of vegetable oil	Soybean crushing capacity (tonnes per annum)
CP Feeds (including Sunseed Oil)	Yes	Yes	Yes	180 000
Mount Meru	No	Yes	Yes	320 000 (combined)[b]
Capital Oil Refinery Industries (CORI)	No	Yes	Yes	
Export Trading Group (ETG)	No	Yes	Yes	
Sungold Food Processing	No	Yes	Yes	
Kelfoods/Proto Feeds	Yes	No	No	—
Conforzi	Yes	No	No	—
Amazon	Yes	No	No	—
Lenzie Milling	Yes	No	No	—

Source: Compiled by authors from interviews in Malawi

Table A10.5 Soybean processors and animal feed producers, Zambia

Company	Animal feed production	Supply of oilcake	Production of vegetable oil
Soybean processors[c]			
Emman Farming Enterprise (EFE)	Yes	Yes	Yes
Zamanita/Parrogate (ETG)	No	Yes	Yes
Mount Meru	No	Yes	Yes
Global Industries (Wilmar)	No	Yes	Yes
Pembe Milling	No	Yes	No
Large feed suppliers			
National Milling/Namfeed (Seaboard)	Yes	No	Yes
Tiger Animal Feeds	Yes	No	No
Novatek Animal Feeds (Zambeef)	Yes	No	No
Simba Milling	Yes	No	No
Olympic Milling	Yes	No	No

Company	Animal feed production	Supply of oilcake	Production of vegetable oil
Ross Breeders (Nutri feeds)	Yes	No	No
Pembe Milling	Yes	No	No
Smaller feed producers			
High Protein Foods	Yes	No	Yes
Consolidated Mining Reef (CMR)	Yes	No	Yes
Antelope Milling	Yes	No	No
Perfect Milling Limited	Yes	No	No
Acropolis Enterprises Limited	Yes	No	No
Chigayo Animal Feed	Yes	No	No
Yielding Feeds Limited	Yes	No	No

Source: Compiled by authors

Table A10.6 Poultry feed producers, Kenya

Producer category	Capacity (tonnes per annum)	Identified players
Tier 1	100 000–500 000	Unga Ltd; Pembe Mills Ltd; Isinya Feeds; Sigma Feeds
Tier 2	5 000–100 000	Approx. 30 companies including Jubilee, Suguna, Empire, Belfast
Tier 3	<5 000	Approx. 100 companies

Source: Compiled by authors drawing on interviews

Notes

a Interview with Malawian poultry producer, 7 July 2022.

b We estimate a total of 500 000 tonnes of crushing capacity in Malawi. Mount Meru is around 100 thousand tonnes, while Sungold is somewhat smaller than the others.

c Mount Meru, EFE and Global Industries each have crushing capacity of around 100th tonnes per annum, while ETG's Zamanita plant is around 200th tonnes. See: https://www.foodbusinessafrica.com/country-focus-grains-and-milling-industry-in-zambia/; https://www.tabj.co.za/agriculture/emman-farming_enterprises.html

11 Competition and the challenges of inclusive economic development: An apparent margin squeeze in poultry farming in Malawi

Timothy Gondwe, Grace Nsomba and Simon Roberts

With poultry being the main source of animal protein in Malawi, demand has grown strongly, particularly from the mid-2000s, due to high levels of economic growth and urbanisation. Commercial broiler and layer production is estimated to have now surpassed rural poultry (CASA 2020). Poultry also has strong backward linkages to the production of maize and soybean for animal feed.

Commercial poultry growth requires investment in breeding operations of the fast-growing global breeds and in the rearing of broiler chickens. Chickens can be sold live (as is the case in much of Malawi) or processed and distributed through the cold chain to end consumers (Bagopi et al. 2016; Ncube at al. 2017). By comparison, rural or 'backyard' poultry production involves rearing local chickens in smallholdings for both eggs and meat with relatively low amounts of feed inputs.

Countries with good conditions for producing the constituents of animal feed should have competitive commercial poultry industries, as the low costs of these combined with the right breeding stock can provide a competitive cost base for poultry production. Industry competitiveness and the ability of smaller poultry producers to compete and grow to supply poultry to consumers depend on the prices and processing of the inputs through the value chain. This in turn depends on competition in the key input markets.

In Malawi, there have been major changes in the pricing and supply of the key inputs, both animal feed and poultry breeding stock, which have undermined smaller producers. We evaluate the impacts of these changes on the competitiveness of small and medium-sized poultry producers drawing from fieldwork interviews and data gathering in 2021 and 2022, as set out in the working paper on which this chapter is based (Gondwe et al. 2022). Our analysis identifies a margin squeeze on smaller producers, which made them unviable. This is as a result of the likely exercise of market power by the large upstream businesses integrated across breeding, soybean processing and animal feed supply. It points to the importance of effective competition enforcement at the national and regional level if smaller producers are not to be excluded and there being no harm to consumers.

Chapter 11 starts with an overview of the poultry value chain and market outcomes, focusing first on value chain linkages, integration and concentration, and then looking at market outcomes. Then it provides an assessment of these market outcomes and explores the possible exclusionary conduct. Next, the chapter conducts a test for a margin squeeze in the Malawi poultry industry, looking at input costs and prices, and assessing evidence for the exclusion of smaller producers, followed by a discussion on the findings. Finally, it provides an analysis of the basis for higher upstream prices, with an assessment of soybean price movements and then concludes with motivations for further investigations and suggestions for avenues to provide support for small and medium producers.

Overview of the poultry value chain and market outcomes

Competitive poultry production depends on linkages along the value chain for competitive supply from breeding stock and feed to poultry production and distribution (see chapter 10 by Nsomba et al., in this book). In this overview, we set out the main levels in the value chain and concentration in Malawi followed by market outcomes in terms of feed components, feed prices and chicken prices.

Value chain linkages, integration and concentration

Across different countries in east and southern Africa, the broiler production model has evolved in different ways. In some countries, such as South Africa and Zambia, the large integrated companies have incorporated contract growers to rear the birds (Ncube et al. 2017). In the case of Malawi, smaller producers source their own inputs and compete independently with a few large integrated companies. Contract farming has not been implemented widely and was introduced by the largest poultry company only from 2019.[1] The majority of small and medium-sized independent producers sell their broilers live, as do large-scale producers.[2]

Poultry production in Malawi has been an important source of income for urban and rural subsistence producers. It is a key driver of livestock sector growth, particularly through private sector investments, which have created employment and largely substituted poultry imports (CASA 2020). Chicken is the fastest-growing category of livestock in Malawi. For instance, between 2015 and 2019, the chicken population increased by 112% (CFTC 2020). In terms of meat production, however, chicken ranked second after pork in 2019, accounting for 31% of meat production in 2019. Commercial broiler/egg production constituted over half the national flock, while the 2018 census recorded that 1.3 million smallholder households keep or own chickens in Malawi.[3] The important backward and forward linkages with production, maize and soybean farming mean that poultry production can contribute to poverty reduction through income generation for poultry farmers and traders, as well as the production of value-added poultry products (Bosiu & Goga 2019; CFTC 2020; Gereffi & Fernandez-Stark 2016; Ncube et al. 2017).

Rural poultry farming is usually based on a mixed flock of less than 100 birds, dominated by local dual-purpose chickens that are raised in a free-range, low-input system. These take much longer to grow than broiler chickens and they are sold in local markets. Rural poultry is difficult to improve through intensification with higher levels of feed because the higher costs of production outweigh the increased gains. Rural flocks have recently started to include the introduction of imported exotic breeds, such as Kuroiler from India and Sasso from France[4], which are faster growing if commercial feed is used.

The commercial poultry market in Malawi is made up of many small-scale farmers (with optimal flocks of up to 500 birds) alongside a very few large vertically integrated producers with one company, Central Poultry (CP), having the lion's share.[5] Commercial poultry production is concentrated around urban areas in Blantyre, Lilongwe and Mzuzu, focusing on broilers and layers.

Cobb 500 and Ross 308 are the broiler breeds used by small, medium and large-scale commercial poultry producers. Central Poultry owns the Malawi franchise for Cobb and keeps parent stock for hatching eggs and sales of day-old chicks. Other hatcheries keep parent stock for Ross, sourcing through Country Bird and Irvine's in Zambia and Zimbabwe (Goga & Roberts 2023).

Concentration at the level of breeding and supply of day-old chicks is striking (see Table 11.1). Central Poultry (CP) holds approximately 87% market share in terms of supply of day-old chicks into its own broiler production operations and the supply to independent producers. Central Poultry is a fully integrated broiler producer that breeds and rears Cobb 500 broilers for sale to independent producers as day-old chicks (DoC), and it sells broilers into the retail market as fresh or frozen chickens.[6] Central Poultry is also dominant in broiler production, with a share of the Malawi market of approximately 80%.

Table 11.1 Commercial poultry producers and estimated market shares 2022, Malawi

Company	Breeding and DoC supply	Feed	Broiler production
Central Poultry	~87%	~40%	~80%
Kelfoods/Proto Feed	~11%	~40%	<4%
Lenzie Milling (Charles Stewart)	~1%		
Conforzi	~1%		
Amazon	<1%		<1%
Other, small and medium scale			~15%

Source: Compiled by authors from interviews conducted in Malawi

The commercial animal feed industry is also highly concentrated, with two main producers being Central Poultry and Kelfoods, jointly accounting for around 80% of feed sales (Table 11.1). Lenzie Milling is the only independent large-scale poultry feed producer, having previously been linked to Charles Stewart Hatchery. There are two other very small feed producers, Conforzi and Amazon.

There are, however, very large oil crushers that produce vegetable oil (for human consumption) and oilcake for animal feed as co-products. In addition to CP Feeds, there are four substantial soybean processors that could supply important feed components: Capital Oil Refinery Industries (which we understand has close links with CP Feeds): Export Trading Group (ETG): Mount Meru: and Sungold (Table 11.2). However, we understand that ETG, Mount Meru and Sungold are not feed producers in Malawi. These producers of vegetable oil therefore play a critical role in supplying oilcake inputs to the animal feed producers, which then supply poultry producers. The soybean derived inputs are also crucial for small poultry producers that opt to mix their own feed. The terms on which the feed producers can source oilcake are clearly important for their competitiveness.

Table 11.2 Soy oilcake, soymeal and commercial animal feed producers in Malawi, 2022

Company	Animal feed production	Supply of oilcake / soymeal	Vegetable oil	Soybean crushing capacity (tonnes per annum)
CP Feeds (including Sunseed Oil)#	Yes	Yes	Yes	180 000[7]
Capital Oil Refinery Industries#	No	Yes	Yes	320 000 (combined)[8]
Export Trading Group (ETG)	No	Yes	Yes	
Mount Meru	No	Yes	Yes	
Sungold Food Processing	No	Yes	Yes	
Kelfoods/Proto Feeds	Yes	No	No	–
Conforzi	Yes	No	No	–
Amazon	Yes	No	No	–
Lenzie Milling	Yes	No	No	–

Source: Compiled by authors from interviews in Malawi

Notes: # related by family

Central Poultry, together with its sister company Sunseed Oil, is a highly integrated poultry producer, both in terms of breeding stock and feed production into broiler production. The other feed mills and soybean crushers operate at one or two levels of the value chain. Central Poultry's size and vertical integration raise questions about the terms on which it supplies independent third parties compared to its in-house operations.

Market outcomes

The 2021 harvest season saw prices at the harvest in April and May at around $500/t for soybeans and $150/t for maize (see Nsomba et al. 2022). The soybean prices at the time were very similar to those in South Africa and compared with prices in Zambia of around $400/t. The Malawian maize prices were substantially below South African prices (around $230/t) and in line with prices in Zambia. The production of soybeans had increased substantially to over 400 000 tonnes in 2020 compared to 223 000 tonnes the year before. This underpinned the significant net exports of soybeans and oilcake. Malawi is generally self-sufficient in maize.

Malawi prices of soybeans then increased dramatically over 2021, almost trebling to around $1 400/t by the end of the year (Figure 11.1) while international prices were around $600. Maize prices meanwhile remained stable.

Figure 11.1 Prices of maize and soybean

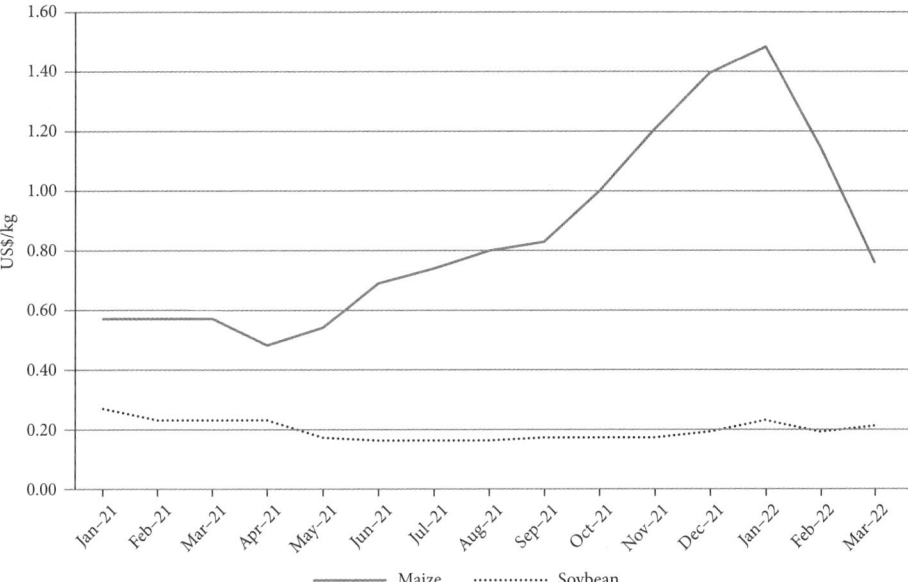

Source: Compiled from interviews in Malawi

Feed prices also increased substantially. Against these price increases, poultry prices increased by approximately 39% over the same period (Figure 11.2). There was also an increase in the prices of day-old chicks during the same period. This price of breeding stock can be added to the feed price to estimate the costs of producing chicken. The cost of day-old chicks increased in June of 2021, when Central Poultry raised the price of day-old chicks from approximately $0.65 to $0.88 per chick, and the second-largest supplier, Kelfoods, followed suit.[9]

Assessing market outcomes and possible exclusionary conduct

These findings led us to ask two important questions. First, what was the impact of the increase in input prices relative to poultry prices on the viability of small- and medium-scale broiler producers? And second, do the market outcomes reflect competition, or do they reflect the exercise of market power by a dominant firm or a group of large firms with the aim of excluding smaller rivals?

Here, we assess whether indeed there has been an exercise of market power to undermine independent producers, based on the high levels of concentration at different levels of the value chain coupled with vertical integration.

Figure 11.2: Prices of maize and soybean against feed and day-old chicken costs, per kg of chicken meat

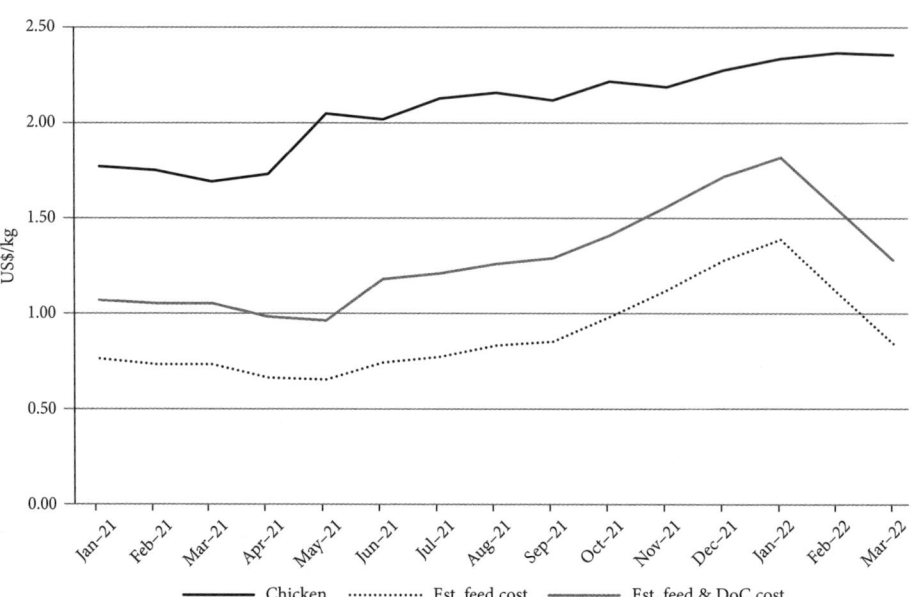

Source: Compiled from interviews in Malawi

Many industries are characterised by vertical production relationships, where the production of a final product requires inputs from suppliers at various stages of the value chain. Vertical integration within one firm may realise efficiencies from better coordination (Ncube et al. 2017). At the same time, however, it means large firms may be able to exploit their position of dominance in upstream levels to restrict competition in downstream markets. It must be noted though that having the ability to do this does not necessarily mean the dominant firm would have the incentive to exclude competitors, nor does it mean that the conduct would have a wider anti-competitive effect.

One way in which a vertically integrated firm with substantial market power at upstream and downstream levels can undermine competition is by exerting a margin squeeze on non-integrated rivals. This is illustrated in the diagram in Figure 11.3. The diagram shows how this theory of harm involves the dominant upstream firm supplying the main inputs raising the price, P_{inputs}, relative to the downstream price that its integrated downstream poultry production business charges to customers (Figure 11.3). The result is that the non-integrated smaller downstream poultry farmers find that their margin is squeezed between the higher input price and the downstream price for poultry.

Figure 11.3 Diagram depicting the possibility of margin squeeze

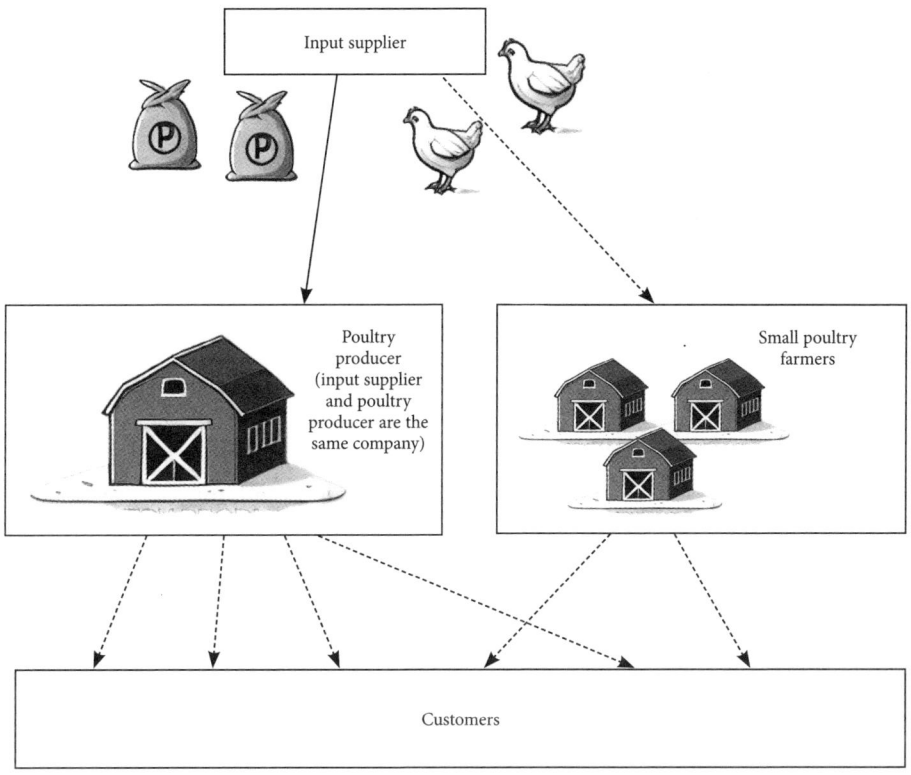

Source: Authors' construction

The ability of the dominant firm to unfairly undermine the downstream competitors depends on the alternatives available to independent poultry farmers to source inputs and whether they can charge higher prices downstream (to pass on the higher costs). If this is not the case, then the downstream rivals, the small independent poultry farmers, are undermined and could exit the market. Even if the downstream firms do not exit, this may represent unfair competition and an exclusionary abuse of dominance.

In the downstream market, it is necessary to assess the prices that are set by the dominant firm and the effect on its competitors. If the dominant firm and its competitors are supplying close substitutes, the smaller rivals will not be able to charge higher prices while still maintaining their sales levels. Customers will instead switch to the dominant firm's products in the downstream market.

In addition to the ability to exclude non-integrated downstream rivals, we also need to think about the incentive to do so and the effects on competition. The test on incentives considers why the firm would want to undermine its customers (even while they are also competitors)? If the dominant firm is simply realising efficiencies, which may be passed onto consumers in the form of lower downstream prices, then this will render non-integrated rivals less able to compete. However, in and of itself, this is not evidence of the abuse of dominance.

The test can rather be framed in terms of whether the conduct of the dominant firm makes economic sense without there being an anti-competitive rationale. One way of answering this is by examining whether the vertically integrated firm's downstream business would be commercially viable at the prices it is charging to independent businesses (Fumagalli et al. 2018; Roberts 2023). If it would not be viable, then a competitor that is 'as efficient' as the dominant firm would be driven out of business.

There are various reasons why the dominant firm may want to unfairly undermine its downstream rivals, even while these are also its customers. First, the firm's position and market power upstream may be bolstered by undermining downstream competition. Downstream competitors may support entrants and smaller rivals upstream and hence weaken the dominant firm's position. Second, reducing competition downstream can increase the stability of collusion upstream, if there is more than one large upstream supplier. Third, there may be limits on the exertion of market power upstream, for example, through regulation or because of imperfect alternatives such as imports.

The assessment of likely anti-competitive effects through the 'as-efficient competitor' test indicates whether the conduct will have the effect of unfairly undermining competition. It is important to note that, in practice, the competitors may have different business models and strategies, as they have been positioning themselves to survive and grow in the context of the dominant firm that they are up against.

The test uses the dominant vertically integrated firm's prices and margins to consider whether they make commercial sense in terms of normal competition 'on the merits', or whether they are set to exclude non-integrated rivals. We consider a dominant firm that supplies a product or service to its own subsidiary that is an indispensable input to actual or potential competitors. The price set on this input may be found to be capable of excluding efficient competitors if the margin that can be made does not cover the reasonable downstream costs of production and supply. The cost benchmark here is usually the long-run average incremental cost of the dominant firm's subsidiary. In other words, the price for the input charged to third parties is applied to the subsidiary and, if it does not cover the relevant costs of the subsidiary for the appropriate increment of output, then it would not be commercially viable on a stand-alone basis (see Fumagalli et al. 2018; O'Donoghue & Padilla 2006; OECD 2010).

The test for whether there is a margin squeeze in Malawi poultry

We assess whether there has been a margin squeeze on smaller and independent poultry producers through applying the main test explained earlier in the chapter to the data gathered on the increased feed and breeding stock prices. In doing so, we need to take into account the other costs of poultry production and the prices at which chickens were sold to consumers. We use a range of estimates to consider these variables.

We first have to consider if there is a dominant and vertically integrated producer of inputs and poultry that has the ability to engage in conduct that may be exclusionary. In terms of these conditions for a possible margin squeeze in Malawi poultry, Central Poultry is evidently dominant in the supply of broiler day-old-chicks in Malawi and in downstream broiler supply (Table 11.2). Central Poultry is also a very large and likely dominant producer of poultry broiler feed, although there is one other large supplier. We also note that Central Poultry processes and crushes soybeans and maize, which are important inputs to animal feed (Table 11.3). We analyse the implications of these dynamics further below.

Given these industry characteristics and the position of Central Poultry, we can consider Central Poultry's conduct as both an upstream supplier of inputs and a downstream supplier of broiler chickens, in Malawi sold largely in the form of live chickens. In terms of whether the pricing constitutes a margin squeeze, the main test seeks to assess whether the prices upstream and downstream being charged by the dominant firm make sense in the absence of an anti-competitive rationale and whether they undermine competition. To do this, we can assess whether the downstream operation of the dominant firm could trade profitably based on the upstream price charged to its competitors. We also consider if there are any objective justifications for Central Poultry's pricing arrangements.

Input costs and prices

There are two essential inputs into broiler production: feed and day-old chicks. There are other components, including vitamins and mineral supplements and vaccines, which can be administered separately. There are also labour, energy and chicken litter costs. We have established the prices charged by Central Poultry for day-old chicks and for poultry feed through the cycle from starter, grower to finisher feed to grow a broiler of about 1.9 kg, which we understand is the approximate weight of the broilers produced by Central Poultry. We also have the price at which Central Poultry vendors sold its chickens to consumers and have made an estimate of the price charged by Central Poultry net of the vendor margin. We have separately estimated the costs of vaccines and other inputs for the birds.

The costs of labour and energy depend on the efficiency of the production plants. We understand that Central Poultry has large-scale facilities, which will mean lower average labour and energy costs, notwithstanding the need for major upfront investments. We estimate these costs separately on what, based on our understanding from the interviews, is a conservative basis. We also separately include an estimated mortality rate, and we consider the sensitivity to different estimates.

Technical efficiency is critical for the overall competitiveness of broiler production. The feed conversion ratio (the amount of feed used to produce a kilogram of meat) is a good indicator of the production efficiency of any producer. Lower values of the feed conversion ratio indicate high production efficiency in that smaller amounts of feed are required to produce a kilogram of meat. Based on efficiency levels in international markets and interviews, we estimate the feed conversion ratio of Central Poultry to be 1.6 to 1.8.[10] Some independent producers have higher conversion ratios (around 1.9 to 2.0), however, we apply the more efficient estimates.

We have also cross-checked our assessment with interviews, which established that basic costs per unit of production (for a 1.8–2 kg bird) are structured as follows: feed, 70%; day-old chick, 20%; energy, 5%; and labour, 3%. Our assessment is in line with these broad proportions, noting that the prices being set by Central Poultry over time will in themselves impact on the actual proportions.

There are other costs such as investments in production facilities and including phytosanitary requirements that do not vary with broiler production. As feed constitutes the majority of production costs, this cost (and the availability and price competitiveness of soybean and maize, which are the main constituents of feed) is critical.

In terms of day-old chicks, interviews with market participants indicated that prices increased from Malawi kwacha (Mwk) 495 per bird in April/May 2021 to Mwk700 in June/July and, by November/December 2021, prices had increased again to Mwk800. We also assess feed costs for November/December 2021 when compared with April/May 2021. The end of the year is a very important period as it is when broiler chickens are being reared for the festive season in December and January, considering the six-week rearing time. We understand that other suppliers set similar prices for key inputs as Central Poultry.[11]

We assess the prices of inputs and estimates of production costs against the selling prices for chickens in the November/December 2021 period. We compare this with the chicken prices in the first half of 2021, before the substantial price increases in animal feed and its constituents, using April/May 2021 for our assessment. We note that Central Poultry had price increases between these time periods, for both essential inputs of feed and day-old chicks, increasing by approximately 100% and 62% respectively.

Market data and interviews indicate that in December 2021, vendors sold Central Poultry broiler chickens in the market in central Malawi at approximately Mwk2600, up from Mwk2400 in April. We consider the Central Poultry price per bird at the production facility, that is, after netting off a conservative estimate for transport costs and margins to vendors, calculated as the Central Poultry retail price less 10%. This gives a wholesale price in December 2021 of Mwk2340. From the input costs and wholesale price, we calculate the margins over different estimates of input costs, and for 1.6 and 1.8 feed conversion ratios (Table 11.3). These are presented as average variable costs to produce a 1.9 kg bird.

Table 11.3 Calculation of Central Poultry margins per 1.9 kg bird (Mwk)

	Nov/Dec 2021	April/May 2021
DoC, per chick	800	495
Central Poultry feed price/kg	514 [a]	260 [b]
Feed cost @ 1.6 conversion for 1.9 kg bird	1 562	790
Feed cost @ 1.8 conversion for 1.9 kg bird	1 757	889
AVC, for only DoC and feed @1.6 conversion	2 362	1 285
AVC, for only DoC and feed @1.8 conversion	2 557	1 384
Vaccines, drugs, litter [c]	46	46
Energy and labour @ 5% of cost price [d]	117	108
AVC, incl vaccines, energy and labour @ 1.6 conversion	2 525	1 439
AVC, incl vaccines, energy and labour @ 1.6, mortality 4%	2 623	1 493
AVC, incl vaccines, energy & labour @ 1.8, mortality 4%	2 833	1 602
CP wholesale price ex-producer [e]	2 340	2 160
CP chicken price per bird to customer	2 600	2 400
Margins of price over:		
AVC: DoC and feed, @ 1.6 conversion	−22	875
AVC: DoC, feed, vaccine, energy, labour @ 1.6	−185	721
..with 4% mortality, @ 1.6 conversion	−283	667
..with 4% mortality, @ 1.8 conversion	−483	558

Source: Authors' own calculations

Notes:
a This is based on a combination of 14% starter feed (at Mwk28368/50 kg), 28% grower feed (at Mwk24881/50 kg) and 58% finisher feed (at Mwk25430/50 kg).
b Estimated from maize and soybean prices, and from interviews.
c From interviews for November/December 2021 prices, assumed to be the same throughout 2021.
d Estimated at 5% of price ex-producer.
e Assuming 10% difference between vendor price and ex-producer price, from interviews.

The findings

The findings are striking. The combination of input costs and wholesale prices yield negative margins in November/December 2021 even when we consider only day-old chick and feed costs, and with the most efficient conversion ratio at 1.6. Including additional costs that have to be incurred and an estimate of mortality rates means much larger negative margins. Including the additional costs (but not all costs of running the facility) at the 1.6 conversion ratio means Central Poultry would have been losing 283 kwacha on each bird sold, or a negative margin of −12% if they had incurred the input prices that they charged to independent poultry producers. We note that negative margins mean no return on the investments made, and no account for management time and other overheads.

Therefore, if Central Poultry had charged its downstream broiler production division the same input costs that it charged independent producers at the end of 2021, it would not have traded profitably.

A reasonably efficient competitor would have to incur these and additional costs, and would likely have higher costs in other areas such as labour and energy, for which we have used extremely low estimates. For example, estimates from other producers were that labour and energy costs collectively were equivalent to around 8% of the wholesale price. This would therefore mean even more negative margins.

By comparison, in the first half of 2021, based on our initial estimates, the margins were positive.

Evidence of exclusion

The evidence on the margin squeeze being exerted by Central Poultry's pricing is consistent with indications of the closure of operations of small- and medium-scale poultry producers around the time, due to them being unable to compete with Central Poultry.

We understand that representations were made to the authorities about the inability of independent producers to compete. In response, some undertakings were made by Central Poultry that it would not sell to rural areas in competition with independent producers. However, this means subjecting consumers in these areas to *higher* prices rather than ensuring that independent producers are better able to compete effectively through ensuring competitive input costs – and meaning lower wholesale prices to consumers as well.

Analysis of the basis for higher upstream prices

The margin squeeze is a combination of upstream input prices and the downstream price for chickens. To consider whether the squeeze is more the result of the upstream higher prices or low downstream prices, we consider the upstream prices and the alternatives available to small- and medium-scale poultry producers.

Establishing commercial hatcheries requires substantial investments and the sourcing of breeding stock from the two main multinational companies, Cobb-Vantress (Tyson Foods) and Aviagen. Breeding is standardised globally through the operation of these multinationals and the regional producers to which they license their breeds. The prices of the day-old chicks in Malawi, however, appear to be very high by international comparison. The price of Mwk800 at the end of 2021 was almost exactly US$1 per chick. International prices were around US$0.40, notwithstanding the fact that the main poultry breeders and producers in the United States (US) have been operating cartels (Roberts 2023).[12] It also compares with an average price in South Africa in the second half of 2021 of R8.27 or around US$0.55 (Goga & Roberts 2023; SAPA 2021). Prices in neighbouring Zambia from which chicks could have been obtained were also high, at around US$1 (16 Zambian kwacha) at the time.[13] The high day-old chick prices in Malawi have a significant material impact on the costs of poultry producers, as reflected in Table 11.3.

To understand feed costs, we need to assess the developments in the markets for the main components of maize and soybeans and their processing (including where crushing of soybeans to produce oilcake as a co-product of vegetable oil). The major change in the period is the increase in the soybean price during 2021. While other inputs for feed such as vitamins and minerals, along with vaccines, are important, they are a relatively small proportion of feed costs (see Table 11.3).

Assessment of soybean price movements

The soybean prices in Malawi trebled from the prices paid to farmers at the harvest in April/May 2021 to the prices at the end of the year. Soon after the 2021 harvest, the prices of soybean were around MwK350/kg ($450/t) and rose to Mwk800/kg ($1000/t) in January of 2022.[14] Prices reported in the market by some market participants spiked to above $1 400. In the same vein, oilcake prices rose dramatically, from around MwK450/kg ($570/t) at the beginning of the season to MwK1 050/kg ($1 330/t) in January of 2022.[15]

The increased soybean prices did have significant effects on the price of animal feed. Lenzie Milling, for instance, revised prices four times over the 12 months to March 2021, even with reformulating to use less soy oilcake.[16] As reflected in Table 11.3, CP Feeds doubled the feed prices from March/April 2021 to December 2021. This is one of the main factors in the margin squeeze finding from our analysis.

The high soybean and oilcake prices may suggest that there was a scarcity and prices therefore increased to the same level as the price of imports. However, given Malawi's soybean production estimates for 2021 and increasing exports into the east and southern African regions, the shortage appears to have been artificial. In addition, the price levels to which soybeans increased were in fact far above competitive import prices.

The trade data indicate that Malawi was a substantial net exporter of soybeans and oilcake in 2021, as production outstripped local demand by a large proportion. Large volumes of exports were made to countries in the region at prices substantially below the local prices being recorded in the second half of 2021. This is reinforced by interviews that indicated oilcake was being exported to countries such as Kenya, Tanzania, South Africa and Zimbabwe.[17] Concerns have been raised over prices of oilcake surging in the 2021 harvest year, significantly raising the costs of inputs into animal feed and, as a result, animal feed itself.

The exertion of market power to set high local prices while exports were being made is supported by buyers reporting price discrimination, apparently according to whether they were local or export buyers. For example, one large buyer looked to source for export and was offered an export price of $600/t for oilcake in January

2022, yet when the buyer was revealed to be a local customer, it was instead charged a price of around $1 000/t.[18] In fact, the buyer was able to import from South Africa at prices around $800–900, indicating that local prices were pushed to levels even above the import prices that could be realised by large-scale traders and importers.

The ability to set different prices to export customers and to local customers is a very strong signal of substantial market power on the part of the sellers. To support the elevated local prices, there have to be firms selling at lower prices into the export markets even while they could achieve higher prices in the local market. Either a single firm must be able to control the additional volumes over the local demand to be able to unilaterally create artificial conditions of scarcity, denying local customers the export volumes, or there must be coordination between the main traders and processors of soybeans.

Conclusions

The poultry industry is a significant sector within agriculture in Malawi. It is an important and relatively low-cost source of protein for household consumption and has wide participation by small-scale producers in rearing and selling chickens. It has key backward linkages to maize and soybean farming, and hence to large numbers of small-scale farmers.

The developments we have analysed in this chapter raise major concerns about how well markets have worked. Farmers of maize and soybeans have received low prices for their crops, while poultry producers have been charged very high prices over the second half of 2021 and into 2022 for the key inputs of day-old chicks and animal feed. There are extremely high levels of concentration at these levels of the value chain and the market outcomes are indicative of the exertion of market power to distort markets. This is evident in the pricing of day old-chicks and feed to small- and medium-scale producers.

When we assess the input prices relative to the prices charged by the large vertically integrated poultry producer, we find that a margin squeeze was exerted on small and medium independent poultry producers in the second half of 2021 with a likely exclusionary effect, thus harming competition and participation in the industry. The same large-scale producer also controls the pricing of live broiler chickens given its market share and sales into markets where small- and medium-scale producers also sell their birds.

Efforts to establish fairer market conditions for smaller poultry producers sought to prevent large-scale producers from selling to the retail markets being targeted by the smaller producers. Our analysis indicates that attention should rather be paid to the pricing of the inputs that render the independent producers uncompetitive and, very importantly, that there are major competition issues that require investigation. These include the apparent margin squeeze exerted by the main vertically integrated producer and the reasons for the high prices of soybeans and its derivative oilcake used for animal feed.

At the same time, policy support for greater rivalry through empowering small- and medium-scale producers to engage in commercial feed production could provide an avenue to discipline market power in future. Such a strategy may be combined with support for aggregation and storage of the main feed components to achieve better prices for farmers at the harvest time and to support small and medium feed and poultry producers in being able to source feed inputs.

Notes

1. Interview with Small and Medium Poultry Farmers Association, 4 March 2022.
2. Interview with Small and Medium Poultry Farmers Association, 4 March 2022.
3. Government of Malawi – National Statistical Office, 2018 Population and Housing Census (PHC) – Final Report, Zomba; Interview with Small and Medium Poultry Farmers Association, 4 March 2022.
4. The Sasso breed is produced by Hendrix, which is in a joint venture with Cobb (Goga & Roberts 2023).
5. Interview with Small and Medium Poultry Farmers Association, 4 March 2022.
6. See: http://www.centralpoultrymw.com/
7. Crushing capacity of 70 000t, with storage capacity of 40 000t in March of 2022. The yield from soybean crushing is 17–19% soybean oil, with the remainder being oilcake. Interview with Sunseed Oil, 18 March 2022.
8. Of this, Mount Meru is estimated to be around 100 000t (https://pdf.usaid.gov/pdf_docs/PA00W6VG.pdf) and Sungold is relatively small; we estimate a total of 500 000t of crushing capacity in Malawi.
9. Note the DoC price increase impact is calculated per kg of meat, noting that a chicken is typically around 1.8 to 2 kg each.
10. Based on Professor Timothy Gondwe's expertise in the industry and international benchmarks.
11. Although some much smaller entrants have had lower prices, such as Thanzi Chicks, which entered as a day-old chick supplier in late 2020. Interview with small producer, July 2022.
12. See: End-User Consumer Plaintiff's Fifth Consolidated Amended Class Action Complaint [Redacted Version], filed, 7 August 2020, United States District Court, Northern District of Illinois Eastern Division. Tyson Annual Report 2021 on Form 10-K SEC filing, page 79. Consolidated Amended Class Action Complaint, Broiler Chicken Grower Litigation filed in United States District Court for the Eastern District of Oklahoma, 10 July 2017. Second Amended Consolidated Complaint in Civil Action No. 1:19-CV–2521-SAG, in US District Courts for the District of Maryland, filed 2 November 2020. Settlements of these cases have been reached by the main producers.
13. See: https://www.agribusinesszambia.com/kwacha-appreciation-set-to-positively-affect-the-prices-of-day-old-chicks/
14. Interview with feed producer, March 2022.

15   Interview with feed producer, March 2022.

16   Interview with feed producer, March 2022.

17   Interview with large transporter, March 2022.

18   Interview with feed producer, March 2022.

References

Bagopi E, Chokwe E, Halse P, Hausiku J, Humavindu M et al. (2016) Competition, agro-processing and regional development: The case of the poultry sector in South Africa, Botswana, Namibia and Zambia. In S Roberts (Ed.) *Competition in Africa*. Cape Town: HSRC Press

Bosiu T & Goga S (2019) *Governance of poultry value chains – A comparative perspective on developing capabilities in South Africa and Brazil*. Working Paper Series 10/2019, Centre for Competition, Regulation and Economic Development, University of Johannesburg

CASA (2020) *Poultry sector strategy – Malawi*. Lilongwe: Commercial Agriculture for Smallholders and Agribusiness. Accessed October 2022, https://www.casaprogramme.com/wp-content/uploads/CASA-Malawi-PoultrySector-analysis-report.pdf

CFTC (2020) *Assessment of competition and consumer protection issues in the Malawi poultry industry*. Competition and Fair Trading Commission Malawi sector study

Fumagalli C, Motta M & Calcagno C (2018) *Exclusionary practices: The economics of monopolisation and abuse of dominance*. Cambridge: Cambridge University Press

Gereffi G & Fernandez-Stark K (2016) *Global value chain analysis: A primer* (2nd edition). Durham, North Carolina: CGGC (Center on Globalization, Governance & Competitiveness) Duke University

Goga S & Roberts S (2023) *Multinationals and competition in poultry value chains in South Africa, Zambia and Malawi*. Working Paper Series 2023/11, Centre for Competition, Regulation and Economic Development, University of Johannesburg

Gondwe T, Nsomba G & Roberts S (2022) *Competition and the challenges of inclusive development: An apparent margin squeeze in poultry farming in Malawi*. Working Paper No. 2022/10, Centre for Competition, Regulation and Economic Development

Ncube P, Roberts S, Samboko P & Zengeni T (2017) *Identifying growth opportunities in the Southern African Development Community through regional value chains: The case of the animal feed to poultry value chain*. WIDER Working Paper No. WP 2017/4, Helsinki, UNU-WIDER

Nsomba G, Roberts S, Tshabalala N & Manjengwa E (2022) *Assessing agriculture & food markets in Eastern and Southern Africa: Implications for regional competition enforcement*. Working Paper No. 2022/1, Centre for Competition, Regulation and Economic Development

O'Donoghue R & Padilla J (2006) *The Law and Economics of Article 102 TFEU*. Oxford: Hart Publishing

OECD (Organisation for Economic Cooperation and Development) (2010) Margin squeeze: Key findings, summary and notes. *OECD Roundtables on Competition Policy Papers, No. 105*. Paris: OECD Publishing. https://doi.org/10.1787/cb1e895c-en

Roberts S (2021) Economic analysis and evidence in abuse cases. *OECD Roundtables on Competition Policy Papers, No. 269*. Paris: OECD Publishing. https://doi.org/10.1787/63e6d5f0-en

Roberts S (2023) Competition, trade and sustainability in agriculture and food markets in Africa. *Oxford Review of Economic Policy* 39(1): 147–151

SAPA (2021) *Subsistence and Small Commercial Farmer Stats Report* 2H2021. Johannesburg: South African Poultry Association

12 An analysis of competition dynamics in South African digital markets for travel and tourism

Itumeleng Lesofe and Siphosethu Tetani

The tourism sector plays a significant role in African economies. In South Africa, the sector is a significant contributor to employment and inclusive growth. Unlike most sectors, tourism displays less concentration levels and vertical integration throughout its extensive value chain.[1] Although various sources attest to the difficulties of conducting a detailed scoping of the tourism value chain for South Africa given the country's large geographic scope, there is general consensus on the role of small businesses in the sector (Hudson 2023).[2] For example, the results of a survey conducted by the Tourism Business Council of South Africa in 2020 showed that 58% of companies that operate in the tourism industry generate less than R5 million in annual revenue.[3] A majority of those businesses, about 70%, operate in the accommodation and hospitality levels of the value chain. The survey results are consistent with Hudson's study findings, namely, that small businesses play a key role as providers of alternative accommodation services such as bed and breakfasts, guesthouses, self-catering holiday apartments and home rentals, backpacker lodges, and camping places (Hudson 2023). Small businesses are also pivotal as primary providers of tourism road transport, as well as tourism activity organisers, craft producers and souvenir shops. In other subsectors such as restaurants, food and beverages outlets, tour operators and agencies, medium- and large-sized enterprises are more prevalent.

According to Statistics South Africa, the South African travel and tourism sector's contribution to gross domestic product (GDP) as a share of the total economy was about R234 663 million in 2022, constituting 3.5% of the total GDP.[4] The sector is also significant for employment in the country. During the same period, there were about 733 385 jobs in the tourism sector in South Africa, contributing 4,9% to total employment. The prospects for the South African tourism sector are also positive. Interestingly, the World Travel and Tourism Council (WTTC) believes that the country has enormous potential and estimates that the South African travel and tourism sector will grow at an average annual rate of 7.6% over the next decade, outstripping South Africa's overall growth rate.[5]

It is evident that the ultimate recovery of the tourism sector will benefit the tourism economy enormously, as well as create opportunities for firms operating within the tourism ecosystem, including small businesses. Travel and accommodation digital platforms, in particular online travel agents (OTAs), are proving to be among the most efficient and convenient ways in which service providers can interact with and sell their products and services. These include hotels and other alternative accommodation providers, for both domestic and international holidaymakers, who enjoy the convenience of browsing for products and concluding transactions online.

The accelerated penetration of smartphones in recent years has made the OTAs even more popular and, arguably, a suitable alternative to traditional brick-and-mortar travel agents. However, it appears that domestic digital platforms actually have a limited role to play in the growth and development of the tourism economy. This is because South African markets that provide online intermediation platform services are dominated by global platforms that are better equipped with digital capabilities.

In May 2021, the Competition Commission of South Africa (CCSA) launched the Online Intermediation Platforms Market Inquiry (the OIPMI or Inquiry) to look into various digital markets in South Africa, including tourism markets. In its final report released in July 2023, among other things, the CCSA found that some global platforms engage in anti-competitive practices that make it difficult for other platforms, including domestic platforms, and business users in South Africa to compete effectively and grow.

Chapter 12[6] analyses competition distortions arising from the implementation of price parity clauses (PPC) by OTAs in travel and tourism. It also examines the role and impact of search engines, particularly Google, on competition in travel and tourism platforms. The chapter starts by giving overviews of digital platforms as well as accommodation intermediation services in South Africa and the key players that provide these services. Then it continues with a discussion on PPCs and their impact on competition, with particular focus on the South African experience. Next, the chapter explores the role of Google, as the dominant search engine, on competition and the impact of Google SERP ranking on competition, and finally concludes with some key findings and motivations for further action.

Digital platforms and their benefits to consumers and business users

Travel and tourism digital platforms are used as intermediaries for suppliers of travel and accommodation products, (business users) to connect and sell their products, such as hotel rooms, car rental days, flights and other forms of transport, to consumers online. Many benefits and efficiencies have been brought about by the vast growth in adoption of digital platforms in the travel and tourism sector. Tourism destinations with higher adoption levels of travel and tourism digital platforms derive more benefits and attract more tourists when compared with those that largely rely on the traditional methods (Lopez-Cordova 2020). The global OTAs market has been growing at an average rate of 4.99% since 2018 and reached $599.27 billion in 2023.[7] It is estimated that the market will continue to grow and reach $807.88 billion in 2028.[8] Thus, the use of travel and tourism digital platforms is likely to ensure the sustainability and relevancy of the tourism sector (Chamboko-Mpotaringa & Tichaawa 2021).

Consumers and business users benefit differently from the use of digital platforms. From the consumer perspective, travellers benefit from the variety that the platforms bring. The platforms' ability to aggregate many business users of a specific category allow consumers the convenience of browsing and comparing all the offerings of different business users from a single point, without searching each business user's website individually.

Over and above convenience, consumers also enjoy the benefits of efficiencies that are brought by digital platforms. Travellers have a preference for service providers that can respond to their queries and requests quickly (Chamboko-Mpotaringa & Tichaawa 2021). Digital platforms provide a medium for businesses to connect and interact with their customers in real time, and these interactions and experiences bring instant gratification to customers and help to build loyalty and trust. Platforms also collect data on customer tastes and demand patterns from users and, in turn, use such data for targeted marketing with tailored information (Chamboko-Mpotaringa & Tichaawa 2021; Lopez-Cordova 2020). Targeted marketing benefits consumers by offering them services and products that are closer to their needs. This tailored information reduces the time spent by consumers searching and planning for their trips (Lopez-Cordova 2020).

On the business user side, travel and tourism digital platforms allow business users to become more discoverable and compete for a broader customer base. The adoption and use of digital platforms exposes business users to customers who they would not otherwise have had access to. Digital platforms induce a greater demand for the business users' offerings, especially for emerging business users, as these platforms bridge the gap between limited access to potential customers for business users and lack of information about tourism opportunities for consumers (Chamboko-Mpotaringa & Tichaawa 2021). The lower search costs on platforms also allow business users, including those that ordinarily would have been less popular, to be more discoverable and attract interest from international travellers (Lopez-Cordova 2020). According to the United Nations, the use of global platforms is even more important for local business users in developing countries in order to attract international travellers (UNCTAD 2020).

Travellers adopting digital platforms for finding accommodation have also facilitated the wider use of peer-to-peer lodgings, such as those found on platforms such as Airbnb (Lopez-Cordova 2020). This has created a new channel for business users previously excluded from the market to reach their audience (Short et al. 2021). For instance, in South Africa, a study conducted by Genesis Analytics showed that Airbnb has lowered the barriers to tourism entrepreneurship, with 45 500 active hosts nationally (Short et al. 2021).

Types of travel and accommodation intermediation services in South Africa

There are different types of travel and accommodation intermediation platforms operating in South Africa. Online intermediation platforms are those digital marketplaces that facilitate transactions between businesses and consumers. In accommodation, intermediation platform services are provided by OTAs. These services are utilised by accommodation providers, usually at a fixed commission fee, to market their accommodation and make it available for reservation. The reservation systems used by OTAs make it possible for consumers to conclude transactions on the platform.

Next to OTAs are metasearch engines. The primary service of a metasearch engine is the provision of price comparison tools, which enable consumers to search for and compare services and products offered by business users, such as airlines and OTAs, as well as compare their prices and rates. Unlike OTAs, metasearch engines are primarily used by business users to generate leads and not for the purposes of consumers concluding transactions on the platform. Metasearch engines redirect interested consumers to the websites of the relevant business users where transactions can then be concluded. They generate revenue on a cost-per-click basis, and not on a commission-fee basis.

The other categories of intermediation platforms are those that enable consumers to compare prices of various car rentals, those for flight tickets and those for long distance buses. Intermediation platforms in these categories account for a small proportion of the sales in each segment. This is because the suppliers have alternative distribution channels that consumers generally prefer, such as airline websites, the car rental operators' own websites, and in-store sales (CCSA 2022: 32–34).

The CCSA's Inquiry found that of the existing online travel and accommodation intermediation platforms, accommodation is by far the largest category, accounting for between 70% and 80% of revenues earned in 2019 and 2020. The remaining categories of online intermediation platforms each account for less than 5% of the overall travel and accommodation revenues (CCSA 2022: 14). Given the significant contribution made by accommodation intermediation platforms to overall travel and accommodation revenue, we focus largely on competition dynamics and key competition issues arising in this category. Next, we look at the leading players in this category.

Key players in the provision of accommodation intermediation platform services

The South African market for the provision of accommodation intermediation platform services is dominated by international OTAs. Booking.com alone has consistently accounted for more than 50% of the market. The second largest player is Airbnb, followed by Expedia. The popularity of international brands is attributable to several factors, including the extensive investments made by these brands in the development of their platforms, access to substantial financial resources that enable them to compete aggressively on Google Search, and the unmatchable discounts and loyalty programmes that they offer. These benefits ensure that the global brands enjoy popularity even among domestic holidaymakers. Importantly, it appears that this popularity has had a negative impact on the ability of domestic OTAs to grow and compete effectively.

Collectively, domestic OTAs account for less than 10% of the market. Unlike global OTAs, the success of domestic platforms is dependent on their ability to attract local travellers. For example, it is unlikely that a group of travellers from the United States would use a domestic platform such as Afristay to book accommodation for a holiday in Cape Town. Instead, such travellers are more likely to use Expedia or Booking.com, as they are well-known brands in their home country. For the same reason, tourists from China are more likely to use an OTA like Agoda, rather than a lesser known South African platform such as SafariNow.

In an effort to remain in business, some domestic OTAs have resorted to developing niche markets that cannot be easily penetrated by global platforms. For example, Tripco, under the brand name Lekkeslaap, employed a unique strategy when it entered the market by targeting Afrikaans-speaking tourists.[9] The platform also focused on brand building to earn the loyalty of its customers as opposed to capturing clicks from Google. Lekkerslaap has since built sufficient brand-trust. According to Similarweb, about 30% of consumers who visited the Lekkeslaap site in 2021 did not visit any other site subsequently.[10] Given such consumer loyalty and the unique experiences for Afrikaans-speaking tourists, it is unlikely that global platforms would match or be able to replicate Lekkeslaap's offerings in that niche market. It is this segmented approach that has helped Tripco to survive in the market.[11] Previously, other platforms also gained traction by relegating their services to small towns-based business users instead of those in the metropolitan areas. This strategy lowered the costs for Google paid search as the large global players would not compete on the key terms for such areas. However, some players have noted that this strategy is no longer as effective, although they continue to use it. Global players have since built a product portfolio all over the country that allows them to bid in destinations or markets that were previously considered niche (CCSA 2022: 70).

Based on submissions received for the Inquiry, the CCSA estimated market shares in the provision of accommodation intermediation platform services are as follows (Table 12.1):

Table 12.1 Accommodation platforms estimated market shares based on commission revenues

Accommodation platforms	Commission revenues (%)		
	2018	2019	2020
Booking.com	50–60 %	50–60 %	50–60 %

Accommodation platforms	Commission revenues (%)		
	2018	2019	2020
Agoda	0–5 %	0–5 %	0–5 %
Airbnb	15–20 %	20–30 %	20–30 %
Expedia	5–10 %	5–10 %	0–5 %
Other global	0–5 %	0–5 %	0–5 %
Tripco (Lekkeslaap/Travelground)	5–10 %	5–10 %	5–10 %
SafariNow	0–5 %	0–5 %	0–5 %
Afristay	0–5 %	0–5 %	0–5 %
Other domestic	0–5 %	0–5 %	0–5 %

Source: OIPMI Provisional Report, CCSA (2022: 16)

The figures show that the position of most of the players in the market remained constant, at least for the period 2018 to 2020. Notably, Booking.com's dominance remained unchallenged while one of its closest competitors, Expedia, lost market share in 2020.[12] This entrenched market position may explain some of the competition distortions identified by the CCSA in the Inquiry report, which we discuss later in the chapter.

It is clear that none of the domestic platforms experienced significant growth during this period despite having implemented various competitive strategies. While the full recovery of the travel and tourism sector will benefit the South African economy overall, it appears that local platforms will continue to face aggressive competition from global players and may not enjoy the gains from the recovery as much.

Price parity clauses and their impact on competition in digital markets

It is common practice in many industries for parties in a vertical relationship to apply price parity clauses (PPCs) in their contractual dealings with one another. While PPCs, also known as most-favoured nation clauses (MFNs), may have certain benefits, it has been observed that their implementation may also give rise to competition concerns. Colangelo (2017) explains:

> As a matter of fact, recent case law testifies that one of the key concerns of competition authorities is the use by online platforms of a type of agreement generally traced to the category of Most Favoured Nation Clause (MFN), typically included in B2B long-term contracts, where the supplier undertakes to guarantee the best price conditions to the intermediary concerned as compared with any other dealer. The competitive assessment of such clauses (also known as parity clauses) is controversial in both traditional and digital markets. At first sight, they appear to offer potential benefits to consumers, at least in terms of price

transparency and reduction of transaction costs; however, they also give rise to competition concerns, as they may serve to acquire or strengthen monopoly pricing. Their recurrence in the digital environment has revitalised an ongoing debate on the likely effects of these clauses on competition. (Colangelo 2017)

A distinction is drawn between wide and narrow PPCs. Wide PPCs require a business user to commit to the agreement that prices offered to consumers through an intermediation platform or marketplace will always be competitive with any of the prices available – including prices offered by the business user on its own website or on other intermediation platforms. In other words, the business user is required to guarantee that its prices on other sales channels will never be cheaper than those offered on the intermediation platform. Narrow PPCs, on the other hand, require business users to guarantee that the prices offered to consumers through the intermediation platform will always be competitive with the prices offered on the business user's own website. In other words, narrow PPCs guarantee that the prices on the business user's website will never be cheaper than the prices on the platform (CMA 2014).

The need to use PPCs is often triggered by the existence of multiple digital platforms serving the same purpose in a particular market. The ability of consumers to use multiple platforms in parallel and the ability of business users to connect to multiple platforms with ease, while at the same time being able to use their own sales channels, also necessitate the implementation of PPCs.

Advantages and disadvantages of PPCs

The common economic justification for PPCs is that they help digital platforms protect their investment and brand value (Gürkaynak et al. 2017). It takes time and substantial capital investment to build a platform that business users and consumers regard as reliable, safe and user-friendly. The importance of scale and the existence of network effects in digital markets also means that firms cannot avoid making extensive capital investment to build platforms that can attract as many consumers and business users as possible. It is therefore important for the investing platform to ensure that any opportunistic behaviour by either business users subscribed to the platform or other third-party platforms is curtailed. From this perspective, PPCs are seen as a way of preventing free riding, that is, consumers using the OTAs to search and compare service providers and prices, but concluding the transaction on any other alternative channel that maybe offering lower prices, including the business users' own websites. Essentially, PPCs guard against undesirable consumer behaviour of possibly using the investing platform to obtain information but ultimately spending on a different channel. If this is allowed, it may make it difficult for the investing platform to reap the benefits of its investment and may even discourage it from making any future investments (Colangelo 2017).

The non-inclusion of PPCs in contractual arrangements between digital platforms and business users may drive business users to encourage consumers to switch sales channels before transactions are concluded on the platform. The option to conclude transactions on the business users' own websites may assist such business users to avoid paying commission fees to digital platforms (Gürkaynak et al. 2017).

Conversely, the use of PPCs, especially in markets where large platforms have a presence, may disincentivise business users from accepting offers from smaller platforms that may be willing to sacrifice commission fees in order to offer cheaper products on the platform. Similarly, new entrants may be prevented from entering the market with cheaper offerings that would enable them to attract customers. Thus, the use of PPCs may disincentivise the adoption of low-price entry strategies that may be beneficial to the competitive process.[13] As explained by the United Kingdom's Office of Fair Trading:

> If a platform ties a substantial share of sellers it can impede the effective entry of rival platforms. A new platform can attract buyers by giving them the opportunity to buy goods at lower prices, but if sellers cannot charge lower prices on the new platform this is not a viable option. This may discourage it from entering even if it is more efficient than the incumbents.[14]

Accordingly, when viewed from this perspective, PPCs may have foreclosure effects on rivals and potential entrants. In turn, this may be detrimental to both business users and consumers. Nonetheless, Gürkaynak and others caution that a market that deters low-cost/low-quality entry through the use of PPCs may actually incentivise high-cost/high-quality entry and this may lead to more competitive outcomes. In this regard, PPCs may encourage innovation and product differentiation as opposed to price competition (Gürkaynak et al. 2017). While there may be merit in this proposition, it is unlikely to hold true for middle-income countries such as South Africa, where new platforms or potential entrants, especially domestic firms, do not have substantial financial resources and often enter the market as low-cost platforms. As observed by Andreoni and Roberts (2022):

> Most middle-income countries do not have large domestically owned multinationals able to invest substantial resources at early stages of technology development, scaling-up and commercialisation. Similarly, these countries lack public resources to compete with the two leading countries… (Andreoni & Roberts 2022)

Effective competition regulation requires a holistic approach that takes into account the prevailing economic, social and environmental circumstances in a country (UNCTAD 2015). In middle-income countries, competition policy is expected to complement other government policies in achieving sustainable and inclusive growth and development (UNCTAD 2015). It is therefore expected that competition authorities in such countries be more inclined toward interventions that seek to promote an environment conducive for smaller indigenous platforms, rather than exposing them to aggressive competition strategies of global platforms, largely driven by substantial capital investments that local platforms may never be able to match. The main objective for developing countries is to ensure contestability of local markets and meaningful participation in these markets by local firms. Once these markets have become contestable and conducive to effective participation by local firms, it should be possible for these firms to grow and ultimately be able to compete in the global markets.

A study conducted by Boik and Corts (2016) shows that the adoption of PPCs by an incumbent is likely to encourage entry when the potential entrant has a business model reasonably similar to the incumbent's. Therefore, PPCs may distort the choice of a business model by a new entrant towards one similar to that of the incumbent (Boik & Corts 2016). In essence, PPCs may result in the foreclosure of low-cost platforms if the incumbent is a high-cost platform, which, in turn, may limit entry by small local firms and ultimately restrict consumer choice.

Compounding the situation is that PPCs discourage competition based on commission levels and have a propensity to raise commission fees charged by digital platforms (CMA 2014; OFT 2012). This then puts the affected business users under pressure to either absorb the loss occasioned by increased commission fees, or to pass on these increases to consumers by raising prices across their distribution channels (Chappatte & O'Connell 2022). A lack of competition on commission fees may also result in digital platforms not seeing the incentive to price differently in order to increase their bookings. Platforms implementing PPCs can also increase their commission without any concerns about potential price disparities and loss of sales volumes (OECD 2013).

Another criticism of PPCs is that they may facilitate a concerted practice or outright collusion among digital platforms (Samuelson et al. 2012). As Chappatte and O'Connell (2022) observe, PPCs, especially wide PPCs, spread rapidly and can easily become industry standard as they often create a strong incentive for competing platforms to implement similar PPCs. Another criticism of PPCs is that they may facilitate a concerted practice or outright collusion among digital platforms (Chappatte and O'Connell 2022). This then makes the market in which PPCs are implemented susceptible to a concerted practice. In some instances, intermediation platforms, especially those operating in oligopolistic markets, may deliberately use PPCs to make sure there is sufficient transparency in pricing and to discourage or disincentivise discounting by business users (Thomas 2019). From the business user side, PPCs may enhance the business users' ability to monitor adherence to collusive agreements (OECD 2013).

The impact of PPCs on competition in the provision of accommodation intermediation platform services in South Africa

As indicated earlier, the Inquiry was launched by the CCSA in May 2021. It sought to investigate, among other things, the impact of PPCs on competition in the provision of accommodation intermediation platform services. In its report, the CCSA found that the implementation of PPCs in this market raised competition concerns. It established that at least five OTAs implemented PPCs and that most of these platforms used wide PPCs; only one platform used narrow PPCs (CCSA 2022: 120).

While there is no evidence to suggest that enforcement mechanisms as radical as the delisting of non-compliant accommodation providers have been adopted, the CCSA found that there were alternative enforcement tools used by OTAs to ensure adherence to PPCs. These included accommodation providers being penalised on ranking on the platform and concerns about the possible loss of their special status that boosted ranking on the platform. No adherence to PPCs also results in OTAs refusing to spend money on marketing the rooms of the offending accommodation providers through paid media. Most importantly, accommodation providers are often reminded of their contractual obligation to implement PPCs and the ramifications of non-compliance, which may include the termination of contract (CCSA 2022: 121). This instils fear in business users, especially those that are heavily dependent on platforms.[15]

The main argument that has been advanced in favour of wide PPCs in South Africa is that they ensure that OTAs recoup their investment and marketing costs incurred in promoting accommodation providers. Without wide PPCs, the contention goes, accommodation providers may distribute rooms at higher prices on OTAs and this may cause consumers to merely use OTAs to search and compare rooms, and then conclude transactions on other distribution channels that may offer cheaper prices. Despite this contention, the CCSA took the view that competition is better off without wide PPCs because these clauses reduce price competition across platforms and are likely to entrench the position of the leading platform in the market (CCSA 2022: 124).

According to the CCSA, evidence submitted to the Inquiry showed that the removal of wide PPCs would lead to a reduction in prices, which would likely benefit consumers. The CCSA noted that there was no evidence to support the proposition that OTAs would be unable to recoup investment in the absence of wide PPCs. Evidence from accommodation providers showed that the absence of wide PPCs would allow them some flexibility in pricing and that they may even be able to run targeted promotions to increase sales (CCSA 2022: 125). Furthermore, evidence from a survey conducted by the CCSA (as part of the Inquiry) showed that a substantial number of accommodation providers would charge lower prices on competing channels without there being the obligation to match prices on all platforms through the PPCs. The CCSA further observed that the use of PPCs, coupled with heavy discounts funded by accommodation providers, creates the impression that certain brands or OTAs are the cheapest and may discourage consumers from shopping around (CCSA 2022: 127).

Two arguments were put before the Inquiry in support of narrow PPCs. First, it was contended that narrow PPCs prevent free riding if accommodation providers are allowed to charge lower prices on rooms, but would conclude transactions on accommodation providers' direct booking channels. Second, narrow PPCs limit the billboard effect. Here, it was argued that by merely being visible on the OTA's platform, the sales of an accommodation provider increase on other distribution channels, so accommodation providers already benefit from the billboard effect (CCSA 2022: 129).

The CCSA took into account evidence that showed that instances of cross-browsing by consumers were very low. Furthermore, evidence before the CCSA showed that actual incidences of free riding were very low too, with at least one OTA estimating that these instances were less than 1%. Just like wide PPCs, evidence before the CCSA suggested that in the absence of narrow PPCs, accommodation providers would have the freedom to adopt pricing strategies of their choice and the distribution mix that suited their needs (CCSA 2022: 131). The CCSA then concluded that the pro-competitive outcomes and consumer benefits arising from no parity are likely to outweigh any efficiencies or free riding concerns that may arise in the absence of narrow PPCs (CCSA 2022: 134).

In its reports, the CCSA noted that overall, both wide and narrow PPCs, as applied by leading platforms, impede platform competition through lower commissions and prices. Furthermore, PPCs impede potential competition from accommodation providers' own direct booking channels on price, increasing their dependence on OTAs. The CCSA found no compelling evidence to justify the implementation of both narrow and wide PPCs in the provision of accommodation intermediation platform services in South Africa (CCSA 2022: 52).

In its final report, the CCSA identified Booking.com as the leading platform and to remedy the competition distortions arising from the implementation of PPCs, the following remedial actions, which Booking.com were required to implement, were instituted(CCSA 2023: 521–523):

- The removal of both wide and narrow price parity terms from all contracts with accommodation providers in South Africa.

- The removal of both wide and narrow price parity as a requirement for participation in the Genius, Preferred Partner or Preferred Plus programmes, or any other membership programmes.

- [Prohibition of any practices that seek to] incentivise any conduct which has the same effect as a wide or narrow price parity term through the inclusion of price parity as a requirement for promotional or loyalty programmes, or as a factor in the ranking of product search results on the Booking.com platform.

- [Notification of] all South African accommodation providers, in writing, of the removal of the wide and the narrow price parity terms and explaining in a clear and unambiguous manner that they are no longer required to price accommodation on Booking. com at rates the same or higher than their direct online channel or any other Online

Travel Intermediation Platform, including for participation in the Genius, Preferred Partner and Preferred Plus programmes. (CCSA 2023: 522)

Google as an important source of traffic for digital platforms in travel and tourism

In the modern day, search engines have become the central location for obtaining information (Ham 2019). The core function of search engines is to organise and disseminate large volumes of digital information to the users. Internet users enjoy the convenience brought by search engines funnelling search results instantly from a diverse pool of sources (Haris et al. 2017; Van Eijk 2009). Search engines store millions of pages in their database, including sites (Haris et al. 2017). As of 2023, about 64.5% of the global population were internet users and 98% of that population used search engines (Kemp 2023). Similarly, most of the online platforms' customers begin their journey on search engines to reach the platforms relevant for their search. As a result, digital platforms are highly dependent on search engines for access to consumers. Google is the most used search engine globally, accounting for 93% market share, among the likes of Bing, Yahoo and Netscape (Kemp 2023).

This chapter also looks at the impact of Google on competition in digital markets, in particular in travel and tourism. The sections that follow discuss the operations of Google, as an important source of consumer traffic for digital platforms and the impact of developments in Google operations on platform competition.

In travel and tourism, search engines are the primary point of information for travellers, making them the most important avenue for digital platforms to attract consumer traffic (Fesenmaier et al. 2010; Le 2019). The main objective of platforms is to attract consumer traffic, convert the traffic into bookings and ultimately monetise it (CCSA 2022: 51). Search engines are the most preferred tool and, according to Fesenmaier, the 'first step' for travellers looking for accommodation, as the search engines enable users to easily get reliable information, without physically inspecting their options (Fesenmaier et al. 2010). A research study by Expedia showed that 71% of travellers chose search engines as the most used information source in the beginning of their travel planning process (Le 2019). Expedia's study also showed that travellers relied heavily on search engines for information in the beginning of their trip planning process, and moved to OTAs in the later stages of the process, once they had narrowed their options (Le 2019). In another research study by Naletova, it was found that 94% of leisure travellers and 80% of business travellers frequently used search engines as the main source of information for accommodation in their trip planning process (Naletova 2017, as cited in Le 2019).

In most countries, Google is a dominant player in the search engines market. In South Africa, Google holds what appears to be an entrenched position of dominance with 93% market share, followed by Bing with only 5% market share.[16] All the other players each hold less than 1% market share. This makes digital platforms operating in South Africa, including those in travel and tourism, reliant on Google as the most important source of consumer traffic.

To illustrate the importance of Google for travel and tourism platforms operating in South Africa, in the last two years from March 2021 till February 2023, some travel and tourism platforms derived more than 50% of their consumer traffic from Google. Bookings.com and AirBnB are the only platforms among the selected platforms that derived more traffic from direct searches than organic search to their own websites. However, both platforms still derive significant traffic from Google. Notably, all the selected platforms derive less than 20% of traffic from paid search, except Booking.com. Figure 12.1 shows the flow of consumer traffic to five travel and tourism platforms by traffic source.

Figure 12.1 Sources of traffic to travel and tourism platforms in South Africa

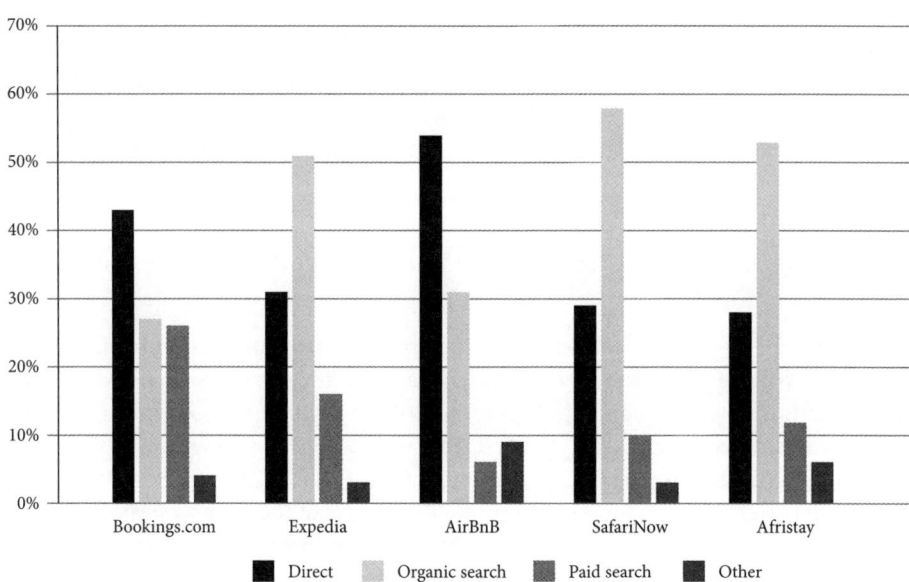

Source: Authors' compilation using Similarweb data

The impact of Google's operations on competition in travel and tourism

When Google first entered the search market in the early 2000s, it was a small start-up firm that simply enabled consumers' easy access to digital information.[17] During that period, achieving visibility and prominence was not a challenge, even for small firms wishing to advertise their service offerings on Google with limited financial resources (CCSA 2022: 42). Over the years, Google gained critical scale and started to exert its market power by employing aggressive monetisation strategies.

These monetisation strategies affect the ability of small advertisers to attract customers.[18] The economic clout that Google has acquired in this time is evident in the numbers: In 2020, Google had a market value of $1 trillion and annual revenue exceeding $160 billion.[19] Its aggressive strategies have earned the search engine the title of gatekeeper of traffic to digital platforms' websites – due to its monopoly position in search advertising in many jurisdictions.[20]

To maintain this position, Google employs a number of different practices. For example, it uses software known as web crawlers to discover publicly available web pages.[21] When a user enters a search on Google, the software uses algorithms to provide the most relevant information from the web pages based on the search terms and rank the information on the search engine results page (SERP) accordingly. Digital platforms compete for traffic on Google by striving for their content to become the most relevant in different searches and to be prominent on the SERP (CCSA 2022: 74). Discoverability of platforms on Google is highly dependent on their ranking on the SERP. The search results that are ranked higher and on the landing page of the SERP receive the most attention from consumers (CCSA 2022; Le 2019). According to Murray, the first ranked search results in organic search on Google earn the highest click at 33%, while the second and third ranked earn 15% and 9%, respectively.[22] As a result, platforms engage in search engine optimisation (SEO) and search engine marketing (SEM) to improve their ranking and prominence on Google.

SEO is a technique by which websites are optimised to achieve the highest ranking on the SERP for selected keywords (O'Neill & Curran 2011). SEO helps to improve the websites' ranking in organic search results. SEM, on the other hand, is a technique where marketers participate in a bidding process on keywords for their websites to appear on top of organic search results on the SERP on the search of those keywords, and pay for clicks (Cantallops et al. 2013). On the SERP, the top four slots and last three slots are reserved for paid search results (CCSA 2022: 81–82). In South Africa, Google distinguishes paid search results from organic search results by labelling the paid results as 'Sponsored'. However, there is no clear evidence to show if consumers distinguish between paid search results and organic results. The undisputed element is that paid search results get most prominence as they are not affected by changes in algorithms and are guaranteed a higher ranking (Cantallops et al. 2013).

Over the years, Google has implemented various changes to the SERP, both for organic and paid search results (CCSA 2022: 87). These changes include algorithm updates for organic search results, the introduction of Google hotels and ranking of paid searches (CCSA 2022: 88). Given the importance of Google to these businesses, changes on the SERP also affect the ability of the platforms to compete for consumer traffic.

Changes in paid search results

This section looks at the changes Google has made to the SERP and their impact on travel and tourism platforms. According to the CCSA, these changes affect mostly small and medium enterprises (SMEs). Therefore, we also focus on the impact of Google paid search on the ability of the SME travel and tourism platforms to compete in the market. The participation of SMEs is important for an inclusive platform market. Most local travel and tourism platforms in South Africa are SMEs. Their ability to compete with large and global platforms for visibility on Google is imperative in ensuring their sustainability and contestability of the local market.

For SEM on Google, competitors bid on key terms and the advertiser with the highest bid for a particular term gains higher ranking each time a user searches that particular key term and pays the rate for each click (CCSA 2022: 86; Rossello 2015). As illustrated earlier in the chapter, paid search results play a significant role in travel and tourism platforms. Platforms invest significant portions of their revenue on Google Ads, bidding to attain favourable ranking. The continuous developments in the algorithms affecting ranking also amplify the need for platforms to attain the highest rank in paid search (CCSA 2022: 94). However, the established platforms have more resources to outbid SME platforms, giving the established platforms a competitive advantage. Although this may generally be viewed as a natural outcome in a competitive process, it has negative effects for inclusivity in digital markets.

The labelling of paid search results on the SERP should distinguish paid search results from organic search results. However, Google has implemented several changes to the labelling of paid searches. As part of the Inquiry, travel and tourism platforms made submissions to the CCSA, contending that the current labelling of paid search makes paid search results indistinguishable from organic search (CCSA 2022: 82). This is one way in which Google leverages its market power in search advertising, by seeking to extract more rents from its customers. The conduct results in consumers clicking on paid search results more often than organic search, causing the advertising costs for digital platforms to increase. The increased advertising costs further magnify the barriers for SME platforms to effectively compete in the respective markets. In the past, Google identified paid search results distinctively, by shading the results on the SERP in different colour shades, with bold borders. With changes over the years, before the release of the CCSA Inquiry's provisional report, paid search results were distinguished by only a small 'Ad' on the left of each paid search result, with neither colour shading nor borders.

Over and above the lack of proper classification of paid search results, Google has also increased the number of slots allocated to paid search results on the SERP, pushing organic search results further down. Before 2016, Google SERP would allow a maximum of eleven paid search results, with a maximum of three results on top of the organic search result and eight on the right-hand side of the search results (CCSA 2022: 82). The search engine removed the right-hand side results and added an additional slot for paid search results on top of the organic search. This further denies the SME platforms without sufficient resources an additional opportunity for visibility. Overall, the prioritisation of paid results in Google SERP disadvantages small platforms while propelling the global platforms with large financial backing to gain prominence.

Changes in algorithms for organic search results ranking

According to O'Neill and Curran (2011), when it started in the 1990s, SEO was easily manipulated, but the subsequent continuous algorithm changes have made it difficult for businesses to manipulate it and achieve higher ranking (O'Neill & Curran 2011). In the current form, SEO favours high-quality advertisers.[23] This is in line with the evidence submitted by travel and accommodation platforms operating in South Africa to the CCSA (CCSA 2022: 48). The SEO algorithm developments ultimately influence ranking on organic search and limit the discoverability of platforms without financial resources and expertise to exploit SEO. Google confirmed to the CCSA that it implements thousands of algorithm updates annually and, according to the search engine, these are implemented to improve the quality and usefulness of search for consumers.[24] It appears that this creates tension between the interests of consumers and platform competition (Berman & Katona 2013).

Another way in which Google seems to have entrenched its market power is through self-preferencing, which further undermines the ability of platforms to gain greater visibility on the SERP. Over and above the algorithm developments, Google also launched its own Travel Unit, which includes 'Hotels', 'Flights' and 'Things to do'. The Hotels Unit is a hotel metasearch engine that enables consumers to search for and book hotels online.[25] Google includes results from the Google Hotels Unit on the SERP. This has caused a global outcry, including from travel and tourism platforms, because it effectively means that Google gives ranking preference and space to its own products. The effect is to further push down organic search results and thus affect the visibility of digital platforms that rely on Google for traffic – in this case, in South Africa (CCSA 2022: 87–88; Vu 2020).[26] There have also been protests about Google's actions of unfairly extracting consumer data from Google search to enhance its own products. The search engine is also moving into the short-term rentals market as it has launched Google Vacation Rentals Feature in some countries, such as the United Kingdom in 2020 (CMA 2020, Appendix P: 58; Vu 2020).

Google's Hotels Unit was launched in South Africa in 2015. It submitted to the CCSA that there have been no changes to the position, size and display of the Hotels Unit since its launch. However, the Inquiry notes that, notwithstanding these claims, Google's Hotels Unit still appears prominently on the landing SERP, occupying a significantly large space, and including more images, hotel reviews and links to YouTube (CCSA 2022: 87–88). These features take up more space and clearly augment the Hotels Unit's visibility, thereby having the effect of pushing down other organic search results.

The impact of Google's changes on competition

To demonstrate the impact of Google SERP ranking changes on discoverability of travel and tourism platforms, we conducted a dummy search for hotels in Cape Town. On the landing SERP, the first two slots are occupied by paid search results by Bookings.com and Marriot. The Hotels Unit appears before other organic search results by competing platforms and occupies double the space allocated to other advertisers. The results of the dummy search are shown in Figure 12.2.

Figure 12.2 Google search results for hotels in Cape Town

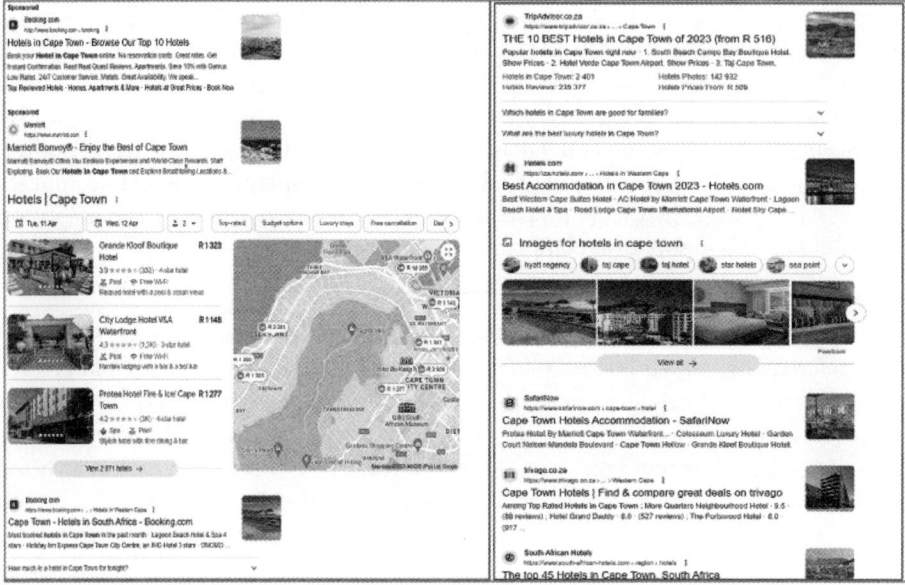

Source: Dummy search conducted by the authors using Google Search, on 18 March 2023

From the image on the left-hand side in Figure 12.2, it is clear that the Google Hotels Unit features prominently in the SERP. Another notable feature from the images is the prominence of Bookings.com on the SERP. The platform appears on top in both paid search results and organic search results. The image on the right-hand side contains organic search results. The second and third slots of the organic search results are occupied by international metasearch engines TripAdvisor and Hotels.com. The only local platform that appears on the landing SERP is SafariNow, in the sixth place, after another insertion of the Hotels Unit's images.

These dummy search results, which are consistent with the findings of the CCSA, give credence to the concern about the impact of Google SERP ranking on the visibility of small platforms and ultimately their ability to compete effectively with large platforms. International firms with substantial financial resources and Google's own services are the biggest winners with the current SERP ranking. It appears that Booking.com is able to outbid all its competitors to get the top position in paid search engine results and to simultaneously exploit SEO to also take the first spot in organic search. It is unlikely that local platforms, without international prominence, can match the expenditure of global platforms for advertising on Google, which is what it takes to become an effective competitor. For instance, the CCSA noted that in 2021, Booking.com's spend on Google paid search was the largest among its competitors, and more than the total revenue of its competitors in South Africa (CCSA 2022: 68). As indicated in the preceding sections, the CCSA noted that most of the local digital platforms in travel and tourism operate low-cost platforms with limited financial resources.

The CCSA further noted that domestic platforms that were thriving before the entry of global platforms have, over the years, lost a significant market share to these platforms. For instance, SafariNow used to be a large digital platform in South Africa and the platform was able to drive consumer traffic to its side by SEO. Currently, paid search seems to be the easier way to acquire traffic for platforms from Google and platforms without enough financial resources are desperately trying to compete. Google has clearly become so ubiquitous that it effectively impedes the ability of small digital accommodation platforms to compete and expand.

CCSA's findings and remedies against Google

Overall, in South Africa, it has been found that while Google was a valuable tool for the acquisition of traffic, the prominence of paid results at the top of the Google SERP and lack of sufficient distinction from organic results, along with its monopoly status, materially restricted intermediation platform competition. This was evident from the way it elevated payment for customer acquisition, which strongly favoured leading platforms with deep pockets from capital-backing and established revenue streams. The CCSA also found that Google's SERP had incrementally become more of its own product and narrowed the range of third-party results on the SERP, which had also pushed down organic results. In relation to the introduction of Google's own competing service offerings on the SERP, such as the Hotels Unit, the CCSA found that Google Search self-preferencing its own specialist search intermediation platforms impeded competition in intermediation platforms (CCSA 2022:47).

To remedy the competition concerns arising from Google's conduct in the market, the CCSA instituted the following remedial actions.

> To improve visibility of SME and HDP platforms, Google is required to:
> - introduce South African platform badges and filtering in the search results for local platforms;
> - introduce a new platform sites unit allowing content-rich display for nonleading South African platforms in travel and shopping;
> - provide R180 million in advertising credits for nonleading South African platforms, with a particular focus on SME and HDP platforms;
> - provide free in-depth technical training to maximise the efficacy of ad campaigns and reduce the effective cost of customer acquisition through general search;
> - provide funding support for SME and HDP digital platforms, including Google product credits, along with startup training and networking; and

- register online profiles for 500 000 SMEs and HDP-owned businesses (CCSA 2023: 510–515).

To address the self-preferencing concerns, Google is required to:
- not treat more favourably, in ranking and related indexing and crawling, services and products offered by Google itself than similar services or products of a third-party. Google shall apply transparent, fair and non-discriminatory conditions to such ranking; and
- implement the changes undertaken in the European Economic Area to comply with article 6(5) of the Digital Markets Act and such implementation, with relevant adaptations to South Africa in consultation with the CCSA, will be considered in compliance with the remedial action above (CCSA 2023: 510–515).

Overall, the remedies imposed by the CCSA favour SMEs and HDP platforms. Given the nature of these remedies, the CCSA's approach in this regard may attract criticism in that it appears to depart from the general principle that competition laws should be applied to protect the competitive process, and not the competitors. However, it should be borne in mind that context matters in the application of competition law.

As one of its objectives, the South African Competition Act (No. 89 of 1998) (the Competition Act) specifically seeks to ensure that SMEs have an equitable opportunity to participate in the economy.[27] In the Inquiry, the Competition Act directed the CCSA to have regard to the impact of any feature of the market that impedes, restricts or distorts competition on SMEs and HPD firms and, where appropriate, to take action that prevents or mitigates such impact.[28] In the context of digital markets, the adoption of a protectionist competition regulation approach is necessitated by the need to avoid 'tipping' and the creation of non-inclusive platforms markets. It remains the responsibility of the CCSA to design remedies that improve the competitiveness of SMEs and HDP firms, and ultimately promote effective competition between these firms and their larger rivals. However, the CCSA should also guard against using its remedial actions to protect inefficient and less innovative firms from competition.

Future outlook of the online travel and tourism platforms in South Africa

The 2018 amendments to the Competition Act empower the CCSA to 'take action' to remedy, mitigate or prevent an adverse effect on competition identified by the agency during a market inquiry process. However, there is an ongoing debate about the scope of the powers conferred to the CCSA, including whether the amendments allow it to make findings and take remedial actions that are binding in nature. This debate is yet to be settled by the courts since the OIPMI was the first market inquiry under the amendments. Despite any ambiguity that might exist on the powers conferred to the CCSA, Google undertook to comply with all the Inquiry's remedial actions and to implement them. Booking.com on the other hand approached the Competition Tribunal to appeal the CCSA's decision on the Inquiry and it appears that it will not be implementing the remedial actions until a ruling is made or, at best, the parties reach an amicable resolution outside the courts.

Compliance by Google will significantly augment the visibility of local platforms and eliminate one of the biggest hurdles to their growth. The CCSA reported that it had received overwhelming evidence from all platform categories, and even from the leading platforms on the critical role of Google for generating traffic. The flagging of South African local platforms and exposing them more to consumers will allow them an equal opportunity to contest consumer traffic, especially for those consumers who have a strong preference for promoting local platforms. The enhanced visibility will also allow the local platforms an equal opportunity to contest for new consumers who might have not yet developed any biased loyalty towards a particular platform.

Notwithstanding the above, it is also noted that despite the significance of Google's compliance and likely impact of local platforms visibility, it cannot be fully guaranteed that the CCSA's intention of a more vibrant and more inclusive platform market will be fully achieved immediately. Visibility is a single part of the challenges to local OTAs' growth. Price competition is another important consideration for consumers, so without the PPCs prohibition being implemented, the local platforms' ability to grow will continue to be hindered to a certain extent. As alluded to earlier in the chapter, the existing travel and tourism platforms' consumers show more brand loyalty towards the leading OTAs. Thus, without innovative price competition strategies, consumers may not be incentivised enough to shift to small platforms. Overall, the CCSA's Inquiry is likely to unlock the potential benefits that could be derived from active participation of local OTAs in the market. However, the full potential benefits may be delayed, pending compliance with the remedial actions that relate to the removal and prohibition of PPCs.

Conclusion

This chapter has shown that digital platforms have an important role to play in the growth and development of the travel and tourism sector in South Africa. However, some of the digital markets in South Africa are characterised by practices that distort competition, especially the ability of domestic platforms to compete effectively with global platforms, which are well resourced. This is notable in the market for the provision of accommodation intermediation platform services where the application of both wide and narrow PPCs has been found to impede competition.

The chapter also shows that Google is an important source of traffic for digital platforms and, by extension, business users in travel and tourism. However, certain of Google's operations and practices have been found to distort competition, especially between small and large digital platforms in South Africa. Lastly, we have demonstrated that proactive competition enforcement by competition authorities often leads to a change in behaviour by the implicated digital platforms. Without active enforcement, there is unlikely to be meaningful change. Given the findings of the CCSA in South Africa, there is a strong possibility that similar anti-competitive practices may exist in many other jurisdictions on the African continent, especially where the same digital platforms operate. Accordingly, proactive enforcement actions may be necessary.

Notes

1   See: Department of Tourism Sector Master Plan, September 2023.
2   See: Department of Tourism Sector Master Plan, September 2023.
3   See: Department of Tourism Sector Master Plan, September 2023.
4   See: Statistics South Africa, Tourism Satellite Account for South Africa, March 2024.
5   See: South Africa's travel & tourism's growth to outpace the national economy for the next 10 years, WTTC, 4 July 2022. Accessed March 2023, https://wttc.org/news-article/south-africas-travel-and-tourisms-growth-to-outpace-the-national-economy-for-the-next–10-years
6   The views expressed and any possible errors are those of the authors and are not the views of the CCSA.
7   See: Online travel market size worldwide from 2017 to 2023, with a forecast until 2028, Statista, 10 June 2024. Accessed July 2024, https://www.statista.com/statistics/1179020/online-travel-agent-market-size-worldwide/
8   See: Online travel market size worldwide from 2017 to 2023, with a forecast until 2028, Statista, 10 June 2024. Accessed July 2024, https://www.statista.com/statistics/1179020/online-travel-agent-market-size-worldwide/
9   See: OIPMI public hearings: Presentation by Tripco. Accessed March 2023, https://www.compcom.co.za/wp-content/uploads/2021/11/Tripco-CompCom-PDF-with-presenter-notes.pdf
10 Data from Similarweb's Audience Loyalty feature.
11 See: OIPMI public hearings: Presentation by Tripco. Accessed March 2023, https://www.compcom.co.za/wp-content/uploads/2021/11/Tripco-CompCom-PDF-with-presenter-notes.pdf
12 Expedia's loss of market shares was attributed to travel restrictions and the fact that it attracts mainly international travellers. See: CCSA (2022: 15).
13 Offering cheaper prices or low-priced products than those offered by incumbents is a common entry strategy often adopted by new entrants; thus PPCs may undermine an entry strategy that may be beneficial to consumers. See: Gurkaynak et al. (2017); Boik and Corts (2016).
14 See: Report prepared by Lear for the Office of Fair Trading. Lear (2012) *Can 'fair' prices be unfair? A review of price relationship agreements.* Rome: Lear.
15 For more information on how PPCs are implemented in South Africa, including various monitoring mechanisms used by OTAs, see Goga (2020).
16 See: Data extracted from Statcounter. Accessed March 2023, https://gs.statcounter.com/search-engine-market-share/all/africa

17 See: United States Department of Justice, 2020. Case 1:20-cv–03010. Accessed March 2023, https://www.justice.gov/opa/press-release/file/1328941/download

18 See: United States Department of Justice, 2020. Case 1:20-cv–03010. Accessed March 2023, https://www.justice.gov/opa/press-release/file/1328941/download

19 See: United States Department of Justice, 2020. Case 1:20-cv–03010. Accessed March 2023, https://www.justice.gov/opa/press-release/file/1328941/download

20 See: CCSA (2022: 75); United States Department of Justice, 2020. Case 1:20-cv–03010. Accessed March 2023, https://www.justice.gov/opa/press-release/file/1328941/download; Briefing document prepared for the European Parliament: Madiega TA (2020) *Regulating digital gatekeepers: Background on the future digital markets act*. Strasbourg: European Parliament.

21 See: United States Department of Justice, 2020. Case 1:20-cv–03010. Accessed March 2023, https://www.justice.gov/opa/press-release/file/1328941/download

22 Murray (2017), as cited in Vu (2020).

23 Google indexing is part of the process for determination of ranking on the SERP. In the Google indexing process, websites with poor quality content are ranked lower, if at all, on the SERP. See: Google Search Central (n.d.) *In-depth guide to how Google Search works*. Accessed March 2021, https://developers.google.com/search/docs/fundamentals/how-search-works

24 Google—Oral submission from Mr Kane in the CCSA public hearing, 4 November 2021, page 6. Accessed March 2023, https://www.compcom.co.za/wp-content/uploads/2023/04/COMPETITION-COMMISSION-OIPMI-GOOGLE-SEARCH.-TRAVEL.-SHOPPING–2021–11–04-DAY–3.pdf

25 See: Barten M (2023) *Tips for hoteliers to grow bookings with Google Hotels*. Accessed March 2023, https://www.revfine.com/google-hotels/#:~:text=Using%20Google%20Hotels-,What%20is%20Google%20Hotels%3F,visibility%20and%20attract%20more%20bookings

26 Lomas N, Travel startups cry foul over what Google's doing with their data, *TechCrunch*, 14 August 2020. Accessed March 2023, https://techcrunch.com/2020/08/14/travel-startups-cry-foul-over-what-googles-doing-with-their-data/

27 See: Section 2(1)(e) of the South African Competition Act (No. 89 of 1998).

28 See: Section 43C(2) and (3) of the South African Competition Act (No. 89 of 1998).

References

Andreoni A & Roberts S (2022) Governing digital platform power for industrial development: Towards an entrepreneurial-regulatory state. *Cambridge Journal of Economics* 46: 1431

Barten M (2023) *Tips for hoteliers to grow bookings with Google Hotels*. Accessed March 2023, https://www.revfine.com/google-hotels/#:~:text=Using%20Google%20Hotels-,What%20is%20Google%20Hotels%3F,visibility%20and%20attract%20more%20bookings

Berman R & Katona Z (2013) The role of search engine optimization in search marketing. *Marketing Science* 32(4): 644–651

Boik A & Corts K (2016) The effects of platform most-favoured-nation clauses on competition and entry. *The Journal of Law and Economics* 59(1)

Cantallops AS, Cardona JR & Matarredona MG (2013) The impact of search engines on the hotel distribution value chain. *Redmarka Revista de Marketing Aplicado* 2(10): 19–54

CCSA (Competition Commission South Africa) (2022) *Online Intermediation Platforms Inquiry Provisional Report*. Pretoria: CCSA

CCSA (Competition Commission South Africa) (2023) *Online Intermediation Platforms Inquiry Final Report*. Pretoria: CCSA

Chamboko-Mpotaringa M & Tichaawa TM (2021) Digital trends and tools driving change in marketing Free State tourism destinations: A stakeholder's perspective. *African Journal of Hospitality, Tourism and Leisure* 10(6): 1973–1974. https://doi.org/10.46222/ajhtl.19770720.204

Chappatte P & O'Connell K (2022) European Union – E-commerce: Most Favoured Nation Clauses. *Global Competition Review*

CMA (Competition and Markets Authority) (2014) *Private motor insurance market investigation final report*. London: CMA

CMA (Competition and Markets Authority) (2020) *Online platforms and digital advertising*. London: CMA

Colangelo M (2017) Parity clauses and competition law in digital marketplaces: The case of online hotel booking. *Journal of European Competition Law & Practice* 8(1): 3

Fesenmaier D, Xiang Z, Pan B & Law R (2010) An analysis of search engine use for travel planning. In U Gretzel, R Law & M Fuchs (Eds) *Information and communication technologies in tourism 2010*. Vienna: Springer. https://doi.org/10.1007/978-3-211-99407-8_32

Goga S (2020) *The impact of digital platforms on competition in the South African tourism industry*. Industrial Development Think Tank discussion paper, CCRED, University of Johannesburg

Google Search Central (n.d.) *In-depth guide to how Google Search works*. Accessed March 2021, https://developers.google.com/search/docs/fundamentals/how-search-works

Gürkaynak G, İnanılır Ö, Dinez S & Yasar AG (2017) Multi-sided markets and the challenge of incorporating multisided considerations into competition law analysis. *Journal of Antitrust Enforcement* 5(1): 100–129

Ham CD (2019) Why is this first? Understanding and analysing internet search results. *Journal of Educational Research and Practice* 9(1): 400–412

Haris AR, Hashim H & Sarijan S (2017) A study on online search by people using search engine. Case Study, Universiti Teknologi MARA

Hudson N (2023) *Challenges and opportunities for small tourism businesses in South Africa: Examining pathways to a more resilient system*. Geneva: International Labour Organization

Kemp S (2023) *Digital 2023 July Global Statshot Report*. Datareportal, 20 July 2023. Accessed December 2024, https://datareportal.com/reports/digital-2023-july-global-statshot#:~:text=The%20reported%20number%20of%20people,higher%20than%20these%20figures%20suggest

Le H (2019) How to enhance search engine optimization in accommodation website on Google search engine. Bachelor's thesis, Oulu University of Applied Sciences

Lear (2012) *Can 'fair' prices be unfair? A Review of Price Relationship Agreements*. Rome: Lear

Lopez-Cordova E (2020) *Digital platforms and the demand for international tourism services*. Research Working Paper No. 9147, World Bank Group, Washington D.C.

Madiega TA (2020) *Regulating digital gatekeepers: Background on the future digital markets act*. Strasbourg: European Parliament

OECD (Organisation for Economic Cooperation and Development) (2013) Vertical restraints for on-line sales. *OECD Roundtables on Competition Policy Papers, No 138*. Paris: OECD Publishing. https://doi.org/10.1787/394faa2b-en

OECD (Organisation for Economic Cooperation and Development) (2015) *Executive Summary of the Hearing on Across-Platforms Parity Agreements*. Paris: OECD Publishing. DAF/COMP/M(2015)2/ANN3

O'Neill S & Curran K (2011) The core aspects of search engine optimisation necessary to move up the ranking. *International Journal of Ambient Computing and Intelligence* 3(4): 62–70

Rosselló LG (2015) Tourism intermediation and the role of Google. Graduate thesis, Universitat de les Illes Balears

Samuelson M, Piankov N & Ellman B (2012) *Assessing the economic effects of most-favored-nation clauses*. Spring Meeting, ABA Section of Antitrust Law

Short R, Scott C, Evans K, Adonis K & Schoeman M (2021) *The foundations of inclusive tourism: The contribution of Airbnb to inclusive growth in South Africa*. Johannesburg: Genesis Analytics

Thomas S (2019) Harmful signals: Cartel prohibition and oligopoly theory in the age of machine learning. *Journal of Competition Law & Economics* 15(2–3): 159–203

UNCTAD (United Nations Conference on Trade and Development) (2015) *The role of competition policy in promoting sustainable and inclusive growth*. Geneva: UNCTAD

UNCTAD (2020) *Digital platforms and value creation in developing countries: Implications for national and international policies*. Geneva: UNCTAD

Van Eijk NANM (2009) Search engines, the new bottleneck for content access. In B Preissl, J Haucap & P Curwen (Eds) *Telecommunication markets: Drivers and impediments*. Heidelberg: Physica-Verlag

Vu J (2020) Globetrotting in a Google run world: Google takeover of travel market risks stifling competition and consumer experiences. *Harvard Journal of Law & Technology Digest* 34. Accessed June 2023, https://jolt.law.harvard.edu/digest/globetrotting-in-a-google-run-world-google-takeover-of-travel-market-risks-stifling-competition-and-consumer-experiences

13 The other platforms, the other consumers: The missing bottom in the South African digital platforms policy debate

Jonathan Klaaren, Tlhalefang Moeletsi, Karissa Moothoo Padayachie and Thando Vilakazi

[1]The Organisation for Economic Cooperation and Development (OECD) defines a digital platform (or online intermediation platforms) as 'a digital service that facilitates interactions between two or more distinct but interdependent sets of users (whether firms or individuals) who interact through the service via the Internet' (OECD 2019b: 21). Digital platforms enable value-creating interactions between producers and consumers through mobile devices, computers and the internet. In other words, digital platforms provide a participatory infrastructure for these interactions. Digital platforms facilitate efficient transactions and enhance market access. They not only reduce search costs but also lower reproduction and verification costs. Additionally, digital platforms have indirectly accelerated innovation by enabling third parties to develop and build upon complementary products and services. As is the case in the global economy, digital platforms in South Africa have been growing in both number and reach. Most of the digital platforms that have achieved the widest reach have been established in the United States and China, with a few platforms outside of these two countries having achieved some success within specific segments (UNCTAD 2020). These digital platforms achieved exponential growth that had never been seen before. The top 10 most valuable firms by market capitalisation as of 2018 included Apple, Alphabet, Amazon, Facebook, Tencent and Alibaba. Each of these firms shared a common feature of having a digital platform to create value through facilitating exchanges between two or more interdependent groups (World Bank 2019a).

Digital platforms in South Africa

As digital platforms have the potential to drive inclusion for businesses and consumers, the emergence of *local* platforms in South Africa can be a catalyst for economic development. Through concerted efforts, they can be extended to previously excluded communities by supporting local platforms that are focused on townships (including peri-urban areas), established by previously disadvantaged entrepreneurs or service micro, small and medium enterprises (MSMEs). Townships have a high prevalence of MSMEs and are characterised by limited connection to mainstream economic activity and short value chains.[2] These MSMEs are often established out of necessity to generate a livelihood and around 65% are informal.

Despite the wide-ranging challenges, a large proportion of South Africa's population resides in townships. This is driven by multiple factors, including the lower cost of accommodation compared to more urbanised areas. Townships therefore host a large population of low-income earners who cumulatively have sizable buying power.

Still, in South Africa, there are unique challenges and opportunities in the digital platform ecosystem that are rooted in the country's broader digital economy and legacy of economic exclusion. On the one hand, the country's socioeconomic divides lead to domestic market fragmentation and hamper the scalability of platforms. On the other hand, digital platforms are usually characterised by winner-takes-all or winner-takes-most outcomes.

General competition issues

Indeed, governments around the world are grappling to understand what the rapid emergence of digital platforms means for regulation, particularly competition regulation. As chapter 12 discusses, not only platform competition but also network effects and the rise of digital gatekeepers have significant implications for market outcomes and for competition enforcement (Andreoni & Roberts 2022; CCSA 2023). As African competition authorities are well aware, market failures in imperfect competition and outright failures in digital markets have large implications for developing economies. This is due to the typically small markets, the presence of entrenched dominant firms and highly concentrated markets, and the limited enforcement reach of competition authorities.

Competition issues in South Africa: The Online Market Inquiry

The South African competition regulator recently embarked on an investigation into the competitive dynamics and potential monopoly problems in the area of online markets. This move brought the Competition Commission of South Africa (CCSA) into alignment with numerous other jurisdictions that are examining economic issues around big tech and its regulation.

In its Online Intermediation Platform Market Inquiry (OIPMI or Online Market Inquiry), the South African agency chose to focus on e-commerce (online classifieds, travel bookings and e-commerce outfits such as Takealot) (CCSA 2023). The Inquiry specifically excluded e-hailing (ride-sharing) services, which were the subject of a previous inquiry. However, also of interest – but not receiving immediate attention – were the financial technology (fintech) and big tech sectors (for example, those firms deriving revenue from digital advertising). The Inquiry indicated its willingness to engage forcefully, noting 'competition law [is required] to not only consider new theories of harm but also to act proactively against potential entrenchment strategies to ensure markets are contestable and prevent irreversible concentration. Ensuring markets are contestable also requires competition policy tools to facilitate access by potential entrants (CCSA 2021).

In spite of the Inquiry, competition policy debates in South Africa have been dominated by the questions related to large transnational platforms versus local platforms. Little attention has been given to platforms that have the potential to enhance inclusion. These platforms usually have limited resources and typically cannot afford representation in policy debates (as in the OIPMI), yet their success could unlock wide and rapid economic development for the country.

This chapter focuses specifically on these kinds of platforms – those that have the potential to enhance inclusion. It aims to provide initial evidence on the impact of these platforms, highlight some of the key challenges they face, and ultimately demonstrate the importance of involving these platforms in policy debates. The chapter starts by setting out the data and methodology used to arrive at the findings. Then it draws from the data and presents the results. Next, the chapter discusses barriers to entry and growth of platforms in South Africa before doing a deep dive into specific categories of platforms. After that, it discusses the overall findings of missing platforms as they relate to the Online Intermediation Platforms Market Inquiry (OIPMI) and provides a critical review of the OIPMI. Finally, the chapter concludes and provides the authors' views of the way forward.

Data and methodology

Data

This study provides a landscape of digital platforms that are fostering economic inclusion in South Africa. The study uses secondary data collected in 2022 to analyse the dynamics, trends and impacts of inclusion-focused digital platforms. A firm-level database of platforms was captured through desktop research and literature reviews aided the analysis.

We used secondary data to assess the potential impacts of platforms, focusing on three broad categories: i) delivery platforms and e-hailing, which comprise logistics and delivery; ii) online classifieds, which include e-commerce, trade and online labour; and iii) travel and accommodation, which comprise booking, rental, and asset-sharing platforms. In total, our sample comprised 210 active platforms in South Africa. Secondary sources (such as Cenfri's list of digital marketplace platforms) were extremely helpful. While the list is not exhaustive, we believe it is sufficiently large as a base for analysis.

Business models of digital platforms are classified according to the types of private relationships that platforms broker: B2P2C (Business to Platform to Consumer), where buyers are individuals and sellers are firms; B2P2B (Business to Platform to Business), where firms are both buyers and suppliers; and C2P2C (Consumer to Platform to Consumer), where buyers are both individuals. However, beyond these broad classifications, there has not been a meaningful and consistent framework for classifying the typologies of digital platforms, despite attempts from studies such as Evans and Gawer (2016), Srnicek (2017), and Kenney and Zysman (2016). The three categories that we have focused on were selected on the basis of their potential to drive inclusion. The emphasis was on delivery platforms, as well as platforms that are MSMEs and/or township based (including peri-urban) and/or black-owned.

Sampling method

We used a convenient sampling framework, where platforms were selected on the basis of data being available. Desktop research was conducted to identify and collect data for the platforms, with a reliance on news websites, published reports, advertisements and interviews, as well as the websites and social media pages of the different platforms. In some instances, we made contact with the platforms to fill gaps and verify some of the data.

Inclusion criteria were determined on the following basis. First, we followed the OECD (2019b: 23) definition of an online platform: 'a digital service that facilitates interactions between two or more distinct but interdependent sets of users (whether firms or individuals) or interacts through the service via the Internet'. We then applied the following criteria:
- The platforms must operate in South Africa.
- The platforms should monitor the completion of transactions or observe the transfer of value.
- The platforms operate within the 'real' economy, that is, platforms that facilitate the exchange of tangible goods, services and labour.
- Platforms are considered active if they were operational at the time that the desktop research was conducted.

This reduced the sample to 90 platforms. Of these, 78 platforms (87% reached marginalised and previously excluded segments of the market in some form. For instance, the majority of the delivery platforms that we sampled are mostly based in townships and service informal MSMEs, were are founded by young black entrepreneurs, of which a fair share are women. The sample is not exhaustive, and no statistical techniques have been used to ensure that it is representative of the population. Our evidence is thus presented as more anecdotal than conclusive.

Tracking the growth of digital platforms in South Africa

This section provides an analysis of the landscape and trends of digital platforms in South Africa, based on our sample. Here, we analyse the dynamics of South Africa's digital platforms and provide evidence on the extent to which local and international platforms are facilitating economic inclusion. It is important to note that our findings are illustrative and not conclusive, as data in this area are scarce. Data on the uptake and usage of platforms in townships were required for our analysis of degrees of inclusion. As these forms of data are difficult to source, we also used anecdotal evidence obtained from the media interviews and data on the number of downloads from Google Play Store.[3]

In our sample, 43% of the platforms were in delivery and e-hailing services, 47% were in online classifieds (38% in e-commerce and trade, and 9% in online labour), and 10% were in travel (1% in car rental) and accommodation (9% (see Figure 13.1).[4]

Figure 13.1 Sample composition of digital platforms across sectors

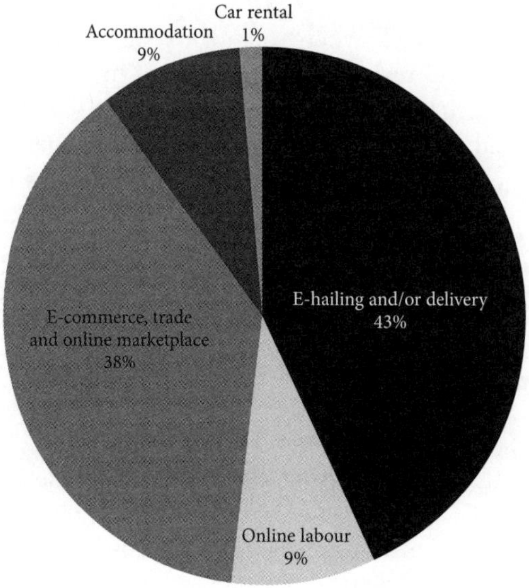

Source: Authors' own compilation

Around 84% of the platforms sampled were based on a B2P2C business model, which is in line with trends in the global digital economy landscape (see Figure 13.2). Inclusion is mainly driven by platforms that were trying to service township communities, particularly in the delivery and e-hailing, and the travel and accommodation categories. In the online classifieds, the impact potential is mainly driven by MSMEs that are located in townships being given access. Gauteng, Western Cape and KwaZulu-Natal were the provinces where most of the platforms were located, with Johannesburg, Pretoria, Cape Town and Durban and their surrounding townships being the most common areas for the launching and operating of the businesses.

Our sample also showed that the local platform space, particularly with regard to inclusion-focused platforms, is nascent. Figure 13.3 shows that most of the platforms are relatively young and that the entry rate started to accelerate from around 2014, when digital platforms were gaining greater prominence in the global economy. The year 2020 also saw a high number of platforms (particularly in delivery and online classifieds) entering the space. This may be associated with the lockdown regulations that were imposed at the peak of the Covid–19 pandemic. The platforms recorded an average of 1 000 downloads but there were some platforms that had

Figure 13.2 Sample composition of digital platforms across business models

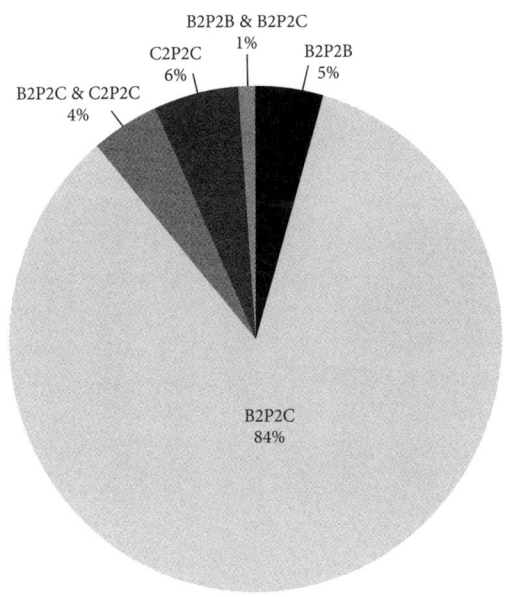

Source: Authors' own compilation

tens of thousands of downloads (and some were reaching hundreds of thousands of followers on Facebook).[4]

A quarter of the platforms had exited the market at the time the desktop research was concluded. As discussed later, exiting the market may be associated with demand- and supply-side challenges in the digital economy in townships, which may be preventing platforms from reaching critical mass and sustainability. Digital platforms function optimally when they have a large market share that generates scale and network effects (as long as the platforms do not abuse their dominance at the expense of consumer welfare) (OECD 2019b). It is thus possible that the recent entry of platforms in our study may represent a saturation on the supply side that may be pushing some platforms out of the market.

Studies have shown that in the short run, foreign platforms usually have the most traction through first-mover advantages within the sector and they usually come into a domestic market having achieved global scale and an accumulation of deep resources. Critical mass and network effects are important for digital platforms and the end-to-end interoperability of the internet, scale without mass, switching costs and data accumulation make it much easier for digital platforms to globalise than for traditional businesses (OECD 2019b).

However, our focus is on locally established platforms, and in the long run, local platforms are more likely to have positive structural and transformative impacts for the domestic economy. For consumers, a local platform does not necessarily

Figure 13.3 The number of local platforms established each year

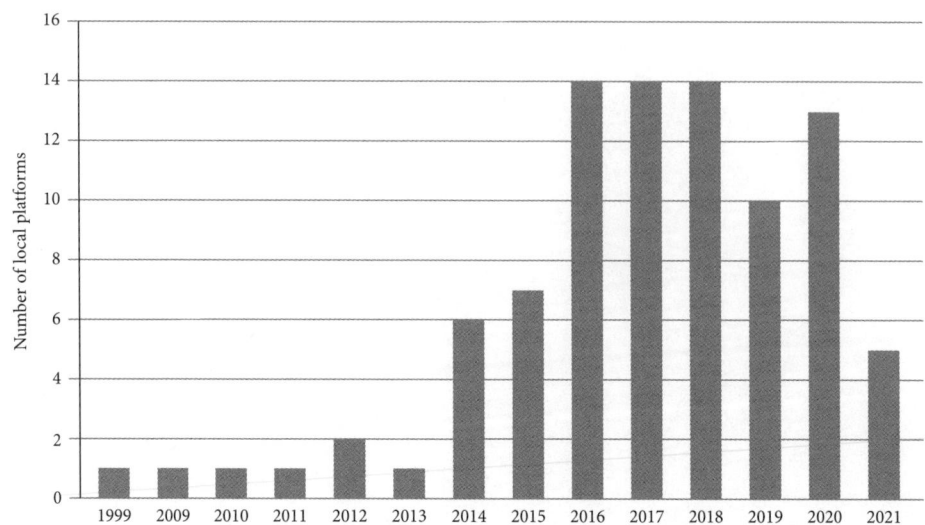

Source: Authors' calculations based on sample

compare to an international platform if the quality is not the same. Nevertheless, for the economy at large, thriving local platforms carry significant structural benefits. Global digital platforms may appropriate large shares of value that are created locally and ultimately contribute to increasing global inequality (Cachalia & Beyleveld 2022). In contrast, local knowledge (for instance, of search habits, traffic conditions and cultural nuances) may bring an advantage to local platforms, enabling them to offer services that are tailored to local users in some instances (OECD 2019b). The technology spill-overs would also remain in the country and help to push the country more towards long-term innovation.

South Africa leads Africa in the development of the digital platforms ecosystem. According to Johnson et al. (2020), South African platforms average 120 000 unique users per month. This is followed by Nigeria (73 000 monthly users), Kenya (34 000 monthly users) and Ghana (15 000 monthly users). South Africa also leads the region in terms of the number of platforms launched. International players identify South Africa as a good entry point into the region, while domestic entrepreneurs launch platforms to try to compete with these players or service domestic needs. A majority of the digital platforms that are active in South Africa have been founded locally.

However, like many markets in the world, the digital economy in South Africa is dominated by global players. The largest locally established platforms typically focus on urban areas and higher-income segments, leaving previously underserved communities behind and further entrenching the legacy of exclusion in South Africa. Indeed, South African platforms, particularly those that focus on the underserved segments of the market, were launched to offer unique propositions for the domestic context. They identify and target market gaps in niches that may be unattractive to foreign transnational platforms. These niche markets may have complexities that local platforms are better suited to overcome because of their on-the-ground understanding. In addition, given the steep learning curves in understanding these markets, the margins may be too low for foreign platforms.

Overall, we do find anecdotal evidence that the economic potential of digital platforms is being realised in South Africa and that economic inclusion, specifically, is being greatly enhanced. First, in e-commerce, accommodation and delivery, local platforms are providing market access to MSMEs, lowering transaction costs, creating efficiencies and improving the quality and price of goods and services (for example, Yebo Fresh and Luntu in e-commerce, and Order Kasi and Kasi Menu in delivery).[5]

Second, our anecdotal evidence also suggests that there has been an inclusive effect through employment. In e-hailing, delivery and accommodation, job creation has mainly been driven by larger international platforms since they have had the most traction. South Africa in the Digital Age (Genesis Analytics 2019) estimates that there are over 20 000 drivers earning an income through e-hailing platforms, while Short et al. (2021) estimates that online accommodation marketplace Airbnb has created an equivalent of 22 000 jobs in South Africa. Local e-hailing and delivery platforms have not yet reached the size to create jobs at that scale, but they do show promise.[6] In a similar way to e-hailing and delivery, growth in e-commerce has the potential to drive inclusion by creating much-needed quality low-skills jobs. In 2020, Yebo Fresh had 50 office and warehouse staff in its operations in the townships of Cape Town[7]. When including drivers and Yebo Fresh's expansion to Johannesburg, there is clearly greater employment creation capacity. Authors such as Mandel (2017) argue that e-commerce creates more jobs in fulfilment centres and logistics than the number of jobs lost in brick-and-mortar retail. According to Mandel (2017), the time that consumers would have previously spent shopping themselves is essentially 'monetised' via fulfilment and delivery charges, whether paid by the seller or the buyer.

Barriers to growth for local platforms that drive inclusion

Several barriers hamper the wide reach and growth of digital platforms in South Africa. Starting with the demand side, across all business models, platform adoption in general and those that are inclusion-focused in particular are constrained by low levels of user readiness. This is linked to South Africa's historical challenges in education in general and digital literacy in particular. The World Bank (2019b) reports that weaknesses in digital skills stem from quality lags in South Africa's education system. While the World Economic Forum's Global Competitiveness Report (2019) shows that South Africa leads African countries in some aspects of digital developments, in the assessment of digital skills among the population it ranks 116th globally. South Africa also ranks at a low 126 out of 157 countries on the World Bank's Human Capital Index, which is below peer African countries with lower GDPs.

Low user readiness is reflected in the low trust in the internet among South Africans. Studies such as OECD (2019a) have demonstrated that consumer trust is essential for widespread adoption of new business models. A survey conducted by Ipsos revealed that only 63% of South Africans trusted the internet in 2022. This showed a decline of 9 percentage points since 2019. In addition to challenges in digital literacy and understanding of the digital economy, low trust in the internet is exacerbated by concerns about online security. According to Ipsos (2022), only 47% of South Africans believed that online security was efficient.

Beyond low levels of user readiness, long-standing structural divides are another key constraint to the growth of digital platforms. South Africa's digital divide along geographical, educational and income lines is well documented. For instance, the National Planning Commission (2020) reports that while South Africa has internet coverage rates that compare favourably with countries in Africa and Asia, it does not perform as well when compared to countries in Latin America with similar incomes. Moreover, comparing South Africa's prepaid mobile data options reveals a high unit cost for low-denomination bundles. This is borne out by the World Bank (2019b), which estimates that the bottom 20% of South Africa's population would have to spend around 12% of their income per capita for 1 GB of mobile data, a figure much higher than the International Telecommunication Union (ITU) average. Effectively, less than half of South Africa's rural population is connected to the internet (National Planning Commission 2020).

The digital divide further narrows an already small market and ultimately exacerbates the challenges for inclusion-focused digital platforms to achieve critical mass. Together with South Africa's broader challenges in digital entrepreneurship, as documented by the World Bank (2019b), the digital divide may also partially explain the number of exits observed in the market.[8]

Strategies for overcoming the barriers

Marketing and educating the market are essential for overcoming low levels of user readiness and trust for B2P2C. However, this is an expensive exercise that requires large upfront investments. This is particularly challenging for inclusion-focused platforms as they generally have limited access to finance. In addition, their lower margins mean that generating revenue to be self-sustaining may often be unattainable. Some local platforms can achieve scale through large corporate partners. For example, Bottles (an on-demand delivery platform launched in 2016) partnered with supermarket retailer Pick n Pay in 2018 to deliver groceries for the supermarket's online orders.[9] However, it is important to note that these examples are exceptions. In most instances, inclusion-focused platforms will not have access to these corporate networks and will therefore not be able to build these strategic partnerships with large corporates. Our analysis shows that they rely more on social media for their service to get exposure, focusing on acquiring followers and educating them about their platforms.

Some inclusion-focused platforms also rely on social media networks to drive adoption among users. Indeed, social network platforms may also provide entrepreneurs from disadvantaged backgrounds with a means of entry without the need for sizeable investments in technology development, as well as the opportunity to determine the demand for a service and at least gain some initial traction. For instance, in addition to its website, Yebo Fresh allows users to place orders using WhatsApp, SMS, email, Facebook light or requesting a 'call back'. BrownSense, an online marketplace for black-owned brands, started off as a Facebook group in 2017 and then leveraged its traffic to launch the website in 2021. Cloudy Deliveries is another delivery platform that enables users to book a delivery via WhatsApp.

Deep dives into categories of digital platforms

This section of the chapter looks at specific categories of digital platforms, particularly as they are used in townships and underserved communities. It also analyses the dynamics of the categories of digital platforms in townships and unpacks how inclusion happens across the different business models. Understanding the dynamics and impact pathways of these inclusion-focused digital platforms is critical for formulating the appropriate competition policy regulation.

Context: Townships and underserved communities

A large proportion of South Africa's population resides in townships. Township economic development is therefore central to South Africa's broad development goals. According to Scheba & Turok (2019), South Africa's townships are characterised by a range of challenges, including:
- low investment in people, places and productive activities;
- high levels of financial leakage and poor resource retention;
- restricted linkages with formal value chains elsewhere;
- poor economic infrastructure (such as banks, business services, logistics, serviced land, industrial areas, business parks and business incubators);
- low-capacity networked infrastructure (such as electricity, water, sanitation systems);
- limited entrepreneurial traditions, business capabilities and vocational skills;
- high population densities with many low-income households with low purchasing power;
- high levels of unemployment, poverty and social ills (such as crime, drug misuse, gangsterism, xenophobia, prejudices against private enterprises);
- inadequate public facilities and social amenities (such as hospitals, schools, colleges, libraries); and
- unsupportive economic institutions and governance arrangements.

Indeed, MSMEs in townships are usually set up out of necessity to generate livelihoods on the part of the entrepreneurs. They are often characterised by their low productive capabilities resulting from challenges such as inadequate capital and skills. According to the Sustainable Livelihoods Foundation (2018), businesses in townships are dominated by informal micro-enterprises.[10] Around 54% are in the food and drinks sectors (including street traders, spaza shops and shebeens), 34% are in the services sector (including hair salons, mechanical and electrical repairs, recycling, churches and early childhood education centres) and 2% are micro-manufacturers.[11] This tiny manufacturing sector does not have significant linkages with wider value chains and external markets (National Treasury 2020) According to Scheba & Turok (2019), the enterprises in townships play a complementary role to formal retailers and this enables them to access a growing segment of low-income earners that cumulatively have sizable buying power.

Aggregate data on the coverage and use of digital platforms for underserved segments is scant, but anecdotal evidence suggests that in these areas, locally developed platforms may be having the most traction. Indeed, local platforms developed by township entrepreneurs may be better positioned to leverage their understanding of the township market based on their lived experience and the niche opportunities that exist. In setting up a platform, their challenge is to understand their competition, identify market gaps in the different sectors and formulate compelling and sustainable value propositions. This must happen while they are navigating the challenges and constraints related to South Africa's digital divide.

Indeed, research has long demonstrated that meaningful competition comes from firms whose service or business model differs from the incumbents as opposed to 'me-too firms' (OCED 2019a). Meaningful competition spurs new ideas, improves the quality of goods and services, provides customers with more choices and lowers prices. While there sometimes may be benefits to 'me-too' firms that replicate the business models of existing dominant firms and leverage second-mover advantages, value creation for customers typically comes from new firms that disrupt the market.

The deep dives that follow look at some of these entrepreneurs and explain their differentiated offerings in more detail. We are focusing specifically on four categories of digital platforms servicing customers in South African townships: online delivery, e-hailing, accommodation and e-commerce.

E-hailing and online delivery platforms in the townships

E-hailing and online delivery are important categories of the digital platform landscape. As illustrated in Figure 13.1 above, e-hailing and online delivery account for 43% of the platforms in our database. E-hailing platforms play a critical role in fostering efficiencies and safety in South Africa's public transportation sector. E-hailing has also provided the market with a cost-effective option when compared with metred taxis, which had been dominant (Dube 2015). Online delivery augments online shopping and facilitates market access. This category improves the efficiency of logistics and assists in overcoming the spatial divides in the South African economy. This subsection analyses the dynamics of this category and unpacks the inclusion effects.

E-hailing platforms

Several e-hailing platforms have been launched locally to try to compete with international ride-hailing platforms Uber and Bolt, which continue to hold the lion's share of the market (WeeTracker 2022). Some of the local platforms have offered the same service as the bigger international platforms, sometimes trying to compete on price. Examples include Ramzy Ride (B2P2C), which was launched in 2018 in Johannesburg, attracting 24 000 followers on Facebook, but eventually exiting the market. Africa Ride was launched in 2016 and operated in Johannesburg, Cape Town and Rustenburg. It had over 500 drivers in 2017, but has also exited the market.[12]

Other local platforms have tried to offer some differentiation in addition to the lower prices. For instance, Local Ride's offerings were a response to safety issues associated with e-hailing in South Africa, such as female safety. The company offers a ride option where female passengers can request a female driver. The option is offered exclusively to women and aims to ensure safety and comfort to both female riders and drivers. Local Ride was launched in in Johannesburg 2019 and operates across the province. The platform currently has over 10 000 downloads on the Google Play Store and is currently active.

There are several e-hailing platforms that were created locally before the service had gained the current level of popularity. Lulaloop is another example of a digital platform that offered differentiation from the incumbents by being more targeted. The platform focuses exclusively on connecting corporate commuters with private shuttles on their way to work. It was launched in Cape Town in 2016 and also operates in Johannesburg, Pretoria, Durban and Gqeberha. It is currently active with over 1 000 installations on the Google Store and over 11 000 followers on Facebook.

Online delivery platforms

Online delivery platforms in the townships include food, retail products and vehicle-hiring services. The delivery services use several modes of transportation, including bicycles, motorbikes and motor vehicles. A majority of online delivery platforms are locally founded but international platforms dominate the market.

Food

In food delivery, several B2P2C platforms connect consumers with local restaurants that offer relatively affordable meals that are not available on incumbent internationally established platforms, such as Uber Eats and Bolt Food. In fact, it is worth noting that some of the incumbent platforms that were locally established, such as Mr D, do not service these previously excluded communities. Township-based entrepreneurs have identified this as a market gap and believe that their food delivery platforms can properly cater for the budgets, tastes and needs of the township market. For instance, Kasi Menus was launched in 2020 and delivered for seven restaurants across Soweto and Ga-Rankuwa townships in Gauteng. In 2020, they had over 2 000 active customers (VUT Research 2020). They have since exited the market.

Another (active) example is Scooter Treats. It uses electric scooters to deliver food and cargo in the townships of South Africa. The platform was launched in 2016 and as of 2020, they were covering 120 square kilometres of Soweto daily, with over 3 000 meals delivered to over 1 000 users.[13] Delivery ka Speed was launched in 2021 in Hammanskraal in Gauteng and the surrounding townships. Through its B2P2C platform, it delivers food from popular fast-food restaurants such as KFC and McDonalds. Within its first three months of launching, it had completed close to 2 500 deliveries.[14]

These food delivery platforms clearly drive inclusion on the supply side by enhancing market access for township-based restaurants. According to Petersen et al. (2021), there are thousands of such informal food businesses across South Africa's townships. The nature of the establishments and food services offered varies widely. There are many street food offerings such as braai grids on the sides of the roads, deep-fried takeaways prepared in shipping containers, and sitting restaurants in 'Shisa nyama' venues.[15] Petersen et al. (2021) note that these food services are geared towards the budgets and preferences of the township economy that are not serviced by the broader mainstream economy. Importantly, while profitability is likely to be modest, these services provide a much-needed shield against the poverty that is prevalent in townships.

Delivery platforms have also been enhancing market coordination in the food delivery space. For example, Order Kasi is a (B2P2C) meal delivery service that exclusively offers food from restaurants based in the township to consumers in and outside the townships. The platform was launched in 2019 in Nyanga in the Western Cape and operates in other townships around Cape Town. It currently has over 1 000 installations on the Google Play Store and over 3 000 followers on Facebook. Another platform, Kasi Eats, launched in 2017 in Pretoria, helps restaurants located in the townships market their menus and manage food delivery orders. Chucks App, launched in 2019 in Soweto, connects consumers with local restaurants looking for a 'kota' – a fast meal that is popular in townships. Chucks reached over 1 000 installations on the Google Play Store, but has since exited the market. Siyeza Deliveries was launched at the height of the Covid–19 pandemic lockdowns in 2020 in the Thembisa township in Gauteng. The platform delivered kotas and African cuisine to Thembisa and the surrounding townships, but has exited the market.

Retail products

Handed is another example of how delivery platforms offer services that are tailored to local needs. Handed is a delivery platform that enables consumers to pay for goods only once they have been delivered. Handed drivers have payment devices and access process payments after the client receives and inspects the goods. Lack of trust by consumers as a constraint to the growth of online shopping in South Africa has been demonstrated by several studies, including Makhitha and Ngobeni (2021). Direct handover addressed this challenge and may potentially increase the conversion of online platforms at no additional cost. The platform was launched in 2019 in Johannesburg and currently services Gauteng, with 350 registered stores.

Another example of local platforms responding to local challenges is Droppa, which allows users in Gauteng to book same-day deliveries from as little as R99. Long delivery times and expensive courier services have been highlighted as some of the major constrains to online shopping in South Africa by studies such as Goga and Paelo (2018).

Truck hire

Delivery platforms servicing townships also encompass on-demand moving services. Established in 2017, Droppa is a B2P2C platform that enables users to book a truck for moving or delivering heavy items on demand. They currently have over 10 000 installations on the Google Play Store. Load It is a B2P2C platform that was launched in 2017 and offers on-demand truck hire services. The platform has over 5 700 followers on Facebook and over 1 000 installations on the driver app. It is available in Johannesburg and Cape Town and services the surrounding townships.

Multiple services and modes of delivery

In a similar way to the larger incumbents, on-demand delivery platforms servicing townships usually have several service lines, delivering food and other consumable and non-consumable goods. eKasi Deliveries is a B2P2C platform that delivers local fast food, liquor and groceries to townships in Gauteng. The platform was launched in 2020 in Vosloorus. It continues to be active, although traction has been low. Cloudy Deliveries was launched in Langa in the Western Cape in 2020 and helps facilitate the exchange of food and other goods between consumers and businesses. Their B2P2P and C2P2C platform has over 3 000 followers on Facebook with 10 bicycles dispatched for deliveries daily as of 2021. eKasi Express Deliveries is a B2P2C platform that delivers fast food, healthcare and medication to townships across South Africa. It was launched in Newlands, Riverhouse and KwaMashu in KwaZulu-Natal in 2020 and has since expanded nationwide although its reach remains limited. Kasi Delivery was launched in 2021 and provides services in Gqeberha and delivers food, goods and documents, although its reach has also been limited. Local Ride was initially launched as a ride-sharing app and its services were expanded to include the delivery of food.

These tech entrepreneurs have also demonstrated adaptability and use different kinds of vehicles to set up their initial fleets. On the low technology end, Cloudy Deliveries uses a fleet of bicycles to make its deliveries. Dash Deliveries also uses bicycles to offer on-demand delivery services within a 20-kilometre radius. Launched in 2018 in Durban, it has recently opened registration for riders across the country. By using bicycles, these platforms can offer prices that are cheaper than the usual market rates. They also make entry easier for gig workers (riders) by not requiring motorbikes or vehicles or licences on the part of the workers. On the high-technology end, Scooter Treats and Delivery Ka Speed use electric scooters to deliver and aim to contribute to the shift towards clean transportation.

Reasons for exiting

Several platforms have exited this space, including the Hunting Chow App, which was launched in 2018 in Soweto and Edenvale to deliver food and drinks, and Ezy Deliveries, which was launched in Vosloorus township in Gauteng in 2020 to deliver fresh produce from retail shops directly to clients. The possible reasons for these exits include limited readiness of the market as discussed earlier in the chapter, possible saturation on the supply side, and inadequate support for the entrepreneurs regarding the resources or funding that is required to scale.

Accommodation platforms in the townships

As reported by the Development Action Group (2022), backyard renting is a major sector in South Africa's townships and informal settlements, providing affordable accommodation to a segment of the market seeking affordable accommodation near to the cities.

In tourism and accommodation, several local platforms have emerged and are providing market access to township-owned establishments for long-term and short-term rentals. Analysis of our sample shows that the entrepreneurs behind such platforms are usually from townships, and they aim to imitate and modify the offerings of bigger platforms that are focused in urban areas. For instance, Amarooms helps tenants find accommodation in townships. Founded in Thembisa in early 2021, they had a reach of 263 townships across the country as of June 2021 (Sowetan 2021).[16] As of 2022, the app had over 10 000 installations on Google Play Store. Another example is the Indlu mobile application, which helps homeowners to register their rooms and tenants to find, pay for and manage their monthly rentals. The app currently has over 1 000 installations and 10 000 followers on Facebook.

Some platforms are not exclusively targeted at townships and were not established by township-based platforms, but nevertheless have significant traction and impact in townships. The LekkeSlaap platform is an example of this. It offers rental bookings and asset sharing across South Africa, including in townships. Established in 2017, it currently has over 100 000 installations on the Google Play Store. These platforms may also help to link township enterprises with new clients.

Township tourism is a growing and lucrative market. According to Scheba and Turok (2019), township tourism has been on the rise in recent decades. Scheba and Turok

(2019) report that township tourism connects affluent international and national residents with township enterprises, bringing spending into the townships with potential multiplier effects on leisure, service, retail and other industries. Thus far, however, this has only been observed in a few townships such as Soweto (Scheba & Turok 2019). Digital platforms may increase tourism in these townships and give more visibility and market access to other townships.

E-commerce platforms in the townships

E-commerce adoption has been increasing in townships, although the sector is still very young. It includes online shopping for fashion and related items, and groceries. E-commerce platforms allow customers to shop for items through digital tools and collection can be provided in-house, through a third party (such as an online delivery option) or customers can collect from designated pick-up points. In townships, e-commerce platforms aim to address challenges such as the long and exhausting commuting experiences from poor public transport and overcrowded supermarkets, when looking to purchase bulk groceries and goods that may not be available at spaza shops. On the supply side, e-commerce platforms also enhance market access for township-based enterprises. A good example of an e-commerce platform fostering inclusion on the demand and supply side is Yebo Fresh. Yebo Fresh is an online shopping service for township communities, delivering groceries to areas that are generally unserved by most formal retailers. The startup now delivers to more than 25 townships in the greater Cape Town and Johannesburg areas, working with a rapidly growing network of spaza shops, prepared food outlets, and other township businesses. Orders are placed via WhatsApp or through the Yebo Fresh team of field sales agents, with Yebo Fresh using a dark store-based fulfilment model to deliver orders within 24 hours.[17]

E-commerce offerings in the townships

Analysis of the platforms in our sample also demonstrates how platforms give township communities access to better quality products. For example, Kasi Meats was launched in 2020 during the height of the Covid–19 pandemic lockdowns to deliver fresh meats directly from the butchery to households in townships around East London in the Eastern Cape. It continues to operate today and has over 4 000 followers on Facebook. A second example is Khula. Launched in 2016, Khula connects households with fresh produce sourced from smallholder farmers. Similarly, Kasi Farmer's Market is an online marketplace that connects township small-scale farmers with consumers looking for fresh produce. The Luntu platform, launched in 2020 in Johannesburg, is an online marketplace where customers may shop for brands and products that have ethical and sustainability standards that consumers consider to be important. For instance, through the Luntu B2P2C platform, consumers can easily filter the online catalogue to find brands that are black-owned, women-owned, owned by people with disabilities, are halal, vegan, locally made or upcycled and recycled. Platforms also provide consumers with products that may otherwise be difficult to source. Examples of this are in the sneaker market, where C2P2C platforms such as Buy My Sneaker and Sneaker Spaza connect consumers looking for second-hand premium sneakers with other consumers who are selling their sneakers.[18]

The e-commerce ecosystem and modus operandi of e-commerce entrepreneurs

On the supply side, for township-based MSMEs and previously excluded entrepreneurs, online shopping presents a market access route with fewer barriers to entry compared to traditional brick-and-mortar retailing. The infrastructure cost for setting up an online retail shop is typically lower than that required for a physical shop, particularly in terms of accessing more affluent segments of the market. For example, the Boxshop's online marketplace provides emerging furniture, fashion and accessory brands with market access that they would otherwise struggle to get at such early stages of their businesses. Technology development companies such as Shopify, Magento and Woocommerce provide affordable services for start-ups to set up online stores without having to code the back-end themselves. Some entrepreneurs use these platforms to establish online marketplaces that drive inclusion through providing market access to brands and SMEs that would otherwise be hidden. The commission charged by these online marketplaces is much lower than that normally charged by physical retailers (for example, Brownsense, Culture Store and iZulu charge a commission of around 15–18%).[19] Even in instances where the platform is more advanced, such as Luntu or Khula, the commission is still low.

Where starting off with a fully fledged website or application is challenging, some online marketplaces leverage social networks as a starting point. Examples are Brownsense and Yebo Fresh. The Brownsense Facebook group was established in 2017 to link consumers and clients with products and services from black-owned businesses. They currently have over 220 000 members on their Facebook group. Traction was leveraged to establish an online marketplace in 2021. Other examples are Kasi Meats, which uses Facebook to deliver fresh meat to townships in East London, and Yebo Fresh, which was launched in 2018 and initially leveraged Unstructured Supplementary Service Data (USSD) and WhatsApp messaging to deliver fresh foods to Imizamo Yethu and other townships around Cape Town directly at the door. At the height of Covid–19 lockdowns, Yebo Fresh was delivering 500 food parcels (56 000 meals) daily in townships around Cape Town (Yebo Fresh 2020). A fully fledged website has since been developed and in 2021, they expanded operations to townships around Johannesburg, with Katlehong, Vosloorus and Thokoza being the first areas targeted. In addition to this B2P2C offering, they also added a B2P2B service where they pick, pack and distribute food parcels to beneficiaries in bulk deliveries to NGOs and NPOs. Yebo Fresh currently has 40 full-time employees.

In addition to serving as an initial market for township-focused and previously excluded entrepreneurs to get market validation and sustainable cash flow before expanding to brick and mortar brick retailing, the rich data on consumer preferences generated by e-commerce adoption enables entrepreneurs to fine-tune their product offering and positioning, thus improving their chances of succeeding. Studies such as those carried out by Ndayizigamiye and McArthur (2014) provide empirical evidence that relative advantage is significantly related to e-commerce adoption.

Digital platforms in South Africa are not only providing market access to township SMEs, but also have a B2P2B offering that enhances the access of MSMEs to suppliers and inputs. For instance, Petersen et al. (2021) report that in food services, the informal micro-entrepreneurs source their inputs from large formal players as well as other informal suppliers. Digital platforms may make it possible for informal enterprises to have better prices when buying from formal suppliers and better logistics when sourcing from informal suppliers. For instance, Zuzela was a Gqeberha-based (B2P2B) ecommerce platform that connected spaza shops and informal traders in South Africa with brands and distributors on a sales app. In this way, Zuzela was making it easier for spaza shops to purchase products at affordable prices — increasing product visibility and price transparency in townships. Products on the platform were organised by suppliers, and informal traders could place their orders on the platform, collect their goods, or receive delivery directly from suppliers and brand owners. Zuzela has since exited the market. Another (active at the time of research) example is Vuleka, which was launched in 2017 in Johannesburg. The platform assists spaza shops in bulk purchases of fast-moving consumer goods (FMCG) from wholesalers at discounted prices. As of 2020, Vuleka had reached over 6 000 informal traders in and around Johannesburg.[20]

Conclusion and the way forward

The OIPMI issued its Final Report and Decision in July 2023. In its process and in its report, the OIPMI did not ignore the township context of local platforms. The Final Report mentions the subject at several points: for example, at pages 12, 90, 96 and 114 (Hodge et al. 2023). However, the specific dynamics of township platforms are largely viewed by the OIPMI through the lens of a broad market dynamic, namely that of local delivery. This is certainly the case for delivery platforms in the townships, as well as for the categories of e-hailing, accommodation and e-commerce to a certain extent. The best-funded market inquiry cannot cover all the bases and choices had to be made about what to research and investigate and what to omit.

Within this context, this chapter has aimed, from a competition perspective, to draw attention to the specific category of digital platforms in the townships and document the empirical investigation. The research on digital platforms in South Africa is thin; our analysis in this chapter has aimed to shed light on some of the local platforms that are driving inclusion in South Africa.

Digital platforms can drive inclusion by democratising markets (OCED 2019b). Digital platforms achieve this by reducing market friction, decreasing search costs, matching consumers and suppliers, and leveraging network effects. In other words, digital platforms reduce transaction costs and information asymmetries between market players in different places (OECD 2019b). Ultimately, by giving consumers more information, convenience, choice and competition, digital platforms may reduce prices and improve the quality of products. The other benefit of digital platforms is their ability to enhance productivity and efficiency, and drive digital innovation and digital transformation. Beyond connecting market players more efficiently, digital platforms may create new digital products or bundle existing products in a new way or create new types of transactions (OECD 2019b). Digital platforms also enable companies and individuals to digitise their processes, enabling industries to function more efficiently.

These inclusive effects of digital platforms vary according to the category of the platform and the business model chosen. Online classified and accommodation platforms drive market coordination and enable resources to be better utilised. They enhance market access and efficiencies for players along the value chain, such as informal or female micro-traders, smallholder farmers and other MSMEs seeking to source inputs or sell outputs. Gig work platforms, including e-hailing and delivery, have major job creation potential in that they can create new income opportunities for low-skilled workers who are typically excluded from mainstream economic opportunities.

By neglecting inclusion-focused platforms in policy discussions, South Africa risks further entrenching the divides that have plagued the nation since the advent of democracy in the country in 1994. Further research and future inquiries should devote a greater share of their investigatory resources towards better understanding and addressing the competitive dynamics of the category of platforms in the townships.

Notes

1. The support of the Omidyar Foundation towards the working paper on which this chapter is based is gratefully acknowledged. See: https://wiser.wits.ac.za/page/african-digital-competition-research-working-papers-webinars-13755

2. A township can be defined as an often underdeveloped and historically racially segregated area located on the periphery of towns and cities, and arising from labour migration towards economic hubs. 'MSME' stands for micro, small and medium enterprises. It is used interchangeably with 'SMME' (which stands for small, medium and micro-enterprises) in this chapter.

3. The Google Play Store is an online store where mobile devices operating the Android software can download mobile applications, games and digital content. It is a digital distribution service operated and developed by Google.

4. Data on 'reach of platforms' in South Africa are scant. We tried to find data on downloads for the Google Play Store for those platforms that had mobile application. In the absence of this data and other data on usage, we use Facebook followers as one of our proxies for reach.

THE OTHER PLATFORMS, THE OTHER CONSUMERS

5   Yebo Fresh is an on-demand e-commerce platform that allows customers to place a grocery order using their website, SMS, email or Facebook light, or by requesting a callback. Luntu is an online marketplace where customers may shop for brands and products that have ethical and sustainable standards that consumers are looking for. Order Kasi and Kasi Menu are delivery services that offer food from restaurants based in the township to consumers in and outside townships.

6   Local platforms that had the largest platforms in South Africa are in the gig work category. These include Kandua, which creates 9.8 work opportunities a day according to their website, and Sweep South, which had created 15 000 jobs by 2019. See: https://www.techinafrica.com/sa-online-cleaning-service-sweepsouth-secured-r50-million-investment/

7   See: Huisman B, From Uber to courier to put food on the table, *Daily Maverick*, 4 June 2020. Accessed November 2024, https://www.dailymaverick.co.za/article/2020-06-04-from-uber-to-courier-to-put-food-on-the-table/

8   According to World Bank (2019), key challenges in South Africa's digital entrepreneurship include policy, regulatory and human capital bottlenecks. The report also highlighted the need to strengthen the numerous digital entrepreneurship support services provided by organisations and increase access to early and growth stage finance.

9   Bottles was eventually acquired by Pick n Pay in 2021 and rebranded to ASAP!.

10 The Sustainable Livelihoods Foundation is a not-for-profit research and community engagement think tank based in Cape Town.

11 A spaza shop, also known as a tuck shop, is an informal convenience shop business in South Africa, usually run from home. They also serve the purpose of supplementing household incomes of the owners, selling small, everyday household items. A shebeen is a drinking establishment (usually in a private home in a township) where liquor is sold or consumed.

12 See: Jackson T, SA's Africa Ride launches to compete with Uber, *Disrupt Africa*, 9 March 2017. Accessed November 2024, https://disruptafrica.com/2017/03/09/sas-africa-ride-launches-to-compete-with-uber/

13 See: Chiothamisi T, Scooter Treats – South Africa's first electric scooter delivery company, *Startup Mag*, February 2021. Accessed November 2024, https://startupmag.co.za/2021/02/scooter-treats-south-africas-first-electric-scooter-delivery-company/

14 Daniel L, This township delivery service uses WhatsApp and electric scooters for fast food drop-offs, *Business Insider South Africa Archives*, 10 October 2021. Accessed November 2024, https://www.news24.com/news24/bi-archive/south-africa-township-fast-food-delivery-with-electric-scooters-2021-10

15 A braai grid is a platform that is usually made from steel and used for flame grilling food. The term 'shisa nyama' venues is used in townships to describe places where food is braaied (barbequed) and served.

16 Vuk'uzenzele G, Free-to-use app connects potential township tenants to backroom landlords, *Sowetan Live*, 30 July 2021. Accessed November 2024, https://www.sowetanlive.co.za/sebenza-live/2021-07-30-free-to-use-app-connects-potential-township-tenants-to-backroom-landlords/

17 Jackson T, SA Food e-commerce startup Yebo Fresh raises $4.5m pre-Series A round, *Disrupt Africa*, 30 January 2023. Accessed November 2024, https://disruptafrica.com/2023/01/30/sa-food-e-commerce-startup-yebo-fresh-raises–4–5m-pre-series-a-round/

18 Buy My Sneaker was launched in 2015 in Vereeniging and has over 4 000 followers on Facebook and over 1 000 installations in the Google Play Store. Sneaker Spaza was launched in 2018 in Johannesburg and currently has over 1 800 followers on Facebook.

19 Brownsense is an online platform that connects buyers to black-owned businesses. Culture Store and iZulu are online marketplaces that offer buyers access to local brands.

20 Jackson T, Gauteng-based retail distribution startup Vuleka plans nationwide expansion in next 12 months, *Disrupt Africa*, 19 August 2020. Accessed November 2024, https://disruptafrica.com/2020/08/19/gauteng-based-retail-distribution-startup-vuleka-plans-nationwide-expansion-in-next–12-months/

References

Andreoni A & Roberts S (2022) Governing digital platform power for industrial development: Towards an entrepreneurial-regulatory state. *Cambridge Journal of Economics* 46(6): 1431–1454. https://doi.org/10.1093/cje/beac055

Cachalia F & Beyleveld A (2022) Exploring legal and policy options to address the competition-inequality nexus: The case of South Africa. In J Broulik & K Cseres (Eds) *Competition law and economic inequality*. London: Bloomsbury Publishing

CCSA (Competition Commission South Africa) (2021) *Online intermediation platforms market inquiry terms of reference*. Pretoria: CCSA. Accessed November 2024, https://www.compcom.co.za/wp-content/uploads/2021/04/44432_09–04_EconomicDevDepartment.pdf

CCSA (2023) *Online intermediation platforms inquiry final report*. Pretoria: CCSA. Accessed November 2024, https://www.compcom.co.za/wp-content/uploads/2023/07/CC_OIPMI-Final-Report.pdf

Development Action Group (2022) *Backyard housing – An essential part of the solution to South Africa's housing crisis: A submission into the proposed New Human Settlements Policy and Human Settlements Bill*. Cape Town: Isandla Institute. Accessed November 2024, https://www.dag.org.za/wp-content/uploads/2023/07/backyard-housing-cso-submission–2022.pdf

Dube SC (2015) Uber: A game-changer in passenger transport in South Africa? *CCRED Quarterly Review November 2015*. Accessed November 2024, https://www.competition.org.za/ccred-blog-competition-review/2015/11/22/uber-a-game-changer-in-passenger-transport-in-south-africa

Evans PC & Gawer A (2016) *The rise of the platform enterprise: A global survey*. New York: The Center for Global Enterprise

Genesis Analytics (2019) Pathways to digital work: A strategy primer for South Africa's digital economy. Accessed June 2023, https://pathwayscommission.bsg.ox.ac.uk/sites/default/files/2021-11/South%20Africa%20Strategy%20Primer%20Accessible.pdf

Goga S & Paelo A (2018) *An e-commerce revolution in retail?* CCRED IDTT Digital Industrial Policy Brief 6, The Centre for Competition, Regulation and Economic Development

Ipsos (2022) *Trust in the internet*. Johannesburg: Ipsos. Accessed November 2024, https://www.ipsos.com/sites/default/files/ct/news/documents/2022-11/Trust%20in%20the%20Internet%2C%20Nov%202022.pdf

Johnson C, Bester H, Janse van Vuuren P & Dunn M (2020) *Africa's digital platforms: Overview of emerging trends in the market*. Insight2impact, Cenfri, FinMark Trust and The Mastercard Foundation

Kenney M & Zysman J (2016) The rise of the platform economy. *Issues in Science and Technology* 32(3): 61–69. https://brie.berkeley.edu/sites/default/files/kenney-zysman-the-rise-of-the-platform-economy-spring-2016-istx.pdf

Makhitha KM & Ngobeni KM (2021) The impact of risk factors on South African consumers' attitude towards online shopping. *Acta Commercii* 21(1): 922

Mandel M (2017) *How ecommerce creates jobs and reduces income inequality*. Washington, D.C.: Progressive Policy Institute

National Planning Commission (2020) *Economic progress towards the national development plan's vision 2030: Recommendations for course correction*. Pretoria: National Planning Commission. Accessed November 2024, https://www.nationalplanningcommission.org.za/assets/Documents/Review%20of%20Economic%20Progress%20NPC%20Dec%202020.pdf

National Treasury (2020) *Cities support programme: township economic series*. Pretoria: National Treasury. Accessed November 2024, https://iudf.co.za/wp-content/uploads/2020/09/Township-Economies-Series-1-Paper.pdf

Ndayizigamiye P & McArthur B (2014) Determinants of e-commerce adoption amongst SMMEs in Durban, South Africa. *Mediterranean Journal of Social Sciences* 5(25): 250–256

OECD (Organisation for Economic Cooperation and Development) (2019a) *Platform companies and responsible business conduct*. Paris: OECD Publishing. Accessed November 2024, https://mneguidelines.oecd.org/RBC-and-platform-companies.pdf

OECD (2019b) *An introduction to online platforms and their role in the digital transformation*. Paris: OECD Publishing. https://doi.org/10.1787/53e5f593-en

Petersen I, Mustapha N, Van Rheede N & Kruss G (2021) *Harnessing innovation in the informal food services sector: Insights for public policy in the age of Covid-19*. UJ-TRCTI Working Paper Series P 2021–06, University of Johannesburg. Accessed November 2024, https://www.uj.ac.za/wp-content/uploads/2022/05/wp6-petersen_final.pdf

Scheba A & Turok I (2019) Strengthening township economies in South Africa: The case for better regulation and policy innovation. *Urban Forum* 31: 77–94. https://doi.org/10.1007/s12132-019-09378-0

Short R, Scott C, Evans K, Adonis K & Schoeman M (2021) *The foundations of inclusive tourism: The contribution of Airbnb to inclusive growth in South Africa*. Johannesburg: Genesis Analytics. https://genesis.imgix.net/uploads/files/Genesis-Analytics-Airbnb-The-foundations-of-inclusive-tourism-13-Sept-2021-Final-report.pdf

Sustainable Livelihoods Foundation (2018) *South Africa's informal economy: Research findings from nine townships*. Cape Town: Sustainable Livelihoods Foundation. Accessed November 2024, http://livelihoods.org.za/wp-content/uploads/2018/05/South-Africas-Informal-Economy.pdf

Srnicek N (2017) *Platform capitalism*. New Jersey: John Wiley & Sons

UNCTAD (United Nations Conference on Trade and Development) (2020) *Digital platforms and value creation in developing countries: Implications for national and international policies*. Geneva: UNCTAD

VUT Research (2020) *Uber Who? Kasi Catering to the Township*. Vanderbijlpark: Vaal University of Technology. Accessed November 2024, https://www.vut-research.ac.za/uber-who-kasi-catering-to-the-townships/

WeeTracker (2022) Decoding Venture Investments in Africa. Accessed November 2024, https://weetracker.com/venture-capital-africa–2022-report/

World Bank (2019a) *Policy and regulatory issues with digital businesses*. Policy Research Working Paper 8948. Washington, D.C.: World Bank

World Bank Group (2019b) South Africa: Digital Economy Diagnostic. Washington, D.C.: World Bank. Accessed November 2024, http://hdl.handle.net/10986/33786

World Economic Forum (2019) *The global competitiveness report 2019*. Geneva: World Economic Forum9. Accessed November 2024, https://www3.weforum.org/docs/WEF_TheGlobalCompetitivenessReport2019.pdf

Yebo Fresh (2020) *Yebo fresh delivers through township turmoil*. Cape Town: Yebo Fresh. Accessed November 2024, https://yebofresh.flywheelstaging.com/delivering-through-township-turmoil/

14 Is the introduction of competition between stock exchanges a good idea?

Paul Anderson and Andre Frauenknecht

A stock exchange is a sophisticated data platform that facilitates the listing and trading of company stocks.[1] These platforms play an important role in the economy by, inter alia, mobilising capital for productive use, providing a framework for good corporate governance of firms and facilitating a transparent mechanism to price securities. However, by their nature, stock exchanges exhibit elements of natural monopoly with features of strong scale economies and network externalities. There is also a widely held view that capital market soundness and the efficient pricing of stocks are best achieved through a single exchange platform.

These characteristics of stock exchanges have traditionally been seen as insurmountable barriers to entry for would-be competitors and a justification for regulators to allow only a single exchange to operate in a given market. However, in the past few decades these barriers have reduced significantly with the rapid rate of technology diffusion and growing sophistication of trading platforms (and its users). This has made the notion of competition between stock exchange platforms more feasible and the prospect of entry a credible threat for incumbent players.

Although many countries may still have a single cash equity exchange, competition is now the norm in a number of jurisdictions including the US, UK, Continental Europe, Canada, Australia and Japan. This wave of new competition is not over, with various trading platforms having recently announced plans to launch in countries such as Mexico and Brazil.

South Africa has not been immune to the trend towards increasing competition. Historically, the Johannesburg Stock Exchange (JSE) has been the sole domestic provider of trading and clearing services for cash equities in South Africa – a market that has stood out internationally for its size and sophistication relative to the national economy. However, changes in financial sector policy, specifically the introduction of the Financial Markets Act (No. 19 of 2012)[2], combined with the general lowering of natural barriers to entry, has – at least in principle – opened the South African market to competitive entry. South Africa now finds itself, like many other international jurisdictions, amid a transition towards competition in cash equity markets with, for example, the licensing of four new exchanges: A2X, ZARX, 4AX and EESE.[3]

South African stock exchanges are regulated by both the Financial Sector Conduct Authority (FSCA) and the Prudential Authority – this has been referred to as the Twin peaks model of financial regulation. The role of the FSCA is to enhance efficiency and maintain integrity of the financial markets, as well as to promote customer treatment, whereas the focus of the Prudential Authority is on maintaining financial stability. The Competition Commission of South Africa (CCSA) still maintains jurisdiction matters that raise concerns related to competition. For example, the merger between the Johannesburg Stock Exchange and Link Market Services was still subject to approval from the CCSA.

Nonetheless, the introduction of competition in capital markets remains a complex issue and involves the consideration of a number of atypical competition impacts. While competition may have the potential to offer benefits to brokers and investors in the form of lower trading fees and increased innovation, it may also introduce additional trading and regulatory costs. Even more fundamental is the potential for competition to impact on the soundness and integrity of the market system and its management of risk.

In this chapter, we provide a framework for considering the various impacts (positive and negative) that competition between stock exchanges may bring. This chapter draws on previous work undertaken for the FSCA in South Africa and focuses on the introduction of competition in cash equity markets (as opposed to other capital markets such as derivatives or bonds).

Chapter 14 first looks at the role and functions of a stock exchange and then outlines the natural monopoly elements of a stock exchange. Next, it explores the features of a well-functioning exchange (including competitive pricing, liquid markets, efficient and orderly price discovery, and innovation) and the potential impact of competition, before showing a possible framework for evaluating the impact of competition between stock exchanges. Then it discusses the hypothesised impacts and international experience of competition (including trading and post trading fees, connectivity costs, trading volume, liquidity and spreads, innovation, price discovery, listing standards and enforcement, market surveillance and member supervision, risk management/clearing). Finally, the chapter explores the potential impact of introducing competition between stock exchanges in South Africa, with a summary of key findings, followed by the authors' concluding remarks.

The role and functions of a stock exchange

A stock exchange provides a platform for companies to list their shares and for these shares to be traded. Exchanges play an important role in the economy by:
- mobilising capital and directing investors' savings for productive use;
- enabling the formation of an efficient, transparent and orderly price[4] for listed securities, as observed in stock exchanges (IOSCO 2011); and
- providing a strong framework for corporate governance through listing requirements (Christiansen & Koldertsova 2008).

The successful execution of a trade on an exchange is facilitated via an intricate value chain of trading and post-trading services. The exact model used to provide

these services can vary – particularly in relation to post-trading services – but at a general level can be broken down into three broad activities: trading, clearing and settlement activities.
- *Trading*: The process begins with a broker placing an order for the trade on a trading platform. This is done on behalf of the broker's client (or in some cases on the broker's own behalf). The trading engine of the exchange determines and facilitates the matching of the buy and sell orders. The trade is executed when order matching occurs and a trading fee is levied for the execution of the trade. The nature and structure of this trading fee can vary substantially from exchange to exchange.
- *Clearing*: This refers to the processes that take place between trading and settlement. Based on the terms of the transaction, clearing prepares the transaction to ensure the obligations related to the transaction will be discharged through the exchange (BIS 2010). This includes the determination of the number and/or value of cash equities of each kind to be transferred by or on behalf of the seller and the monies to be paid by or on behalf of the buyer. This is followed by settlement instruction (processing the matched and netted trades to be sent for settlement). These clearing services can be provided by a central clearing counterparty (CCP) or the exchange itself, as in the case of the JSE. A clearing house or CCP typically puts in place various risk management levers to drive settlement assurance. This may include capital adequacy and margin requirements[5], a default fund and even the clearing house's own financial resources.
- *Settlement*: Settlement constitutes the completion of the transaction. Once the trade has cleared, settlement involves discharging the obligations arising from the transaction – that is, the actual transfer of ownership of money and securities – and then settlement is complete (Oxera 2007). These settlement activities (and related services) can be provided directly by a central securities depository (CSD) or by central securities depository participants (CSDPs) (which maintain an account with the CSD).[6,7]

Figure 14.1 presents a stylised illustration of these categories across the value chain for the provision of trading and post-trading services undertaken by the JSE.

Trading services for cash equities can potentially be undertaken by various forms of trading platforms – the different types of exchanges in a market strongly shape the nature of competition that will emerge:
- *A traditional exchange*: This type of exchange competes to attract a wide range of firms to list cash equities on the exchange, and competes in trading. In some cases, these exchanges may also offer post-trading services, while in other instances post-trading services could be outsourced to a CCP. Where entrants seek to replicate this model, they will tend to compete head on with traditional incumbent exchanges. However, it is uncommon for entrants to attempt to enter with a full traditional cash equities exchange. Rather, entrants tend to differentiate themselves by using one of the alternative forms of exchange below.

Figure 14.1 Stylised illustration of the value chain for the provision of trading and post-trading services by the JSE for cash securities

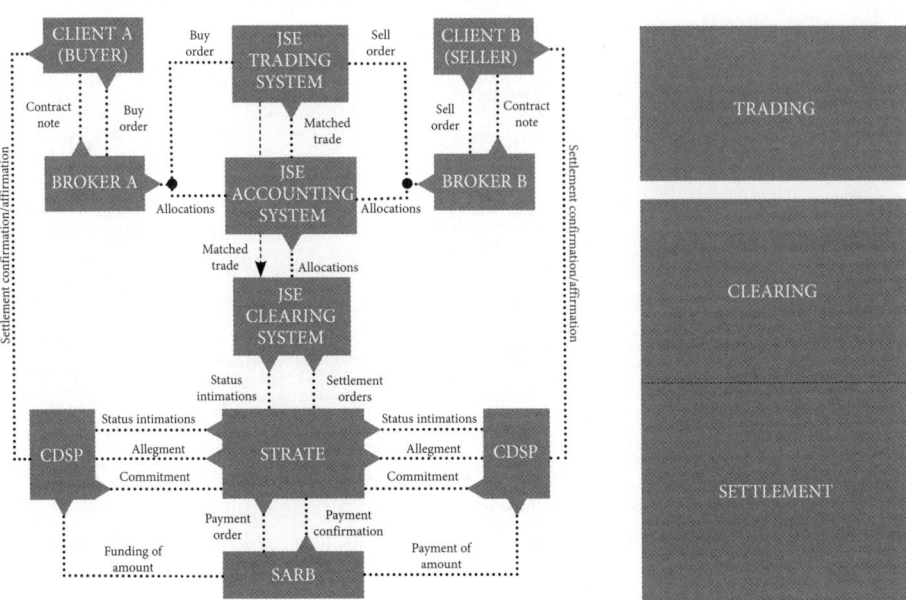

Source: www.jse.co.za, cash equities

- *A niche or alternative exchange*: These trading venues also compete to attract firms to list cash equities and offer trading of these securities. However, these exchanges tend to cater for different cash equities than the incumbent and focus on niche listings. For example, these exchanges may focus on a particular type of restricted cash equities or a particular size of listing. These forms of exchanges tend not to list the same cash equities that are also on the incumbent's exchange, and therefore direct trading competition with the incumbent is often limited. South Africa has seen a number of entrants, such as EESE[8] and 4AX[9], who have (broadly) followed this approach.
- *A secondary listings exchange*: These trading venues tend to focus on listing only those cash equities that are already listed on a traditional incumbent exchange.[10] This form of exchange does not directly compete in attracting listings vis-à-vis the traditional exchange. However, it does compete head on with the traditional incumbent exchanges in trading the securities listed on both platforms. Such a proposition typically appeals to investors looking for low-cost access to the most liquid securities available in the market. In South Africa, A2X is an example of such a platform.[11]

The natural monopoly elements of a stock exchange

By their nature, stock exchanges (and cash equity markets more generally) exhibit elements of natural monopoly with features of strong scale economies and network externalities. These characteristics have traditionally been seen to pose a very high natural barrier to entry for competing exchanges:

- The strong economies of scale arise from the fact that the provision of infrastructure for trading, clearing and settling in cash equity markets can be costly and largely fixed. This includes the initial set-up costs for the trading and post-trading systems, as well as ongoing costs for facilitating trading services.[12] Since many of the costs are fixed, this creates a natural competitive advantage for larger venues that can attract volume and reduce average costs per transaction (whether in trading or post-trading activities).
- Exchanges can also benefit from network externalities and the concentration of investor demand in a single market, because prospective buyers and sellers are drawn to markets with the highest liquidity. This is due to the fact that the more buyers and sellers that are on an exchange, the greater the likelihood of orders being matched (and the less likely the trade will impact price).

However, in the past few decades, a number of these barriers to entry in trading have significantly reduced with the rapid rate of technology advancement and growing sophistication of trading platforms and its users (Oxera 2012). The demutualisation of company stock and introduction of automated trading, in particular, has reduced barriers to entry in cash equities trading and significantly lowered the costs of setting up an exchange. Furthermore, as competition for trading software has increased, the cost and availability of trading systems to potential entrants has also fallen – arguably, to a point where these trading systems have become more 'commoditised' and open to competition. The technology advances also mean that brokers (on behalf of investors) can more easily access multiple exchanges and instantaneously compare prices across venues. This ability to instantaneously trade across venues effectively lowers the network externalities for an exchange.

As a consequence, the features of a natural monopoly traditionally associated with trading cash equities have weakened over time, and the prospect of entry has become a credible threat to the incumbent exchanges. Indeed, new trading platforms have been established in a number of jurisdictions over recent decades, including the United States (US), United Kingdom (UK)[13] and Continental Europe, Canada[14], Australia[15], South Korea[16], Japan[17] and more recently Mexico[18] and South Africa[19].

Technology advances have also lowered the cost of post-trading systems. However, in general, the extent to which barriers to entry have significantly reduced for post-trading services is more ambiguous. For example, many of the efficiencies from consolidation, such as netting, remain a feature of post-trading services. As a result, the introduction of competition has been most intense in terms of trading activities, although entry has also occurred in relation to clearing (for example in the UK).

The lowering of natural barriers to entry for exchanges and the observation of entry in a number of countries suggest that the natural monopoly features do not necessarily preclude the possibility of competition between exchanges. However, it is important to recognise that although barriers to entry have reduced over time, aspects of economies of scale and network externalities still exist. As such, even where entry occurs, security markets are likely to tend towards an oligopolistic structure with a relatively small number of competing exchanges, and/or exchanges competing on a differentiated basis. The extent of feasible competition will also depend on the overall size of a given market.

Even though the introduction of competition between exchanges may now be feasible, it should be noted that it has the potential to bring with it *both* benefits and costs. It is a weighing up of these benefits and costs that is at the heart of any assessment of the impact of multiple exchanges, and a topic we deal with in more detail in the remainder of this chapter.

Features of a well-functioning exchange and the potential impact of competition

A well-functioning cash equity market is one that embodies, among other things, elements of competitiveness, efficiency and market soundness. The introduction of competition between exchanges can potentially impact these elements in different ways – some positive and some negative. Below, we discuss the keys aspects to a well-functioning exchange. This allows us to ultimately develop a framework for assessing the impact of competition on capital markets in the section that will follow.

Competitive pricing

Economic theory recognises that the introduction of competition reduces the ability of the incumbent to exploit its market position through higher prices, and eliminate monopolist rents. Well-functioning cash equity markets would be characterised by competitive trading costs. Competitive pricing will imply that trading is more affordable for investors. This would be the case where the exchange covers its cost and makes a reasonable return on investment, but where monopolistic rents are not earned. This also assumes that only efficient costs are incurred.

However, it is important to recognise that competition may also introduce material additional costs into the system, which could increase aspects of the total trading costs for brokers (and ultimately investors).

Liquid markets

In general, liquidity refers to the ease with which a security can be sold or purchased, without the transaction causing significant price movements in the process. This implies that there is sufficient demand in the market to support the market price of the financial asset. This leads to capital markets that exhibit low transaction costs, immediacy (that is, trade execution within a short time frame) and minimal loss to nominal values (Oxera 2012; Sarr & Lybek 2002). The two most commonly considered components of liquidity are market breadth and market depth.

- *Market breadth*: This represents the spread of multiple buyers and sellers in the market. A common measure of market breadth is the bid ask spread. The more liquid a market with multiple buyers and sellers is, the more the bid ask spread will tend to tighten (where tightness indicates low transaction costs such that the difference between buy and sell prices is low). The tighter the bid ask spread is, the lower the implicit cost of going in and out of a transaction is likely to be (Sarr & Lybek 2002).
- *Market depth*: This relates to the ability of the market to absorb a sale position without impacting the price. The depth of a market therefore describes the impact of large trade volumes on price movements (Sarr & Lybek 2002). Where markets are deep, it means that even larger transactions can be absorbed without affecting prices (BIS 2000).

Liquidity is a critical feature of any well-functioning cash equity market because it contributes to increasing investor confidence and reduces the implicit costs of trading for investors (IOSCO 2007). Introducing competition between exchanges will divide volumes between platforms where they compete through trading common cash equities. This has the potential to fragment or weaken liquidity. However, to the extent that brokers have access across the venues and/or the overall trading volumes are increased through competition, then this may not necessarily be the case.

Promotion of good corporate governance

A key feature of a well-functioning exchange is the promotion and regulation of good corporate governance of their listed firms.

The demutualisation and the subsequent self-listing of stock exchanges[20] prompted much debate around this regulatory role of exchanges (Christiansen & Koldertsova 2008). The debate centres on the potential for conflicts of interest to arise between the commercial and regulatory role of exchanges. The reason for this is that one of the dimensions in which exchanges can conceivably compete to attract listings to their platform is by lowering the standards required of listed firms. Lowering listing standards (and ongoing monitoring requirements) could also be a way for an exchange to streamline its own costs.

The counter perspective to this is that lowering listing standards may compromise the confidence in the exchange, which is also important for attracting investors. it is Therefore not necessarily the case that exchanges do have a strong incentive to lower standards.

Efficient and orderly price discovery

For the allocation of investors' funds to be socially optimal, it is important for prices of cash equities to be efficient, in that they convey all the information relating to the cash equities and the underlying asset that is publicly available at that time. Efficient pricing minimises transaction and search costs. Disclosure requirements for firms, as well as real-time information flows on price movements to brokers, play an important role in facilitating efficient price formation.

A well-functioning exchange will also ensure that the price formation occurs in an orderly and transparent manner (which ultimately engenders the confidence of investors). This would include surveillance activities to ensure the prevention of manipulative behaviour to deliberately distort market prices. Relevant to this would also be appropriate listing requirements (and the monitoring thereof), which impose a standard of good corporate governance on listed firms.

The introduction of competition could potentially have an impact on market integrity if fragmentation of trading volumes makes price formulation less efficient by splitting up the price discovery process across more than one venue.[21] Competition could also impact market integrity if it undermines the orderly formation of prices by incentivising exchanges to inappropriately reduce listing standards, or if it makes individual surveillance functions less effective.

Strong risk management

Risk management is critical for the soundness of financial markets, particularly where it applies to post-trading services (IOSCO 2018). This is important to ensure the efficiency of securities settlement and robustness of clearing. The management of these encompasses the following:

- The management of operational risks pertaining to operational failures such as human errors, insufficiencies in information systems or disruptions in systems.
- The management of credit risk, which refers to the risk that the participant or entity will not have the ability to fulfil their obligation fully when due or at any time in the future.
- The management of liquidity risk, which relates to the inability to meet the financial obligation when due, although the party concerned would able to meet this obligation in the future; this means that the seller of the asset anticipating the payment may have to borrow or liquidate assets to complete other payments (IOSCO 2018).

A market participant failing to meet its obligations may cause other participants to not settle obligations as expected (BIS 2008). The contagion effect of systemic risks such as this means that system disruptions of this kind might spread, resulting in liquidity shortfalls and the risk that settlement does not take place across the market (BIS & IOSCO 2012). For example, the inability to complete settlement and the transfer of assets means financial institutions will face costs such as replacement costs or in some cases, credit losses (BIS 2008).

Having multiple trading venues may reduce risks in the sense that if one of the venues was to cease functioning, an alternative would still exist for trading to continue. However and probably more fundamentally, competition can also potentially weaken the integrity of the system if it makes these functions of risk management less effective.

Innovation

Innovation is an engine for growth that facilitates the initiation of new capabilities. This is central to capturing competitive gains, addressing challenges in the market, increasing productivity and achieving efficiency in market outcomes. Innovation in cash equity markets is particularly relevant given the rapid technological advances that continually make new and more sophisticated functionality available (Capgemini 2017). Innovation can also take the form of exchanges differentiating their offering to target a particular set of investors or firms looking to list. This potential expansion in the investor group may open up the market to a wider pool of traditionally excluded investors and promote financial inclusion. Recently, several innovations have impacted the financial markets. The increased use of artificial intelligence (AI) and machine learning (ML), expansion of fractional share trading, and growth of robo-advisors have modernised investment strategies and broadened market access. Furthermore, an increasing number of user-friendly retail investing platforms have democratised participation in the financial markets.[22] Lastly, there has been increased interest in using blockchain technology for securities trading, clearing and settlement.[23]

Developing a framework for evaluating the impact of competition between stock exchanges

In light of the differing impacts that competition could have on the various facets of securities markets, we have developed a conceptual framework that breaks down the competition assessment across nine key indicators of market health. These nine indicators are drawn from the discussion above and constitute dimensions of either:
1. all-in cost of trading;
2. innovation; or
3. market soundness.

This conceptual framework is presented in Figure 14.2.

For each of these indicators, we proceed to consider:
- what the hypothesised impact of competition may be;
- evidence from other markets that have experienced competitive entry; and
- the potential outcomes that might be experienced in South Africa given the characteristics of the local market.

It should, however, be noted that the operations of exchanges – and even more so the competitive dynamics between exchanges – occurs across multiple dimensions, many of which are interrelated. This conceptual framework is therefore a deliberate simplification that focuses on the core issues to enable the main impacts of competition to be teased out and better understood.

Figure 14.2 Conceptual framework to assess the impact of competition

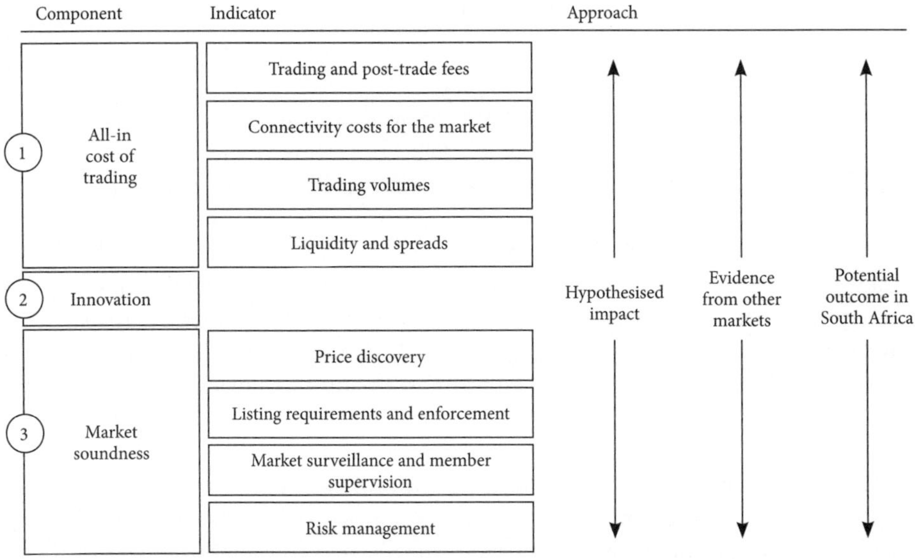

Component	Indicator	Approach
1. All-in cost of trading	Trading and post-trade fees / Connectivity costs for the market / Trading volumes / Liquidity and spreads	Hypothesised impact → Evidence from other markets → Potential outcome in South Africa
2. Innovation		
3. Market soundness	Price discovery / Listing requirements and enforcement / Market surveillance and member supervision / Risk management	

Source: Genesis Analytics

Hypothesised impact and international experience

International markets that have introduced competition between exchanges provide useful insights into the potential effects of competition – although, as with most international benchmarking exercises, there is no perfect comparator for a particular home country. Utilising the conceptual framework developed above, and drawing on the hypothesised impacts in literature, the following lessons can be drawn.

Trading and post trading fees

Hypothesised impact: *Economic theory suggests that the key benefit from the introduction of competing exchanges will be downward pressure on trading and post-trading fees, while other fees such as data and membership charges may also be positively affected.*

In the US, Europe Australia and Canada, the introduction of competition in trading has significantly reduced the cost of executing trades. There is also evidence that competition in clearing has reduced post-trading costs in Europe. Furthermore,

competition has had an impact on how fees are structured, for example by introducing pricing formats that incentivise the enhancement of liquidity. Examples are the following:
- In Europe, the implementation of MiFID (Markets in Financial Instruments Directive) in 2007 led to a rapid increase in competition among exchanges. Aggregating across all financial centres, the cost of on-book trading in equities fell by 60% between 2006 and 2009, on a per transaction basis (Oxera 2011). It is also reported (Oxera 2011) that following an increase in competition from new CCPs, there was a reduction in clearing fees on a per-transaction basis across all financial centres[24] of 73%, from 2006 to 2009.[25]
- In Australia, following the entry of an 'admit-to-trade' competitor, Chi-X Australia, ASX's headline trade execution fees were reduced from 0.28bp to 0.15bp (applicable in 2011) (Oxera 2012). This is a 46% reduction in the incumbent's fees.
- In response to competition in Canada, a study indicates the incumbent exchange, TSX, reduced the per-transaction fee charge by nearly 80% from 2006 to 2010 (Garriott et al. 2013).

The US is one of the first markets to experience competition between trading venues (Brown et al. 2006). Evidence suggests that competition and the size of the market have contributed to the US now having among the lowest trading fees in the world. This benefit of competition would be welcomed, although the following caveats should be noted:
- While trading fees are an important cost component to brokers, trading fees are by no means the only component taken into consideration when making the decision to trade on an exchange. Features of an exchange such as liquidity are also fundamentally important to brokers, as they inform the implicit cost of trading in the market.
- For an investor, trading fees are but one component of total transaction costs. In the case of South Africa, for example, this includes a brokerage fee, Strate settlement fees, an investor protection levy, securities transfer tax for buy-side transactions and value-added tax.

Connectivity costs

Hypothesised impact: *The introduction of competition is likely to increase connectivity and internal costs for brokers participating in the market for trading cash equities, to the extent that these brokers choose to connect to multiple exchanges.*

The types of costs affected include once-off and ongoing costs, such as the following:
- *Direct connection costs*: Connecting directly to an exchange entails registering as a 'trading participant' (or market participant), which includes a connection fee. Connecting to additional exchanges will increase this connection cost.
- *In-house broker costs*: In-house broker costs are typically incurred for adjustments to internal systems to allow for the consolidation of liquidity from multiple

venues. Other internal costs may be incurred such as back-office accounting system upgrades plus an additional staff complement.

International evidence confirms that introducing competition between exchanges increases costs faced by market participants that choose to access multiple trading platforms. While connectivity costs have increased in countries where competition has been introduced, the various countries and market participants experience this cost impact differently.

International experience has shown that these costs can impact segments of brokers in different ways. In Australia and the UK, for example, the brokerage services market has become stratified, with large brokers directly connecting to multiple exchanges, and smaller brokers connecting either to a single exchange or to multiple exchanges indirectly through the large brokers.

Trading volume

Hypothesised impact: *High trading volumes are one of the drivers of liquidity in the market and can also lower average transaction costs. Academic studies generally predict that trading volumes will increase following competitive entry because of: (i) reductions in transactions costs, and (ii) the extent to which competition intensifies the prevalence of high-frequency trading (HFT) and innovations in order functionality, such as dark pools.*

This has been borne out in practice and in academic studies. The UK and Europe in particular have experienced an increase in trading volumes that coincided with the introduction of competition. The elasticity of trading volume to transaction costs in particular has been studied by several academics:

- Looking at the impact on 23 stock exchanges from 1980 to 1989, Ericsson and Lindgren (1992) found the elasticity of trading volume to transaction costs to be between −1.2 and −1.5.[26]
- Jackson and O'Donnell (1985) examined the impact of total transaction costs on trading volume in the UK and found the short-run elasticity to be −0.5 and the long-run elasticity to be −1.7.
- Lindgren and Westlund (1990) considered the impact of transaction costs on the Stockholm Stock Exchange and found elasticity ranges from −0.9 to −1.

These elasticities imply that as transaction costs fall, volumes are expected to increase by a factor of the anticipated change in costs, particularly in the long run, where the percentage increase in volumes will exceed the percentage reduction in transaction costs.

Liquidity and spreads

Hypothesised impact: *The level and quality of liquidity in a market determine the implicit costs of trading. Introducing multiple exchanges will divide volumes between platforms where they compete through trading common securities. Although this* *fragmenting of volumes could have the potential to lead to the deterioration of overall liquidity, this is not necessarily the case. For example, if liquidity across venues is sufficiently accessible to participants using the latest technology, it may not be the case that the likelihood of order matching will be reduced, or that search costs would be prohibitive. Indeed, technology advances have meant that participants can now relatively easily interact with liquidity across exchanges.*

In general, the studies and experience tend to indicate that the introduction of competition has had an overall positive impact on bid ask spreads and market depth (Chen & Duffie 2021; Degryse 2009; Garriott et al. 2013; Gresse 2017).

Gresse (2017) found that, in Europe, an increase in lit[27] market fragmentation narrowed bid ask spreads with the reduction being more pronounced for large stocks than mid-cap stocks. In Canada, the market quality impact measures (also measured by relative spreads) of the S&P/TSX 60 stocks, trading on TSX, were found not to be adversely affected by the entry of Chi-X in 2008.[28] Further, relative spreads of the S&P/TSX 60 stocks, estimated as bid ask spreads divided by prices, were found to drop to a lower equilibrium following Alpha's entry in 2008. Market depth was also observed by the authors to improve following Alpha's entry (Garriott et al. 2013). Chen & Duffie (2021) also found that despite fragmentation reducing market depth on individual equity exchanges, this does not suggest that overall liquidity is worsened; in fact, the authors suggest that market fragmentation leads to more aggressive order submissions. Lastly, studies find that the entry of Chi-X into the market has resulted in an improvement in spreads in Australia (Aitken et al. 2015; Aitken et al. 2013).

Some studies also show that this impact can vary depending on the size of the stock, with smaller stocks less likely to display a positive impact (Haslag & Ringgenberg 2016). Haslag and Ringgenberg (2016) found that fragmentation results in reduced bid ask spreads for large stocks in the US, however, were not the necessarily the case for small stocks as fragmentation is found to increase bid ask spreads. The authors also found similar mixed results with respect to the impact of fragmentation on market depth.

In summary, international studies on the impact of fragmentation from the US, Europe, Canada and Australia are mixed in their approaches and findings. This international experience is summarised in Table 14.1 below.

Table 14.1 Summary of empirical literature on the impact of fragmentation from 2000 to 2021

Overall impacts of fragmentation on market quality		Summary impact	
		Spreads	Depth
US	• For large stocks, fragmentation results in reduced bid ask spreads and improved price efficiency. • For small stocks, fragmentation is found to increase bid ask spreads and worsen price efficiency. • Fragmentation is also found to be associated with increased depth for large stocks and reduced depth for small stocks.	Large stocks: ↓ Small stocks: ↑	Large stocks: ↑ Small stocks: ↓
Canada	• The relative spread of the S&P/TSX 60 stocks fell to a lower equilibrium after Alpha's entry in late 2008, and fragmentation was not at any point associated with worsening spreads.	Large stocks: ↓	n.a.
Europe	• Overall, lit fragmentation is found to generally result in tighter spreads for all stocks. However, the depth of small stocks falls with lit fragmentation.	Large stocks: ↓ Small stocks: ↓	Large stocks: ↑ Small stocks: ↓
Australia	• Overall, the entry of Chi-X into the market has been found to be associated with an improvement in market quality, evident in reduction in spreads and increase in depth of Australia's larger indexed stocks.	Large stocks: ↓	Large stocks: ↑

Source: Consolidation of various sources

Innovation

Hypothesised impact: *Innovation is a widely anticipated outcome of the introduction of competition in cash equity markets.*

This prediction has been confirmed as new entrants or incumbents responding to competition have introduced innovations. Some of the more common instances have been new order functionality (block trades, smart order routing, dark pools, etc.), new fee models to attract liquidity (rebates, maker-taker pricing models), high-frequency/low-latency trading, and differentiated operational/business models employed by exchanges.

Table 14.2 presents examples of innovation that have been introduced in various countries where competition has been experienced.[29]

Table 14.2 Examples of the impact of competition on innovation in selected countries

	Forms of competition	Types of innovation as result of competition and response of incumbents
US	• Cross-trading of NYSE-listed stocks on the Consolidated Stock Exchange, 1885–1926 • Dual-listing of stocks on NYSE and NASDAQ, 2004	• Advances in order functionality such as odd-lot trading[30]. • Launch of dual-listing programme, which enables members to list on the NASDAQ, as well as trade on the New York Stock Exchange. • Development of LINQ, a blockchain[31] technology that simplifies share management and the use of capitalisation table for private companies.
Europe	• Introduction of competition following MiFID, 2007	• Advances in automated trading and SOR technology. • Advances in interoperability following post-trade fragmentation. • European blockchain LiquidShare improves the speed, transparency and security of post-trade services.
Australia	• Introduction of Chi-X (an ATS), 2011	• Advances in technology have facilitated an increase in dark pools. • Launch of new bulk-order functionality such as VolumeMatch[32]. • Development of a new data centre facility in order to adhere to the demand for co-location services. • Implementation of blockchain in post-trading services for better management of clearing and settlement of equities and recording of shareholding.
Canada	• ATS allowed by regulator to operate in 2001, but meaningful entrants emerge, 2009	• Development of new trading fee packages; further, TMX Group launched TMX Select, offering lower trading fees. • Incumbents introduced own new electronic trading platform with lower prices. • Advances in order functionality, for example dark pools, regulated as ATSs and subject to regulatory requirements.

Source: Consolidation of various sources

Price discovery

Hypothesised impact: *A price is efficient if it incorporates all the information relating to a security and the underlying asset that is publicly available at that time. This is usually assumed to be the case if the observed price of a security reflects the full sum of demand for and supply of that security. By its very nature, competition means that all sources of demand and all sources of supply are no longer present in one trading venue. Therefore, the introduction of competition may worsen the informational efficiency of share prices.*

In practice, competitive markets have counteracted this risk through environments that are friendly to price-equalising arbitrage, as well as a host of regulations intended to highlight relative prices. Examples are various forms of price consolidation and rules to govern interaction of orders such as best execution and automatic volatility rules. In some cases, the regulatory framework chosen has given primarily responsibility to the regulator for consolidating trade data (US), while in other cases

the incumbent or data vendors have played a central role aggregating trade data (Australia and Canada):
- In the US, Congress dealt with data fragmentation by mandating a consolidated tape for the market (Aite Group 2013).
- In Australia, the Australian Securities and Investments Commission (ASIC) did not prescribe a regulated consolidated tape and it was believed that private vendors would be able to provide this consolidation service (Aite Group 2013). However, minimum data consolidation operating standards were implemented to ensure completeness and quality of price information, as well as robustness and reliance of service (ASIC 2011).
- In Canada, with the introduction of ATSs in 2001, the regulator also put in place Universal Market Integrity Rules to maintain the integrity of the market under competition (TSE Regulation Services 2001). However, it was only in 2009 that a single consolidated source of pre- and post-trade information was created.
- In Europe, with the recent introduction of MiFID II, European regulators are aiming to provide a regulated consolidated tape for the whole market to deal with data fragmentation.[33]

Listing standards and enforcement

Hypothesised impact: *A commonly cited concern with the introduction of competition in cash equity markets is the potential for a so called 'race to the bottom' in regulatory standards.*[34] *A counter-view has been that exchanges are also likely to have the incentive to compete through the integrity of their market, to attract investors and issuers.*

Although theoretical literature posits a race to the bottom in listing requirements (Chemmanur & Fulghieri 2006; Christiansen & Koldertsova 2008), there is no strong empirical evidence to suggest this has been the case in other markets where competition between exchanges has been introduced. This may be because competing exchanges have the incentive to raise their standards of supervision and enforcement to attract market participants and listings. Many exchanges view regulation as an integral part of their brand proposition and as a competitive advantage (Coffee Jr 2002). The lack of empirical evidence may also be due to the fact that often competition has been in the form of multilateral trading facility and ATS-type platforms where this concern is less likely arise.

International experience highlights two primary models used to manage primary market regulation under competition:
- The first option is to centralise issuer regulation, either in an independent body constituted in the private sector or in a state regulator.
- The second alternative is to decentralise issuer regulation and to retain this function within each of the competing exchanges (potentially with some cross-exchange oversight and guidance from the regulator).

Neither centralisation nor decentralisation is a foregone response to competition, as both models are observed.

Market surveillance and member supervision

Hypothesised impact: *Prudent supervision of the market and its participants fosters fairness and accuracy of trades and reassures buyers and sellers of the market's integrity.*

Once competition has been introduced, supervising market and member activity becomes more challenging as activity occurs across multiple independently competing infrastructures. An example is detecting market abuse such as insider trading or price manipulation in the context of fragmented trading – particularly if this regulatory function is delegated to individual exchanges (as is currently the case in South Africa). Similar to listings, theoretical literature points to 'race to the bottom' type concerns – namely that there could be an incentive for exchanges to compete through reducing the level of regulatory oversight (Chemmanur & Fulghieri 2006; Christiansen & Koldertsova 2008).

A review of international markets indicates that while this risk is recognised, there are a number of different approaches that can effectively deal with the surveillance of the market and its members following fragmentation. In certain cases, competition has resulted in a degree of centralisation of surveillance functions, either to a national regulator or through the creation of an independent, self-regulatory organisation (SRO) in the private sector (UK and Australia). In other instances, the exchanges have continued with their regulatory functions, but this has tended to also be accompanied by some degree of parallel market surveillance by the regulator (US). This has often been expressed as a 'thin layer' of cross-market surveillance by the regulator while exchanges perform their own market surveillance.

Risk management/clearing

Hypothesised impact: *The management of risk is especially relevant to post-trading services offered by exchanges, which conclude with the final settlement of obligations between counterparties to a trade. Introducing competition in post-trading services may in theory reduce the effectiveness of risk management.*

Multiple exchanges may reduce the effectiveness of post-trading risk management if this distorts the view of risk exposures faced by market participants. The functioning of effective risk management systems can also be reduced to the extent that there are key operational differences in the underlying models of multiple clearing facilities, for example different settlement cycles.

Two approaches to the introduction of competition in other jurisdictions stand out: the centralisation of risk management/clearing functions in a single entity (US, Canada and as an interim measure in Australia), and the decentralisation of clearing across multiple infrastructures (Europe, India and the UK). The decentralisation of post-trading services is a complex undertaking and has typically been accompanied by guidance and/or standards for risk management as well as requirements for a high level of alignment, and even interoperability, between the post-trading services of players (UK, Europe and recently Australia).

The staggered approach to introducing competition in cash equity markets, which has been applied in Australia, is noteworthy. Here, competition was first introduced at the trade execution level in 2011, and then only some five years later was it decided to also allow competition in post-trading services – albeit with a set of guidance and standards for market operators following careful consultation with the industry.

In summary, introducing competition can introduce increased uncertainty and risk in the absence of cooperative arrangements between exchanges or some form of centralised clearing.

Potential impact of introducing competition between stock exchanges in South Africa: Summary of key findings

Ideally, regulatory bodies and competition authorities would want to assess the impact of introducing competition across stock exchanges. This chapter aims to present a framework for these agencies to evaluate the effects of introducing such competition. Figure 14.3 provides an overview of the key considerations when considering the introduction of competition, particularly in relation to trading costs, market soundness and innovation. While the introduction of competition has merit, there exist important factors that regulatory bodies and competition authorities should be weary of. Overall, these factors should remain as key considerations for South African regulatory bodies and competition authorities as liberalisation in this market persists. This section illustrates how this framework can be applied in practice, shown below in Figure 14.3.[35]

Figure 14.3 Summary of main findings

	Indicator	Direction of impact	Description of impact	Outcome for the market
All-in trading costs	Trading & post-trading fees	↓	Reduction in trading & clearing and settlement fees (15%–40%) resulting in market savings (R167m–R446m).	●
	Connectivity costs to the market	↑	Increase in costs but likely to be outweighed by gains in trading fee reductions (R31m–R89m).	◐
	Trading volumes	↑	Growth in volumes, additional growth possible depending on the extent of innovation (0.4%–5%).	●
	Liquidity and spreads	↓ ↑	Overall neutral/positive but may vary by size of stock.	●
Innovation		↑	Improved technology and capital expansion.	●
Market soundness	Price discovery	—	Neutral impact if rules and tech in place.	●
	Listing standards and enforcement	—	Risk of lower quality but can be managed by with regulatory adjustments.	●
	Market surveillance and member supervision	—	Increased uncertainty and could result in cost duplication if not managed.	●
	Risk management (post-trade)	↓	Increased risk and uncertainty in the absence of cooperative arrangements between exchanges or some form of centralised clearing.	◐

As an indication, assuming a 15% to 40% reduction in trading fees, which is in line with other jurisdictions, competition between multiple exchanges could bring benefits in the form of lower trading fees and improved volumes. Estimated gains from lower trading fees are relatively modest – ranging from R167 million to R446 million in annual trading fee reductions.

The consequence of competition for the implicit costs of trading (for example, spreads and market depth) is somewhat more ambiguous, with the overall impact likely to be neutral to positive. International research and experience do, however, suggest that the impact on implicit trading costs may not be uniformly positive across all types of equities, with those of smaller firms potentially at a disadvantage.

Although the introduction of multiple exchanges would raise connectivity costs for market participants, this is likely to be outweighed by the benefits yielded through lower trading costs in other areas.

Competition between exchanges is also expected to stimulate innovation in the sector. This innovation may be expressed in many different ways such as: enhanced technological applications and sophistication; and improved and differentiated operational models, which may target an expanded set of firms and investors.

Therefore, the introduction of multiple exchanges is likely to lower the all-in trading costs for the market and enhance innovation.

However, when considering the impact of competition on cash equity markets, the impact on all-in trading costs is only half of the story. Consideration also needs to be given to the impact that multiple exchanges will have on the soundness of the market and its underlying integrity. The area of highest risk – and where measures to mitigate this risk need to be most carefully thought through – relate to instances where competing exchanges also offer post-trading services, and the complications that result in the clearing and settling process. Nevertheless, with the correct measures in place, these risks may be largely mitigated and managed. This may include, for example, allowing line of sight through increased interoperability and greater cooperation among competing clearing platforms. In Australia, such arrangements for competing clearing houses are currently governed by specific minimum standards.

Conclusion

This chapter contributes to theoretical literature assessing the potential impact of introducing competition into cash equity markets. The overall finding of this study is that the introduction of multiple exchanges would be likely to have a net positive impact on cash equity markets in South Africa – but only as long as the potential risks to market soundness are sufficiently managed. This has a number of important implications for both financial regulators (who are usually responsible for the introduction of competition through the licensing of exchanges) and competition authorities.

For financial regulators, it is important to note that the way in which competition is introduced, as well as the measures put in place to actively manage potential risks, would be critical in shaping whether such an opening of the market will be beneficial to the country. Therefore, competition can be encouraged, but a thoughtful regulatory framework would need to be put in place to ensure that the soundness of the market is not compromised.

For competition authorities, the reduction of traditional barriers to entry means that competition between stock exchanges is now possible, and even likely. Furthermore, as these markets develop, it can be expected that the incumbent exchanges would, in many cases, continue to hold a dominant position. As such, competition authorities would need to ensure the incumbent does not use its strong position to limit effective rivalry. This would likely be a particularly important consideration where the incumbent offers services to rivals (for example where it offers some form of regulatory function or post-trade services). Given the need for cooperation and interoperability between players, it would also be important to ensure subtle forms of collusion do not dampen the rivalry between players. These investigations would require careful cooperation between competition and financial regulators given the sector specific nuances at play and the multifaceted elements impacting both traditional competition and market soundness.

Notes

1. We thank Nonhlanhla Msimango for her research contributions. The authors of this chapter are employees at Genesis Analytics. The views expressed in this chapter are those of the authors and do not necessarily represent the views of Genesis Analytics.

    This chapter was originally based on research and analysis conducted in 2019. While efforts have been made to update the context to ensure an accurate description of the cash equities environment as of 2024, it is important to note that the core findings are rooted in the 2019 research. The authors assert that the conclusions drawn remain valid and relevant.

2. The Financial Markets Act (No. 19 of 12012) laid the groundwork for the licensing of additional exchanges.

3. ZARX no long holds a licence. EESE and 4AX have rebranded to Integrated Exchange (I-Ex) and Cape Town Stock Exchange (CTSE), respectively.

4. Orderly price formation is ensured through surveillance activities that protect against prices being affected by market manipulation, abuse by dominant investors or technical problems.

5. The calculation of capital adequacy measures members' credit risk, liquidity and solvency, and is used to flag potential financial stress of a trading member. Clearing houses may also require that the parties commit collateral (margin) to reduce the loss that the clearing house or CCP would incur if parties to the transaction fail to meet their obligations.

6. In South Africa, primary custody and settlement (C&S) is provided by the central securities depositary, Strate, and can be thought of as the 'wholesale' component of C&S, which is then 'retailed' to the end customer by the CSDPs, which provide secondary C&S. Other services that may attract additional fees can include netting, custody and record keeping activities.

7   The settlement activities also require the CSDPs' accounts held at the SARB to be debited and credited.

8   EESE has been rebranded to Integrated Exchange (I-Ex). The expanded service offers bonds and notes in addition to cash equities.

9   In 2021, the 4AX stock exchange was rebranded to Cape Town Stock Exchange (CTSE).

10 Once more, these players offer trading and post-trading services or choose to outsource post trading services.

11 These types of platforms have strong similarities to so-called ATSs and MTFs that occur elsewhere in the world and whose main focus is on competing in relation to trading activity.

12 This includes costs relating to functions such as surveillance of transactions, listings and members, dissemination of information and clearing services.

13 In the UK, like Europe, the introduction of MiFID expanded entrance of competition to MTFs after 2007 such as the introduction of Chi-X Europe (rebranded to Cboe Europe equities).

14 The Canadian securities market saw the emergence of Alpha Trading Systems (now Alpha Exchange) in 2008, which is an alternative trading system, trading securities listed in TSX.

15 The Australian securities market saw the introduction of competition in 2011. Chi-X, launched in October 2011, is an alternative trading venue whose operations include all of ASX counters. The launch of this platform ended the ASX's exchanges long-standing monopoly in exchange-traded equity.

16 Founded in 1996, the Korea Stock Exchange (KRX) introduced competition in 2005. Korea saw the integration of KRX, Kosdaq and Korea Futures exchange, leading to Korea's sole exchange under the name KRX.

17 Tokyo stock exchange (TSE) was founded in 1878. Before the merger of TSE and Osaka's exchange (OSE) in 2013, first entrance in the market was by Nagoya in 1886, an alternative trading venue, followed by entry of OSE, focusing on derivatives market, in 1949.

18 Founded in 1894, the introduction of competition occurred in 2017. BIVA, an alternative private securities exchange, was launched in July 2018. Currently, BIVA has 64 equity listings.

19 In 2017, the landscape of the South African securities market changed, with four (only three operational) new cash equity exchanges being launched.

20 The process of demutualisation began with the Stockholm Stock Exchange in 1993.

21 For example, such inefficiencies may have the implication of in any way distorting or delaying information flows to investors.

22 Examples include Robinhood in the USA and Easy Equities in South Africa.

23 Recently, an argument suggesting that economic rents realised from latency arbitrage – latency arbitrage refers to a strategy that exploits delays in transmission of market data or trade execution across different trading platforms – inhibits innovations and is likely to favour an inefficient market design has been advanced (Budish et al. 2019).

24 Financial centres are defined as the country in which the investor, client or security is initially issued (domiciled).

25 When measured in terms of cost per value of transaction, the results of a change in clearing fees and trading fees have been found to be more mixed as a result of changes in trading behaviour – on average, trade sizes across markets have been falling as high-volume trading has grown.

26 An elasticity is a measure of the responsiveness of one variable to another. For example, in this case, an elasticity of trading volume to transaction costs of –1.5 implies that for a percentage decrease in transaction costs, trading volumes will increase by 1.5%. The negative informs us that there is an inverse relationship between the two variables and an elasticity greater than unity informs us that the demand is elastic.

27 Gresse (2017) makes a distinction between markets with multiple open and transparent order books that compete for the order flow, referred to as 'lit fragmentation', and markets where order flow is partially internalised off-exchange by dealers.

28 Due to Alpha's entry coinciding with the financial crisis, the authors note the difficulty experienced in isolating the impact of entry.

29 Not all of the innovation observed in these markets may be as a direct result of competition, but these innovations have coincided with the introduction of competition and certainly are likely to have been enhanced by introduction of competition.

30 An odd lot is an order amount for a security that is typically less than the standard 100 shares for stocks.

31 Blockchain or distributed ledger technology (DLT) is a digital ledger that permanently records transactions, thereby limiting the tampering of data by securing the transmission of data.

32 This order functionality allowed for large orders to be executed that would have minimal impact on the market price.

33 European Securities and Markets Authority (ESMA) website 'MIFID II'. Accessed April 2024, https://www.esma.europa.eu/policy-rules/mifid-ii-and-mifir

34 The rationale for a 'race to the bottom' in listing standards is that exchanges may compete to attract listed cash equities by reducing the quality of primary market regulation so as to reduce regulatory costs.

35 These quantifications were illustrative of the potential impacts at the initial competition of this study.

References

Aite Group (2013) *Market fragmentation and its impact: A historical analysis of market structure evolution in the United States, Europe, Australia, and Canada.* (Commissioned by BM&F Bovespa). Boston, Massachusetts: Aite Group

Aitken M, Chen H & Foley S (2013) *How beneficial has competition been for the Australian equity marketplace?* Sydney: Capital Markets Cooperative Research Centre

Aitken M, Chen H & Foley S (2015) The impact of fragmentation, exchange fees and liquidity provision on market quality. *Journal of Empirical Finance* 41: 140–160

ASIC (2011) *Guidance on ASIC market integrity rules for competition in exchange markets.* (Also reflected in 2015 guidelines on market integrity rules.) Australian Securities and Investments Commission

BIS (2008) *The interdependencies of payment and settlement systems.* CPMI Papers 84, Bank for International Settlements

BIS (2010). *Market structure developments in the clearing industry: Implications for financial stability.* CPMI Papers 92, Bank for International Settlements

BIS and IOSCO (2012). *Principles for financial market infrastructures.* CPMI Papers 101, Bank for International Settlements

Brown Jr WO, Mulherin JH & Weidenmier MD (2006) *Competing with the NYSE.* Working Paper No. 12343, National Bureau of Economic Research

Budish E, Lee RS & Shim JJ (2019) *A theory of stock exchange competition and innovation: Will the market fix the market?* Working Paper No. 25855, National Bureau of Economic Research. https://doi.org/10.3386/w25855

Capgemini (2017) *Top ten trends in capital markets 2017 – Trend 05: Evolution of data management and analytics into a strategic function.* Paris: Capgemini

Chemmanur T & Fulghieri P (2006) Competition and Cooperation among Exchanges: A theory of cross-listing and endogenous listing standard. *Journal of Financial Economics* 82(2): 455–489

Chen D & Duffie D (2021) Market fragmentation. *American Economic Review* 111(7): 2247–2274

Christiansen H & Koldertsova A (2008) The role of stock exchanges in corporate governance. *OECD Journal: Financial Market Trends* 2009(1): 209–238

Coffee Jr JC (2002) Racing towards the top: The impact of cross-listings and stock market competition on international corporate governance. *Columbia Law Review* 102: 1757

Degryse H (2009) Competition between financial markets in Europe: What can be expected from MiFID? *Financial Markets and Portfolio Management* 23(1): 93–103

Ericsson J & Lindgren R (1992) Transaction taxes and trading volume on stock exchanges: An international comparison. Department of Finance Working paper No. 39, Stockholm School of Economics

Garriott C, Pomeranets A, Slive J & Thorn T (2013) Fragmentation in Canadian equity markets. *Bank of Canada Review* 2013(Autumn): 20–29

Gresse C (2017) Effects of lit and dark market fragmentation on liquidity. *Journal of Financial Markets* 35: 1–20

Haslag P & Ringgenberg M (2016) *The causal impact of market fragmentation on liquidity.* WFA Center for Finance and Accounting Research Working Paper No. 14/003, Olin Business School at Washington University

IOSCO (2007) *Factors influencing liquidity in emerging markets.* Report of the International Organization of Securities Commissions Emerging Markets Committee (December 2007). Madrid: IOSCO

IOSCO (2011) *Regulatory issues raised by the impact of technological changes on market integrity and efficiency.* Report by the Technical Committee of the International Organization of Securities Commissions (June 2011). Madrid: IOSCO

IOSCO (2018) *Recommendations for liquidity risk management for collective investment schemes.* Report by the Board of the International Organization of Securities Commissions (February 2018). Madrid: ISOCO

Jackson P & O'Donnell A (1985) *The effects of stamp duty on equity transactions and prices in the UK Stock Exchange.* Bank of England Discussion Paper No. 25, Bank of England

Lindgren R & Westlund A (1990) How did the transaction costs on the Stockholm Stock Exchange influence trading volume and price volatility? *Skandinaviska Enskilda Banken Quarterly Review* 2(1990): 30–35

Oxera (2007) *Methodology for monitoring prices, costs and volumes of trading and post-trading services.* Report prepared for the European Commission DG Internal Market and Services (July 2007). Oxford, Brussels: Oxera Consulting Ltd

Oxera (2011) *Monitoring prices, costs and volumes of trading and post-trading services.* Report prepared for the European Commission DG Internal Market and Services (May 2011). Oxford, Brussels: Oxera Consulting Ltd

Oxera (2012) *What would be the benefits of changing the competitive structure of the market for trading and post-trading services in Brazil?* Prepared for Comissão de Valores Mobiliários (June 2012). Oxford, Brussels: Oxera Consulting Ltd

Sarr A & Lybek T (2002) *Measuring liquidity in financial markets.* Working Paper No. 02/232, International Monetary Fund

TSE Regulation Services (2001) *Universal Market Integrity Rules* No. 200–033

15 E-commerce business models: Insights from micro- and small enterprises in South Africa

Aarti Krishnan and Reena das Nair

[1]The growth of food technology (foodtech), such as e-grocery, restaurant delivery, food safety tech and food waste management tech, as part of food e-commerce, is increasingly becoming an important pathway to development and economic transformation.[2] We distinguish 'foodtech' from 'agritech', which represents technological innovations with the potential to bring about improved agricultural techniques and practices for increased agricultural productivity and output (Das Nair & Landani 2020). Foodtech broadly captures any technology applied to the way food is produced, processed, sold, distributed or served.[3] E- grocery and restaurant delivery broadly fall under the remit of food e-commerce. Food e-commerce can contribute towards supporting the inclusion and expansion of micro- and small enterprises (MSEs) in value chains (Krishnan & Das Nair 2021).

The focus on food e-commerce, especially in a value chain or production network context, has largely focused on labour in relation to large food platforms such as Deliveroo (Zeng et al. 2017). For example, studies have shown how gig workers have been underpaid and have faced difficulties regarding precarity of working conditions (Lord et al. 2023; Uchiyama et al. 2022). Other studies focus on the broader systems of competition, from an antitrust perspective this means studying the impact that large platforms have had on competition in terms of various leveraging, exclusionary and exploitative practices to preserve or enhance market power (CCSA 2023; Goga et al. 2019; Khan, 2017).

Much less focus has been on food e-commerce MSEs themselves, who provide food-related services to end users (Reardon et al. 2021). Recent research suggests that food e-commerce MSEs have been able to outperform brick-and-mortar competitors in terms of reaching a more spread-out consumer base (Bai et al. 2021). Research has also shown that food e-commerce MSEs are more risk-taking and have a larger range of products than brick-and-mortar food retailers (Chaochotechuang & Mariano 2016). However, MSEs on e-commerce platforms are often squeezed by high participation costs (for example, platform charges) and face other substantial barriers to entry (Ezeomah & Duncombe 2019; Foster et al. 2018; Kos & Kloppenburg 2019).

Existing research has also insufficiently accounted for the way in which MSEs are embedded in food e-commerce value chains: this means the various ways in which they network with other value chain actors. This, in turn, has implications for how they upgrade (improve value addition) within value chains. Along with value and governance[4], embeddedness is one of the three principal elements in the global production network (GPN) analysis of economic development (Henderson et al. 2002). Building on pioneering contributions to the social sciences (Granovetter 1985; Polanyi 1944), the concept of embeddedness in GPN research refers to how lead firms anchor in localities as well as in terms of how network relationships are produced and reconstituted (Hess 2004). While network embeddedness is a key component of GPN analysis, it has not been studied from perspectives of intermediary MSEs in digitally driven value chains, particularly in the context of African countries. This chapter therefore seeks to answer the following research question: How are MSEs embedded in food e-commerce value chains, and what are the implications for economic, social and environmental upgrading in South Africa? Effective competition at different levels of food e-commerce value chains is a critical enabler to MSE participation and upgrading.

In South Africa, food value chains are highly concentrated at almost every level. At the breeding level of key seed inputs, for instance, only a handful of international firms operate. Similarly high levels of concentration exist at the distribution level of key seeds such as maize, wheat, sorghum, soya and sunflower (CCSA 2021). In midstream food and beverage manufacturing markets, the largest 20 enterprises contribute to 50% of income. Concentration levels are even higher within specific narrower product markets (CCSA 2021; Stats SA 2017). In downstream grocery retail markets, five large supermarket chains control 64% of the national market (CCSA 2019). These high levels of concentration are reflective of the high barriers to entry in many markets, which are exacerbated for MSEs

With limited participation by MSEs in the South African economy overall, and persistently high unemployment levels (especially for informal and low-income workers) at over 32% in 2023 (Stats SA 2023), foodtech may offer opportunities for greater inclusion and integration of MSEs and associated employment. This would be possible at different points in value chains such as food processing, packaging, nutrition, food software, delivery, retail and catering – both through facilitating the participation of MSEs in food processing and as intermediate foodtech platforms themselves.

Within foodtech, this chapter focuses on MSEs in e-grocery and restaurant marketplaces. Both are broadly part of food e-commerce, which offer physical as well as digital modes of service delivery. Most food e-commerce occurs through platforms, which essentially provide intermediation services for all the components of a digital market. Firms that participate in e-grocery and restaurant marketplaces are often therefore referred to as 'platformised firms'.

There are a number of types of businesses that are relevant to this study. *E-groceries* operate at either the level of business to consumer (B2C) or business to business (B2B). B2C is defined as businesses that sell grocery-related goods and products directly to the end customers, typically via a website with an online shopfront or an online marketplace. Business to business (B2B) in turn operates by providing grocery-related products from one business to another, through either marketplaces or online auctions. *Restaurant marketplaces* include virtual (ghost or cloud) kitchens or physical restaurants selling to customers either directly online, or omnichannel[5], or through aggregators or tie-ups with logistic providers (B2C), and businesses that sell to other businesses (B2B) such as to the hospitality sector, other restaurants and virtual marketplaces.

To answer the research question, we collated a novel dataset of 135 formal firms to better understand the foodtech landscape in South Africa. Following this, primary data collection for the case studies was conducted through in-depth interviews with two owners of food e-commerce MSEs – one an e-grocery and the other a business that runs a restaurant marketplace. This was complemented by interviews with service providers (companies providing blockchain services) and members of the Intergovernmental Fintech Working Group (IFWG).[6]

The research found that the MSEs interviewed were embedded in networks with upstream and downstream actors (for example input providers, subcontractors, super platforms), which was marred with low levels of trust and limited bargaining potential for them. MSEs were exploited by more powerful actors in the network, and seemed to experience social downgrading, that is, scarcity of permanent contracts, precarious job conditions and environmental downgrading. However, despite contested network embeddedness, some economic upgrading (in terms of better profits) was experienced, suggesting that some trade-offs exist.

Chapter 15 starts by setting out the conceptual framing to map foodtech value chains and to understand the issues that arise with respect to governance and upgrading. Then it assesses the complex demand- and supply-side networks that are formed for platformised MSEs to unpack the quality of network relationships (including the power structures, competition, and stability that have emerged) and to evaluate the value creation and capture trajectories (the cross-network effects). Next, it provides a landscape of foodtech value chains in South Africa based on the database of firms compiled. Finally, the chapter describes in-depth case studies in two selected segments of restaurant marketplace and e-grocery, respectively, followed by the authors' concluding remarks and policy recommendations and actions.

Overview of actors in the value chains and production networks

This section provides a brief value chain and production network mapping, which is a starting point to understand the various connections and linkages between actors, and the power dynamics that underpin them. This forms the basis for understanding how MSEs are embedded in value chains or production networks.

Platformised MSEs are both suppliers and users or consumers of services. They serve multiple businesses and consumers physically as well as digitally. When catering to end customers, the platformised MSE is a supplier of services; when purchasing services from suppliers, it is a consumer of services (Xie et al. 2022). It is thus critical to understand the value chain and unpack network embeddedness from both the demand- and supply-side perspectives. The demand-side perspective is when the MSE itself demands services from a range of actors (for example telecom providers and 'super platforms' such as Uber Connect or Uber Eats); and the supply-side perspective is when the MSE supplies services (for example to the final customers).

E-grocery and restaurant marketplaces consist of a mix of traditional value chain actors (for example brick and mortar companies), as well as platform-related actors, as Table 15.1 shows.

Table 15.1 Value chain actors in e-grocery and restaurant marketplaces

Demand/ supply side	Ecosystem of actors	Actors in South Africa
	Core network: *The most direct links to the MSE*	
Supply	Direct customers	Household consumers (high income, middle income, low income).
Demand	Direct subcontractors and suppliers	Wholesalers, retailers (small, medium, large), MSEs in food and beverage processing, spaza shops, other cloud/ghost kitchens, other intermediaries.
Demand	Distribution and logistics partners	Food aggregators, logistics and transport specialists.
Supply	Workers/labour/ employees	Delivery workers, workers in-house for cooking and packaging, cleaning companies.
	Business network: *Secondary actors who are connected to core network actors*	
Demand	Platform providers and operators	Platform owners and operators, including software and hardware developers.
Demand	Service providers	Data processing centres / web service providers / mobile money, food advisory services, local computing services, application programming interface (API) developers.
Demand	Service partners and operators	Network/Telecom operators.
Demand	Fixed asset or machinery providers	Kitchen-related mechanisation, food catering equipment suppliers.
Demand	Sources of capital	Local: Commercial banks, government departments through support programmes, development finance institutions International financial actors and donors; the World Bank, the United Kingdom (UK) Department for International Development (DFID), Food and Agriculture Organization (FAO), foundations; donor funding is also applied in the form of incubation spaces and business development training; other private financial actors such as venture capitalists, angel investors, private equity and debt financing.
Supply/ Demand	Trade and industry associations (global and local)	For example: Global System for Mobile Communications (GSMA) representing global interest of mobile operators. In South Africa, there are numerous industry associations in different food value chains, including Milk SA, Fruit SA, Consumer Goods Council of South Africa (CGCSA).

Demand/ supply side	Ecosystem of actors	Actors in South Africa
	Extended network: May or may not be directly connected to the firms participating, but are critical to its functioning	
Demand	Universities, technical and vocational education and training (TVET) and research organisations	Crucial actors in facilitating human capital development and as spaces for incubating talent, for example: the Food and Beverage Sector Education Training Authority (SETA); the Wholesale and Retail SETA; and other key public institutions such as the Council for Scientific and Industrial Research (CSIR).
Demand	Government agencies and regulatory bodies; standards bodies	Various regulations that apply to food products[7], as well as cross-cutting standards bodies such as the South African Bureau of Standards and the International Standards Organisation; other cross-cutting regulatory bodies include the Competition Commission of South Africa.
Demand	Social media / advertisers	Facebook, Instagram, WhatsApp, X (formerly Twitter).
Supply	Other competitors	Offering similar value propositions or related.
Demand	Continental and global organisations and regulatory bodies	Supranational unions such as the African Union have pushed for digital 'ag' investment as part of the Comprehensive African Agricultural Development Programme Agenda 2063. Intergovernmental organisations such as the United Nations (UN), the World Trade Organization (WTO) and the Organisation for Economic Cooperation and Development (OECD).
Supply/ Demand	Non-governmental organisations (NGOs)	Local NGOs.

Source: Authors' construction drawing on Hein et al. (2020), Kapoor et al. (2021) and Parker et al. (2017)

Conceptual framing

One of the key tenants of global value chains/production networks is the concept of embeddedness, which unpacks how social relationships between both firm (for example MSEs and non-firm actors (for example states and institutions) are constituted and reconstituted because of the quality of interactions within the relationship (Henderson et al. 2002). One of the key forms of embeddedness is related to network embeddedness (Hess 2004; Krishnan 2023). This section of the chapter assesses the network embeddedness of MSEs in foodtech value chains, followed by a discussion of two related concepts – network architecture and network stability. The section ends with a focus on the upgrading of MSEs in food e-commerce value chains or production networks.

Network embeddedness of MSEs in foodtech value chains

The concept of embeddedness dates to Polanyi's (1944) pioneering work *The Great Transformation*. With the rise of markets, rather than the economy being embedded in social relations, Polanyi argued that social actions are embedded in the economic system (Polanyi 1944). While his concept of embeddedness focused on more abstract relationships between economies and societies, Granovetter (1985) focused on actors and their networks to further the concept in the context of ongoing social relations. Within the global-production networks (GPNs) framework[8] put forward by Henderson et al. (2002), the concept of embeddedness is explained as the social relationships between both firm and non-firm actors (such as the state) across multiple interrelated geographies. The emphasis is on how lead firms embed themselves in networks and regions (Henderson et al. 2002). Even within global value chain analysis, actors are embedded in broader institutions (such as the WTO and various standards organisations) that can span multiple countries (Gereffi et al. 2005).

Network embeddedness is explained as the 'degree of connectivity within a GPN' (Henderson et al. 2002: 452), which focuses on the architecture and durability of inter-firm relations, as well as the broader institutional network structure, which includes horizontal actors, such as non-firm actors. Network embeddedness is a product of a process of trust building between network agents that engender stable relationships. Through repeated interactions that players in a network have with each other at different levels of the value chain, relational embeddedness is developed over time (Granovetter 2017).

For the purposes of this study, unpacking the relational nature of networks requires an understanding of the levels of cohesion, cooperation or contestation, power structures and trust between MSEs and other related network actors in the value chain (Gereffi 2019; Neilson et al. 2018). Drawing on the work of other studies (for example: Alford & Phillips 2018; Barrientos 2019; Hess 2004; Krishnan 2023), two key categories of network embeddedness are explained and evaluated: network architecture and network stability. Each category is covered from both the demand- and supply-side perspectives of platformised MSEs.

Network architecture

Network architecture captures the nature of the relations between actors connected in a network (Krishnan 2023). Krishnan sets out there are three main aspects within network embeddedness:
- *Power and bargaining/competition*: This demonstrates asymmetric power relations, usually in the form of control over resources, between platformised MSEs and other demand- or supply-side actors (as shown in Table 15.1) within the value chain. A lack of symmetric relations in digital markets may result in the abuse of market power by core actors or business network actors in the form of exclusionary or exploitative conduct that creates barriers to entry or excludes MSEs. The degree to which platformised MSEs are bound by relations of common interest, purpose, routines and varying degrees of mutuality explains the nature of the power balance in relation to other value chain actors.

- *Intensity of interactions*: Repeated interactions between platformised MSEs and other demand- or supply-side actors are shown to foster cohesiveness and build cooperation between actors. 'Repeated' refers to the frequency of interactions between core and business network actors (Foster & Graham 2017).
- *Quality of networks:* This measures the quality of information transmitted and types of transactions (for example, tech transfer) that occur between platformised MSEs and core and/or business network actors. The relative level of strength of the interactions includes quality of information transmitted and types of transactions that occur between platformised MSEs and core and/or business actors. For instance, high-quality transactions relating to transfer of high levels of training, technology knowledge, support and feedback are shown to improve the processes of absorption and internalisation of training and technology (Heeks et al. 2021; Krishnan & Foster 2018).

Table 15.2 shows three categories of network architecture with examples of indicators for demand- and supply-side perspectives under each category. These indicators are inductively developed through interviews and can be used to capture the nature of network architecture.

Table 15.2 **Network architecture: From demand- and supply-side perspectives**

Network architecture (main pillar)	Indicators demand side	Indicators supply side
Power, bargaining and competition	• Input offerings • Services offerings • Access to markets (costs, terms and conditions)	• Change in customer base • Service delivery performance • Market share • Main competitors
Intensity of interactions	• Interactions with suppliers (cooperative vs contested) • Intermediaries • Supplier support	• Changes in interactions with customers
Network relationship quality	• Ease/Difficulty negotiating with suppliers • Financing • Knowledge transfer • Capabilities • Hiring skilled professionals	• Complaints • Trust with customers

Source: Authors' construction

Network stability

The original GPN framework points to stability in a network occurring when lead firms through trust creation attempt to develop a cooperative culture between themselves and local actors (Henderson et al. 2002). Understandings of trust within relational embeddedness can be drawn on to extend the concept of stability in networks from a perspective of platformised MSEs. Stability in a network can be seen as arising from trust-building processes when non-lead firm actors embed into

GPNs. Thus, when embedding, non-lead firm actors may earn or ascribe trust to or from other actors in new networks (Krishnan 2023). From studies in this space (Coe & Yeung 2015; Srinivasan & Venkatraman 2018; Wood et al. 2019), there are two main indicators developed to explicate network stability (see Table 15.3):

- *Trust building*: Increased dependency on certain suppliers or service providers causes locking into certain relationships (demand and supply side) that may be exploitative of the MSE or exclusionary to rival suppliers, ultimately leading to either trust creation or reduction.
- *Access and reach:* Barriers or ease of expansion and lack of access to consumers, productive resources and scope of enlarging the scale of operations can reduce trust.

Table 15.3 shows two categories of network stability from the demand- and supply-side perspectives. As with network architecture, the demand- and supply-side indicators for each category were inductively developed through our interviews to understand network stability.

Table 15.3 Network stability

Network stability (main pillar)	Indicators demand side	Indicators supply side
Trust building	• Ease of finding alternative suppliers • Negotiation and trust building	• Dispute settlement procedures • Customer support provisioning
Access and reach	• Support provision (for example training) • quality of enabling environment	• Access to new customers • Quality of available infrastructure

Source: Authors' construction

Network architecture and stability are not mutually exclusive concepts and have considerable overlaps and feedback loops that affect how MSEs embed into foodtech value chains. Understanding demand- and supply-side perspectives of how MSEs are platformised provides an understanding of the complex relations MSEs need to navigate in a digital context.

Upgrading of MSEs in food e-commerce value chains/production networks

Upgrading is a central tenet of value chain/production network analysis. Gereffi's (1999: 51–52) seminal definition refers to upgrading as the 'ability of a firm or an economy to move to more profitable and/or technologically sophisticated capital and skill intensive niches'. It accounts for the possibilities of transforming inputs (such as data, raw materials or intermediary goods) into products that can be monetised for commercial use (Neilson et al. 2018). Within networks, upgrading does not occur in isolation, and is modified or co-created through forces of interactions of actors and processes (Ramaswamy 2009). The ability to upgrade is closely linked to the how the value chain is governed, which in turn is a function of the power that lead players hold and exert.

Upgrading has been expanded by Humphrey and Schmitz (2002) to include the:
- introduction of new and more sophisticated products (product upgrading);
- implementation of new methods to transform inputs through superior technology and/or industrial organisation (process upgrading); and
- move into new production tasks in the same industry, also known as functional upgrading.

For the purposes of this study, we focus on product and process upgrading, understood as changes in revenues, profits, new asset accumulation, productivity and product diversification. Similar indicators have been used across global value chains (GVC) studies (Krishnan & Foster 2018; Pasquali et al. 2021). Both product and process upgrading can be viewed as forms of economic upgrading, although not exclusively.

Another form of upgrading is social upgrading, which mainly relates to improving labour working conditions. Within GVC analysis, social upgrading outcomes include those of the various labour governing processes and strategies. This concept of upgrading draws upon the International Labour Organization's 'decent work' framework. The most commonly used indicators to measure this form of upgrading are changes in the number and permanency of jobs, improvements in the type of contracts, wage changes (including wage improvements and reductions in wage inequality between workers), and improvements in the quality of working conditions, such as health and safety, unemployment insurance, social protection and working hours. Immeasurable aspects relate to principles of social justice and non-discrimination (Barrientos & Smith 2007), including the empowerment of workers, greater rights and the possibilities of creating positive externalities such as improvements in health, education and food security for workers, their households and communities (Barrientos et al. 2011, Bernhardt & Milberg 2011). In contrast, the concept of social downgrading represents a decline in measurable and immeasurable aspects of working conditions. Social upgrading and downgrading are both non-linear processes and can differ significantly across worker types.

The third form of upgrading is referred to as environmental upgrading, which essentially relates to performing tasks that reduce or mitigate environmental impacts on actors in the value chain (for example De Marchi et al. 2019; Krishnan et al. 2023). Much of the discussion around the environment deals with how the resources of specific actors can be appropriated and used indirectly, or how costs and risks of environmental upgrading can be passed on by more powerful actors to less powerful actors in the value chain.

The foodtech landscape in South Africa: E-grocery and restaurant marketplaces

This section maps out the landscape of MSEs in foodtech in South Africa. South Africa has one of the fastest-growing foodtech industries in Africa

(Frost & Sullivan 2018). The most common segments within foodtech in South Africa are e-grocery and restaurant marketplaces, followed by innovative foods and in-store retail.

We collated a novel dataset of 135 formal firms from publicly available sources[9] that have been in operation at least since 2018 to identify companies within various foodtech segments. These firms include startups and incumbent firms, comprising digital and omnichannel firms (Table 15.4). Large incumbents appear to be more active in the e-grocery segment, while startups and mid-sized firms are more active in restaurant marketplaces.[10]

Table 15.4 Foodtech segments in South Africa based on lower caseuthors' compiled dataset (as of 2020)

Foodtech by segmentation	No. of firms	% of total number of firms[11]	Employee ranges	Food coverage
E-grocery	40	32	Startups: 0–50 Midsized established firms: 101–250 Incumbents/large firms: 500–10 000	Processed groceries, fresh fruit and vegetables, wines and spirits
Restaurant marketplace	78	56	Startups: 0–50 Midsized established firms: 101–250 Incumbents/large firms: 500–10 000	Hospitality, catering, food processing, restaurants
In-store retail and restaurant tech	7	5	Startups: 0–50 Incumbents: 500–3 000	Retail technology
Cloud retail infrastructure	47	34	Midsized firms: 101–250	Developer application programming interfaces (APIs), information technology, cloud computing, machine learning, data visualisation, geospatial, software as a services (SaaS)
Midstream technologies	6	4	Startups and mid-sized: 0–100	Warehousing, geospatial, transport
Home and cooking tech, and online restaurant meal kits	2	1	Startups: 0–50	Kitchenware, meal kits
Innovative foods	10	7	Midsized and incumbents/large firms: 51–250	Nutrition, proteins, biotechnology

Source: Authors' compilation from LinkedIn, Agfunder, Crunchbase and Tracnx

We focus on e-grocery and restaurant marketplaces. As noted, both fall within food e-commerce, which offers both physical and digital modes of service delivery.

E-groceries

E-groceries are e-commerce services, which are either B2C or B2B. South Africa's B2C e-commerce as a percentage of total retail market sales stood at 1.9% in 2019, compared to 0.5% in Kenya, and 3.3% in Nigeria (Euromonitor 2021). E-grocery B2C firms range from the large, well-established supermarket chains, such as Shoprite's Checkers Sixty60, Pick n Pay through ASAP!, which it now owns, and Woolworths Online (Dash). Particularly since Covid–19, all supermarkets have been offering growing e-commerce and delivery options through small niche providers. Examples are Faithful to Nature, which provide organic products, and Zulzi, Sir Fresh and Green Butler, which offer online fresh produce delivery. There are also smaller, less formal superettes and spaza shops that are starting to use platforms to reach customers. These players frequently use large third-party service providers for home and business deliveries, such as Uber Eats and NetFlorist.

B2B e-commerce, in turn, operates by providing products from one business to another, through either marketplaces or online auctions. For instance, even in the informal 'spaza' shop[12] space in township areas, digital apps such as Vuleka and Spazzap have been developed. These offer ordering systems that help spaza shop owners purchase goods collectively from manufacturers and allow them to build credit profiles to buy stock on credit. Uber Connect, a relatively new product offering in South Africa, which allows users to send packages through the app, also supports B2B models. This is discussed in the next section.

Restaurant marketplaces

Restaurant marketplaces include virtual kitchens or physical restaurants, known as ghost kitchens or cloud kitchens. They sell to customers either directly online, through omnichannels, or through aggregators or tie-ups with logistic providers (B2C). They also include businesses that sell to other businesses (B2B) such as to the hospitality sector, other restaurants and virtual marketplaces.

Examples of B2C restaurant marketplaces in South Africa are virtual kitchens such as The Ghost Kitchen, SmartkitchenCo, the Slick Restaurant Group, Saffron Kitchen and the Dark Kitchen.[13] Although these are small businesses, over the past 10 years and accelerating markedly during the Covid–19 pandemic, they have collectively emerged as a distinct business model. There have been huge increases in delivery services for prepared, prepacked and frozen ready-to-eat meals, particularly those that are marketed as healthy meals. The increases are also related to growing health trends among middle-to-high income consumers (for example, FitChef, Fitfood4u and Clenergy). B2B restaurant marketplace models, which on-sell to other businesses, include those that sell ingredients or partly cooked food to other restaurants, catering businesses and small businesses for resale to end consumers.

The case studies

To understand how MSEs are embedded in food e-commerce value chains, and what the implications have been for economic, social and environmental upgrading in South Africa, we undertook case studies on two types of food e-commerce MSEs – e-grocery and restaurant marketplace. As part of the case studies, we conducted in-depth interviews with the owners of an e-grocery MSE and a restaurant marketplace MSE respectively. This was complemented by interviews with blockchain service providers and members of the Intergovernmental Fintech Working Group (IFWG) as previously noted. Value chain mapping was performed for each of the MSEs. This determines the input–output (I/O) structure of each task and the various stakeholders involved (Frederick 2019). Mapping the I/O structure of the value chain enables an understanding of the key functions, the incentive for participation of different actors and the types of transactions that occur between actors. Data were transcribed and analysed using Nvivo to develop the key themes in the study – network embeddedness and upgrading.

Case study on MSE 1: E-grocery

MSE 1 is a digital platform that started operating in April 2020 to support local spaza shops in townships to stay afloat during the Covid-19 pandemic by enabling customers to place online orders. It was initially started to reduce customer time spent in small spaza shop spaces during Covid-19, but still allowing them to continue shopping locally. Through its website, MSE 1 set itself up as a 'local store connector' platform. On the supply side, its customers, which are spaza shops, register their stores to access the local market. This allows customers to shop from their local stores by simply submitting their grocery list through their mobile phones and collecting their order once they have received confirmation. With only three employees, in 2020 1 200 spaza shops, restaurants and other township-based businesses had registered with the platform, and it started to look at how it could expand its offerings.

As shown in Figure 15.1, MSE 1 offers platform services to spaza shops, allowing them to register on the platform at no cost. Spaza shops can reach multiple customers in their local area. MSE 1 also provides a unique customer-to-business (C2B) offering, by allowing customers to create customised 'grocery lists', which are then uploaded onto the platform. MSE 1 then, in effect, provides a matchmaking service, linking the 'lists' of customers to offers and deals provided by the registered spaza shops. Once the matchmaking has been completed, the spaza shops offer click-and-collect options, or they contract logistics operators to deliver the groceries. MSE 1 also provides spaza shops with a range of complementary services, from website development to search engine optimisation tools, the registering of own domains, user forums and disk space for data collection on their cloud. Spaza shops can enhance their own technical capabilities by creating their own webpages.

Figure 15.1 E-grocery value chain mapping for MSE 1

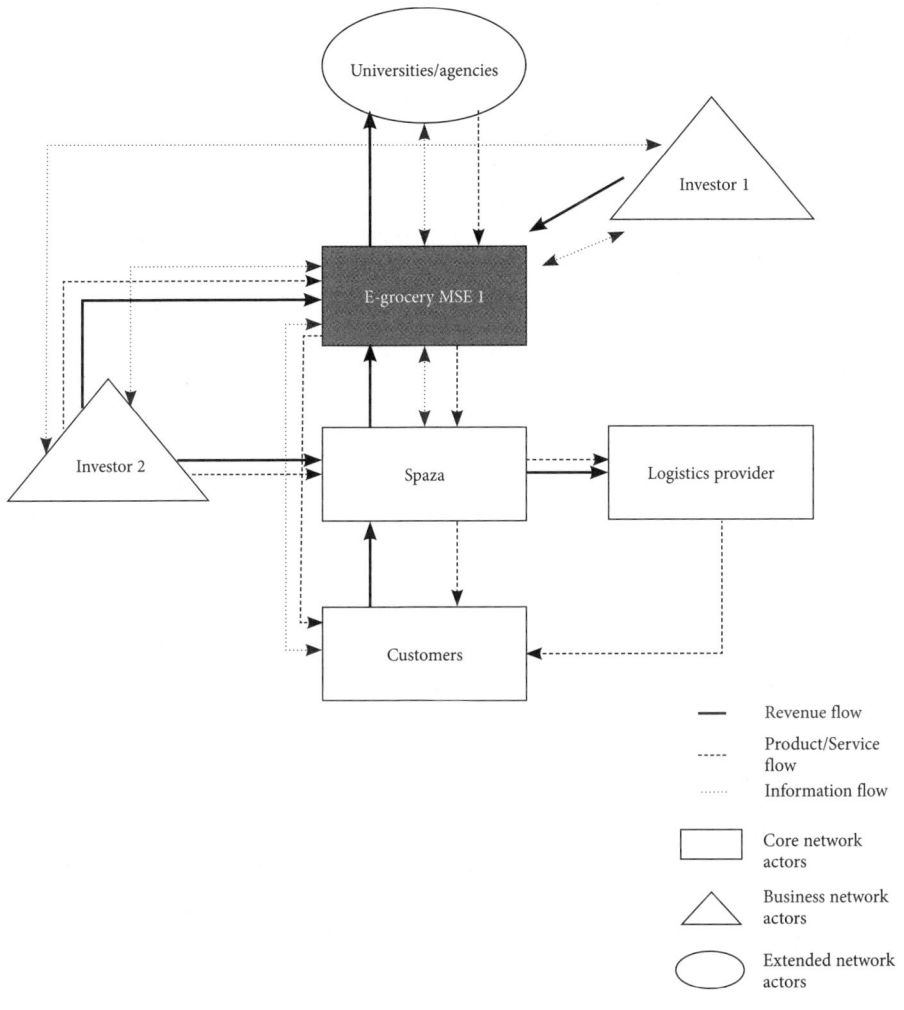

Source: Authors' construction

MSE 1 has partnerships with two investors. Investor 1 is an angel investor involved in the funding of the platform through seed funding and acquiring new capital. Investor 1 also assists with marketing and education. Investor 2 is a global investment bank that provides grant funding for MSE and tech development. It also assists spaza shops to formalise their businesses more.

Analysis of network embeddedness: The supply side

Table 15.5 provides a brief overview of the key findings of the case study for MSE 1. As part of network embeddedness, we first unpack network architecture, followed by network stability. MSE 1 is connected to spaza shops in its current township area of operation, thus focusing on small, informal retailers. However, it is looking to expand to include MSE food processors and spaza customers in new geographic regions and to offer home delivery, thereby connecting to new actors. In terms of the long-term viability, at present, registering is free of charge for spaza shops. However, charges range from ZAR150–1 200/month for other website development services. This is a heavily subsidised model that facilitates increased adoption and participation. However, this is not enough to run the platform, and without suitable funding and sustainable business models, the long-term prospects of MSE 1 remain weak. Thus, the current network architecture (through the connections and the business model structure and strategy) limits the potential for expansion.

Despite being given the support to register, the success of the relationship with spaza shops has been mixed for several reasons. Spaza shops lack awareness of the benefits of digital trading and being omnichannel, and due to their limited digital and technological capabilities, spaza owners are unable to use the online ordering system efficiently. The lack of trusted payment systems is another significant factor that reduces overall trust in the viability of digital footprints. This can lead to difficult relationships with spaza shops. There is a lack of trust due to the novelty of digital systems in townships. Spaza shop owners are used to doing business informally as barter systems and fear being looted. Therefore, many join but do not optimally use the services. Furthermore, many spaza shop owners and operators are illegal migrants, which is a disincentive for creating formal digital footprints. Overall, there are significant opportunities for improving workforce capabilities by, for example, creating specialised training and developing accelerators for supporting business development beyond pilot stages.

In terms of network stability, our results suggest that there is a lack of dispute settlement options with customers. MSE 1 does not have a defined refund management process or money-back guarantees, as they currently do not charge any fees. There are no spaces where complaints can be discussed face to face in the current business model. However, future business models include the incorporation of clear protocols for resolution of issues. Also, with respect to network stability, in terms of communication channels, there is a strong dependence on word of mouth, because reaching via social media is difficult, and marketing through radio and flyers has proven to be more successful in attracting spaza shops. Table 15.5 provides a summary for MSE 1 with respect to aspects of network embeddedness.

Table 15.5 MSE 1: Network embeddedness (supply side)

Network architecture	Current situation and challenges
Power, bargaining and competition	
Power of suppliers	No major constraints were highlighted in terms of access and pricing at this stage.
Change in customer base and customer segments	• Limited to spaza shops in current township area of operation. • Looking to expand to include linking MSE food processors to spaza shops/customers. • Looking to expand into new geographic regions and offer home delivery.
Service delivery performance	• Free registration currently for spaza shops. • Charges range from ZAR150–1 200/month for other website development services. • Can still grow customer base in township spaz shops. • Currently heavily subsidised; needs clear business strategy for sustainability.
Main competitors	• Similar matchmaking services exist, but in different regions. • Platforms that provide combined e-grocery and delivery services targeting middle-to-high-income consumers who are not direct competitors also exist. • Large supermarket chains with their growing online delivery options expanding in townships.
Market share	Unknown; likely < 0.5%.
Intensity of interactions	
Changes in interactions with customers	• Mixed interactions with spaza shops. • Initial lack of awareness of benefits of digital trading and being omnichannel. • Limited digital/technical capabilities of spaza shops. • Lack of trusted payment systems reduces trust in developing digital footprints.
Network relationship quality	
Complaints	Lack of trusted payment systems led to difficulty finding new customers (due to word of mouth) to use the app.
Trust with customers	• Lack of trust due to the novelty of digital systems in townships. • Spaza shops used to doing business informally; fear being looted. • Many spaza shop owners/operators are illegal migrants – unwilling to create formal digital footprints.
Network architecture (low overall)	Significant opportunities to improve capabilities of workforce by creating specialised training; and developing accelerators for supporting business development and expanding beyond pilot stages.
Network stability	**Current situation and challenges.**
Lock-in and dispute settlement	
Dispute settlement procedures	• No defined refund management process or money back guarantees, as no fees are currently charged. • No spaces where complaints can be discussed face to face in the current business model (future business models will incorporate clear protocols for resolution of issues).
Customer support provisioning	Limited customer support, mostly in other services offered (for example, website development).
Access and reach	
Access to new customers	• With a growing database, there is increasing ability to access new customers. • Reaching via social media is difficult, and marketing through radio and flyers has proven to be more successful to attract spaza shops.

Network architecture	Current situation and challenges
Quality of available infrastructure	Poor quality infrastructure, especially lack of payment systems, high costs of hiring own logistics and distribution, and difficulties finding warehousing.
Network stability (relatively low overall)	Limited trust in relationships between MSE 1 and spaza shops due to lack of education and capabilities to effectually use apps and a reluctance to formalise; there is the ability to grow the consumer base, but MSE 1 needs to demonstrate greater accountability and transparency.

Source: Authors' construction

With the above understanding of how MSE 1 is embedded in food e-commerce value chains, we proceed to assess the impact on economic, social and environmental upgrading by MSE 1. Table 15.6 summarises our findings.

Table 15.6 MSE 1: Economic and social value creation or lost/upgrading

	Value creation or value loss indicators (per year)	Measurement and outcome
Economic	Annual revenue/sales value	+20% (increase primarily due to website services, not e-commerce) – value is created.
	Annual profit margins	n.a. (since the e-commerce service is not charged for in the pilot phase).
	Product diversification	Spaza shops who have registered have bought other web services – value is created.
	Productivity (outputs/inputs)	Spaza shop sales increased by +55% sales during the pandemic – value is created.
	Investment in new assets	Technical and marketing managers – value is created.
Social	Current employees	Three; no change.
	Employees on permanent contracts	n.a.
	Employees on part time contracts	n.a.
	Women employees	Only one; not much change.

Source: Interview with MSE 1, 15 January 2021

The results suggest that despite having relatively low levels of network architecture and stability, some value creation has occurred. Most value creation has occurred through economic upgrading, that is, there has been an increase in revenue, product diversification and overall productivity. There was limited evidence of social value creation. Given the nature of MSE 1's offering, no environmental value creation was expected. For this MSE the market power of large suppliers did not have a direct impact.

Case study on MSE 2: Restaurant marketplace

MSE 2 is a virtual kitchen and food delivery firm that can be categorised as a restaurant marketplace. On the demand side, it is a consumer of products and services from core and business network actors. On the supply side, it provides virtual kitchen offerings as a type of restaurant marketplace. MSE 2 operates out of a modular shipping container that is leased from manufacturers for a period of one year (and then renewed). It has been running since 2012 and provides home-style cooking for catering, events and professionals. Its main customers are middle and lower-middle income consumers in urban areas in Johannesburg and the surrounding southern suburbs (mainly Meredale, Mondeor, Ridgeway, Winchester Hills, Suideroord and Melville), particularly near office or business parks.

MSE 2 has five employees, including a director, a chef and three support staff in the virtual kitchen. The shipping containers are offered as turnkey solutions, as they arrive with a fully fitted kitchen and required equipment, tablets, a point-of-sale (POS) system and other hardware and software necessary to run it. This type of virtual kitchen is relatively low-tech in nature and can be run without high technical capabilities. Such models therefore enable the employment of low-to-medium-skilled staff. The benefit of using shipping containers is that they can be located close to key hubs of consumers, allowing for flexibility of location. MSE 2's virtual kitchen model primarily aggregates direct orders from customers, as well as receives orders through Uber Eats and Uber Connect (business network actors) (see Figure 15.2).

While the shipping container virtual kitchen is mobile and low-cost, it tends to have limited cold store space and smaller-sized kitchens, limiting the breadth of items that can be put on the menu. Therefore, along with preparing some of the orders, MSE 2 orders food from other food manufacturers who pre-prepare certain menu items, and package and sell them to MSE 2. These are then reheated, value is added through some customisation (for example adding some extra garnish or sauces) and food is sold to consumers.

Most of MSE 2's relationships are intermediated through a broker who connects them to key suppliers and negotiates bulk deals on their behalf.

The virtual kitchen has applied for food safety standards such as Hazard Analysis Critical Control Points (HACCP) certification. This is captured under the circle of extended network actors. HACPP is not a compulsory food safety standard in South Africa. Acquiring and monitoring the standard come at a significant cost, and monitoring is required on a yearly basis including through audits to maintain the standard.

Network embeddedness: Demand- and supply-side perspectives

The results for the demand-side analysis in Table 15.7 indicate that there were predominantly asymmetric relationships with suppliers such as Uber Eats and Uber Connect, platforms on which they operate and that charge hefty commissions (over 30% of each transaction). Despite trying, MSE 2 has been unable to negotiate better terms of participation. Furthermore, operating costs such as those of their business network (for example renting the containers and internet services) are also on the

Figure 15.2 Restaurant marketplace value chain mapping for MSE 2

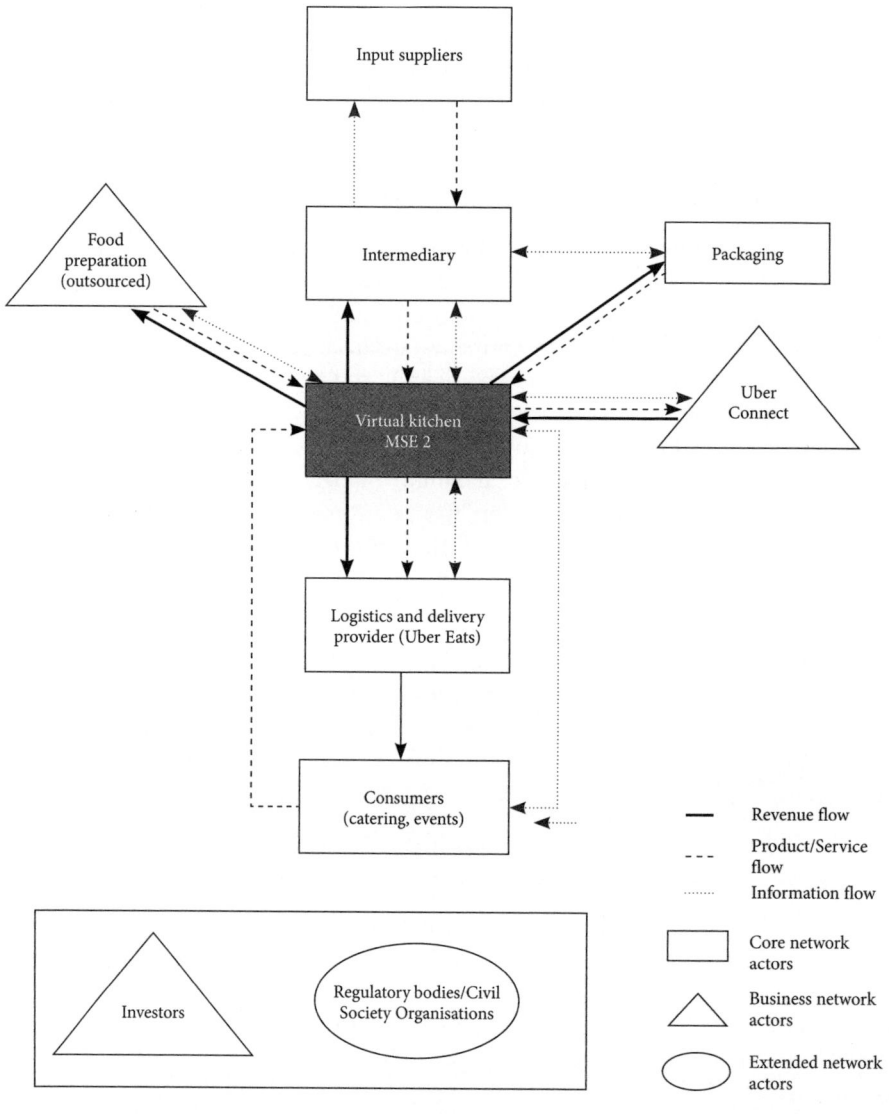

Source: Authors' construction

rise, and here they have again failed to negotiate better prices. There is no direct relationship with supplier services.

However, the relationship is not as asymmetric when it comes to dealing with input suppliers, such as providers of food and packaging. Relationships with input suppliers are relatively symmetrical, where they are often given bulk discounts, and have more ability to negotiate for cheaper prices or new products through the broker.

Thus, the interactions are much more cooperative. However, the intermediary (the broker) often takes a 0.1% commission on the overall transaction. Issues such as network quality, financing, knowledge transfer and finding professionals with the right managerial and technical skillsets have all proven extremely difficult to resolve, reflecting the struggles MSEs broadly experience as they attempt to enhance their current position. There are also broader issues, such as poor-quality infrastructure, especially the lack of payment systems for such small businesses, the high costs of hiring own logistics and distribution, and difficulties in finding warehousing.

Table 15.7 MSE 2: Network embeddedness (demand side)

Network architecture	Demand side perspective: Current situation and challenges
Power, bargaining and competition	
Power in relation to input suppliers	• Costs include those for inputs and packaging • Relationship with main input suppliers navigated through an intermediary/middleman/broker who negotiates for bulk deals and lower prices on behalf of MSE 2.
Power in relation to supplier services	Commission charges of the business network, including Uber Eats and Connect (platform provider), are high, with over 30% per-order; reduces overall profits.
Intensity of interactions	
Interactions with suppliers (cooperative vs contested)	• Cooperative interactions with input and packaging suppliers, mediated through known middleman. • No rent extraction perceived through middleman; viewed as a one-stop-connection allowing for efficiencies.
Intermediaries	• Value chain not vertically integrated; intermediated by a middleman. • High dependence on intermediary.
Supplier support	No direct interaction with main suppliers, thus no support provided.
Network relationship quality	
Ease/Difficulty to negotiate with suppliers	• Intermediary created one-stop shop to connect with all suppliers, making direct negotiation less relevant. • Negotiations with distributors and platform providers (Uber) more difficult; no agency in deciding contract terms.
Financing	• Extremely difficult to get credit from commercial banks; interest rates over 10%. • Donor funding and development financial institution funding difficult to access, and competitive. • Very few accelerators running, which are funded by venture capitalists or other investors; firms like MSE 2 have yet to scale or develop detailed business plans eligible for advanced financing.
Knowledge transfer	• Relatively difficult to connect with universities; and very difficult to connect with government, primarily due to lack of clear information on whom to approach and what services exist.
Managerial and technical capabilities	• Relative difficulty in accessing educational institutions, the Sector Education and Training Authority, and TVET organisations. • Lack of information on whom to approach and where to obtain specific managerial capabilities necessary.

Network architecture	Demand side perspective: Current situation and challenges
Hiring skilled professionals	Extremely difficult to find maintenance operators, data scientists, marketing managers and user interface professionals, especially due to high costs and a small number of people who have the niche requisite capabilities.
Network architecture (relatively low overall)	**Relatively poor/low network architecture, with low-quality interactions with network actors, and lack of bargaining power to negotiate better credit or contract terms.**
Network stability	**Current situation and challenges**
Lock-in and dispute settlement	
Ease of finding alternative suppliers	Uncertainty on finding alternative suppliers, as most deals occur through intermediary.
Negotiation and trust building	Difficult relationship with last mile delivery/distribution such as Uber due to high commissions charged; low bargaining capability.
Access and reach	
Support provision	• During Covid–19, Uber did not provide any specific support on their platform; relatively better relations with input suppliers through intermediary, as it helped negotiate for delays in payments.
Quality of enabling environment	Poor quality infrastructure, especially lack of payment systems, high costs of hiring own logistics and distribution, difficulties finding warehousing.
Network stability (low overall)	**Mixed relations with suppliers, mostly low levels of bargaining and flexibility**

Source: Authors' construction

The results for how MSE 2 embeds into supply-side networks in Table 15.8 show that the customer base has increased by over 40% since inception, especially the middle and middle-low income consumers. In order to improve their delivery performance, MSE 2 joined Uber Eats, as it would provide them with reputational capital, which they did not have when they were marketing produce only through social e-commerce (for example Facebook). There was an increase in positive feedback from customers, which helped visibility and growth. This also increased overall trust. Thus, while there were tensions with asymmetric power relationships with key suppliers and high costs in terms of commissions paid to super platforms, there was more trust earned by customers. This speaks to network effects of such platforms, defined as the increase of the value of a product or service as the number of other people using it increases (CCSA 2023; Yoo n.d.). In our case study, customers join Uber given the large number of other customers already on the platform, in turn building greater trust for the platform. The implication is that these super platforms hold substantial market power and are able to charge high commissions to users.

Table 15.8 MSE 2: Network embeddedness (supply side)

Network architecture	Supply-side perspective: Current situation and challenges
Power, bargaining and competition	
Change in customer base and customer segments	• Customer base increased by over 40% since inception (a compound annual growth rate, or CAGR, of 4.5% per year from 2012). • Customer segments primarily middle and middle-low income consumers.

Network architecture	Supply-side perspective: Current situation and challenges
Service delivery performance	• Prior to 2018, MSE 2 delivered food through hiring local drivers; however, this created various issues in relation to 'who' was accountable for quality (food arrived late or cold, or the order was incorrect). • To mitigate issues related to accountability, a third party (Uber) has been used instead since 2019.
Main competitors	• Smaller local foods restaurants, rather than large incumbent chains (that do not supply ethnic food). • Many are informal and located close to consumers; many started home deliveries during Covid-19.
Market share	• Unknown, likely <0.5%. • Covid-19 reduced MSE 2's market share, since the number of competitors increased with many informal home-based entrepreneurs setting up food delivery services.
Intensity of interactions	
Changes in interactions with customers	• Increase in interactions with customers, especially in terms of receiving feedback and trying to scale up operations. • Transactions with customers in terms of orders have increased from 20 in the year of inception (2012) to approximately 1 200 per year in 2019.
Network relationship quality	
Complaints	• Relatively few complaints as many clients approach MSE 2 through referrals and networks, rather than social media advertising or because of MSE 2's online presence.
Trust with customers	• Other than referrals, MSE 2 has faced significant difficulties in accessing new customers through social media campaigns and flyers.
Network architecture (relatively high overall)	**Clients acquired through networks, and close relations are maintained to promote loyalty and trust in MSE 1**
Network stability	**Current situation and challenges**
Lock-in and dispute settlement	
Dispute settlement procedures	• MSE 2 has a discount policy; if they receive complaints, customers are given 10% discount off their next purchase. • MSE 2 is yet to introduce a defined refund management process given the small customer base.
Customer support provisioning	No service support
Access and reach	
Access to new customers	Relatively open market with less competition, but low financing prevents expansion into new markets.
Quality of available infrastructure	Poor quality infrastructure, especially lack of payment systems, high costs of hiring own logistics and distribution, difficulties finding warehousing.
Network stability (low overall)	**Difficult to access new customers and limited infrastructure access prevents expansion**

Source: Authors' construction

With respect to the implications of network embeddedness on upgrading of MSE 2, our results suggest that despite having relatively low levels of network architecture and stability, some value creation has occurred for MSE 2 (albeit from a low base). For instance, most value creation has occurred through economic upgrading, that is, there has been an increase in sales and profit margins as well as overall productivity (Table 15.9). However, product diversification is limited to home delivery, and the range of products sold has not substantially changed over the last eight years; and there have been almost no investment in new assets to expand the business. Social upgrading was much more limited. For example, the number of employees has grown by only two over the last eight years, and no new or women employees have been hired. Furthermore, no staff are on permanent contracts, and employment terms are precarious. Similarly, environmental downgrading has occurred, with an increase in the use of electricity and non-renewable fuel, as well as an increase in plastic and tinfoil packaging, which are not recyclable. However, no food waste is generated, which is a positive environmental outcome.

Table 15.9 MSE 2: Economic and social value creation or lost/upgrading

	Value creation or value lost indicators (per year)	Measurements and outcomes
Economic	Annual revenue/sales value	+35% (range of revenue: R600 000–R1 500 000) – value is created
	Annual profit margins	+200% (until 2019) –80% (2020) – value is created
	Product diversification	Home delivery (along with collection); limited menu change – value is created
	Productivity (outputs/inputs)	48% – value is created
	Investment in new assets	10% (for example kitchen equipment) – value is created
Social	Current employees	+40% (increase from three to five employees) – value is created
	Employees on permanent contracts	0 – value is lost
	Employees on part-time contracts	+100% – value is lost
	Women employees	0 (only one as chef since inception) – value is lost
Environmental	Electricity costs	+25% (2020: R30 000) – value is lost
	Fuel costs (non-renewable)	+35% (2020: R15 000) – value is lost
	Use of cold store	Yes – value is created
	Waste generation (as % of sales)	0% – value is created
	Packing material (share of total packaging)	Tinfoil: +40%; Plastic: +60%; Paper: –5% – value is lost

Source: Interview with MSE 2, 7 September 2020

Conclusions and policy recommendations

Contributing to the empirical literature on global production networks (GPNs), this chapter aimed to better understand how MSEs are embedded in food e-commerce value chains in South Africa – in particular, how they network with other value chain actors and what the implications are for value creation and upgrading. Effective competition at different levels of food e-commerce value chains is a critical enabler to MSE participation and economic upgrading, particularly when super platforms are used to access customers.

We highlighted the importance of assessing network embeddedness of MSEs in terms of network architecture and stability from both demand- and supply-side perspectives. We sought to assess the complex demand- and supply-side networks that are formed for platformised MSEs The aim was also to assist in categorising and unpacking the quality of network relationships (power structures, competition and stability), to better understand actual value creation and upgrading of MSEs.

The results for both MSE 1 and 2 showed that, overall, there was significant scope to expand in niches of the market that have been neglected (low-income areas, poorer households and informal spaza shops). This has facilitated the creation of new forms of value creation economic upgrading, especially in relation to productivity, profits and product diversification. However, networks with suppliers and consumers remain unstable largely due to lack of trust in the relationships. This was particularly evident in the experience of MSE 1. There remain unclear protocols on who is accountable if there are disputes between spaza shops and customers or if refunds are demanded, along with having low bargaining power with large service suppliers, which have resulted in unbalanced power structures. MSE 2 has faced difficulties because it depends on third parties with considerable bargaining power skewed against them for delivery services and high commissions charged (for example, Uber Connect and Uber Eats).

Challenges to growth are exacerbated by poor coordination with other business and extended actors (such as finance providers and the government), which prevent the proliferation of the MSEs Intra-firm factors, such as lack of STEM (science, technology, engineering and mathematics) and managerial capabilities, and missing horizontal services, such as affordable payment systems, are holding back both MSEs 1 and 2, inhibiting their ability to compete, grow and develop comparative advantages in the foodtech space. We also find that social upgrading is limited in terms of continued low levels of employment, the lack of permanent contracts and the persistence of job precarity. In one of our case studies, environmental downgrading occurred, with increased electricity and non-renewable fuel use, as did increased use of non-recyclable plastic and tinfoil packaging, although less food waste was generated.

From the assessment above, we conclude by offering some policy priorities and actions to create a more enabling environment for foodtech MSEs to embed and create value by upgrading in value chains or production networks.

A competitive digital economy is critical to enabling MSEs in foodtech to participate and grow in food value chains.

Particularly in platformised markets, a few large players can grow into dominant platforms as a result of network effects. Concerns around the abuse of these dominant positions emerged in our case studies with respect to the use of powerful platforms like Uber. There is no neutral or open space for negotiation of terms of contracts, especially with large platforms.

The Competition Commission of South Africa's recent Online Intermediary Platforms Market Inquiry (report released in July 2023) recognised this as a challenge. Based on the experiences of MSE 2, as well as the evidence heard during the course of the inquiry, we concur with the recommendations of the inquiry for the creation of a more competitive digital economy. The inquiry found that the two leading food delivery platforms (Uber Eats and Mr D Food) charged much higher commission fees to independent restaurants than large chain restaurants, and that this difference was not based on underlying costs of serving these different groupings. Higher commission fees tend to be passed on to customers in the form of higher prices, which negatively affects their relative competitiveness. The inquiry recommended that Uber Eats standardise its tiered commission fee structure by allowing independent restaurants to self-select from a range of commission fees associated with different levels of service and different charges based on their needs (CCSA 2023).

The inquiry also stipulated that Mr D Food offer promotional rebates and monthly advertising credits for independent restaurants. In principle, this (and the similar action by other super platforms) should benefit MSEs like MSE 2 and allow them to better embed in networks. However, greater advocacy is required to ensure that MSEs are aware of these recommendations and aware of the recourse they have if large platforms abuse their power. Although not currently a direct concern with the MSEs we interviewed, amendments to the Competition Act (No. 89 of 1998) aim to protect them from the possible abuse of dominance from input sellers and final product buyers through the new price discrimination and buyer power provisions. Support generally is needed to create an enabling ecosystem of support for these MSEs. For instance, collective sourcing, logistics and warehousing can reduce costs. However, the appropriate competition exemptions, if applicable, need to be granted, in addition to industrial policy support tools.

Network relationships, including between large, established firms and MSEs in foodtech, need to be developed. This could take the form of a foodtech task force that deals with issues related to the full value chain of foodtech MSEs and that addresses some of these issues through public–private partnerships (PPPs), including as part of the Agriculture and Agro-processing Masterplan (AAMP).[14]

Partnerships with businesses and extended networks to access *funding*, including preferential interest rates, loans, credit lines, grants and tax breaks, for foodtech MSEs should also be developed. Financial products could also include, from government's side, a 'shock support fund' to create a buffer during times of shock.

Commercial finance is unaffordable for MSEs, and 'patient' development finance is needed.[15]

Strengthening accelerators and setting up sandboxes to allow more MSEs to experiment and participate in the foodtech space are important to develop novel business models and to build trust in the digital economy. Similarly, improving traceability infrastructure for market access through digital systems that can verify adherence to standards, labour and environmental practices can enhance trust in foodtech MSEs.

The lack of an available and affordable skilled workforce (for example, STEM, marketing, managerial and social media skills) is a significant factor that prevents the expansion of MSEs. Creating specialised STEM education, as part of general education skills at school level, or even as short-term diploma programmes for professionals is critical. PPPs are important in this regard, as is utilising the Food and Beverage(SETA, the Wholesale and Retail SETA and the CSIR to more effectively develop foodtech, as advocated for in the AAMP. This needs to be complemented by further research on the way MSEs are embedded in food e-commerce value chains, and the implications of this on how they upgrade within value chains.

Notes

1. This chapter is an iteration of a working paper: Krishnan A & Das Nair (2021) *Supporting inclusion of small, medium and micro enterprises (SMMEs) in foodtech in South Africa*. Working Paper 2021/07, Centre for Competition, Regulation and Economic Development–Industrial Development Think Tank, University of Johannesburg. Accessed April 2022, https://static1.squarespace.com/static/52246331e4b0a46e5f1b8ce5/t/614459c93d5b4115601dadf0/1631869392958/IDTT_4_PB_Supporting_inclusion_of_SMMEs_in_foodtech_in_South_Africa_202107.pdf
2. See Appendix C for the Authors' characterisation of different foodtech segments.
3. Das Nair R & Krishnan A, Combating Covid–19: The promise of foodtech in SA, *Daily Maverick*, 24 May 2020
4. Often defined as the control lead firms have on their suppliers (for example, Gereffi et al. 2005).
5. Omnichannels are multiple channels, including online and brick-and-mortar.
6. The IFWG comprises officials from National Treasury, the Financial Intelligence Centre, the Financial Sector Conduct Authority, the National Credit Regulator, the South African Reserve Bank, the South African Revenue Service and the Competition Commission of South Africa.
7. Regulations include The Foodstuffs, Cosmetics and Disinfectants Act (No. 54 of 1972) and the Agricultural Product Standard Act (No. 119 of 1990).
8. A network of firms, government, civil society and other actors bound together through how they organise various tasks and the power structures within (Henderson et al. 2002).
9. From LinkedIn, Agfunder, Crunchbase and Tracnx, through key word searches of 'foodtech + South Africa'; 'food tech'; 'food delivery'; and 'food platforms'.
10. The authors note that this is by no means a complete dataset of all firms that exist in this space and that it is limited to companies found in 2020, but absent any other publicly available dataset, this forms the base for the research in this chapter and could be valuable for future additions and tracking of foodtech MSEs.
11. Due to overlaps of the functioning of firms across foodtech segmentations, the percentage of total does not add up to a 100, as there has been double counting.
12. A spaza shop or a tuck shop is a small informal convenience shop business in South Africa, often located in peri-urban, township areas and rural areas. Spaza shops sell daily foods and convenience products in variable quantities.
13. See: https://www.businesslive.co.za/fm/life/food/2020-08-27-the-rise-of-the-dark-kitchen-trend-in-sa/
14. See: https://www.namc.co.za/aamp-about-aamp/
15. See: https://www.competition.org.za/ccred-blog-thinkingaheadsa/2020/4/30/the-nature-of-funding-matters-making-development-finance-work-for-south-africas-smes-in-the-covid-19-crisis;
https://www.competition.org.za/ccred-blog-structural-transformation/2020/4/20/structural-transformation-competition-and-economic-power

References

Alford M & Phillips N (2018) The political economy of state governance in global production networks: Change, crisis and contestation in the South African fruit sector. *Review of International Political Economy* 25(1): 98–121

Bai C, Quayson M & Sarkis J (2021) Covid–19 pandemic digitization lessons for sustainable development of micro-and small-enterprises. *Sustainable Production and Consumption* 27: 1989–2001

Barrientos S (2019) *Gender and work in global value chains: Capturing the gains?* Cambridge: Cambridge University Press

Barrientos S, Gereffi G & Rossi A (2011) Economic and social upgrading in global production networks: A new paradigm for a changing world. *International Labour Review* 150(3–4): 319–340

Barrientos S & Smith S (2007) Do workers benefit from ethical trade? Assessing codes of labour practice in global production systems. *Third World Quarterly* 28(4): 713–729. DOI: 10.1080/01436590701336580

Bernhardt T & Milberg W (2011) *Does economic upgrading generate social upgrading? Insights from horticulture, apparel, mobile phones and tourism sectors.* 'Capturing the Gains' Working Paper 2011/07, University of Manchester

CCSA (Competition Commission of South Africa) (2019) Grocery retail market inquiry final report, non-confidential. Accessed November 2023, http://www.compcom.co.za/wp-content/uploads/2019/12/GRMI-Non-Confidential-Report.pdf

CCSA (2021) *Measuring concentration and participation in the South African economy: Levels and trends.* Accessed November 2023, https://www.compcom.co.za/measuring-concentration-and-participation-in-the-south-african-economy-levels-and-trends/

CCSA (2023) *Online intermediation platforms market inquiry final report and decision.* Accessed November 2023, https://www.compcom.co.za/wp-content/uploads/2023/07/CC_OIPMI-Final-Report.pdf

Chaochotechuang P & Mariano S (2016) Alignment of new product development and product innovation strategies: A case study of Thai food and beverage SMEs. *International Journal of Globalisation and Small Business* 8(2): 179–206

Coe NM & Yeung HWC (2015) *Global production networks: Theorizing economic development in an interconnected world.* Oxford: Oxford University Press

Das Nair R & Landani N (2020) *Making agricultural value chains more inclusive through technology and innovation.* WIDER Working Paper No. 2020/104, Helsinki: UNU-WIDER

De Marchi V, Di Maria E, Krishnan A & Ponte S (2019) Environmental upgrading in global value chains. In S Ponte, G Gereffi & G Raj-Reichert *Handbook on global value chains.* Cheltenham: Edward Elgar Publishing

Euromonitor (2021) *The future of food retail: A spotlight on e-commerce.* London: Euromonitor Accessed May 2022, https://www.euromonitor.com/the-future-of-food-retail-a-spotlight-on-e-commerce/report

Ezeomah B & Duncombe R (2019) The role of digital platforms in disrupting agricultural value chains in developing countries. In P Nielsen & Kimaro HC (Eds) *Information and communication technologies for development. Strengthening southern-driven cooperation as a catalyst for ICT4D.* International Conference on Social Implications of Computers in Developing Countries, ICT4D 2019. IFIP Advances in Information and Communication Technology (Vol. 551). Cham: Springer. https://doi.org/10.1007/978-3-030-18400-1_19

Frederick S (2019) Global value chain mapping. In S Ponte, G Gereffi & G Raj-Reichert *Handbook on global value chains.* Cheltenham: Edward Elgar Publishing

Foster C & Graham M (2017) Reconsidering the role of the digital in global production networks. *Global Networks* 17(1): 68–88

Foster C, Graham M, Mann L, Waema T & Friederici N (2018) Digital control in value chains: Challenges of connectivity for East African firms. *Economic Geography* 94(1): 68–86

Frost & Sullivan (2018) *African B2C eCommerce growth opportunities, forecast to 2020, global digital transformation.* San Antonio: Frost & Sullivan

Gereffi G (1999) International trade and industrial upgrading in the apparel commodity chains. *Journal of International Economics* 48: 37–70. https://doi.org/10.1016/S0022-1996(98)00075-0

Gereffi G (2019) Global value chains and international development policy: Bringing firms, networks and policy-engaged scholarship back in. *Journal of International Business Policy* 2: 195–210

Gereffi G, Humphrey J & Sturgeon T (2005) The governance of global value chains. *Review of International Political Economy* 12(1): 78–104

Goga S, Paelo A & Nyamwena J (2019) *Online retailing in South Africa: An overview.* Working Paper No. 2/2019, Centre for Competition, Regulation and Economic Development, University of Johannesburg. Accessed November 2023, SSRN: https://ssrn.com/abstract=3386008

Granovetter M (1985) Economic action and social structure: The problem of embeddedness. *American Journal of Sociology* 91(3): 481–510

Granovetter M (2017) *Society and economy: Framework and principles.* Cambridge, Massachusetts: Harvard University Press. https://doi.org/10.2307/j.ctv24w64km

Heeks R, Gomez-Morantes JE, Graham M, Howson K, Mungai P et al. (2021) Digital platforms and institutional voids in developing countries: The case of ride-hailing markets. *World Development* 145: 105528

Hein A, Schreieck M, Riasanow T, Setzke DS, Wiesche M et al. (2020) Digital platform ecosystems. *Electronic Markets* 30, 87–98

Henderson J, Dicken P, Hess M, Coe N & Yeung HWC (2002) Global production networks and the analysis of economic development. *Review of International Political Economy* 9(3): 436–464

Hess M (2004) 'Spatial' relationships? Towards a reconceptualization of embeddedness. *Progress in Human Geography* 28(2): 165–186

Humphrey J & Schmitz H (2002) How does insertion in global value chains affect upgrading in industrial clusters? *Regional Studies* 36(9): 1017–1027. DOI: 10.1080/0034340022000022198

Kapoor K, Bigdeli AZ, Dwivedi YK, Schroeder A, Beltagui A et al. (2021) A socio-technical view of platform ecosystems: Systematic review and research agenda. *Journal of Business Research* 128: 94–108

Khan LM (2017) Amazon's Antitrust Paradox. *Yale Law Journal* 126(3): 710–805. Accessed November 2023, https://scholarship.law.columbia.edu/faculty_scholarship/2808

Kos D & Kloppenburg S (2019) Digital technologies, hyper-transparency and smallholder farmer inclusion in global value chains. *Current Opinion in Environmental Sustainability* 41: 56–63

Krishnan A (2023) Embeddedness beyond the lead firm in global production networks: Insights from Kenyan horticulture. *Environment and Planning A: Economy and Space* 55(8): 1859–1883. https://doi.org/10.1177/0308518X231170194

Krishnan A & Das Nair R (2021) *Supporting inclusion of small, medium and micro enterprises (SMMEs) in foodtech in South Africa*. Working paper April 2021, Centre for Competition, Regulation and Economic Development–Industrial Development Think Tank, University of Johannesburg. Accessed November 2023, https://static1.squarespace.com/static/52246331e4b0a46e5f1b8ce5/t/614459c93d5b4115601dadf0/1631869392958/IDTT_4_PB_Supporting_inclusion_of_SMMEs_in_foodtech_in_South_Africa_202107.pdf

Krishnan A, De Marchi V & Ponte S (2023) Environmental upgrading and downgrading in global value chains: A framework for analysis. *Economic Geography* 99(1): 25–50

Krishnan A & Foster C (2018) A quantitative approach to innovation in agricultural value chains: Evidence from Kenyan horticulture. *The European Journal of Development Research* 30: 108–135

Lord C, Bates O, Friday A, McLeod F, Cherrett T et al. (2023) The sustainability of the gig economy food delivery system (Deliveroo, UberEATS and Just-Eat): Histories and futures of rebound, lock-in and path dependency. *International Journal of Sustainable Transportation* 17(5): 490–502

Neilson J, Pritchard B, Fold N & Dwiartama A (2018) Lead firms in the cocoa–chocolate global production network: An assessment of the deductive capabilities of GPN 2.0. *Economic Geography* 94(4): 400–424

Parker G, Van Alstyne M & Jiang X (2017) Platform ecosystems. *Mis Quarterly* 41(1): 255–266

Pasquali G, Krishnan A & Alford M (2021) Multichain strategies and economic upgrading in global value chains: Evidence from Kenyan horticulture. *World Development* 146: 105598

Polanyi K (1944) *The great transformation: Economic and political origins of our time*. New York: Rinehart & Company

Ramaswamy V (2009) Leading the transformation to co-creation of value. *Strategy Lead* 37(2): 32–37

Reardon T, Heiman A, Lu L, Nuthalapati CS, Vos R & Zilberman D (2021) 'Pivoting' by food industry firms to cope with COVID-19 in developing regions: E-commerce and 'copivoting' delivery intermediaries. *Agricultural Economics* 52(3): 459–475

Srinivasan A & Venkatraman N (2018) Entrepreneurship in digital platforms: A network-centric view. *Strategic Entrepreneurship Journal* 12(1): 54–71

StatsSA (2017) *Manufacturing industry: Financial, 2017. Report No. 30-02-03*. Pretoria: Statistics South Africa

Stats SA (2023) *P0211 – Quarterly Labour Force Survey (QLFS), 4th Quarter 2022*. Pretoria: Statistics South Africa. Accessed January 2024, https://www.statssa.gov.za/?p=16113

Tsan M, Totapally S, Hailu M & Addom BK (2019) *The digitalisation of African agriculture report 2018–2019*. Wageningen: The Technical Centre for Agricultural and Rural Cooperation

Uchiyama Y, Akhir MNM, Wang Y, Lim B & Pazim KH (2022) Working conditions of online food delivery gig workers from a consumer perspective in China: A lesson for Malaysia. *Contemporary Chinese Political Economy and Strategic Relations* 8(2): 324–IX

Wood AJ, Graham M, Lehdonvirta V & Hjorth I (2019) Networked but commodified: The (dis)embeddedness of digital labour in the gig economy. *Sociology* 53(5): 931–950

Xie X, Han Y, Anderson A & Ribeiro-Navarrete S (2022) Digital platforms and SMEs' business model innovation: Exploring the mediating mechanisms of capability reconfiguration. *International Journal of Information Management* 65: 102513

Yoo C (n.d.) *Network effect: Global dictionary of competition law*. Concurrences, Art. N° 12232. Accessed November 2023, https://www.concurrences.com/en/dictionary/network-effect

Zeng Y, Jia F, Wan L & Guo H (2017) E-commerce in agri-food sector: A systematic literature review. *International Food and Agribusiness Management Review* 20(4): 439–460

Appendix C

Figure A15.1 Diagram showing foodtech segments

(see next page)

Source: Author's construction, drawing on Tsan et al. (2019)

VERTICAL SEGMENT: DEFINITION OF FOOD SEGMENT

In-Store Retail & Restaurant

AI or robots in stores and restaurants: shelf stacking, assisting (inventory management)

Point of sale (POS) systems
Merges sales, inventory and customer management (inventory management and optimization, minimization of wastage and food loss)

E-Grocery: Online stores and marketplaces for sale and delivery of processed & unprocessed food and agricultural products to consumer

On-demand enabling Tech: Involves crowdsourcing customer feedback and providing data analytics; data aggregation/curation, building digital assets

Food waste and surplus management
Upcycling to create new food products

3D food printers
Additive manufacturing to personalize food (for instance, printing chocolate into desired shapes). (e.g. Foodini)*

Online restaurants and meal kits start-ups: Offer culinary meals and sending pre-portioned ingredients to cook at home

Restaurant marketplaces: Online tech platforms delivering food from a wide range of vendors (food as a service provision) (e.g. Uber Eats)

Cloud Retail Infrastructure

Real time decision making at the front end: Includes pricing and margin management, and loyalty programme management, while back end can include omnichannel order fulfilment

In-Store Retail and Restaurant

Food safety
Tech to sanitise food and prolong shelf life such as food testing devices and sensors and pathogen test kits

Traceability technology
Such as blockchain used by various organizations to trace the origins of food, and the various transactions along the way (e.g. Fairtrade blockchain for food standards).

Food/agricultural processing tech
Precision technologies, fortification (products or services that leverage innovative techniques to improve food ingredient functionality).

Food packaging
Based on IoT, NFC and RFID technology for food monitoring. E.g. water soluble and biodegradable thermoplastic pellets for packaging, natural and biodegradable packaging.

Home & cooking tech: Smart kitchen appliances that are consumer facing or devices that help restaurants manage business effectively. These also include wearable nutrition tech, such as AI apps to analyse nutrition information.

Innovative foods or 'Food-as-software': where food can be designed including plant – based, insect-based, immune-boosting, cell-based, artificial proteins and protein fermentation (process that allows programming micro-organisms to produce almost any complex organic molecule).

Home & Cooking Tech

Mid-stream tech

HORIZONTAL SERVICES: DEFINITION

Warehouse management systems such as RFID sensors to track-and-trace data to the entire supply chain and real-time visibility into inventory levels

GPS technology to accurately locate vehicles, monitor freight movement and consolidate shipments

Logistics and transport

Intelligent Transportation Systems, which use multimodal systems for increasing safety and reliability, travel speeds, traffic flow and for reducing risks, accidents rate, carbon emissions and air pollution

Fintech solutions

Payments (entities that perform part or all of the functions required to send and/or receive value from one party to another via any digital channel)

Lending: entities that facilitate the borrowing of money or financing assets for individual consumers and/or small businesses with traditional and non-traditional financiers through internet, cloud or app-based platforms.

Savings & deposits: entities that are deposit-taking and provide digital banking services as well as savings products and layby arrangements using mobile technology.

Insurtech: entities that provide part or all of the insurance value chain functions

Investments: entities that provide digital platforms for investment

Financial planning & advisory: entities that use artificial intelligence and/or robotics to provide financial advice to individuals or small businesses by recommending suitable savings, investment or credit products and managing financial wellness

Capital raising: equity or debt funding platforms that allow businesses or individuals to raise funds for investment purposes or charitable causes.

285

About the authors

Paul Anderson is the managing partner in the Competition and Regulation Economics practice at Genesis Analytics. With nearly 20 years' experience, he provides economic analysis and expert advice on competition, trade and regulatory matters across Africa. He holds a master's degree in economics from the University of Cape Town, and has authored and presented numerous papers in the competition field.

Jason Aproskie is a principal economist at the Competition Commission of South Africa. He has extensive experience in the competition and regulation field in both the private and public sectors. A published author, Jason has also testified as an expert economist at the Competition Tribunal and National Energy Regulator of South Africa. He holds a master's degree in economics from the University of Cape Town.

Tessa Bleazard is a senior economist at the Competition Commission of South Africa, with experience in competition law and economics. Prior to joining the Commission, she worked as an economic analyst in the Department of Research at the South African Reserve Bank. She holds a Bachelor of Commerce honours degree and a MCom in economics from Stellenbosch University.

Michael-James Currie is a director of Primerio. His regulatory and commercial law practice is pan-African and he has practised across several countries and regional blocs. He is also widely recognised as a leading competition law practitioner across Africa. He is a regular speaker and author who has published several articles, papers and opinion pieces on competition law.

Reena das Nair is the executive director of the Centre for Competition, Regulation and Economic Development and associate professor and programme coordinator for the MCom in competition and economic regulation degree programme both at University of Johannesburg. Reena provides training and capacity building for regulators and competition professionals in east and southern Africa. Her research interests include competition dynamics in food value chains, barriers to entry for small, micro- and medium enterprises and women-owned enterprises.

Joshua Eveleigh is a managing associate at Primerio and has experience in all aspects of competition law. Joshua is a regular speaker and has authored papers focusing on competition law. Joshua also regularly drafts comments to competition law legislation on behalf of numerous organisations.

Andre Frauenknecht is a principal economist in the Competition and Regulatory Economics practice at Genesis Analytics, with over 14 years' experience. He has worked on diverse competition matters across a wide range of industries and sectors.

He holds a master's degree in economics from the University of Cape Town. Andre has co-authored and presented papers at leading competition conferences.

Timothy Gondwe is a professor of animal science (breeding) at Lilongwe University of Agriculture and Natural Resources with experience in training, research, outreach and consultancy in animal agriculture, especially poultry, goats, pigs and dairy cattle. He obtained a PhD at the University of Göttingen, Germany, in 2004. He has published in the field of animal agriculture, ranging from breeding, feeding and production systems to marketing.

Wang'ombe Kariuki is a competition policy, economics and law consultant, and former director general of the Competition Authority of Kenya. He was instrumental in the development of the Kenyan Competition Act (No. 12 of 2010), as well as in the development of the Common Market for Eastern and Southern Africa Competition Commission's regulatory capacity. He was also the founder member and the first chairman of the African Competition Forum.

Jonathan Klaaren is a professor of law and society at the University of the Witwatersrand, where he teaches competition law and other subjects. He is a former head of the School of Law and is part of the Wits Institute for Social and Economic Research.

Aarti Krishnan is a lecturer in sustainability and innovation at Alliance Manchester Business School, University of Manchester and a senior research associate at the South African Research Chairs Initiative, University of Johannesburg. She obtained her PhD at the University of Manchester in the UK. She has previously worked at ODI Global and has experience and published in the fields of global value chains, production networks, sustainability, digital technologies and green finance.

Itumeleng Lesofe is a principal analyst at the Competition Commission of South Africa and holds an LLM in corporate law from the University of Pretoria. He previously served as technical director for the Online Intermediation Platforms Market Inquiry, which focused on digital markets in South Africa, and he has published several articles in the field of competition law and economics.

Maletuma Malie is a sales and development manager at the Johannesburg Stock Exchange, South Africa. She holds a MCom in competition and economic regulation from the University of Johannesburg. She is a seasoned financial industry professional.

Angella Kachipapa Mhone is a senior analyst at the Competition and Fair Trading Commission of Malawi. A trained economist with a master's degree in economics from the University of Essex in the UK and Bachelor of Social Science in economics from the University of Malawi, Angella is an experienced professional in competition and consumer protection law in Malawi and has researched and published in the field.

Tlhalefang Moeletsi is a manager at Genesis Analytics and a former consultant to the World Bank. He holds a master's degree in economic science from the University of the Witwatersrand.

Inonge Mulozi is a senior analyst at the Competition and Consumer Protection Commission of Zambia. She obtained her Master of Philosophy in competition law and policy from the University of Lusaka, Zambia. With expertise in competition law, strategic management and industrial policy, she actively investigates competition and consumer protection cases and conducts market studies.

Priscilla M Njako is the manager of the Buyer Power department at the Competition Authority of Kenya. She obtained her LLD from the University of Pretoria in South Africa. She has an interest in dynamic enforcement of policy to address the needs of developing economies and is a frequent commentator on the intersection between competition policy and inclusive economic development.

Grace Nsomba is an economist and researcher at the Centre for Competition, Regulation and Economic Development at the University of Johannesburg (UJ) and a PhD student at UJ. She has an MCom in competition and economic regulation from the University of Johannesburg and a BCom Hons in economics from the University of Pretoria. Grace's research has specialised in competition and economic development in east and southern Africa.

Rosebela A Oiro is a senior analyst for policy, research and advocacy at the Competition Authority of Kenya. She obtained a master's degree in economics (international trade and finance) at Kenyatta University in Kenya. She has previously worked at the Consumer Unity Trust Society – Africa Resource Centre and has experience in trade, competition, and consumer protection.

John Oxenham is the managing partner of Primerio and has practised in the regulatory, commercial litigation and antitrust fields locally and across the African region for over 20 years. He is recognised as a leading competition practitioner by many professional platforms and has published numerous papers and opinion pieces on competition and regulatory law locally and internationally.

Karissa Moothoo Padayachie is a PhD student in economics at the University of Johannesburg (UJ), focusing on the relationship between market power and inequality in South Africa. She currently works at the Centre for Competition, Regulation and Economic Development at the University of Johannesburg, and has worked as an economist at the Competition Tribunal of South Africa.

Genna Robb is an economics director at the UK's Competition and Markets Authority. She holds an MSc in economics from the University of Warwick. She has previously worked as an economist at the Competition Commission of South Africa and the University of Johannesburg, as well as in consulting. She has experience and publications in the field of competition and regulatory economics.

ABOUT THE AUTHORS

Simon Roberts is a professor at the University of Johannesburg in the Centre for Competition, Regulation and Economic Development; research professor at the SOAS University of London; and a special advisor at the Shamba Centre for Food and Climate. Simon has been an economics director at the UK Competition and Markets Authority and the chief economist at the Competition Commission of South Africa.

Chilufya P Sampa is a special advisor on competition law and policy at the Shamba Centre for Food and Climate. He served as executive director of the Competition and Consumer Protection Commission in Zambia for 11 years. He also served on several boards nationally and regionally. Chilufya has a bachelor's degree in business administration, a master's degree in economic policy management and a bachelor's degree in commercial law.

Siphosethu Tetani is a senior economist at the Competition Commission of South Africa. She holds a master's degree in economics from the Nelson Mandela University. She has experience working on abuse-of-dominance investigations, merger and acquisitions, policy research and market inquiries. Her areas of research interest include competition regulation and policy, and industrial policy and development.

Thando Vilakazi is associate professor of economics at the University of Johannesburg. He serves as a part-time member of the Competition Tribunal of South Africa and served as executive director of the Centre for Competition, Regulation and Economic Development from 2019 to 2024.

Index

Note: The index is arranged alphabetically in letter-by-letter order. The use of italics indicates figures, while the use of **bold** indicates tables. Some notes are included.

A

AAC solutions *see* augmentative and assistive communication solutions
AAMP *see* Agriculture and Agro- processing Masterplan
abuse of buyer power
   as 'abuse of dominance' 63–66
   in Competition Act in Kenya 83–87
   in emerging markets 58–73
   and prohibition of in Kenya 22, 26, 78, 85–86
   as public interest provision 66–68
   remedies obtained through enforcement for 85–86
   in South Africa 63–69
abuse of dominance 5–7, 51–52, 61, 63–66
   access and reach as indicator of network stability 262
accommodation platform services 187 189, **188–189**, 222–223
ACF *see* African Competition Forum
administrative penalties 109, 114, 121–123
AfCFTA *see* African Continental Free Trade Area
African Competition Forum (ACF) 10, 24, 25, 51, 54
African Continental Free Trade Area (AfCFTA) ix, 2, 9, 38–57
   Protocol 9, 24, 45
African Market Observatory (AMO) x, 154, 161
   Agriculture and Agro-processing Masterplan (AAMP) 278, 279
   AIM see Alternative Investment Market under London Stock Exchange
alternative exchange 233, 234
alternative trading systems (ATSs) 234n11, **245**, 246
AMO *see* African Market Observatory
   anti-cartel laws and enforcement 109, 123, 124
   in South Africa 121–122

anti-competitive conduct and arrangements ix, x, 8, 34, 110, 137, 175
   effects 39–40, 60, 95, 137, 138–139
   self-reporting of and absolution from fines 34
   see also substantial lessening of competition
antitrust laws and enforcement 28, 111, **112**
ASEAN *see* Association of South East Asian Nations
ASIC *see* Australian Securities and Investments Commission
Association of South East Asian Nations (ASEAN)
   cooperation model 40–41
   Experts Group on Competition 41
ASX *see* Australian Securities Exchange
Australian Securities and Investments Commission (ASIC) 245
Australian Securities Exchange (ASX) 235n15, 241

B

B2B *see* business-to-business
B2C *see* business-to-consumer
Babelegi Workers and Industrial Supplies CC 64, 65–68, 99–101
bargaining power 60, 260
barriers to entry into market 7–8, 143
Botswana
   approach to merger evaluation 3
   establishment of prioritisation plans by 4
   integrated agency enforcement model 4
   jurisdiction of 3
Brazil as international comparative benchmark 155
businesses, rules for inherently powerful 5–7
business models, e-commerce 255–285, *284–285*
business owners and consumers, benefits of digital platforms to 185–186
business-stealing effects 131

business-to-business (B2B) 189, 256. 257, 265
business-to-consumer (B2C) 256, 257, 265
buyer power 5
   and buyer power abuse across Africa 5–6, 59
   distributional implications of 6
   concerns 22–23
   in emerging markets 58–76
   framework 69, 73
   in Kenya 22, 69–72, 83–84
   legislation against abuse of 5, 6–7
   meaning of 59–61
   in South Africa 61–69
Buyer Power Enforcement Guidelines 63, 68–69
Buyer Power Guidelines 63, 64, 66, 68–69, 70, 84–85, 87

C
CAC *see* Competition Appeal Court *under* South African competition-related authorities and agency
CAK *see* Competition Authority of Kenya *under* Kenyan competition-related authorities and agency
Canada, Universal Market Integrity Rules 246
CAR *see* Cumulative Abnormal Return
cartels and cartel enforcement and penalisation 8, 28–34, 36, 40, 49–51, 109–129
   see also cartels, fight against in *under* Zambia
CAT *see* Competition Appeal Tribunal *under* United Kingdom competition-related authorities and agency
CCC *see* Competition Commission *under* Common Market for Eastern and Southern Africa
CCPA *see* Competition and Consumer Protection Act 24 of 2010 *under* Zambian competition-related legislation and legislative bodies
CCPC *see* Competition and Consumer Protection Commission *under* Zambian competition-related authorities and agency
CCPs *see* central clearing counterparties
CCSA *see* Competition Commission of South Africa *under* South African competition-related authorities and agency
CEEC *see* Citizens Economic Empowerment Commission *under* Zambian competition-related authorities and agency

cement 33–34
   producers, merging of *see* Lafarge/Holcim *under* global and continental *under* mergers
central clearing counterparties (CCPs) 233, 241
Central Securities Depository (CSD) and Participants (CSDPs) 233
Chicago-school narratives 82, 136
clearing as central process in trading (post-) service value chain 233
climate change, resilience in face of 7, 161
CMA *see* Competition and Markets Authority *under* United Kingdom competition-related authorities and agency
code of practice 86
collusion 27, 28, 29, 30, 33, 36, 38, 39, 40, 43, 50, 51, 53, 115, 121, 122, 174, 192, 250
COMESA *see* Common Market for Eastern and Southern Africa
Common Market for Eastern and Southern Africa (COMESA) ix, 2, 3, 9, 38, 41–42, 44, 53
Competition Commission (CCC) x, 23, 38, 41–48, 52–53, 142
Competition Regulations and Rules 24, 41, 42
   amendments to (2015) 42
   article 3(2) 41
   integrated agency enforcement model 4
   member states 43
   Merger Assessment Guidelines 41
competition 7–8, 28
   buyer power in law and practice in field of 58–61
   and the challenges of inclusive economic development 167–183
   and competitiveness in regional animal feed to poultry value chain in ESA 154
   cross-border ix, x, 2, 9, 10–11, 39, 40, 41, 43, 44, 49, 50, 51, 52, 161
   digital market 137–138, 189–195
   downstream 60, 68–69, 136–137, 139, 155, 172, 174, 175
   and economic development ix, 167–183
   framework for 239–247, *240*, **243–245**
   law and policy 1, 58, 77–94, 105, 116, 123, 209
   in southern African countries 28, 39, 40, 48, 105
   in the United States 78, 80, 81–82
   legislation ix; 6–7

see also anti-cartel laws and enforcement; antitrust laws and enforcement; Federal Competition and Consumer Protection Act 2019 *under* Nigeria; Kenyan competition-related legislation and legislative bodies
  overall findings and implications for 158–160, *159*
  potential impact of 131–132, 133, 134, 234–236, *248*, 248–249
  and power 260
  and regional integration in soybean and animal feed to poultry markets 147–166, **164–166**
  upstream 137, 140, 172, 174, 175
competition agency, making of 15–26
competition authorities 3–5, 36, 38, 40, 41, 52–54, 59, 98, 109, 123, 143, 144, 161
  see also Association of South East Asian Nations
competition culture 36–37
competition protocol ix, 24, 40–41
competition regimes, building and establishment of in Africa ix, 1–14, 106
competition standard, substantial lessening of 95–108
competitive pricing 236
competitive threats 141
concentration
  along value chains 147–151, 168–170, **169, 170**
  and barriers to entry of markets 77–78
  global 44
  and market power 1–2, 7, 8, 77, 96, 256
    of poultry and animal feed suppliers in Malawi 169
    of poultry suppliers in ESA 149–150, **151**, 155, 156
connectivity costs 241–242
consumer detriment and welfare 68, 100–101, 102, 104, 106
  standard 60, 61, 66, 73
consumer groups 97
contracts, basic minimum for 86–87
co-ownership and networks of poultry-related alliances 151–153, *152*, *153*
corporate governance 231, 232, 237, 238
corporate leniency policies 4, 34–36, 50
cost benchmark 174
costs 138, 154, 174, 241–242
Covid-19 pandemic

CCSA investigations during 64
  effect on financial stability 22
  enforcement of competition during crisis 15, 20–22, 25, 26
  excessive pricing of surgical masks during 65
  firms' ability to increase prices during 67
  number of local digital platforms entering market due to 212
  price gouging cases in South Africa during 99–100
  price increase thresholds set during 100
  recovery from 23
  shocks associated with 2, 7
cross-border markets ix, x, 40, 43, 161
CSD and CSDPs *see* Central Securities Depository and Participants
Cumulative Abnormal Return (CAR) 119, 121, **127–129**
customers, downstream 20, 140

D

dawn raid 29, 30, 32–33, 35, **112**, 113, 114, 116
demand- and supply-side perspectives on network embeddedness 271–276, *272*, **273–275, 276**
deoxyribonucleic acid (DNA) sequencing technology 132–133
  see also Illumina/PacBio *under* merger assessments by the Competition and Markets Authority
Designated Service Provider networks (DSPs) 104
Digital Competition Expert Panel 137
digital markets
  and jurisdictions 79
  and marketplaces 79, 184–210
digital platforms
  to growth for local that drive inclusion 215–217
  benefits of to consumers and business owners 185–186
  categories of 217–225
  and consumers 185–186, 208–230
  established by MSMEs and previously disadvantaged entrepreneurs 208–226
  Google as an important source of traffic for 195–196, *196*
  market, competition from nascent firms in 131

Dis-Chem case *see Competition Commission of South Africa v Dis-Chem Pharmacies under* South African competition-related cases
display advertising *see* Meta/GIPHY *under* United Kingdom merger-related cases
distribution of effects, unequal 96–97
distribution rights 155–156
DNA sequencing technology *see* deoxyribonucleic acid sequencing technology
dominance, abuse of 5–7, 51–52, 61, 63–66
dominance threshold 64, 67
dominant buyers and firms 68, 70, 131, 132, 172, 173–174, 175
DPP *see* Director of Public Prosecutions *under* Zambian competition-related authorities and agency
DSMI *see* Data Services Market Inquiry *under* Competition Commission of South Africa *under* South African competition-related authorities and agency
DSPs *see* Designated Service Provider networks

E

EAC *see* East African Community
East African Community (EAC) 24, 50
  Competition Authority 24
eastern and southern Africa (ESA) region 147–166
  see also Kenya; Malawi; South Africa; Zambia
e-commerce
  business models 255–285, *284–285*
  ecosystem and entrepreneurs 224–225
  platforms and offerings in townships 223–225
  value chains 255–256, 262–263, 277, 279
econometric approach 117–121
economic dependence 67–68
economic policies ix, 2, 98, 103, 105, 160
Economic Recovery Strategy for Wealth and Employment Creation (2003) 15
ecosystem, e-commerce 224–225
EDM *see* elimination of double marginalisation
effects
  of change in competition 101–105, 106
  and policy 98
  of transaction in competition 101–105, 106
  unequal distribution of 96–97

efficient market hypothesis (EMH) 113, 114
e-groceries, case studies 265, 266–270, *267*, **269–270**
elimination of double marginalisation (EDM) 137
EMH *see* efficient market hypothesis
employment 48, 85–86, 184, 215, 256
entrepreneurs, modus operandi of e-commerce 224–225
entry and expansion
  incentives 144
  in merger control 142–143
  threat of 133, 134
ESA region *see* eastern and southern Africa (ESA) region
estimation
  procedure 116–117
  window 114, 116, *118*, 119, 120
European Commission, imposition of fines for engagement in buyers' cartel 58
European Economic Area 202
European Union
  and competition law 82
  consumer-focused theory of protection 82
  Digital Markets Act 81
  article 6(5) 202
  GlaxoSmithKline v Commission 82
  historical trends in competition law and enforcement in 82
  jurisdiction, enforcement of abuses of buyer power in 58
event, definition of 114
event studies
  building blocks of 114–117
  history of 111–112, **112**
  methodology 112–117
  selection criteria for 114–116, *115*
  timeline for *118*, 118–119
event window 114, 116, 117, 118, *118*, 119, 120, 121, **127–129**
evidence 133, 136, 144, 176, 178
exclusionary conduct 20, 67, 171–174, *172*, *173*
exiting, reasons for upstream 222
External Competitive Impact 133

F
Facebook 131, 141
  /Instagram merger 132
fees, trading and post-trading 240–241
Fertiliser Input Support Programme (FISP) 30–31
FISP *see* Fertiliser Input Support Programme
food e-commerce value chains/production networks, MSEs in 262–263
food industry, mergers in *see* National Foods Ltd/Pure Oil Industries *and* Zambeef/Zam Chick and Zamhatch *under* regional and national *under* mergers
food production and systems transformation 7–8
foodtech value chains 259–260
foreclosure 140, 141–142
  vertical 137, 138, 139, 140
framework, for evaluating competition between stock exchanges 239–247, *240*, **243–245**
free trade 110
see also African Continental Free Trade Area
FSCA *see* Financial Sector Conduct Authority *under* South African competition-related authorities and agency

G
Gabon, competition law in 83
global duopoly in poultry breeding stock 148
global production network (GPN) 255–256, 260, 261–262, 277
global system for mobile telecommunications (GSMT) network 19
global value chains (GVCs) 263
Google 141, 188, 199–201, *200*
  acquisition of companies by 131
  CCSA's findings and remedies against 201–202
  Hotels Unit 199–200, *200*
  impact of operations on competition 196–199
  as source of traffic for digital platforms 195–196, *196*
  searches on 188
GPN research and analysis *see* global production network research and analysis
GRMI *see* Grocery Retail Market Inquiry *under* Competition Commission of South Africa *under* South African competition-related authorities and agency

GSMT network *see* global system for mobile telecommunications network
GVCs research and analysis *see* global value chains research and analysis

H
HACCP certification *see* Hazard Analysis Critical Control Points certification
harm
  to competition and consumer welfare 19, 39, 60, 96–98, 99, 101, 102, 132, 142, 167
  to labour 103
  potential for 142, 144
  theory of (ToH) 39, 100, 132, 138, 140, 144, 172, *173*, 209
Hazard Analysis Critical Control Points (HACCP) certification 271
HDPs *see* historically disadvantaged persons
healthcare services, right of access to 104
historically disadvantaged persons (HDPs)
  abuses against 72
  digital platforms of in South Africa 208–226
  firms and suppliers 66
  Google-based platforms of 201
  offence to require/impose unfair prices/trading terms against 66
  platforms of in CCSA-imposed remedies 202
  see also Competition Act 89 of 1998 *under* South African competition-related legislation

I
ICN *see* International Competition Network
incentives
  to market entry 143
  strategies for overcoming 216–217
innovation 131, 132, 139, 239, 244–245
international best practices 72, 110
International Competition Network (ICN) 17, 23–24
  Steering Group 24, 25

J
Japan Fair Trade Commission 17
Johannesburg Stock Exchange (JSE) 35, 110, 115, *115*, 231, 232, 233
  Stock Exchange News Service (SENS) 116–117
JSE *see* Johannesburg Stock Exchange

K

Kenya
  abuse of buyer power in Competition Act in 83–87
  bifurcated agency enforcement models in 4
  Buyer Power Department 6
  buyer power in 4, 10
  cartels in 50
  competition law in 83, 87
  contribution of MSMEs to GDP of 87
  delays in payment in 85
  digital markets and platforms in 3, 18–19
  employment challenges in 85
  importers of oilcake/meal 143
  jurisdiction of 3, 4
  market inquiries in 2, 5, 10–11
  market and sector surveillance 21, 87
  merger control in 4
  poultry markets, structure of in 147
  prioritisation plans by 4
  regulatory and enforcement developments in 58–76
  Retail Sector 16
  soybean and animal feed to poultry market outcomes in 154–158, *155*, *157*
  special compliance process in 5
  value chain concentration in 149–151, **151**
Kenyan competition-related authorities and agency 6, 15
  Annual Competition Symposium 17
  Competition Authority of Kenya (CAK) 6, 15–26, 41, 42, 49–50, 60, 61, 69, 70, 71–72, 73, 84–85, 86, 87
  Board 15
  Business Continuity Plan 20, 25
  Case Management System 20
  code of practice for retail suppliers and buyers 23
  enforcement strategy 25–26
  Enterprise Resources Management 20
  focus on internal capacity and enforcement strategies 18, 23, 25
  investigations into abuse of buyer power 22–23
  Strategic Plan 18, 23
  Competition Tribunal 15, 61, 70, 71, 72, 84
  Coronavirus Emergency Response Committee 21
  High Court 15
  National Assembly 24, 25
  National Competition Agencies 24
  National Treasury 15–16, 17, 22
  Parliament 16–17, 19, 25
  State Corporation Advisory Committee 16
  Director-General 16
  State Corporations in Kenya 16
Kenyan competition-related cases
  Majid Al Futtaim Hypermarkets Limited v Competition Authority of Kenya and Orchards Limited 70–71, 72, 84–85
  Unilever Kenya 23, 71–72
Kenyan competition-related legislation and legislative bodies
  Competition Act 12 of 2010 6, 15, 18, 69, 70, 72, 73, 83–87, 88
  amendments to 69, 70, 72, 78
  Competition Amendment Act of 2016 6, 22, 24
  Restrictive Trade Practices and Monopolies Act of 1988 83
Kenyan economy 22, 23, 85, 86–87
Kenyan medium and small enterprises 22
Kenya Vision 2030 16

L

labour, harm to 103
Lafarge/Holcim case *see* Lafarge/Holcim
law and enforcement in African markets 77–94
licence holders in poultry industry 148–149, 150
liquidity and spreads 242–244
liquid markets 236–237
listing standards and enforcement 246
London Stock Exchange 35
  Alternative Investment Market (AIM) 47
Lusaka Stock Exchange 35, 47

M

Malawi
  analysis of market outcomes in 154–158, *155*, *157*
  apparent margin squeeze in poultry farming in 8, 167–183, *173*
  input costs and prices in 175–177, *177*
  production of soybeans in 147
  structure of poultry markets 147
  test for margin squeeze in 174–177
  value chain concentration in 149–151, **151**
market competition *see* competition
market context 99–101
market entry 143

295

market inquiries 4, 5, 51–52
see also Data Services Market Inquiry *under* Competition Commission of South Africa *under* South African competition-related authorities and agency; Grocery Retail Market Inquiry *under* Competition Commission of South Africa *under* South African competition-related authorities and agency; Online Intermediation Platform Market Inquiry *under* Competition Commission of South Africa *under* South African competition-related authorities and agency
market model *118*, 118–119
market outcomes 154–158, *155*, *157*, 170–174, *171*, *172*, *173*
market power 63–64, 65–66, 98, 102–103, 105, 131, 137, 151, 152, 155, 159, 171, 174
markets
　adjusting of law and enforcement to address challenges of African 77–94
　ensuring fair and open ix
　liquid 236–237
　relevant 67
　see also digital markets
market search costs 96–97
market share 64, 65
Markets in Financial Instruments Directive 240, **244**
market surveillance and member supervision 246–247
Massmart, acquisition of by Walmart 103
Mauritian Competition Commission 44
Mauritius
　establishment of prioritisation plans by 4
　integrated agency enforcement model 4
　jurisdiction of 3
Mediclinic case *see* Competition Commission of South Africa v Mediclinic Southern Africa (Pty) Ltd and Another *under* South African competition-related cases
Mediclinic/MMHS merger in South Africa *see* Mediclinic/Matlosana Medical Health Services *under* merger
medium and small enterprises (MSEs) in value chains 255–285, *267*, **269–270**, *272*, **273–275**
Memoranda of Understanding (MoUs) 17, 23, 34

merger
　Facebook/Instagram 132
　Google/Waze 132
　Mediclinic/Matlosana Medical Health Services (MMHS) 101, 103–105
merger assessments by the Competition and Markets Authority
　Illumina/PacBio 132–133
　Meta/GIPHY 134–136, 141–142
　PayPal/iZettle 133–134
　Tobii/Smartbox 139–140
merger control 4, 137
merger regulation and policy 79
mergers
　and cartels, core challenges of 38–57
　see also Mediclinic/Matlosana Medical Health Services *under* merger
　ceding of jurisdiction over 42
　distributive impact of 104
　employment losses following 48
　global and continental
　　Bayer/Monsanto (2017) 43, 44–45
　　Lafarge/Holcim (2014) 39, 43–44
　horizontal 144
　of multinational firms, anti-competitive ix
　notifications and evaluations of 42
　price effects of 95, 96
　regional and national
　　National Foods Ltd/Pure Oil Industries (Zimbabwe, 2016) 45–47, *46*
　　Zambeef/Zam Chick and Zamhatch (CCC, 2016) 45, 47
　review of 41
　threshold 24, 41, 42, 45, 47, 53
　vertical effects of 136–142, 144
　control of 137
　see also merger
merger-specific effects 101
Meta *see* Meta/GIPHY *under* United Kingdom merger-related cases
methodology
　and data 210–211
　event study 112–117
　potential limitations in 120–121
MFNs *see* most-favoured nation clauses
micro, small and medium enterprises (MSMEs)
　misuse of buyer strength against 22
　sustainability 85–86
MiFID *see* Markets in Financial Instruments Directive

MNOs *see* mobile network operators
MNVOs *see* mobile virtual network operators
mobile network operators (MNOs) 19
mobile point of sale (mPOS) services *see* PayPal/iZettle *under* United Kingdom merger-related cases
mobile virtual network operators (MNVOs) 19
models, e-commerce business 255–285, *284–285*
modes of delivery, multiple 221–222
monopolists 137
monopsony 59–60
most-favoured nation clauses (MFNs) 189–190
MoUs *see* Memoranda of Understanding
mPOS services *see* mobile point of sale services
MSEs *see* medium and small enterprises
MSMEs *see* micro, small and medium enterprises
multiple services and modes of delivery 221–222

N
network architecture 260–261, **261**
network embeddedness
   demand- and supply-side perspectives on 271–276, *272*, **273–275**, 276
   of MSEs in foodtech value chains 259–260
   supply side of 267–270, **269–270**
networks
   of alliances and co-ownership 151–153, *152*, *153*
   quality of 261
network stability 261–262
New Zealand, Commerce Commission 58
niche exchange 233, 234
Nigeria, Federal Competition and Consumer Protection Act 2019 83
non-parametric approach, Theil's 119–120, 121, **127–129**
non-pricing terms 69

O
OECD *see* Organisation for Economic Co-operation and Development
OFT *see* Office of Fair Trading *under* United Kingdom competition-related authorities and agency

OIPMI *see* Online Intermediation Platform Markets Inquiry *under* Competition Commission of South Africa *under* South African competition-related authorities and agency
oligopolistic market structures in ESA 159–160
OLS methodology and estimates *see* Ordinary Least Squares methodology and estimates
online delivery platforms
   food 219–220
   retail products 221
   truck hire 221
online travel agents (OTAs) 184–185, 187, 188, 193, 194, 203
Ordinary Least Squares (OLS) methodology and estimates 118, 119–120, 121
Organisation for Economic Co-operation and Development (OECD) 24
   competition committee 22
OTAs *see* online travel agents

P
paid alignment model 134–136
paid search results 197–198
payment terms 71
PayPal *see* PayPal/iZettle *under* United Kingdom merger-related cases
personal liability 124
personal protective equipment (PPE) 99–100
policy and policy recommendations 26, 98, 208–230, 277–279
poultry market structure and supply 147, 148–158, **151**, 168–171, **169, 170**, *171*
poultry value chains 154–160, *155*, *157*, *159*
power and bargaining/competition 260
PPCs *see* price parity clauses
PPE *see* personal protective equipment
PPPs *see* public–private partnerships
price discovery 237–238, 245–246
price gouging cases *see* Babelegi Workers and Industrial Supplies CC v The Competition Commission of South Africa *under* South African competition-related cases; Competition Commission of South Africa v Dis-Chem Pharmacies *under* South African competition-related cases; price gouging cases, investigation of by *under* Competition Commission of South

297

Africa *under* South African competition-related authorities and agency
price increases
   in poultry value chains 154–158, *155*, *157*
   unequal effects of 96
price movements, soybean 179–180
price parity clauses (PPCs) 189
   advantages and disadvantages of 190–192
   impact of on competition
   in accommodation intermediation platform services 192–195
   in digital markets 189–195, 203
   implementation of by online travel agents 185
prices
   during compliant period 67
   in the ESA-based poultry value chain 178–180
   share 111
pricing
   anti-poor 97
   on average 97
   competitive 236
   lack of 158–159
   policies and strategies 104
   and supply of key inputs 167
   unfair and excessive 65, 69, 99–100
prioritisation and policy 3–4, 98
production networks
   actors in value chains and 257–259, **258–259**
   upgrading of MSEs in 262–263
production plants 175
public interest 100
   in merger review and control 47–48, 72–73, 104
   provisions 63, 66–68, 101, 103, 106
public policy 98, 103, 105
public–private partnerships (PPPs) 278

Q
quality of care 102

R
REC *see* Regional Economic Community
regional competition challenges and enforcement 8–9, 156
Regional Economic Community (REC) 52, 53, 54
regional integration ix, 147–166, **164–166**
regional value chains (RVCs) 39, 160
restaurant marketplaces 265
   case studies 270–276, *272*, **273–275**, **276**
restrictive business practices 51–52
Retail Sector Code of Practice 86
   Principles of Fair and Ethical Dealing 86
Retail Trade Code of Africa (RTCP) 6
returns
   calculation of normal and abnormal 116, **127–129**
   company share prices 109–134
risk clearing 247
risk management 238–239, 247
RTCP *see* Retail Trade Code of Africa
rules for inherently powerful businesses 5–7
RVCs *see* regional value chains

S
SACU *see* Southern African Customs Union
SADC *see* Southern African Development Community
sampling method 211
search engine
   marketing (SEM) 197, 198
   optimisation (SEO) 197, 201, 209
   results pages (SERPs) 197–198, 199–200, 201, *200*
secondary listings exchange 234
seed and agro-chemical industries *see* Bayer/Monsanto *under* global and continental *under* mergers
self-interrogation in Africa 83
self-regulation 71, 72
self-regulatory organisation (SRO) 247
SEM *see* marketing *under* search engine
SENS *see* Stock Exchange News Service *under* Johannesburg Stock Exchange
SEO *see* optimisation *under* search engine
SERPs *see* results pages
sim toolkit (STK) and charges 19, 20
SLC *see* substantial lessening of competition
small and medium-sized enterprises (SMEs)
   abuses against 72
   buying power and 5–6
   effect on 85, 197–198
   empowerment of 28
   favouring of platforms of 202
   firms 66
   improvement of platform visibility of 201
   offences against 66
   potential impact of mergers on 48
   producers and suppliers 23, 33, 66, 86

role played by 5, 70
support of 36
SMEs *see* small and medium-sized enterprises
social media market *see* Meta/GIPHY *under* United Kingdom merger-related cases
South Africa
  approach to merger evaluation 3
  average cartel prosecution period in 122
  bifurcated agency enforcement models in 4
  buyer power in 10, 61–69
  cartels and cartel legislation in 8, 110–111
  competition in 5, 83, 105, 184–207, 209–210
  corporate leniency policy in 4
  costs of private healthcare in 104
  digital platforms and consumers in 208–230, *212*, *213*, *214*
  e-commerce building models in 255–285, *284–285*
  food e-commerce in 255–285, **258–259**, **261**, **262**, **264**, *267*, **269–270**, *272*, **274–275**, **276**, **285**
  intermediation services in 187
  jurisdiction of 3
  legal frameworks in 4
  Mediclinic/Matlosana Medical Health Services (MMHS) merger in 101, 103–105
  on-demand delivery platforms servicing townships in 221–222
  outlook of online travel and tourism platforms in 202–203
  priority sectors and government policy 98
  public interest provisions in 101
  small enterprises in 47
  support for employees in 47
  travel and accommodation intermediation services in 187
  Twin Peaks model of financial regulation in 231
  see also Johannesburg Stock Exchange
South African competition-related authorities and agency 67, 117, 124
  Competition Appeal Court (CAC) 61, 64, 65–66, 67, 99, 104, 105, 110
  Competition Commission of South Africa (CCSA) 5, 6, 10, 17, 23, 31, 34, 37, 41, 44, 60, 61, 62, 63, 64, 66, 67–68, 69, 73, 97, 99–101, 103–104, 110, 115, 116, 121, 122, 124, 187, 188, 189–190, 197–198, 200–202, 203, 232
  Data Services Market Inquiry (DSMI) 97
    findings and remedies of against Google 201–202
  Grocery Retail Market Inquiry 61–63
  Online Intermediation Platform Markets Inquiry (OIPMI) 5, 185–203, 209–210, 215, 278
  price gouging cases 64, 99–100
  Competition Tribunal 61, 64, 65, 67, 99, 100, 103, 104, 110, 111, 114, 122
  Constitutional Court 66–67, 104, 105
  Financial Sector Conduct Authority (FSCA) 231–232
  National Prosecuting Authority 122
  Prudential Authority 231–232
South African competition-related cases
  Babelegi Workers and Industrial Supplies CC v The Competition Commission of South Africa 64, 65–68, 99–101
  Competition Commission of South Africa v Dis-Chem Pharmacies 64, 65, 67–68, 99–101
  Competition Commission of South Africa v Mediclinic Southern Africa (Pty) Ltd and Another 66–68
  Competition Commission v Babelegi Workwear Overall Manufacturers and Industrial Supplies CC 64, 65–68, 99–101
  Mediclinic/MMHS 101, 103–105
  Sasol Chemical Industries Limited v Competition Commission 65
  Walmart Stores Inc v Massmart Holdings Ltd (73/LM/Dec10) [2011] ZACT 42, 101, 103, 105
South African competition-related legislation
  Competition Act 89 of 1998 6, 61, 62, 63–64, 65, 66, 67–68, 69, 70, 72–73, 99, 100, 101, 103, 105, 110–111, 122, 188, 202
  Competition Amendment Act of 2018 6, 63–69, 97, 99
  Financial Markets Act 19 of 2012 231
South African digital markets for travel and tourism 184–207
South African digital platforms policy debate 208–230
South African perspective on SLC standard 95–108
Southern African Customs Union (SACU) 49
Southern African Development Community (SADC) 40

299

SPLC *see* substantial prevention or lessening of competition
spreads and liquidity 242–244
SRO *see* self-regulatory organisation
STK and charges *see* sim toolkit and charges
stock exchanges
    features of well-functioning 236–239
    framework for evaluating competition between 239–247, *240*, **243–245**
    introduction of competition between 231–254
    potential impact of *248*, 248–249
    natural monopoly elements of 234–236
    niche 233, 234
    role and function of 232–234, *234*
    secondary listings 234
    traditional 233
    see also Johannesburg Stock Exchange; London Stock Exchange; Lusaka Stock Exchange
substantiality and magnitude 99–101
substantial lessening of competition (SLC) 95–108, 135, 139–140, 142, 144
substantial prevention or lessening of competition (SPLC) 95
see also substantial lessening of competition
supply limitations and shortages 155
supply side of network embeddedness 267–270, **269–270**

T

target firms 131–132
test
    as-efficient competitor 174
    on incentives 173–174
    margin squeeze in Malawi poultry 174–177
testing framework 117
tests for competition matters x
Theil's non-parametric approach 119–120, 121, **127–129**
Tobii *see* Tobii/Smartbox *under* United Kingdom merger-related cases
ToH *see* theory of *under* harm
tourism and travel, competition dynamics in 184–207
trading 233
    and post-trading fees 240–241
    volume 242
traditional exchange 233
transaction, effects of 101–105

travel and accommodation intermediation services 187
travel and tourism, competition dynamics in 184–207, *196*
trust building in network stability 262

U

Uganda, imports from 148, 152
uncertainty 130–136, 144
UNCTAD *see* United Nations Conference on Trade and Development
United Kingdom (UK)
competition authorities 143
see also Competition and Markets Authority *under* United Kingdom competition-related authorities and agency
    merger assessment and control 130–146
    theories of health 132
    thinking in merger assessment 130–146
United Kingdom competition-related authorities and agency 130, 132
    Competition and Markets Authority (CMA) 97, 130, 131, 132–136, 139–142, 143, 144
    Merger Assessment Guidelines 132, 138, 143
    Competition Appeal Tribunal (CAT) 130n1, 135–136, 139–140, 142
    Office of Fair Trading (OFT) 142
    see also London Stock Exchange
United Kingdom merger-related cases
    CHC/Babcock 143
    ICE/Trayport 139–140
    Illumina/PacBio 132–133
    Meta/GIPHY 134–136
    PayPal/iZettle 133–134
    Tobii/Smartbox 139–140, 142
United Nations Conference on Trade and Development (UNCTAD) 24
United States of America
    antitrust and merger policy and enforcement 79–82
    Brandeisian tradition and views 78–79, 81
    Clayton and Federal Trade Acts of 1914 81
    competition law and political economy 80
    Department of Justice 34, 58
    dialysis market in the 101–103, 105
    economic welfare model 78
    enforcement of competition law in 78
    Federal Trust Commission 34

historical trends in competition law and enforcement 81–82
Horizontal Merger Guidelines 102
jurisdiction 58
market concentration in 78
Robinson-Patman Act of 1936 81
Sherman Act of 1890 81
Unstructured Supplementary Service Data (USSD) 19–20
USSD *see* Unstructured Supplementary Service Data

V
value chain
  concentration 149–151, **151**
  linkages across ESA 148–149, *149*
  integration and concentration 168–170, **169**, **170**
  mapping 266
  strategies and practices 102
value chains
  actors in production networks and 257–259, **258–259**
  e-commerce 255–256, 262–263, 277, 279
  in foodtech 259–260
  pricing in ESA poultry 154–158
vertical integration and vertically integrated firms 147, 148, 149, 172, 174, 175
volume-based discounts 60, 69

W
Walmart case *see* Walmart Stores Inc v Massmart Holdings Ltd (73/LM/Dec10) [2011]
  ZACT 42t *under* South African competition-related cases

Z
Zambia
  approach to merger evaluation 3
  bifurcated agency enforcement models in 4
  cartels, fight against in 27–37
    auto repair (2010–2013) 28, 29–30
    bread (2015) 31–32
    cement (2021–2022) 33–34, 36
    fertiliser (2011) 28, 30–31, 36
    fish fingerlings 32–33, 34, 37
    negative impact of 109
    poultry (2018) 33
  establishment of prioritisation plans by 4
  jurisdiction of 3
  marketing in 45
  market outcomes in 154–158, *155*, *157*
  poultry markets structure 147
  soybean production in 147
  special compliance process in 5
  value chain concentration in 149–151, **151**
  see also Lusaka Stock Exchange
Zambian competition-related authorities and agency x, 1
  Citizens Economic Empowerment Commission (CEEC) 32
  Competition and Consumer Protection Commission (CCPC) 27, 28, 29, 30, 31–33, 34, 35–36, 42, 49–50
  Board of Commissioners 28–29, 31
  Competition and Consumer Protection Tribunal 29, 30, 31, 34
  Competition and Tariff Commission Zimbabwe 45
  Director of Public Prosecutions (DPP) 34
  Zambia Information Communication and Telecommunication Authority (ZICTA) 33
  Zambian Competition Commission (ZCC) 28
  Zambia Public Procurement Authority (ZPPA) 30
Zambian competition-related case
  Frederick Jacob Titus Chiluba v Attorney General, Appeal No. 125 of 2002 30
Zambian competition-related legislation and legislative bodies
  Competition and Consumer Protection Act (CCPA) 24 of 2010 28–34
  Competition and Fair Trade Act 28
  Supreme Court 30
ZCC *see* Zambian Competition Commission *under* Zambian competition-related authorities and agency
ZICTA *see* Zambia Information Communication and Telecommunication Authority *under* Zambian competition-related authorities and agency
ZPPA *see* Zambia Public Procurement Authority *under* Zambian competition-related authorities and agency